THE BEST *of British* WOMEN

Printed and bound by Bath Press, England
Typeset by Mainline Typesetters Ltd, St. Leonards-on-Sea
B/W origination by GH Graphics, St Leonards-on-Sea

Front cover illustrations:
Clockwise from top left: Anita Roddick, Selena Scott, Anouska Hemple, Kate Adie, H.M. Queen Elizabeth, Juliet Stevenson

Rear cover illustrations:
Left to right: Patti Boulaye, Beth Chatto, Sister Wendy Beckett

Spine illustration:
Delia Smith

ISBN 0 951863 12 6

First published in Great Britain in 1993 by Best of British Publications, Eldon Lodge, 52 Victoria Road, London W8 5RQ. Tel 071-937 4276. Fax 071-937 1137

THE BEST *of British* WOMEN

CONTENTS

ACKNOW

THE TEAM

In addition to the people whose contributions are acknowledged on this page, I would particularly like to give credit for the skill and dedication of the following members of the BEST OF BRITISH team, without whose efforts the books would not have been produced at all:

THE RESEARCHERS

The job of gathering and collating formation on the number of people featured in the BEST OF BRITISH is one requiring a great deal of patience, perseverance and, not least, charm. The reward has been the opportunity of speaking to and getting to know the most extraordinary and successful members of our society in every walk of life. The research team burned the midnight oil for many months, chivvying and cajoling for information, photographs ad biographies and I would particularly like to mention Angela Breheny, Jenny Tobin, Donna Allen-Eggison, Lloyd Stanton, Patrick Fuller, Sandi Mollod, Kim Bolton, Debbie Collinson and Jonny Ffinch.

THE WRITERS

The principal writers, Richard Bundy, Amelia Maiden and Richard Dawes, who summarised, expanded and edited the information provided until man and machine became one.

THE ART DEPARTMENT

Art director John Clement, ably assisted by Tasha Miller, who made the pictures fit the text and the text fit the pages.

Accountancy Age Newspaper; Acorn Entertainments; Dr Helen Agnew, Institute of Physics; Linda Agran, Paravision; The Airds Hotel; Amanda, Laister Dickson Ltd; Carol Ames, Eagle Star Investment Managers Ltd; Anderson O'Day Gallery; Stuart Anderson; Annely Juda Fine Art; Dr Barbara Ansell; Eve Arnold; Arts Review Magazine; Dr Margaret Ashwell, British Nutrition Foundation; Association of British Introduction Agencies; Aurelia PR; Austin-Desmond Gallery; Kit Bailey, Adastra; Martin Bailey; Roy Bailey; Lorraine Baldry; Dennis Ball, The Foundry; Nick Ballantine; Prof John Barrow, Univ of Sussex; Guy Batham, National Federation of Spiritual Teachers; BBC News Publicity; BBC Picture Publicity; BBC Publicity Office; The Beeson Gallery; Sasha Behrendt, Storm; Jean Bennett; Hazel Bently, International Journal of Alternative & Complementary Medicine; Beverley Cable PR; Lt David Bird; Dr Carol Black; Tim Bourne, Amalgam Gallery; William Boustead, The Toffee Shop, Penrith; Wendy Bridgman; British Film Institute; British Institute of Management; The British Tourist Board; Nikki Brokenshire, Mail on Sunday; Twink Burton, Alison Price Catering; Ann Bush, Alan Mann Helicopters; Elizabeth Butler-Sloss, Royal Courts of Justice; Liz Calder, Bloomsbury; Campaign Magazine; Eileen Campbell, Thorson Publications; Dee Carpenter; Axel Chaldecott, Howell Henry Chaldecott Lury; Julie Ivelaw Chapman, Chester Music; Stephanie Churchill; Nick Clarke, English National Ballet; Classical Music Magazine; Tony Cobb, Royal College of Art; David Cole, British Microlight Commission; Helen Constantindes, PBJ Management; The Cooling Gallery; Graham Coombs, British Rail; Jackie Cooper; Paul Cordy, Dail Mail; Sue Cottam, Design Council; Anne Cox, Thorson Publications; The Crafts Council; Ilse Crawford, Elle Deco; Creative Review Magazine; Alan Cristea, Waddington Gallery; Paul Crocetta; Alan Crompton-Batt; Dianne Crowder, Shell UK; Jane Curtis; Andy Cutting; Marcelle D'Argy-Smith, Cosmopolitan; Beverly D'Silva, Cosmopolitan; Jackie Daya, Reed Regional Newspapers; Sally Dellow, Prime Performers; Clarissa Dickson-Wright, Books for Cooks; Mike Dinsdale, English Karate Commission; Steve Dixon, Caterer's Magazine; Michael Donovan, Alison Hargreaves; Sarah Doukas, Storm; April Ducksbury, Models One; Richard Dudley, The Custome Studio; Mairi Eastwood, Eastwood Consulting; Janet Eiger, London Contemporary Dance School; Andrew Eliel, Egon Ronay Guides; Elle Magazine; Dr Brent Elliott; Peter Ellwood, TSB; John Emmett; John and William Emmett; Michael Endicott, Institute of Complementary Medicine; Yvonne Eskenzi, London Enterprise Agency; Mary Evans, British Council on Ballroom Dancing; Baroness Ewart-Biggs; Steven Farish; E Fellows; Andrew Ferguson; Scott Findlay; Folk Roots; Jose Fonseca, Models One; John Fordham, Evening Standard; Annie Forster-Firth; William Fotheringham, Cycling Weekly; Erika Frei;

EDGEMENTS

Gabbitas Truman & Thring; Gerry Gajadharsingh; Rosie Gerrard-Wright; Robin Gibson, National Portrait Gallery; Peggy Gibson; Rod Gilchrist, The Mail on Sunday; Martin Glanville, CBD Research Ltd; Johnny Gold, Tramp Nightclub; Joy Goodman; Goring PR; Paul Green, London Regional Transport; Henrietta Green; John Grig, British Dietetic Association; Isaac Guillory; Philip Gunn; Tim Haigh, Psychic News; Hairdressers Journal; Theresa Hale, Hale Clinic; Robin Hall, CINVen; Rev Douglas Hamilton-Ashby; Harold Holt Ltd; Paul Harris; Harrison Parrott Ltd; Anne Harvey; Richard Havers, Rushman-Lloyd Communications; Carol Hayes; Clare Henry; Peter Heppel, The Stage; Simon Higman, BBC; Hilary Shaw Management; Mark Hindle, The Mousetrap Cheese Shop; Mark Hindle; Lt Peter Hingley, Royal Astronomical Society; Chris Hodgekins, Jazz Services; Jane Holden, West Riding Milk Testing Service; John Home; Horrowitz Music Management Ltd; Barry Hugman, British Boxing Association; Ian Hutchinson; IMG Artists; Independent Television News Press Office; Hugh Inge-Innes-Lillingston; Brian Ingles; Ingpen & Williams; J Gurnett Personal Management Ltd; JRA Management; Jeremy James, Helicopter Club of Great Britain; Helen Jameson, Lilliput Ltd; Pervella Jeffries, Spotlight Casting; John Roseman Associates; John Kenny; Elizabeth Kershaw, Harpers & Queen; Leslie Knevitt, Prince of Wales Innovation Awards; Nicolas Lander, Financial Times; Jean Lee, Corporate Hospitality & Event Association; Tac Lee, Harrods; Dr Robert Lefever; Suzanne Lewis; Lies Askonas Ltd; Hugh Lillingston; Jo Lloyd, Automobile Association; Ashley Lloyd-Jennings; Joanne Logan, Predictions Magazine; London Weekend Television Press Office; John Lowe; Edward Lucie-Smith; Anthony Lyman-Dixon, Arne Herbs; Mainline Typesetters Ltd; Arthur Map, British Ju Jitsu Association; Marlborough Fine Art; Jack Masserik, The Guardian; Martin Matthews; Anne Mayer, Royal Court Theatre; Leslie Mayer, London Fire Brigade; Sam McCarthy, British Marble Board of Controls; Helen McKay, Associated Newspapers; Rod McNeil, Theunissen; Greig McPherson, P Wigham-Richardson Ltd; Deidre McQuillen, Food Journalist; Jane McWhirter, All Hallow's Clinic; Anna Mei, Chadwick Gallery; Peter Miall, National Trust; Maureen Michaelson; Mike Henton Photography; John Miles; Bobbie Mitchell, BBC Photo Library; Edward Mitchell, NEVS; Modern Painters Magazine; Jonathon Monckton, Research Council for Complementary Medicine; Kate Moon, Speakeasy; Debbie Moore, Pineapple Studios; Becky Morris, Smallworld Music; Robert Morris, Koestler Chair of Parapsychology; Stephen Morris; Jonathan Morrish, Sony Music; Martin Mortimer, Tomorrow's World, BBC; National Pawbrokers Association; James Nicoll; Richard O'Donoghue, The Society of Designer-Craftsmen; Terry O'Neil; Dr Paul Oldershaw; Tony Ortzen, Psychic News; The Oxford Gallery; PR Unlimited; Sue Parker, Blank Space Studios; Brad Parsons, Elite Premier; Brian Pearse, Midland Bank; The Photographers Gallery; Pomeroy Purdy Gallery; Margarita Porter; Stephen Pottle, Designer Sale Studio; PR Consultants Association; Kim Prior, You & Your Wedding; E Pugh, The Society of West End Theatres; Peter Pugson, Pugson's Food & Wine; Dr Richard Ralph, London Contemporary Dance School; Christopher Ramus; John Renbourn; Mark Rhodes, Angels & Bermons; Jo Richardson, MP; Gloria Ricks, National Magazine; William Robson; Roger Forrester Management; Barry Rolfe, Royal Aero Club of the UK; Gwen Rolfe, Martial Arts Commission; Michael Roosen; Derek Ross, British Airways; Prof rchie Roy, Univ of Glasgow; The Royal Geographical Society; Nicky and Nigel Rushman, Rushman-Lloyd Communications; Annette Russell, Tuff; Debbie Saldana, Prime Performers; Katrina Scetter, Larraine Ashton; Amber Webster, John Swannell Studios; Bert Weedon; The Welsh Tourist Board; Charles Westhead; Barbara Westmore, Harper Collins; Carol White, Elite Premier; Dr Roger Whitehead, Dunn Nutrition Centre; Andrew Wickham; Beverley Wickham; John Williams, British Bridge Union; Stan Willis, Society of Golden Keys; Shane Wilson, Expedition Advisory Centre; Women in Film & TV; Women's Journal; Celia Wood, Jazz Services; Chris Wood; Alex Woodcock-Clarke.

A MAJOR DECISION

At the time of going to press, we learned that John Major is proposing to adopt the Best of British method of nomination for the sadly anachronistic honours system. This is enormously pleasing to us, because the whole ethos of the Best of British is to acknowledge excellence in every field regardless of political favour. The honours system has long been a mystery to the man in the street; some jobs, particularly in the Civil Service, seem to carry such honours as CMG (call me God), KCMG (kindly call me God) and GCMG (God calls me God) as part of the promotional package. The range of honours available has also been remarkably confusing, for instance, in the 1992 New Year's list two television personalities were honoured, one with the CBE and one with the MBE, a nice but baffling distinction. When honours were first bestowed on members of Parliament they were a form of recompense for those who sacrificed their time performing a service to the community. Nowadays, being an MP is an extremely well-paid job when jobs are not easy to come by and to present a knighthood to someone who has done little or nothing except vote in the right direction, sit on the back benches and keep his nose clean seems a long way from slaying dragons or searching for the Holy Grail. In a rapidly changing society in which the Queen pays tax, her children make telephone calls like ordinary mortals and the Courts occassionally admit their fallibility. THE BEST OF BRITISH would like to welcome Mr Major's decision which, like this book, is intended to recognise people for what they do and not for what they are.

Martin was born in Worthing in 1946 and educated at the local secondary modern school. He became a freelance photographer and local radio journalist on leaving school, before co-founding Lyle Publications, in 1968. He has a rare talent for restoring period buildings – the larger the better – and left his mark in the South of England for the five years after leaving Lyle, until, in 1979, he started Miller's Antiques Guide, now the biggest selling antiques yearbook in the world. Martin's obsession with property has stayed with him and he is a director and co-founder of the highly successful Kent-based company, Milroy Developments. In 1984, he bought Chilston Park, at the time an uninhabitable virtual ruin, which he opened in 1985 as a country house hotel. The success of Chilston has been a tribute to Martin's vision and it now boasts 40 bedrooms, all individually furnished with antiques, and two stars in the restaurant guide for its food. Martin lives in Eldon Lodge, in Kensington, a Victorian mansion which, again, he restored from the uninhabitable. Aside from the Best of British books, Martin's recent publishing successes have included The Miller's Christmas Book, various books on period styles and details and the Essential Address Books. His latest venture is The Martin Miller Design Partnership, through which he combines his knowledge of antiques and buildings with his flair for decoration and restoration for the benefit of selected clients.

INTRODUCTION

When Martin Miller first conceived the idea of THE BEST OF BRITISH yearbooks, he did so with more knowledge than most people would have had of the scale of the undertaking. He had, after all, been publishing books since he co-founded Lyle Publications in 1968 and could boast amongst his publishing achievements MILLER'S ANTIQUES PRICE GUIDE, the biggest selling yearbook in the world. The first edition of THE BEST OF BRITISH MEN and its companion volume, THE BEST OF BRITISH WOMEN, have taken four years from conception to production.

The first problem was to decide on the categories, over 135 of them in each volume, and, realising that it was impossible to include every possible field of endeavour in a single volume, it was reasoned that, as a yearbook, we could concentrate on certain areas for 1993 which we may leave out in 1994. For instance, 1992 being an Olympic year, we have emphasised the achievements of our Olympians and, particularly, Paralympians at the expense of our association footballers, cricketers and boxers, who will get their turn in 1994.

The next major consideration involved establishing the criteria for 'the best'. Obviously, there are any number of areas in which this is a very subjective judgement – for instance, the best pub is often the pub where you are best known and the best smoked salmon to some may be thoroughly offensive to others. It was reasoned that there were two reliable ways to judge standards of excellence and the first of these – and the easiest – was by taking the results of current awards. The second method was by recommendations. Thus, ten names were extracted from one leading exponent in a given field and then ten from each of them and so on until a broad consensus was reached. In this way it became possible to say that, whilst people appearing in the book are not indisputably 'the best', there are very few better. To ascertain this information, a team of expert and experienced researchers was assembled, each with a specialised knowledge of a particular field. With 12 researchers working full time, the information started to flood in and the book began to take shape.

It was our intention to include under the various categories only those people who are currently active at the top of their chosen fields of endeavour and who have made a particular impact in the past year. This has left room for a separate section entitled HALL OF FAME, dedicated to those people who may not have made a particular contribution in 1992, but whose impact on British life over the years is impossible to ignore. Thus, Ian Botham may no longer be amongst the top five cricketers in the country, but as a fund-raiser, TV performer and personality, he certainly deserves a place among THE BEST OF BRITISH. The HALL OF FAME also contains people whom media exposure has brought to prominence, sometimes through no achievement of their own.

Finally, there are some, although very few, people who requested that they should be left out of the book – there is, for instance, a well-known omission in the Horse Racing section – and their wishes have been respected.

Should the reader find what he considers to be a glaring omission – or an unfair inclusion – he is welcome to contact us with nominations for the 1994 BEST OF BRITISH.

HOW TO NOMINATE

If you wish to nominate anyone for inclusion in the 1994 BEST OF BRITISH book, in an existing category or one which you may feel we have overlooked, then fill in the form at the back of the book and send it to us. To avoid defacing your book you may reproduce the form as often as you wish.

ELDON LODGE · 52 VICTORIA ROAD · KENSINGTON · LONDON · W8 5RQ

071-937 4276

MOYRA BEAVES

Moyra Beaves became general manager of Sheraton Belgravia in 1992, her role being to reopen the hotel after major refurbishment and to rebuild the business base. During her tenure, the hotel has twice been awarded the top Sheraton customer service award, and Moyra's management team has been nominated for the Harold Geneen Award, ITT's highest accolade. Moyra qualified as a metallurgist in 1966 and worked variously as a sales promoter, air stewardess and technial representative before joining the hotel industry with the Hilton Hotels Corporation, where she was director of sales in their European office in 1988. She joined Sheraton ITT on a "fast track" programme to become a general manager in 1988, having never previously worked in a hotel.

CLAIRE MacDONALD

Lady MacDonald and her husband Godfrey James, High Chief of the clan Donald, the Lord MacDonald, run their home on the Isle of Skye, Kinloch Lodge, as a small hotel. It is set on a sea loch with a hill behind the house and provides ten simple bedrooms. The house is full of family portraits and furniture and is, she says, not at all grand and smart, but relaxed and very much more a house than a hotel. Claire's main interest, apart from people, has always been food and the guests who come to Kinloch – many of them regularly two or three times a year – come for the relaxation, the walks, the bird and otter spotting and the eating. Claire has published ten cookery books, with another due out this year, and writes regular columns for The Field, a Glasgow newspaper and the Aberdeen Press and Journal.

ANNE VOSS-BARK

Anne Voss-Bark owns the Arundell Arms in Lifton, Devon, probably the premier fishing and sporting hotel in England. Originally an actress, Anne and her first husband Gerald Fox-Edwards, moved to the hotel because of Gerald's poor health. Since his death in 1973, Anne has developed and run the business herself. In 1978 she won the Cavendish Cup for the most successful woman hotelier of the year. Anne has been in the forefront of promoting British fishing hotels here and in the USA, has edited a book on West Country flyfishing, and is chairman of the South West Fishery Advisory Committee of the National Rivers Authority. She is a member of the national executive of the British Hospitality Association and a local magistrate. Anne is now married to Conrad Voss-Bark, a former BBC parliamentary correspondent.

ANOUSKA HEMPEL (LADY WEINBERG)

Blakes Hotel was created by the multi-talented Anouska Hempel out of two Victorian mansions in South Kensington. Originally with 28 rooms, it has grown with the acquisition of further houses to 46 rooms. Although not in a fashionable area, Blakes quickly became accepted as a hotel for fashionable people, renowned as it is for protecting the privacy of its clients. It is the London base for film personalities such as Robert de Niro, Mickey Rourke, Michael Douglas, Jack Nicholson and Ali McGraw. Fashion designers Giorgio Armani, Christian Lacroix, Karl Lagerfield, Claude Montana and Issey Miyake also make Blakes their London home, as do leading businessmen from around the world. Blakes' restaurant is noted as one of the best in London. Having created the archetype of the small, luxury hotel – much imitated in London and elsewhere – Anouska Hempel has recently designed another hotel soon to be opened in London's Bayswater.

SALLY BULLOCH

Sally Bulloch, the youngest of six children, was educated at drama school and, while there, she says she spent more time playing a little horror in the St Trinians films than studying. She didn't achieve any passes at GCE. On leaving school, she went to work as nanny for comedian Peter Cooke's family in Hampstead and then went to Malta, where her celebrity connections in London led to a radio interview, which itself led to a radio programme of her own on BFBC Malta. On her return to England, Sally joined the Athenaeum Hotel as a reservations clerk and, in ten years, worked her way up to sales and PR manager. She left briefly to run her own PR company and then to take over as general manager of the Draycott Hotel for two years. In 1989 she moved to the Pelham Hotel as general manager, returning to the Athenaeum in 1991 as executive manager. She will be responsible for the massive refurbishment at the hotel, due for completion in 1994. Sally believes that training as an actress and a nanny has stood her in good stead as a hotelier.

Photograph by Nicky Rushman

SALLY CLARKE

Sally Clarke is one of the great innovators of the London restaurant scene. Her "no choice" dinners at Clarke's restaurant could have been regarded as a high risk idea, but the quality of the ingredients, the cooking, and the imagination in selecting the menus have ensured their long term success. Sally was born in Guildford and acquired her diploma in Hotel and Catering Operations at Croydon Technical College. She took the Cordon Bleu Advanced Certificate Course in Paris, and returned to England from 1976 to 1979 to work at Leith's, rising to head teacher at the School of Food and Wine. From 1979 to 1983 she was in California, largely with Michael McCarty, and it was here that her ideas for her own, eclectic restaurant really gelled. She opened Clarke's restaurant in 1983, the shop in 1988 and the bakery in 1990, and all go from strength to strength.

RUTH WATSON

Ruth Watson is the proprietor of the Fox and Goose Inn in Fressingfield, Suffolk. Born in 1950, Ruth was a graphic designer for ten years, and it was only when she and her husband bought Hindlesham Hall in 1984 that her enthusiasm for food and wine was given full rein. However, it was food, not rooms, which really excited Ruth, and in 1990 she bought the Fox and Goose with the express intention of "buying good produce and cooking honest food". Her main hobby is eating out, and her heroes are Simon Hopkinson, Alastair Little and Shaun Hill.

SIMONE GREEN

Simone Green came from Manchester to London in the 1960s to work in advertising, and soon discovered that working in a Soho agency largely involved having lunch. It was a short step to the thought that providing the meal might be as enjoyable, and more fulfilling, than merely eating it. Hence, she founded Odettes, with two former colleagues, in 1976. In 1977 she became sole owner and has, she says, been serving a long apprenticeship ever since. Situated a short walk from Primrose Hill and Lord's cricket ground, Odette's has a faithful following both locally and from further afield, so it would appear that her "apprenticeship" has been well served.

VERONICA SHAW

Before entering the catering world, Veronica Shaw achieved the distinction of being the youngest ever headmistress of a comprehensive school. In 1977 she opened a lunchtime bistro serving English food. Two years later she set up Shaw Food, initially supplying location food for her husband's film company, but soon doing food photographic work for commercials. By 1981 Shaw Food was working 24 hours a day, and expansion was becoming so great that a restaurant with large kitchens was required, and Veronica's opened its door, in Bayswater, in 1983. Veronica's immediately started offering British historical and regional dishes at a time when they were yet to become fashionable, and approval and acclaim were intant. The restaurant is the flagship of Veronica's operations and has won many awards – partly because early English foods is highly compatible with modern health conscious eating.

PRUE LEITH

In 1992 Pure Leith, as chairman of the Restaurateurs Association of Great Britain, was awarded the Catey Special Award for her outstanding contribution to the industry. Prue discovered food when she arrived in Paris from South Africa at the age of 19 and, after a Cordon Bleu course in London, set up her own outside catering etablishment in 1962, working from a bed-sit in Earls Court. In 1969 Leith's restaurant opened and has continued to be a feature of London entertaining, serving 80 people with sumptuous food in the Grande Luxe style. Six years later Leith's School of Food and Wine opened in Kensington, and has sustained a reputation for excellence throughout the catering world. In 1976 Leith's Farm in the Cotswolds was acquired, and supplies the group with speciality produce. Although Prue retains overall control of all the arms of her business, she believes strongly in delegation, without which the group would not prosper as it has continued to do.

HILARY BROWN

Hilary Brown studied for three years at the Glasgow College of Domestic Science, graduating in Food and Nutrition. After a year at teacher training college, she taught home economics for two years. In 1975 Hilary and her husband David bought a little restaurant called La Potiniere, in Gullane, East Lothian. For the past 17 years they have run the restaurant entirely on their own, serving a daily changing, no choice menu. Hilary does all the cooking totally unaided, and won her first AA Star in 1977, her first Egon Ronay Star in 1985, and her Michelin Star in 1991. David has won many accolades for his wines. In 1990 they published La Potiniere and Friends.

JULIA CHALKLEY

Julia Chalkley began her cooking career when she joined a cruise company, and her efforts at steering a 70ft narrow boat proved so disastrous that she was relegated to the galley to cook for the 16 passengers and crew. After two seasons she went to work for Popjoys restaurant in Bath, both front of house and in the kitchen, and from there she joined the Ebury Wine Co as head chef, setting up and managing a new bar. In 1988 she set up Gilberts in South Kensington, with partner Ann Wregg, and it is now recognised as serving some of the best food in London, in a welcoming, civilised atmosphere, and accompanied by some of the best wine. Julia is featured in the book, The Women Chefs of Britain.

SONIA BLECH

Sonia Blech's cooking career took off when she and her husband Neville bought a run down pub in Wales in 1972. Sonia gave up her job teaching medieval history at Brunel University three years later to cook full time at the pub. Despite their great success the couple moved back to London in 1980 and set up Mijanou, feeling that for their teenage children it was no longer fair to live in such a remote place. Sonia's "artisanale" philosophy has not changed since those early days. Uninterested in trends and passing fads she is still fiercely independent in her cooking, following her own instincts and making everything at Mijanou from pasta to bread and petits fours with fresh, natural ingredients.

JOYCE MOLYNEUX

Joyce Molyneux was born in Birmingham and left college in 1949 to work in industrial catering for a year, before spending nine years in the kitchen of the Mulberry Tree Restaurant in Stratford-on-Avon under D J Sutherland. She then moved to Bath to work for George Perry Smith at the Hole in the Wall. Under George's aegis, she opened the Carved Angel, in partnership with Tom Jaine, in July 1974. Her partner is now Meriel Boydon. In November 1990, in conjunction with Sophie Gregson, she published the Carved Angel Cookery Book.

PATRICIA HEGARTY

Patricia Hegarty read English at London University, got married and brought up two children before achieving a lifelong ambition to restore and live in a romantic old house in the country. Work on her family owned house and landscaped garden in Herefordshire led to a new career as cook, gardener and hotelier. She has spent the last 18 years developing the skills and techniques necessary to produce English country house food and run an 18th century walled kitchen garden with dedication to the promotion of traditional English country ways of life, adapted to the 20th century. Her book, An English Flavour, published in 1988, records her many recipes and ideas.

ROSE GRAY

Rose Gray has a degree in fine arts and started her career teaching art at a comprehensive school. In 1965 she set up a design team, designing paper and furniture, and subsequently wood-burning stoves, which led to her opening a French Crèperie in London in 1970 and a mobile one for pop concerts, etc. From 1981-85 she lived in Italy, studying Italian cookery and gardens, and in 1986 she set up an Italian restaurant in New York. In 1987, with Ruthie Rogers, she started the River Cafe in Hammersmith, which has been one of the great restaurant successes of recent years – Best Italian Restaurant, 1988 – Best of the Best New Restaurants 1989, etc. Rose has been awarded the Academia Italiana della Cucina, and appeared in the BBC's Hot Chefs. The River Cafe Cook Book is published later this year.

BETTY ALLEN

Eric and Betty Allen bought The Airds Hotel in 1978. Although Betty had had no experience or training, she soon gained a number of awards including a Michelin Star, three AA Rosettes and a consistently high score in the Good Food Guide. In 1986 she received the Scottish Field/Bollinger Award for the Best Scottish Restaurant, and in 1987 she was one of only two in Scotland to be made Chef Laureate by the British Academy of Gastronomes. The hotel is one of only four members of Relais & Chateaux in Scotland.

CAROLE EVANS

Carole and her late husband John came to The Roebuck in Shropshire in 1983. Since then CArole set about gradually developing Poppies, the Inn restaurant, which led to her being awarded a Michelin Red M in 1990. In 1992 she won the Pub of the Year award. Carole uses as many fresh local ingredients as possible, and produces food which not only draws on current fashion, but includes many traditional recipes.

MARION JONES

Marion Jones has held a Michelin Star longer than any other British woman chef. She changed her career from secretarial to catering in the mid-1970s and, with husband Robin, bought a Victorian bakery in Malvern Wells, which they converted into the 24 seater Croque-en-Bouche. In 1981 she received stars from both Michelin and Egon Ronay. Her style of cooking is influenced by her love of gardening; she grows many herbs, salads and vegetables for the restaurant, and her cooking, with a Provincial French base, melds Italian and Oriental influences to give strong, individual flavours. Robin and Marion have no staff other than washing-up help.

BABA HINE

With an interest in cooking, but no formal training, Baba Hine found Michael Harris at the Bell Inn in Ashton Clinton, as his PA. She met and married Denis Hine, and in 1965 they took over the Red Lion in Weobley, with much success. In 1970 they bought the Three Cocks Hotel in Breconshire and Baba embarked on her cooking career, discovering a real flair for food. She's been cooking ever since. In 1978 they moved to the Corse Lawn House Hotel where, says Baba, son Giles will eventually take over front of house, but not the kitchen.

FRANCES ATKINS

Frances Atkins trained in hotel management at Bradford Polytechnic, while working in all departments of the Box Tree in Ilkley. She took up a position in Edinburgh, and moved to the contintent, where she spent a year developing her skills in a royal patisserie in Copenhagen. On her return she became the first ever female head chef in Scotland, when she joined Dalhousie Castle. Her career was interrupted for ten years by her first marriage, but in 1984 she opened her own restaurant in Buckinghamshire, called Atkins. Demand dictated that larger premises be acquired, and she was recognised by the Good Food Guide. In 1988, with her second husband, she bought Farleyer House, in Perthshire, and turned it into a country house hotel. They have sold the hotel side of the business and Frances now concentrates on being executive chef.

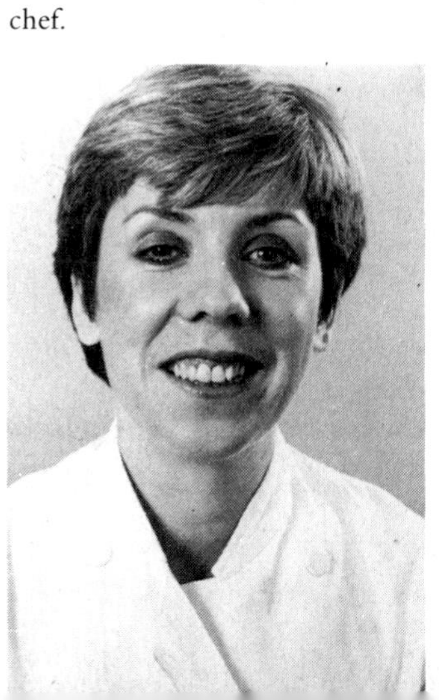

SHEILA PERERA

Sheila Perera is executive housekeeper at the five-star Gleneagles Hotel, the luxury golfing resort in Scotland. Originally from Dunfermline, Fife, Sheila graduated from Strathclyde University in 1970 with a BA in Hotel and Catering Management. She then joined Trusthouse Forte's personnel and training division, working at St George's Hotel in Liverpool for 18 months before assisting in opening two hotels – Dublin's International Airport Hotel and Jamaica Pegasus Hotel, where she remained as executive housekeeper for 18 months. She then worked in South Africa and Sri Lanka before transferring to the Pierre Hotel in New York. She returned to the UK as training manager at the Hyde Park Hotel and executive housekeeper at the Westbury Hotel. She became executive housekeeper at Gleneagles in 1983. In 1987 she was voted Housekeeper of the Year and received the Catey Award for the Caterer and Hotelkeeper magazine. She is married to Allan, who also works at Gleneagles, and they have three children.

MARY KAMAL

Mary Kamal's career began in 1960 at the Jury's Hotel in Dublin, but she was introduced to supervisory work at the Skyway Hotel at London's Heathrow, where she was senior floor housekeeper and later catering supervisor. In 1965 her employers took over catering at No. 3 passenger building and she was assigned to supervise one of the restaurant/bars. She was later head cashier for J. Lyons and Co, the parent company, but returned to housekeeping in 1976 when she accepted the position of assistant housekeeper at the 700-bedroom Cunard Hotel. She later moved to the Europa in Mayfair, and to hotels in Germany. She returned to the UK for the £20 million refurbishment of the Hyatt Carlton Hotel. She is now executive housekeeper of the Lanesborough at Hyde Park Corner.

FLEUR McIVER

When Birmingham's five-star Swallow Hotel was named by the catering industry as Hotel of the Year in 1992, the judges made special reference to "attention to detail and service of every member of staff" – but the award must have brought particular pleasure to Kent-born Fleur McIver, its young head housekeeper. Still only 24 years old, she recruits and trains room staff and chambermaids to her own high standards. She has no trade secrets – "it's the right materials and good old elbow grease", she says – and the results speak for themselves through the hotel's 98 rooms and suites. The Swallow is a favourite with business leaders, show-business personalities, politicians and sports competitors.

PAT McDONALD

Convent-educated Pat McDonald got her early training at Dublin's Russell Hotel and is now head housekeeper at the five-star Cliveden at Taplow, Berkshire. In her 20s, she held this position at hotels in Gibraltar, then moved to the Oatland Park Hotel in Weybridge, Surrey. She was involved in the pre-opening of the Embassy House Hotel in London's Queensgate and was head housekeeper there from 1981-83. The rest of the decade saw her as deputy head housekeeper at Forty Seven Park Street and as executive head housekeeper at the Halcyon Hotel in Holland Park. She was appointed to her present job in 1987. Pat is a member of the UK Housekeepers Association.

DENISE BATESON

Denise Bateson realised from an early age that the hotel business – and housekeeping in particular – was the one in which she wanted to make her career. Born in Leicester in 1954, she was educated at Beauchamp College and Southend College and later worked as a trainee housekeeper at Wolverhampton's Park Hall Hotel. Before the age of 20 she was assistant head housekeeper at the Magnum in Leicester, which she left to broaden her experience in Johannesburg, South Africa, at the Sunnyside Park Hotel – as head housekeeper. From 1976-79 she was assistant director of housekeeping at the city's Carlton Hotel, then moved to the Detroit Plaza in Detroit, Michigan. She returned to the UK in 1980 to be executive housekeeper at the five-star Sheraton Park Tower Hotel in Knightsbridge – the European flagship of the international ITT Sheraton group. Denise has received many accolades in her career, most recently the Caterer and Hotelkeeper magazine's prestigious Catey award, but she says nothing gives her more fulfilment than enabling other employees to learn and realise their own potential. She somehow finds time to organise events for worthy causes, her latest being a charity fashion show which was featured in the leading trade magazines.

DEBORAH PRESTON

Deborah Preston's career developed via "progressively larger hotels", moving from floor housekeeper to deputy housekeeper to head housekeeper over a five-year period. Her first executive position was at the 800-bedroom Strand Palace Hotel in London, where she was executive housekeeper for six years. She then spent five years as a lecturer on accommodation management, returning to a more familiar routine as housekeeping executive at the Grosvenor House in Park Lane, where she remained for another six years. During her time there, she supervised many improvements and developed new systems to meet the changing needs of the industry. In 1992 she moved into the luxury country home market as accommodation manager at Danesfield House in Marlow, Buckinghamshire.

SHANE STEED

The Old Eight Bells in Robertsbridge, East Sussex, had been closed for some time when the brewery sold it to Shane Steed 18 years ago. She re-named the pub the Salehurst Halt and set about a substantial refurbishment programme, creating a traditional small country pub with traditional values and excellent food. A wide cross-section of clientele is catered for – the clergy, farm labourers, traditional craftsmen, Swiss car dealers and race-horse owners among them, and all without the aid of electronic games machines or chips-with-everything. Shane is ably supported in the business by her loyal assistants, her two sons and, occasionally, her husband Trevor, who follows his own profession elsewhere.

SUSAN FRANKLAND

Licensee of the Dobermann Inn, near Stowmarket in Suffolk, Susan Frankland has spent her life in the county. All her family had been connected with the licensed trade at some time, but she set off on a career in the 1960s and 1970s, breeding, judging and showing Dobermanns. Her name became a by-word for quality and she travelled throughout the UK and Europe judging. After her divorce in 1981, she started a business renovating and selling houses and, when an old tenant pub in Framsden came on the market, her skills in this field came to the fore. After only three weeks, the Dobermann Inn was born. Over the years her formula of good value, wide choice, relaxed atmosphere and immaculate hygiene have ensured her continuing success. She follows her family tradition of customer care above all things.

SUSAN LINDSAY

With her husband George, Susan Lindsay has been in the beer business for 15 years, and at the Nursery Inn in Heaton Norris, Stockport, for 12. Susan's policy is to provide good beer, good food, friendliness and cleanliness. With no music or pool tables, the Nursery is a pub where, she says, conversation is alive and kicking. Susan enjoys cooking wholesome food – her favourites are steak and kidney pie, fresh fish, roasts and curries, and she is delighted that what started as a part-time job has turned into a way of life.

PAULINE TYLER

Born in East London, Pauline Tyler was married to policeman Charles at the age of 17, and the mother of three children by the time she was 21. She discovered at an early age that she had a natural ability to turn her hand to any number of skills and was soon very proficient at dressmaking, cooking, knitting and hairdressing, and was much in demand among a wide circle of friends. When her husband retired from the police, the chidren were already leading their own lives and Pauline and he decided to realise a long-held ambition and buy a pub. After a year of searching they bought the Wooden Fender, a small country pub in Colchester. The quality of Pauline's food was soon appreciated, leading to the building of an 84-seater restaurant. As a tribute to their success, Charles was voted Innkeeper of the Year for the Eastern region for 1991/92.

SANDRA MILLS

Born in Tanzania of British parents, Sandra Mills came to England when she was 17 years old to do a hairdressing course and decided to stay. She worked in London's West End, where she eventually bought her own shop which she ran for four years before selling it and going to catering college. Sandra met her husband Steve when she was the franchisee of the catering in a snooker club and he was an area manager. Together they bought a very run-down pub, the Five Bells in Grantham. After five years of hard work, their gamble has paid off and they offer good food, good beer and en suite accommodation to a very appreciative clientele.

ALICE PERCIVAL

Alice Percival was born in Kenya and convent educated. After finishing school in Klosters she studied in Paris. In 1957 she married an army officer stationed in London, where she embarked on a modelling career which lasted until the arrival of her first baby, three years later, when the family moved to Essex. In 1976 she entered a partnership in a new seafood restaurant as chef/manageress and, although self-taught, she was much praised in several publications, including the Good Food Guide. The celebrated food writer of the time, Fanny Cradock, a customer who became a friend, dedicated a book to Alice. There followed several years of outside catering and directors' lunches. In 1986 Alice's husband died and she and her three children moved to a large Edwardian house near the centre of Cambridge. For three years the house was filled with boisterous students but, now that her family has left, she has upgraded the rooms and provides bed and breakfast accommodation of the highest quality for many of the visitors to Cambridge.

SUE O'GRADY

Born in East Sheen at the end of WWII, Sue O'Grady has since found her way across Putney Bridge and may be found dispensing food, drink and backchat at the Imperial Arms, at the bottom of the King's Road. Although Sue's grandmother had a hotel in Richmond, catering was not her first calling and she spent several years in advertising, working for agencies and with her own company, before finding this vocation. With her husband, the redoubtable Cornelius O'Grady, she cut her teeth on the Alma, in Parsons Green, before moving to the Imperial. Sue runs the front of the house and Cornelius the kitchen in this plushly restored Victorian pub, where oysters are flown in daily from County Cork and some of the best lobster, crab and Scotch beef is served alongside simpler fare, all washed down with good claret and fine real ale.

DOREEN WRAIGHT

The Tower Guest House, owned by Doreen Wraight, must qualify as one of the most unusual bed and breakfast establishments in the country. It is, in fact, a converted water tower situated behind her house in Dover. Doreen was born in Nottingham in 1933 and moved to Dover a year later. She married Ron in 1951 and they have three children. In 1966 Ron's work took the family abroad and they had many happy years in the Bahamas and the Grand Cayman Islands before returning to Dover in 1977. They re-bought 98 Priory Hill, the house they had built and sold before their departure. Doreen saw the potential of the old water tower overlooking the town and, after a great deal of hard work, opened it as a guest house in 1981, since when it has served as a friendly haven for visitors from both sides of the channel.

DIANA DUKE

Diana Duke lives at Elmdon Lee, a farmhouse on a 900-acre farm in the undulating countryside near the town of Saffron Walden in Essex. After the death of her husband, she farmed the land herself for ten years until her son Robert finished his studies at agricultural college and joined her. When Robert took over the running of the farm, Diana became a member of the Wolsey Lodge Consortium. She very much enjoys sharing her home with guests from all over the world, many of whom are regular visitors.

SYLVIA GRIFFITHS

A Shropshire girl born and bred, Sylvia Griffiths trained in domestic science before joining BOAC as a stewardess. In 1966 she married a company director of a family corn merchants business. In 1976, with three sons plus a daughter on the way, they moved to The Citadel, a large castellated house built as a dower house by the Hill family. With the children away at school and the bills mounting, they decided to fill the house with paying guests. Eight years on, the business has grown and become extremely successful. Sylvia's year now consists of six months looking after the guests and six months concentrating on the family, the garden, needlework and holidaying abroad.

ELISABETH LUARD

In 1992 Elizabeth Luard won the Glenfiddich Award for the outstanding Cookery Book of the Year for her Flavours of Andalusia. Initially, her reputation was made by a trilogy of books on the basic rural cookery of Europe. European Peasant Cookery (1986), The Barricaded Larder (1988) and Festival Foods (1990). Whenever possible she illustrates her own work, reflecting her earlier career as a wildlife artist. She has a weekly column in the Scotsman, is a contributing editor to Country Living and has recently finished filming a television series titled the Rich Tradition of European Peasant Cookery for SBS Australia.

FRANCES BISSELL

Frances Bissell has been called "the best private cook in Britain" but has been the guest cook at some of the world's leading hotels. She has been the Times cook since 1987 and her writing has appeared in many publications including the Sunday Times, Homes and Gardens and BBC Good Food Guide. She has written several cookery books.

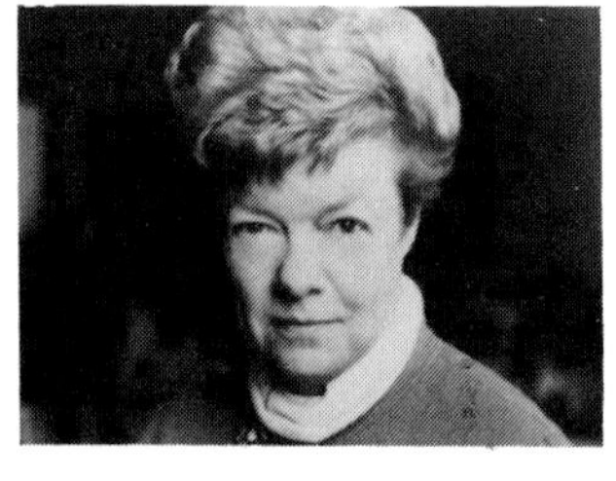

PAMELA VANDYKE PRICE

Pamela Vandyke Price was born in 1923 which, she says, is a good vintage for many classic wines. She acquired an honours degree in English at Oxford and worked in various types of consumer and trade journalism. She has edited Wine and Food, and written regularly for the Observer and the Sunday Times, broadcasted and lectured worldwide. She is a member of various wine fraternities, including being the first woman to be elected as "Dame et Prud'homme" to the Jurade of St. Emilion and has published numerous books on Wine and Food.

ARABELLA BOXER

Half Scottish and half American, Arabella Boxer was educated in England, Paris and Rome. She began writing about food in 1963 and since then has written 12 books and been food editor of Vogue for 16 years. She has won the Andre Simon, Michael Smith and Glenfiddich awards for her books and journalism. She is a founder member of the Guild of Food Writers and is currently writing a new book.

Photograph by Sandra Lousada

JANCIS ROBINSON, MW

Jancis Robinson is the only British journalist to have qualified as a Master of Wine, having passed the notoriously vigorous practical and theoretical exams at the first attempt. She was the award-winning wine correspondent of the Sunday Times between 1980 and 1986 and now writes regularly for the Financial Times and the Spectator in the US. She has written seven books of which Vines, Grapes and Wines has been published in six languages and has been particularly successful in France. She has been chosen by Oxford University Press as editor of a forthcoming Oxford Companion to Wine, a major new work of reference to be published in 1994. Jancis is probably best known as a television presenter, notably with three series of the Wine Programme. With her husband, Nicholas Lander who is Financial Times restaurant correspondent, she has produced as well as presented Matters of Taste, an award-winning series of six documentaries on various aspects of eating and drinking shown three times on Channel 4 in 1991.

FAY MASCHLER

Fay Maschler was born in a Himilayan hill station, and educated in England and New England. Her first serious job was as a copywriter for J. Walter Thompson, in London. She went from there to be assistant features editor at the Radio Times. In 1970 she married publisher Tom Maschler and his enthusiasm for eating good food nurtured her interest in making it, which had started when, aged 12, she was bored and lonely, having moved to Connecticut where she knew no-one. In 1972, Fay won a writing competition run by the Evening Standard. Quentin Crewe had just resigned as restaurant critic, and the prize was doing the restaurant column for three months. Twenty years later she is still doing it. She has three children and, having got divorced in 1986, married novelist Reg Gadney in 1992.

Photograph courtesy of The Evening Standard

SERENA SUTCLIFFE, MW

Serena Sutcliffe is a director of Sotheby's and head of Sotheby's wine department. In 1976 she became a Master of Wine. She is the author of many books, widely translated, her latest work being A Celebration of Champagne and Guide to the Wines of Burgundy. In 1988 she was made a Chevalier dans l'Ordre des Arts et des Lettres by the French Government for her services to literature on French wine. She is married to David Peppercorn, a distinguished Master of Wine, and they live in London.

Courtesy of Sotheby's

JOANNA SIMON

Joanna Simon, 1992 Glenfiddich Drink Writer of the Year and 1992 Qantas Wine Writer of the Year, is one of the new generation of consumers. She has been wine correspondent of the Sunday Times since 1987. Before that, while still in her 20s, she edited Wine and Spirit International. She contributes to a wide variety of publications and is currently working on Discovering Wine for publication in 1994.

Photograph by David Ridge

GAY BIDDLECOMBE →

Gay Biddlecombe is one of England's leading wine producers and a publicist who has helped put English wine on the map. A former newspaper journalist she writes, broadcasts and gives talks on wine. Her book about the establishment of her St George's Vineyard in 1979 is due for publication this year. The vineyard, in Sussex, consists of 20 acres, with a modern winery producing eight wines, including methode champenoise and oak aged wines. She makes wine for other vineyards and runs a wine club whose members "own" a vine at St George's. She exports her wines worldwide. Gay was the first producer to open to the public with a substantial shop and gourmet restaurant, the first to introduce "own label" wines and the first to introduce commemorative wines.

JAN ROBERTS AND FIONA HOLMES ↓

Jan Roberts and Fiona Holmes are brewers with Guinness. Fiona has brewing in her blood; her father spent 32 years with Guinness in Ireland and her husband is a master brewer. She joined Courage Breweries in 1983, after university, as site microbiologist and won the company's scholarship to brewing school. As a brewer she held several positions within brewing and packaging and, in 1990, passed her master brewers' examinations. She joined Guinness in the same year. Jan Roberts was born in Glasgow and studied applied microbiology at Strathclyde University, before taking an MSc at UMIST in biochemical engineering. In 1986 she joined Unilever Research for two years before moving to Guinness to pursue a career in production. She was the brewer for Kaliber, the non-alcohol lager (produced and advertised by Glaswegians!). At present she is involved in production projects and as support for the lager production team.

JULIA BRIDGEWATER ↑

The vineyard at Conghurst in Kent was originally planted by Julia Bridgewater's mother, Barbara, in 1979. Julia took over the vineyard in 1987 and set about expansion. A theatre designer by qualification, Julia was made redundant by the BBC in 1991, and now feels the need to expand and diversify. In the interests of furthering her education Julia studied viticulture and oenology at Plumpton College, and is the first woman ever to gain the City & Guilds Horticulture Phase III Viticulture and Oenology. The exclusive Conghurst Blush, made by Stephen Donnelly at Lamberhurst Vineyards, was the Bronze Award winner in the 1991 Wine Magazine International Challenge.

GILLIAN PEARKES ▲

Gillian Pearkes is the owner of the National Vine Centre, in the Exe valley, where she propagates more varieties of ancient and modern vines than anyone else in the country. She has been fascinated with the ancient culture of the vine since she was 16 years old, and spent ten years experimenting with various vareties, before first planting professionally in 1976, on a steep south-facing rocky slope in Devon, which proved incredibly successful even in cool summers. Also in 1976 she was awarded the Nuffield Travelling Scholarship to France and Germany. In 1980 she started the Yearlstone Viticultural Courses for new growers – an ongoing project. In 1984 she published Vinegrowing in Britain and lectured at the first Cool Climate Viticultural Symposium in Oregan, USA. Gillian is a Fellow of the Royal Agricultural Societies of England, and her National Vine Collection is registered with the Royal Horticultural Society. She is planning the planting of the Ultimate Vineyard for the 21st century, with classic varieties, and the yield kept low to ensure quality.

HELEN TARRY ▼

A farmer's daughter, Helen Tarry attended agricultural college and kept her own herd of cows. Some 15 years ago her love of the land extended to a love of the grape and the resulting wine. She worked with Bernard Theobald on the Westbury vineyard and, amongst others, developed the first pinot noir red wine to be produced commercially in England and the only English red to attain the seal of quality. With the sad death of Bernard Theobald, the original Westbury ceased to be, but Helen is keeping the name alive working her own winery.

MOYRA WILLIAMS ▲

Born and educated in Greenock, Scotland, Moyra Williams won the Duke of Edinburgh's gold award in 1983 and went to Heriot-Watt University where she graduated BSc in microbiology and brewing in 1987. She spent six months in Australia before returning to England to take up a laboratory position at McMullen's Brewery in Hertford. Nine months later she joined George Gale & Co Ltd, the independent Hampshire brewery, as third brewer. Her duties were initially in the brewhouse and fermentation areas, but now she is responsible for beer post-fermentation and packaging. Moyra is a member of the Institute of Brewing and the Brewers' Guild, for which she is very active in the London area. She continues to attend lectures and courses relating to the brewing industry and keeps up her brewing connection with Heriot-Watt University at the annual Former Brewing Students' Dinner, which always takes place on the evening of one of the Five Nations rugby internationals, emphasising the balance of learning and fun in brewing.

CLAIRE HINDE

Having completed the Advanced Cordon Bleu course at Ewart Place in Oxford, Claire Hind began her catering career in traditional fashion, with a season in Val d'Isere. Returning to London in 1984, she quickly became in demand for cooking in the city, where she spent two years polishing her skills before the opportunity arose to start her own business. Her husband owned a building company and, during the course of shopfitting a wine merchant in Fulham, the owner casually mentioned that he wished to lease part of the premises, possibly to a catering company. Claire needed no second bidding and within two weeks had opened Hinde Catering on the Wandsworth Bridge Road. Claire now operates a small, exclusive catering company from her own premises in South Kensington, where she continues to defy the recession.

FIONA BURRELL

Co-principal of Leith's School of Food and Wine, Fiona Burrell was born in 1955 in Birkenhead. She graduated with an HND in Industrial Management, Catering and Domestic Administration at Queen Margaret College, Edinburgh, in 1977, and went on to acquire a second string to her bow in the form of a secretarial qualification. She became assistant to the principal of the Woman & Home Cook School in Edinburgh and, when the school closed in 1978, she became a director of a consortium of the employees who took over the lease, trading as Cookright Ltd. From 1980 to 1981, Fiona was food technician to the Home Economics department of her old college in Edinburgh and, for the next two years, took various freelance jobs in Edinburgh, as a chalet girl and, latterly, in London. She joined Leith's in 1983 as a teacher and worked her way up to become co-principal in 1991. Fiona has contributed to Leith's Cookery Bible (1991) and co-authored, with Prue Leith and Caroline Waldegrave, Leith's Complete Christmas (1992).

LYN HALL

Lyn Hall's career in restaurant management began in 1970. Six years later, having worked her way up to chef in a luxury hotel, she opened her own cookery school, La Petite Cuisine School of Cooking, which was soon regarded as one of the finest in Britain. At the same time, she contributed to a number of books and magazines, which led to a series of apprenticeships in the best restaurants in France, augmented by studies in butchery, patisserie, wine, caking-decorating and bread making. In 1986 she joined a consultancy and extended her experience in the food industry by developing recipes, training staff, creating food for product launches and trouble-shooting in restaurants. She designed and set up an English restaurant which achieved Michelin standard. In 1991 Lyn decided to return to teaching and opened La Petite Cuisine at The Waterside Inn, with Michel Roux. Classes in regional cooking in the French Alps and Bachelor Cooks in London soon followed. The consultancy continues to thrive and Lyn intends to increase her teaching portfolio, and open another school.

SALLY DAVIES

Sally Davies is a diploma graduate of Winkfield Cordon Bleu Cookery College. After completing her course, she worked for Cordon Bleu as a junior teacher for eight months before taking over the restaurant at the General Trading company for a year, followed by running the salad bar at Body's Health Club, in Chelsea. She founded her company, Ingredience, in 1986, providing flexible cuisine for all occasions, formal and informal. Sally lives and works in Fulham.

SILVIJA DAVIDSON

Born in England of Latvian refugee parents, Silvija Davidson developed an interest in Baltic cuisine at home. Her interest in wine was induced during her time at Newnham College, Cambridge, where she read English. Fortunately, Silvija's husband shares her passion for good food and wine and, when she landed a job at the headquarters of the International Wine & Food Society, they jointly seized the opportunity to organise tastings for the London branch of the society. Since winning numerous cookery competitions, including the prestigious Mouton Cadet and TV's Masterchef, Silvija has combined her literary and culinary skills; she currently writes a cookery column for Scotland on Sunday and is a member of the Guild of Food Writers. Silvija feels and The Taste Trials open public tastings (in conjunction with La Vigneronne), which she and her husband run, bear this out. strongly that the enjoyment of the finest produce comes from educating the palate – at any age and both the Marriage of Food and Wine course at Le Cordon Bleu

LADY ELIZABETH ANSON

Party Planners, the longest standing company of its kind in Britain, was founded by Lady Elizabeth Anson in 1960, when she was just 19 years old. She has built up an unequalled reputation since then for helping with the organisation of any party, whether large or small, grand or simple, private or business; from tea parties to large dances, fashion shows to charity balls. A cousin of the Queen, Lady Elizabeth has organised private parties for most members of the Royal Family, and for foreign royalty at home and abroad, including the wedding of the Prince and Princess Michael of Kent in Vienna. Other clients she has organised parties for include Douglas Fairbanks Jnr, Mick Jagger, John Paul Getty and Princess Ira von Furstenberg and companies such as the Rank Organisation, the Royal Ballet, Lloyds Bank and the BBC. She is the author of Lady Elizabeth Anson's Party Planners Book and has recently re-launched Party Planners Products, marketing items specifically chosen by her in Japan and the USA.

CAROLINE NEVILLE

Caroline Neville Associates was set up in 1962, and has established a reputation as one of the most respected and successful in the business. Specialising in consumer public relations, with clients ranging from small companies to the world's largest, the agency's expertise lies in a broad range of areas, including luxury goods, beauty, fashion, the home, the arts, travel and tourism, publishing and personal PR. Among the special events handled recently are the Midsummer Night's Magic Ball at the Dorchester, Queen Charlotte's Birthday Ball Appeal, press relations for the Queen's Cup polo final at Smith's Lawn and the House of Lords vs House of Commons charity swim. Previously, the company handled Cartier International Polo for seven years and helped to create the Cartier Million horse race.

LORNA WING

Lorna Wing is one of Britain's most original party organisers. She has organised dinners for royalty, prime ministers and presidents. Art, public relations and fashion companies too, have had a taste of her imaginative and exquisitely presented food. Lorna ran the highly acclaimed Heal's Restaurant in the mid-1980s and now organises a wide variety of memorable events, private and business, from intimate dinners for two to wedding receptions and corporate lunches for 500. Lorna is the originator of the much-copied fashion for shrinking traditional dishes to canape-size, including fish and chips in tiny Financial times cones and bacon and eggs the size of a 10p piece. Her food can be either serious or light-hearted, but is always inventive and delicious. As well as undertaking food photography and styling for various publications, she acts as consultant to restaurants, food retailers and producers.

JUDI SMITH

Born in the North East of Scotland, in the heart of Aberdeen Angus country, Judi Smith has been interested in quality food all her life. For 26 years she has run her own outside catering business, specialising in private events for 100 to 1,000 people, and working from recommendations. She has always sourced and used the best local (Devon) ingredients before buying from further afield. For the past 12 years, Judi has also been a partner in British Event Caterers, which specialises in public events, providing everything from the marquee to the flowers, food, drink and entertainment for numbers from 1,000 upwards. Work undertaken includes air shows, flower shows, Navy days and special events in Hyde Park. For ten years she ran her own cookery school in the South West and has lectured regularly at La Petite Cuisine in London and around the country. Judi is the marketing executive for Devon Fare Ltd.

JACQUELINE LLEWELYN

After spending several years organising and running parties of all sizes for various London caterers and party planners, Jacqueline Llewelyn set up her own business, specialising in weddings. Jacqueline Llewelyn Weddings Ltd offers a consultancy service to brides covering everything from the legal and administrative processes of marriage to the planning and etiquette of the wedding. Jacqueline's commitment to ensuring that every wedding is as personal as the union it celebrates has etablished her reputation as an authority in her field. She frequently appears on radio and television, is a regular contributor to bridal features and publications and is the author of Debrett's Wedding Guide – The Planning and Etiquette of a Modern Wedding. A graduate of Manchester University, Jacqueline lives in London with her husband, designer and painter Laurence Llewelyn-Bowen.

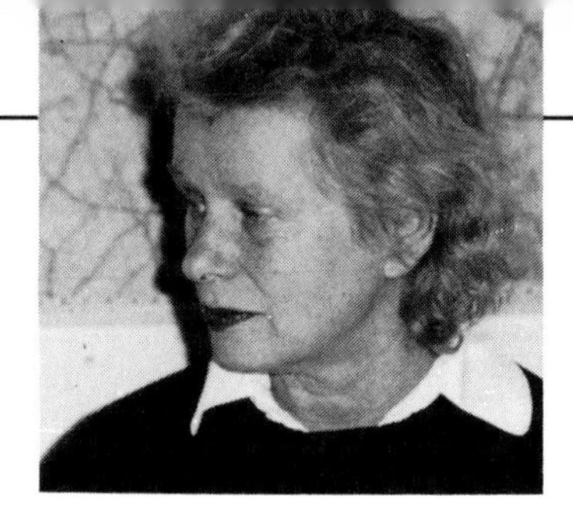

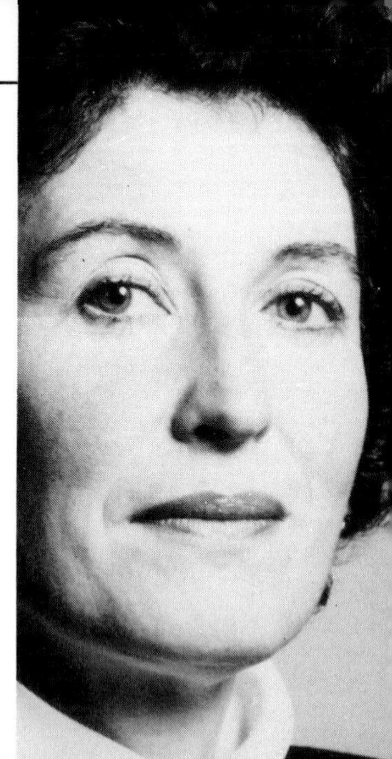

AVRIL ROBERTSON

Avril Robertson was born in Edinburgh and spent her childhood on the island of Coll, before attending Queen's College, Glasgow, where she obtained a certificate in institutional management and large scale catering. Since then she has worked in Ayrshire, Canada, Leamington Spa, Coventry, Preston, Manchester, Bradford and Strathclyde. She has held posts in hotels, restaurants, hospitals, civic catering, department store catering and local authority catering. Her present position is as director of the largest contract catering organisation in Scotland, with 6,500 staff and over 2,000 catering units. She is responsible for a budget in excess of £65 million. Avril Robertson is also a governor of Queen's College, Glasgow, and is a member of the College Council for the Glasgow College of Food Technology.

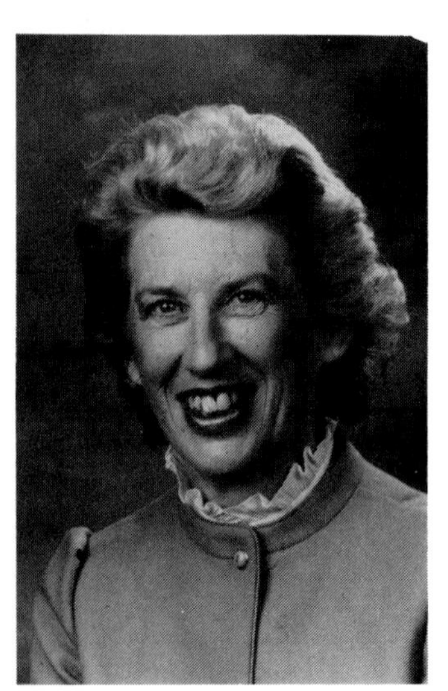

SALLY SPRATT

Sally Spratt founded the Good Eating Company in 1978, catering for directors' lunches, cocktail parties and a wide variety of social functions. In 1984 she set up a sister company, the Good Eating Film Food Company, operating on site with mobile kitchens, for film companies and advertising agencies.

VANESSA BELLAMY, VICTORIA WOODERSON AND MANDY KEEGAN

Victoria Wooderson, Vanessa Bellamy and Mandy Keegan are the joint project managers of WRAP, the company that specialises in providing parties for the film, television and arts industries. Vanessa has been in party planning for 12 years, and has organised parties for clients as diverse as Louis Vuitton and the New Zealand Admiral's Cup team. Victoria, whose great love is dance and the theatre, gained her expertise organising parties in the Caribbean, while Mandy, an enthusiastic singer with her own band, has been organising events since she left college three years ago. Together, they will arrange end-of-picture parties; end-of-tour parties; opening night parties; brunch parties; go-karting parties – any sort of party you want, really.

CELIA BUTLER

Celia Butler began her career in catering working for George Perry-Smith at the Hole-in-the-Wall in Bath in 1968. In 1971 she opened her own restaurant, The Salamander, in Brighton, with a wine bar downstairs. She also provided outside catering for London Livery Halls and the Mansion House, amongst others. She sold the restaurant in 1975 and, in 1976, started Butler's Catering. Celia caters for cocktail parties, suppers and weddings, conferences, business luncheons and dinners, government departments and royal occasions. Her aim is to provide delicious food, temptingly presented.

JUDY TARLO

Born in London and brought up in the United States, Judy Tarlo used to produce a popular nightly talk show on New York's WMCA radio, where she was responsible for booking well-known personalities and arranging special outside broadcasts. Returning to England in 1966, she joined Columbia Pictures and, in 1968, she moved to Rogers and Cowan, as deputy managing director of their international division. After running her own company in Covent Garden, she joined Media Relations Ltd in 1988, and has been responsible for the organisation and publicity of, amongst other things, the BAFTA Award ceremonies, BAFTA tributes, Queen Charlottes Ball, in 1991, the Oscar Night at the Ritz and Joy to the World at the Albert Hall for the past three years.

JANE ASHER

Multi-talented Jane Asher runs several careers simultaneously, as actress, author, caterer, retailer and mother, as well as sitting on many committees and taking an active part in numerous charities. She has written several successful books, including Jane Asher's Party Cakes (1982), Jane Asher's Fancy Dress (1983), Silent Nights for You and Your Baby (1984), Jane Asher's Quick Party Cakes (1986), The Moppy Stories (1987), Easy Entertaining (1987), Keep Your Baby Safe (1988), Children's Parties (1988), Calendar of Cakes (1989) and Eats for Treats (1990). She is currently working on two new books. In October 1990 Jane opened Jane Asher Party Cakes Shop and Tea Room, in Chelsea, which now supplies many of London's leading hotels and restaurants, producing thousands of individually commissioned cakes each year, which are all baked on the premises. Jane Asher also works in journalism and has had a monthly column in the Daily Telegraph and a weekly column in the Independent. She is a fellow of the Royal Society of Arts, a member of BAFTA, an associate of RADA, a governor of the Molecule Theatre and a member of the General Advisory Council to the BBC. Incredibly, Jane Asher still finds time to be one of Britain's busiest and most celebrated actresses.

KATE ADIE

The awards won by Kate Adie for her services to news reporting are too numerous to detail, but include RTS Television Journalism Awards in 1981, 1987 and 1989, Monte Carlo International Television Golden Nymph Awards in 1981 and 1990 (the latter for her coverage of the student uprising in China), the BAFTA Richard Dimbleby Award 1990, when she was also Television and Radio Industries Club News Personality/Presenter of the Year. Kate started work as a studio technician with BBC local radio after graduating in Scandinavian studies from the University of Newcastle-upon-Tyne. She specialised in farming and arts programmes in Bristol, and worked as a director in television outside broadcasts, before moving into news as a regional reporter at BBC Plymouth. Kate joined BBC TV national news in 1979, covering general news stories at home and abroad, was court correspondent for two years, and now specialises in foreign reporting, particularly from the worlds "hot spots". She was appointed Chief News Correspondent in 1989.

ESTHER RANTZEN

Esther Rantzen joined the BBC in 1963, equipped with an MA(Hons) degree in English from Somerville College, Oxford. In 1965 she started work for Ned Sherrin as a researcher and, in 1968, became a reporter for Bernard Braden on Braden's Week. In 1973 she became producer/presenter for That's Life, a programme that has run ever since. Esther's other current series is The Big Time, which started in 1988. During the last 20 years Esther has presented and produced numerous shows and various documentaries about religious and current affairs and social issues. She is a tireless worker for charities, and campaigner on issues concerning mothers and children, and the disabled. She is the founder and chairman of Childline, the president of Meet-a-Mum (combating post-natal depression) and a patron and trustee of numerous charities. She has won many awards for journalism and television, including BBC TV Personality of the Year in 1975, and in 1991 was awarded the OBE.

SUE CARPENTER

Sue Carpenter graduated MA in English from King's College, London, in 1978. She entered the broadcasting world in 1982, as editor of the day and newsreader at Dubai Television. She joined BBC TV Bristol in 1983 and worked there until 1985 as presenter of Points West. She was a reporter for the Holiday Programme from 1984 to 1986 and, in 1985, presented Spotlight, Look East and London Plus for a year and broke into national newsreading on Breakfast Time, News Afternoon and Newsview. In December 1986, Sue transferred to ITN, where she presented all the major news programmes until November 1992. In June 1992 she became narrator for Trans World Sport.

ANNA FORD

Anna Ford read Social Anthropology at Manchester University before taking a post graduate diploma in adult education. She taught in Belfast for four years, and then became a staff tutor for Northern Ireland for the Open University. In 1974 she joined Granada TV as a researcher, working on numerous local and schools programmes. In 1976 she joined the BBC Man Alive team, and then spent a short time working on Tomorrow's World. She joined ITN in 1978, and stayed there until joining TV-am as one of the pioneers in 1981. Since TV-am, Anna has worked as a freelance TV presenter and broadcaster, and has researched and written a book on men. She can currently be seen reading the Six O'Clock News on BBC 1.

JULIA SOMERVILLE

After graduating from Sussex University, Julia Somerville joined IPC, working on Homes and Gardens and Woman's Journal. She spent two years as editor of a computer group's house magazine before joining the BBC in 1973, as a sub-editor in the radio newsroom. She became chief-sub and then a reporter and was made Labour Affairs Correspondent in 1981. In 1984 she joined the Nine O'Clock News and was a senior presenter until moving to ITN in 1987. Julia is a member of the presenting team on ITN's flagship programme, News at Ten, and introduces the Focus on Britain section three times a week.

GLORIA HUNNIFORD

In 1982 Gloria Hunniford left her native Northern Ireland to become the first woman to have her own show on BBC Radio 2. It had taken her 30 years to become an overnight success. She started singing at the age of nine in Northern Ireland and, subsequently, starred on the three television networks and made a couple of records. Broadcasting became her top priority in 1969 starting with news and current affairs and going on to have her own daily radio programme and, ultimately, her own daily TV programme for Ulster Television. Gloria now has her own daily programme on Radio 2, her own chat show on LWT, and appears constantly in quiz shows, holiday programmes et al. She is currently co-hosting "Family Matters" with her daughter. Gloria was Variety Club Radio Personality of the Year 1982, and TV Times TV Personality of the Year 1985.

TANIA BRYER

Tania Bryer was one of the most well-known faces on Sky, and then BSkyB, satellite television until 1992. A graduate of Georgetown University, Washington DC, she founded her own company, Promotion Associates of London, in 1985. She organised fashion shows in hotel restaurants making those locations the fashionable place to be for ladies who lunch. In the late 1980s Tania was offered a modelling contract; a model for three years, she worked in Tokyo, London and New York – where she also took acting classes. Early in 1991, when she was working in the promotions and advertising department of Vogue magazine, Tania was approached by Sky Television and asked to become a presenter. In 1992 she moved from weather to presenting all the channel's lifestyle and fashion features. Late in 1992, she joined the breakfast television channel TV-am. Tania, who enjoys music, theatre, opera and ballet, is a dedicated skier and tennis player.

JULIET MORRIS

Juliet Morris is a presenter and reporter for the BBC television news and current affairs programme for children, Newsround. She writes her own material and has presented both in the UK and abroad – for Newsround and for Newsround Extra. Her many assignments include reports from Israel during the Gulf War and coverage of the Prime Minister's visit to the Vietnamese refugee camps in Hong Kong. Juliet has presented Children in Need, a regular live discussion slot on Going Live! and, in 1993, will present 999 with Michael Buerk for BBC television. A former presenter of Spotlight, the BBC's main daily news magazine programme in the South West, she has also worked in radio – as a reporter for GWR (Bristol) and Radio Orwell (Suffolk).

JILL DANDO

In 1993 Jill Dando presents Holiday '93 for BBC television, from locations including Mexico, Australia and Bournemouth. A graduate of BBC local radio, she worked for BBC Radio Devon's Breakfast Show and the Sunday Morning Show for BBC Radio Bristol. She became a presenter with BBC Southwest''s regional nightly news programme Spotlight and then with the BBC's Breakfast News. In 1991 she co-presented the series Safari UK with Julian Pettifer and, in 1992, worked with BBC News on General Election coverage – appearing in the morning for Breakfast News and in the evening for the Nine O'Clock News. Jill has many other presentation credits, including Children in Need, This is the Day and the Royal television Society Programme Awards for the BBC.

CHRISTINE WEBBER

A former dancer, Christine Webber is a television presenter and agony aunt for the Daily Star. Her earliest ambition to become a singer was thwarted by a teacher who told her that her legs were better than her voice! She was the female lead dancer for the Black and White Minstrel Show until the late 1970s, when she became a presenter for Anglia television. Although Christine worked largely in news, she also interviewed a lion tamer in a cage with six lions, had knives thrown at her in a cabaret act and became a trapeze artist for a day. A presenter with Angiia until 1990, she also worked on medical and social features. Christine is now co-presenter of the Meridian television series Future Perfect. A successful writer, she is awaiting the publication of her second novel.

PAMELA ARMSTRONG

Pamela Armstrong is the main presenter of BBC World Service Television News. She has previously presented ITN's News at Ten, Breakfast Time, Daytime Live and the Pamela Armstrong Show for the BBC, as well as Channel 4's health magazine Well Being. Pamela's ease with the camera is reflected in her ability to communicate at all levels and in the empathy which she has for her guests – whoever they might be. Ever popular with the viewing public, Pamela has made numerous celebrity appearances on game and quiz shows, including Blankety Blank, Tell The Truth, Through The Keyhole and Call My Bluff; she has also appeared as an extra in the comedy series French and Saunders. Her high media profile means that she is always in demand for corporate and conference presentation, Pamela has presented for numerous clients – from Rank Hovis McDougal to Coca-Cola.

JUDI DENCH

A respected theatre name who has also made her mark in popular TV comedy, Dame Judi Dench was awarded an OBE in 1970 and became a Dame of the British Empire in 1988. She was educated in York and at the Central School of Speech and Drama and was with the Old Vic company from 1957-61, playing Ophelia in Hamlet and Juliet in Romeo and Juliet. Through the 1960s and 1970s she consolidated her position as one of Britain's leading actresses and picked up numerous awards, including Best Actress of the Year from the Guild of Television Directors in 1967 for the TV drama Talking to a Stranger. She won a BAFTA Best Actress award in 1985 for the sitcom A Fine Romance, which she starred in alongside her real-life husband Michael Williams. In 1987 she was named Best Supporting Actress for the film A Room With a View.

Her latest success is the BBC sitcom As Times Goes By.

DEBORAH WARNER

Deborah Warner trained at the Central School of Speech and Drama and in 1980 founded the Kick Theatre Company for whom she directed The Tempest and King Lear among others. She was resident director for the Royal Shakespeare Company from 1988-89 and won the Evening Standard Award and the Olivier award for Best Director for Titus Andronicus. In 1991 she directed Hedda Gabler at the Abbey Theatre, Dublin, and the Playhouse, London. In the same year she directed Electra at the Riverside Studios on a UK tour and in Bobigny, France. She has recently been awarded the Chevalier de L'Ordre des Arts et des Lettres by the French government. In the later part of 1993 she will direct Coriolanus at the Salzburg Festival and plans a production of Don Giovanni at Glyndebourne in 1994.

THELMA HOLT

After an acting career, Thelma Holt co-founded the Open Space Theatre along with Charles Marowitz and it became the forerunner of the London Fringe. In 1977 she joined the Round House as artistic and executive director, bringing the best of regional theatre and the Edinburgh Festival to London audiences. In 1985 she joined the National Theatre as head of touring and commercial exploitation. For Peter Hall's company, she was executive producer of the London production of Tennessee Williams' Orpheus Descending, Shakespeare's The Merchant of Venice (with Dustin Hoffman as Shylock) and The Wild Duck. She also produced the acclaimed version of Three Sisters with Vanessa, Lynn and Jemma Redgrave at the Queen's Theatre. In 1992 she produced Hamlet with Alan Rickman in the title role.

TIMBERLAKE WERTENBAKER

Certainly a name to remember, Timberlake Wertenbaker won the Evening Standard's Most Promising Playwright award and the Laurence Olivier Best Play award for Our Country's Good. She was resident writer at the Royal Court Theatre from 1984-85 and one of her later plays, Three Birds Alighting on a Field, won her the Critics Circle Award for Best New Play in 1992. Other plays include Abel's Sister and Inside Out. She adapted Edith Wharton's novel The Children for Channel 4 and has written an original screenplay for the BBC, Do Not Disturb. Her work as a playwright earned her the Whiting Writers Award.

BARONESS O'CATHAIN

Detta, Baroness O'Cathain of the Barbican in the City of London, is the managing director of the Barbican Centre, one of London's most impressive venues for theatre, concerts and film screenings. Prior to her appointment in 1990 she held management positions in industry, most recently with the Milk Marketing Board. Her career had begun with Aer Lingus in 1959 and she remained with them until 1966 as assistant economist. She moved via Tarmac and the car giants Rootes/Chrysler and British Leyland to Unigate in 1976. She was their corporate planning executive, leaving in 1981 to join the MMB. She was awarded the OBE in 1983 and became a life peer in 1991. She is a Fellow of the Royal Society of Arts and the Chartered Institute of Marketing. She has homes in London and Arundel, Sussex.

MAUREEN LIPMAN

Maureen's accolades include a nomination for a SWET Award for Best Comedy Performance as Maggie in Outside Edge and a nomination for a SWET Award for Best Actress for her role in Martin Sherman's Messiah. She won the Laurence Olivier Award for Best Comedy Performance and the Variety Club Award for her performances in the play See How They Run at the Shaftesbury. On TV she has appeared in the award winning The Evacuees written by her husband Jack Rosenthal, Agony (for which she was nominated for a BAFTA for Best Comedy Performance), and Outside Edge and Alan Bennett's Rolling Home, both of which won her BAFTA Award nominations for Best Actress. The lead role in the Thames TV comedy All At No 20 won her the TV Times Best Comedy Actress Award. Her films include Educating Rita, for which she was nominated for a BAFTA for Best Supporting Actress, Water, with Michael Caine and Carry on Columbus. Maureen's one-man show Re: Joyce, about the life of Joyce Grenfell, had four sell-out seasons in the West End and, of course, she is well-loved as Beatie in the British Telecom ads.

HELENA BONHAM-CARTER

Twenty-six year old Helena Bonham-Carter's debut film appearance was in the title role of Lady Jane in 1984. Since then she has appeared in all three of Merchant Ivory's adaptations of E M Forster novels, as Lucy Honeychurch in A Room With A View, in Maurice and, most recently, as Helen Schlegel in Howards End. Her other films include Where Angels Fear To Tread, La Maschera, A Hazard of Hearts, Francesco and Getting It Right. She also played Ophelia in Franco Zeffirelli's Hamlet. Here television credits include The Vision, Arms and The Man, Beatrix Potter and a guest appearance in Miami Vice.

HELEN MIRREN

Helen Mirren was born Ilynea Lydia Mironoff, the grand-daughter of a Tsarist army officer, to an English mother and a Russian father. She grew up in Essex where she received a convent education. Helen made her first film, Michael Powell's Age Of Consent, with James Mason, in 1969, and the following year she joined the RSC and set what has become the pattern for her career, mixing film and stage work in about equal measures – Prime Suspect marked a rare excursion into contemporary TV drama. She won Best Actress awards from Plays and Players for her performances as Nina in The Seagull, directed by Lindsay Anderson and Maggie in David Hare's Teeth 'N' Smiles at the Royal Court. The title role in The Duchess of Malfi won her Best Actress Award from the Vareity Club. Her films include The Long Good Friday, starring role in Cal, for which she won Best Actress Award in Cannes in 1984, Excalibur, The Mosquito Coast, Pascali's Island, The Comfort of Strangers and Where Angels Fear To Tread. Her title or leading roles for television include Cousin Bette, Miss Julie, The Changeling and Dennis Potter's Blue Remembered Hills. She also starred with Laurence Olivier in The Collection and Kenneth Branagh in Coming Through and Cause Célèbre.

PAULINE COLLINS

Pauline Collins is best known for Shirley Valentine and her television roles as Sarah in Upstairs, Downstairs and Thomas and Sarah, and No Honestly, Wodehouse Playhouse and most recently, in Forever Green, now in its third series. In 1987 she starred in the highly acclaimed production of Woman In Mind at the Vaudeville Theatre and in The Colonel's Lady, one of the Tales of the Unexpected plays. In 1988 she played the title role in Shirley Valentine at the Vaudeville for which she won the Olivier Award for Best Actress of the Year. She went on to repeat the success with the film and won a BAFTA Award for Best Actress. She was nominated for an Oscar and Golden Globe Award. For her 1989 performance in Shirley Valentine at the Booth Theatre, New York, Pauline received a host of awards for Best Actress. Last year she starred as Pearl in Shades at the Albery. Her first book, Letter to Louise, was published by Bantam Press last October.

MAGGIE SMITH

Maggie Smith made her debut with the Oxford University Drama Society as Viola in 1952 and since then has been awarded two Oscars, countless Best Actress awards and has received both a CBE and DBE. In 1963 she joined the National Theatre at the Old Vic and appeared in Othello, playing Desdemona opposite Laurence Olivier. Her films include Oh! What a Lovely War, The Prime of Miss Jean Brodie (for which she received a Best Actress Oscar and the Society of Film and TV Best Actress Award), California Suite, for which she won an Oscar and Golden Globe Award, A Private Function, which earned her a BAFTA award, and A Room With A View, which won her a BAFTA, Golden Globe and Variety Club Awards and her fifth Oscar nomination. In 1991 Dame Maggie was awarded the Hamburg Shakespeare Prize. She is a Fellow of the BFI, an honorary DLitt of St Andrews University and a patron of the Jane Austen Society.

VANESSA REDGRAVE

Vanessa Redgrave trained for eight years at the Ballet Rambert School and graduated from the Central School of Speech and Drama in 1958. Her first appearance in London was with her father Michael Redgrave as Caroline Lester in A Touch of The Sun at the Saville in 1958. Her films include The Seagull, directed by Sidney Lumet and The Devils, directed by Ken Russell (1970), Yanks, Julia, Murder on the Orient Express, Howards End (1991), and in 1992 Heartbreak House, The Wall, House of The Spirits and Mothers' Boys. Among her awards are the Golden Globe for Julia, an Emmy and a TV Times award for Playing For Time, the Laurence Olivier Award for Best Actress for Miss Tina in The Aspern Papers. For her performance in The Bostonians she was voted Best Actress by the National Film Critics (USA), and Best Actress at the New Delhi International Film Festival and in the Golden Globe nominations. She received the CBE in 1967, and last year won an award from the Variety Club and the ACE award for Best Supporting Actress in Young Catherine.

DIANA RIGG

Diana Rigg trained at RADA. She joined the Royal Shakespeare Company in 1959 and made her first appearance in London at the Aldwych in 1961 playing roles ranging from Philipe Trincante in The Devils to Madame de Tournel in The Art of Seduction. Back at Stratford her roles included Lady Macbeth and Cordelia. After a year as Emma Peel in The Avengers she rejoined the RSC in 1966 to play Viola in Twelfth Night. She joined the National Theatre in 1971 to play Dottie in Stoppard's Jumpers, Celimene in The Misanthrope and Lady Macbeth. At the Albery she played Eliza Doolittle in Pygmalion in 1974 and returned to the National in 1976 to play Phaedra in Phaedra Britannica. More recently she has been in All For Love at the Almeida in 1991, Berlin Bertie at the Royal Court and Medae at the Almeida. She has appeared in several films including On Her Majesty's Secret Service and Evil Under The Sun. Her television credits include King Lear (Granada), Hedda Gabler (Yorkshire TV), Unexplained Laughter and Mother Love (BBC).

PATRICIA ROUTLEDGE

Patricia Routledge trained at the Bristol Old Vic Theatre School and went on to gain wide repertory experience in Guildford, Worthing and Windsor before landing several leading roles in the West End. Her first venture on Broadway, in Darling of the Day, earned her the 1967 Tony Award as Best Actress in a Musical. Other awards in her distinguished career include a nomination for a Laurence Olivier Award for Queen Margaret in the RSC's Richard III in 1984, the British Comedy Award for Best Comedy Actress for 1991 and the Olivier Award for Outstanding Performance of the Year by an Actress in a Musical for her performance as the Old Lady in Jonathan Miller's Candide. Her work with Alan Bennett is well known: she has starred in several of his plays, including one of his Talking Heads and A Woman Of No Importance, which Bennett wrote for her and which won her the Broadcasting Press Guild (Critics') Award for 1992.

ALISON STEADMAN

Alison's television work includes, for the BBC, Girl, Hard Labour, Nuts In May, Our Flesh And Blood, Esther Waters, Through The Night, Pasmore (with Pete Postlethwaite), Abigail's Party, The Singing Detective (for which she received a BAFTA nomination for Best Actress), Virtuoso, A Small Mourning and Newshounds (for which she received the Chicago Film Festival Gold Award for Best Actress). Other TV credits include Selling Hitler (Euston Films), Gone To The Dogs (Central TV) and Gone To Seed (Central TV). Her film credits include Champions, P'Tang Yang Kipperbang, Number One, A Private Function, Clockwise, The Short and Curlies, Stormy Monday, The Adventures of Baron Munchausen, Shirley Valentine, Wilt, Blame It On The Bellboy and Mike Leigh's Life Is Sweet, for which she won the Society of American Film Critics Best Actress Award. At the time of going to press she was acting in the highly acclaimed Rise And Fall Of Little Voice at the Aldwych.

JANE HORROCKS

Twenty-eight year old Jane Horrocks joined the RSC soon after leaving RADA where she won bronze, silver and gold LAMDA medals as well as a RADA bronze. The media first began to make a fuss of her when she acted in Jim Cartwright's Road, at the Royal Court. Among her TV credits are BBC TV film Heartland, Alive And Kicking, and most recently Bad Girl (written for her) and the much talked about Absolutely Fabulous. Her films include The Dressmaker, Witches, Memphis Belle and Life Is Sweet, the Mike Leigh film for which she won the 1992 Los Angeles Critics Award for her performance as Nicola, the disgruntled teenager. Her latest play, The Rise And Fall Of Little Voice, directed by Sam Mendes, won her wide acclaim from both critics and public alike.

MIRANDA RICHARDSON

Miranda Richardson's first break came in 1979 when she was given a part in Moving at London's Queens Theatre. At the end of the six-month run she went off to gain valuable training working in rep in Derby, Bristol, Leicester and Lancaster. It was while she was playing in The Life Of Einstein at the Duke's Playhouse in Lancaster that director Mike Newell cast her as Ruth Ellis, the last woman to be hanged in Britain, in Dance With A Stranger. Her success in the film brought her the Evening Standard's Best Film Actress Award as well as awards from the Variety Club and City Limits magazine. Other accolades she has earned since then include a nomination for the Laurence Olivier Best Actress Award for A Lie Of The Mind and a BAFTA nomination for Best Television Actress for After Pilkington. Her most recent work in film includes, in 1991, appearing in Mike Newell's Enchanted April and playing an IRA terrorist in Neil Jordan's The Crying Game. Last year she played Jeremy Irons' wife in Louis Malle's Damage.

FIONA SHAW

Born in Ireland Fiona studied philosophy at Cork University before coming to London when she was 21 years old to train at RADA. She left with the Bancroft Gold Medal and joined the National. She has won the Olivier Award for Best Actress three times, all in 1990, for Electra at the RSC Barbican, The Good Person Of Sichuan at the National (both directed by Deborah Warner) and for Rosalind in As You Like It at The Old Vic. Her films include My Left Foot, Mountains Of The Moon, Three Men And A Little Lady and London Kills Me.

JANET McTEER

Janet McTeer's credits include, for the BBC, A Masculine Ending, My Life, 101 Boulevard Haussman, Prince, Portrait Of A Marriage, Yellowbacks, Miss Julie, Precious Bane, Sweet Nothing And Dead Romantic. Her roles for the theatre have included, at the Manchester Royal Exchange, Masha in The Three Sisters, Rosalind in As You Like It, Imogen in Cymbeline, Lady Mary in The Admirable Crichton and Mrs Joe in Great Expectations. For the RSC she has played Titania, Katerina in The Storm and Victoria in Worlds Apart. At the Sheffield Crucible she played Judy in Action Replay, directed by Clare Venables, and Beatrice in The Changeling, directed by Jane Collins.

KAREN HILTON

Born in Liverpool, Karen met her husband to be and future dancing partner Marcus Hilton when they were both children. They have been dancing together for 15 years, six of these as a married couple. On leaving school Karen worked for her father until her dancing career took off. As amateurs she and Marcus became the World Amateur Latin Champions and World Amateur Ten Dance Champions. After turning professional they won the World Ten Dance Championship and then decided to concentrate on Ballroom style. Since that time they have held every major international title including the World, European, British Open, USBC Open, International, UK Open, World Trophy and on 10 October 1992 they retained their world title at the 1992 World Standard Ballroom Championship in Kolding, Denmark.

AMANDA BRITTON

Twenty-seven year old Amanda Britton trained at the Southern Ballet School and the Rambert School before joining the Rambert in 1984. She was in the original cast of Rambert's Touchbase, the first piece Merce Cunningham created for a British company, and she is known for outstanding performances in the substantial solo work, Soda Lake, and the televised Soldat, choreographed by Ashley Page and Strong Language. 1986 saw her moving into choreography with works such as The Second Construction at the Riverside which had music by John Cage and designs by artist Anish Kapoor.
Photograph by Catherine Ashmore

GAYNOR FAIRWEATHER

The current World Professional Latin Champion (with partner Donnie Burns) Gaynor has been dancing since she was 11. She worked as a window dresser, dancing and going in for amateur dancing championships in her spare time. Since turning professional she and Donnie have won nine world professional championship titles: eight World Latin and one World Segue. They are the current champions. In 1992 they received the MBE for their achievements in ballroom dance.

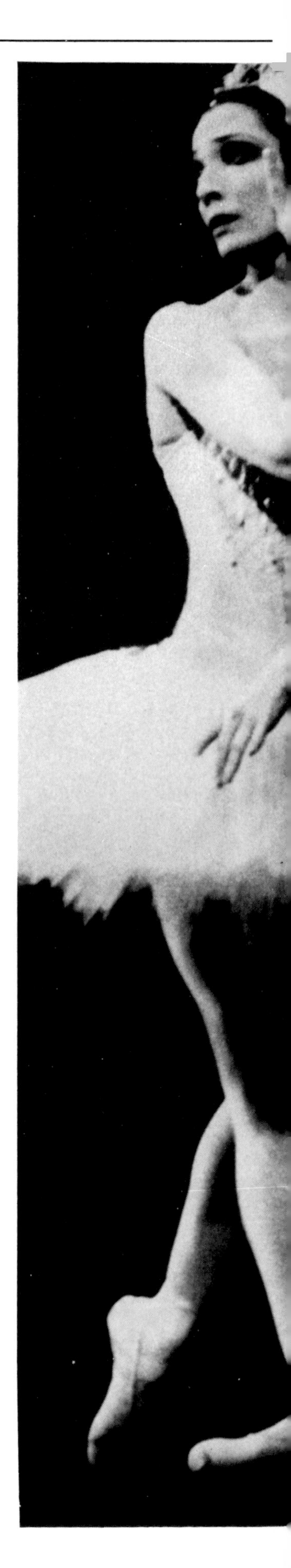

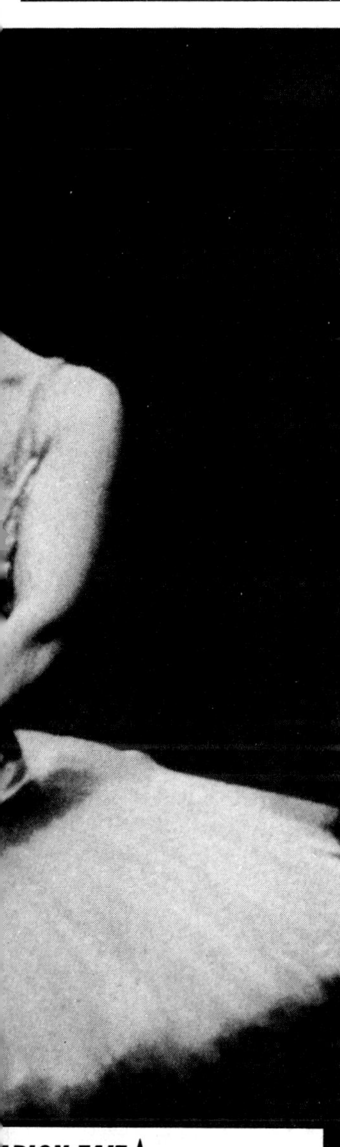

ARLENE PHILLIPS

Arlene Phillips first hit the headlines when her dance group, Hot Gossip with Sarah Brightman, earned top television ratings on the Kenny Everett Show. Today she is one of our most prolific chroeographer/directors. She has worked on ten films including Annie and Monty Python's The Meaning of Life, countless videos with major pop stars and television series and specials for, among others, Tina Turna and Duran Duran. She has also choreographed over 100 commercials in England, Europe and America, including Levis and Coca Cola. The futuristic musical Time was hers as was the RSC's production of A Clockwork Orange, and she created the choreography for Starlight Express, staged in London and on Broadway, Germany, Japan and Australia. Her theatre work includes Lindsay Kemp's acclaimed production of Flowers in London and New York. Most recently she staged and choreographed the Royal Variety Performance for the BBC.

JOSEPHINE JEWKES

English National Ballet's principal dancer since 1992, Josephine joined the company (then the Festival) in 1982, after her training at Solihull School of Ballet, White Lodge and Bush Davies. By 1988 she was dancing major roles with the company, from Juliet in Ashton's Romeo and Juliet to Odette in Makarova's Swan Lake. That year she was awarded "most improved dancer of the year" by Dance and Dancers. She has created many roles during her time with the company in ballets by Bruce, Haigen, Michael Clark, Siobhan Davies and Kim Brandstrup.

Photograph by Bill Cooper

ARION TAIT

arded the OBE in 1992 Marion t is the leading light at the mingham Royal Ballet. A duate of the Royal Ballet School made her debut in Birmingham 1974 with the Girl in cmillan's The Invitation. Critics nediately pinpointed her strong matic talent and superb nnique. Later that year she ame the company's principal cer. Since then she has danced a e variety of roles, appeared on in numerous performances and sted with the Houston Ballet. 1987 she received the first John wson award in recognition of contribution to Sadler's Wells, outstanding performances and creations at home and abroad.

tograph by Tamara

TRACEY FITZGERALD

A very versatile dancer who brings energy and lyricism to everything she does, 29 year old Tracey Fitzgerald is one of the London Contemporary Dance Theatre's major talents. She trained at the Arts Educational School and London Contemporary Dance School, before spending 18 months working with founder member of the ARC Dance Company, Kim Brandstrup. Her most notable role to date was as Euridice (pictured here) in Brandstrup's Orfeo, a production which won LCDT the Laurence Olivier award for 1988.

LINDA JAMES

Linda James graduated from York University with a joint honours degree in History and Politics. She took a post-graduate course in Business and Management in London before joining Sid Robertson Productions as a production assistant in commercials. A year later she had joined Sgrin and was producing programmes for Sianel Pedwar Cymru, the Welsh Fourth Channel. In 1983 she formed Red Rooster Films Ltd with director Stephen Bayly and produced, among other films, Coming Up Roses in 1985, a comedy for S4C which won Best First Feature at Vevey and a Golden Plaque at the International Film Festival in Chicago and Just Ask For A Diamond (1987), also directed by Stephen Bayly, which won Best Adventure Film at the Moscow Film Festival. In 1989 she produced The Gift, a six part TV series for BBC Wales which won second prize for Best Live Action Feature at the Chicago International Children's Film Festival. She is a member of the Board of Governors of the BFI and the National Film and Television School and was chair of the 1992 Edinburgh International Television Festival. She has contributed to many industry seminars and has sat on awards juries for BAFTA and the BFI. She has also run two short courses for the National Film and Television School on Producing The Low Budget Movie. In 1992 she was invited to join the British Screen Advisory Council.

ALISON OWEN

The international, critical and commercial success of Hear My Song has put Alison Owen on the map as a producer. She was nominated as Most Promising New Producer by the Producers Guild of America, and The Guardian critic Derek Malcolm declared: "Few British debuts of recent years have been heralded with quite so much enthusiasm." Alison had earlier worked for the UK division of Limelight Film and Television, setting up projects such as the enormously successful Teenage Mutant Ninja Turtles. She was responsible for promotions and commercials as well as initiating many TV and film documentaries including Channel 4's Teenage Health Freak. After the impact of Hear My Song, she was recruited by Working Title Films to head their schedule of mid-budget productions. Her latest is The Young Americans, a thriller with an international cast. A mother of three, Alsion lives in London.

LYNDSEY POSNER

One of the UK's leading film industry lawyers and a partner in the Entertainment & Media Group of Simon Olswang & Co, Solicitors, Lyndsey Posner qualified as a solicitor in the UK before moving to America in 1978 where she became a member of the Californian Bar. She entered the film industry as an associate in the entertainment department of the Century City law firm Greenberg & Glusker in 1979: the subsequent development and direction of her career is impressive by any standards. In 1981 she joined Columbia Pictures in LA where she began as assistant general counsel and, in rapid succession, rose to become director (1984), vice-president (1985) and senior vice-president (1986) of Business Affairs. In 1987, under the chairmanship of David Puttnam, she became the highest ranking woman executive at Columbia Pictures when she was appointed executive vice-president of Worldwide Business Affairs. She returned to the UK in 1988 with Puttnam, joining him at his company, Enigma Productions, where she was responsible for putting together a $50 million production fund. She also acted as a consultant to Anglia TV and its distribution arm, ITEL. In 1990 she joined Paramount Pictures as executive director of European Business Affairs, before moving to Simon Olswang & Co as a partner in 1991. Her extensive experience of the US film industry makes her unique in the UK.

BEEBAN KIDRON

Born and raised in London, Beeban Kidron was a prizewinning photographer while still in her teens. She worked as an assistant to the legendary Eve Arnold, who encouraged her to travel. After a spot of globe-trotting, she returned to the UK and enrolled at the National Film School, hoping to be a cinematographer. When she switched to directing, her first project was a documentary about the Greenham Common peace camp. It was a prize-winner at the Chicago Film Festival in 1983 and was also shown at the Berlin Film Festival and in Japan. Her first feature film, Vroom, was the centrepiece of the London Film Festival in 1988. She gained a wider audience with the TV success Oranges Are Not the Only Fruit, which was swamped by internatinoal awards, including BAFTA's Best Series award and the Prix Italia. She has since directed Itch for Channel 4, with Alexei Sayle as a man waiting on a traffic island to hitch a lift. Still only 30 years old, Beeban Kidron has recently made her American feature film debut with Used People.

KATYA KRAUSOVA

Katya Krausova came to Britain in 1968 after the Russian invasion of Czechoslovakia. She completed her undergraduate studies in ecomomics and politics at the London School of Economics and did post-graduate studies at St Antony's College, Oxford. She started her TV career researching and producing current affairs documentaries for BBC programmes including Panorama. She became an independent in the music and arts field and has worked with major international artists such as Sir Georg Solti, Claudio Arrau and the Royal Ballet. She produced the first classical music programme on high definition TV in the UK in 1989. Since the recent political upheavel in the world, she has become involved in advising the film and TV industries in Eastern Europe in association with the British government's Know-How fund and the British Council. She is a director of Portobello Films, is married with two children and lives in London.

NORMA HEYMAN

Liverpool born and educated, Norma Heyman started out as an actress and joined World Film Services as a director and script consultant in 1968. She became an independent producer with the formation of NFH Films (her middle name is Frances!) in 1984. The company made the successful film of Graham Green's novel, The Honorary Consul, with a top-notch cast including Richard Gere, Michael Caine and Bob Hoskins. Other successes followed, among them Buster with Phil Collins and and Dangerous Liaisons with Glenn Close and John Malkovich. More recently, Norma Heyman has produced The Clothes in the Wardrobe with Jeanne Moreau and Joan Plowright, seen on BBC TV early in 1993, and The Innocent, directed by John Schlesinger and starring Anthony Hopkins and Isabella Rossellini. In 1992 she received the Simon Olswang Business Award from Women in Film and Television.

SALLY HIBBIN

Born in 1953, Sally Hibbin is a producer with Parallax Pictures. She started out producing documentaries like Live a Life (shown at the London Film Festival) and The road to Gdansk for Channel 4. In 1991 she produced a much-praised documentary about black footballers, Great Britain United. She has since moved into drama, producing the award-winning A Very British Coup and the 1991 European Film of the Year winner, Riff-Raff. Other recent productions are Bad Behaviour and The Estate (aka Raining Stones). She is also a journalist and has written the behind-the-scenes books The Making of Licence to Kill and The Making of Back to the Future.

GINGER CORBETT

Ginger Corbett moved into public relations after working as a production assistant in the independent film sector. Looking after film production for a leading agency, DDA, she went on to head its international division, specialising in film markets and festivals. Along with Sara Keene, she set up Corbett and Keene in 1988 and the company is now recognised as one of the world's leading specialised PR agencies catering exclusively to the film and TV industries. Ginger is married and lives in London, with an office – logically enough – in Wardour Street.

SHEILA WHITAKER

Director of the London Film Festival since 1987, Sheila Whitaker worked for several years in commerce and industry before joining the National Film Archive as head of its collection of stills, posters and designs. She attended Warwick University as a mature student before becoming director of the Tyneside Cinema in Newcastle-upon-Tyne. In 1980 she established the Tyneside Film Festival, now a prestigious annual event. She also set up Tyneside Publications and was general editor. She has contributed to various magazines including Screen and Sight & Sound, and was founder-editor of the literary journal Writing Women.

Photograph by Peter Smith

RENEE GODDARD

Originally an actress, Renee Goddard has been secretary of the European Script Fund since 1989. In the 1960s, she worked in theatre management and was later an assistant producer with the influential Woodfall Films. She moved into TV as Head of Scripts at ATV and in 1972 became a freelance consultant to various international TV companies. In 1980 she became European Consultant and European Editorial Consultant (Fiction and Arts) to Channel 4. She was a consultant to the research phase of the European Script Fund and has been a broadcasting expert to the European Commission's Media 92 programme. Over the years in theatre and TV, Renee Goddard has been active in giving opportunities to freelance writers, directors, script editors and researchers from the Continent. She has two daughters and lives in London.

ANN SKINNER

Now one of Britain's leading independent producers, Ann Skinner started out as a publicity assistant with the Rank Organisation, later working as a production assistant on films like A Kind of Loving, Billy Liar and The L-Shaped Room. She was script supervisor on John Schlesinger's Darling and later worked for him again on Far From the Madding Crowd and Sunday, Bloody Sunday. She formed Skreba films in 1979 (with Simon Relph and Zelda Barron) and its first project was The Return of the Soldier with Glenda Jackson and Julie Christie. She then produced A Profile of Arthur J. Mason, Handel – Honour, Profit and Pleasure, The Gourmet and Heavenly Pursuits. In the late 1980s, the company's film, The Kitchen Toto, won awards at the Tokyo Film Festival. For Channel 4 it made A Very British Coup which won an international Emmy and five BAFTA awards. Ann Skinner is on the Executive Council of the producers' trade association PACT and sits on one of the industry training sub-committees. She is also on the DTI working party examining the British film industry.

ROMAINE HART

Romaine Hart runs Mainline Pictures, which has five cinemas including the Screen on the Green and the Screen on the Hill. It is also an active distribution company, with My Beautiful Laundrette and Baghdad Cafe among its successes. Her family has owned cinemas for three generations and she recalls her father promoting a Tarzan film with a caged lion outside the cinema. She is a director of the British Screen Advisory Council, a member of the BAFTA Council and won a BFI Award for Excellence in 1986.

PHILIPPA CROSS

After gaining an English degree at Oxford, Philippa Cross was entertainments manager at Wembley Conference Centre from 1977-80 and admits she was "lured into television". She joined Granada, where she managed the drama department before moving into Features, where she teamed up with Steve Morrison. After her family moved to Kent she became manager of factual output for TVS. In 1988 the prospect of developing feature films took her back to Granada to be Head of Film Development and gave her another chance to work with Morrison. They hit the jackpot with their first effort, the Oscar-winning My Left Foot, on which Philippa was production executive. This was followed by The Field, which was also covered in glory. They now aim to build on this achievement and have several new TV and feature films in the pipeline.

SARAH RADCLYFFE

Sarah Radclyffe co-founded the production company Working Title in 1984 and it has since become a leader in its field. It produced hit films like My Beautiful Laundrette, Wish You Were Here and Personal Services and has a TV arm, WITV, which made the acclaimed Newshounds which won Best TV Film in the BAFTA awards. Working Title enters the 1990s in close association with recording giant PolyGram, giving it a solid base for expansion. Born in 1950, Sarah Radclyffe has a four-year old son and lives in London.

PREMILA HOON

As head of the merchant bank Guinness Mahon's entertainment and finance activities, Premila Hoon has been involved in structuring the financing of over 50 films. She is also a governor of the British Film Institute. A banker for 14 years, she spent four years as Head of Credit at the London-based subsidiary of Manufacturers' Hanover Trust and financed a wide spread of assets from ships and aircraft to industrial equipment and cars. She has a BSc (Hons) degree in Physics and a Masters degree in Business Administration.

Photograph by Vijay

LINDA MYLES

Arbroath born Linda Myles co-produced one of the most successful films of recent times, The Commitments, which won Best Film, Best Director and best Screenplay/Adaptation awards from BAFTA. A philosophy graduate of Edinbugh University, she was director of that city's International Film Festival from 1973-80 (she is now on the Board), then Curator of Film at the University of California's Pacific Film Archive until 1982. She was later a senior vice-president of Columbia Pictures (1986-88) and joined BBC Television as Commissioning Editor for Drama. Since 1990, Linda Myles has been co-executive director of the East-West Proudcers Seminar which runs training courses for young film and TV producers in Hungary, Czechoslovakia and Poland. She is a Trustee of the Screenwriters' Studio and is on the Board of the Scottish Film Production Fund.

EMMA JOHNSON

Still only in her mid-20s, Emma Johnson has the distinction of being one of the very few woodwind players to have made an international career as a soloist. Performing regularly in the USA, the Far East, Africa and throughout Europe, this talented clarinettist has also achieved great popularity in Britain, appearing on radio and television and regularly playing to sell-out concerts. She was just nine when she began studying the clarinet and, in 1984, won the BBC Young Musician of the Year competition. When she was 18 years old she recorded the Mozart Concerto and has since recorded all the concerti of Weber and Crusell, as well as many other works. As a winner of the Young Concert Auditions in New York, this young virtuoso recently made her New York and Washington recital debuts. She particularly enjoys chamber music and her aim is to expand the repertoire for clarinet.

DAME ELIZABETH MACONCHY

Dame Elizabeth began her long musical career in 1923 when she began her six year studies at the Royal College of Music. From there she went to Prague to study for a further year. Almost as soon as she returned to England in1930 the first public performance of her work took place at the Sir Henry Wood Prom – an orchestral suite entitled The Land. Since then many of her compositions, which include orchestral works, choral pieces, chamber works, songs and operas, have been performed in London and at numerous festivals both in Britain and abroad, as well as on Radio 3. Recently, in 1990/91, her 12 string quartets were recorded on CD by Unicorn-Kanchana. Still active, this distinguished lady is President of the Society for the Promotion of New Music as well as being an Honorary Fellow of the Royal College of Music and of St Hilda's College, Oxford. She was given due recognition for her music in 1987 when the Queen made her a Dame of the Order of the British Empire.

JUDITH WEIR

While still at school, composer Judith Weir studied composition with John Tavener and played in the National Youth Orchestra. She went on to study music at King's College, Cambridge, before spending three years as the Southern Arts Association's Composer in Residence working in schools, adult education classes and community arts projects. Later she held the position of Guinness Composer in Residence at the Royal Scottish Academy of Music and Drama. Her first full-length opera, A Night At the Chinese Opera, was premièred at the Cheltenham Festival in 1987 and subsequently toured and performed in London to great critical acclaim. The USA première of the work took place in Santa Fe in 1989. The Vanishing Bridegroom, her most recent opera, was commissioned to celebrate the 1990 European City of Culture. Other recent projects include a television film – the subject is a contemporary reworking of an early Mozart opera, Il Sogno Di Scipione, and an orchestral work for the Boston Symphony Orchestra.

JOANNA MacGREGOR

Since 1985 Joanna MacGregor's career has developed apace, both in recital and concert appearances. She has played with many of the major orchestras in this country, and made many visits abroad including Singapore, Germany and the Netherlands where she gave several concerts with the Rotterdam Philharmonic Orchestra. Recording exclusively with Collins Classics, Miss MacGregor's outstanding releases to date include music by Satie, Gershwin, Ives, Barber and Britten, and most recently a release of Scarlatti sonatas. Television audiences know her from her appearance in Omnibus at the Proms and from masterclasses for Young Musician of the Year. She has also written a fantasy play for radio entitled Memoirs of an Amnesiac based on the life of Erik Satie and nominated for the Prix d'Italia.

SIAN EDWARDS

In recent years Sian Edwards has made several enormously successful debuts as a conductor and this year will become music director of English National Opera. After graduating from the Royal Northern College of Music she studied at the Leningrad Conservatoire (as it was then) and during this time won the first Leeds Conductors' Competition. Since returning to Britain in 1985 she has worked with many of this country's leading orchestras, making her operatic debut in 1986 conducting a new production of Weill's Mahogany for Scottish Opera. Her debut with ENO was made in 1990 conducting Prokofiev's The Gambler and, in 1991, she conducted the Los Angeles Philharmonic Orchestra for the first time. She now also has many successful tours under her belt, as well as a number of well-received recordings with EMI, many with the London Philharmonic Orchestra.

RITA HUNTER ▲

Rita Hunter is one of the world's leading dramatic sopranos and was made a CBE in 1985 – the same year in which her autobiography, Wait Until The Sun Shines, was published by Hamish Hamilton. By the 1970s she was singing Brunnhilde in Wagner's The Ring under Reginald Goodall, which was subsequently recorded for EMI/Angel and has now been re-released on CD, and making her debut at the Metropolitan Opera in New York in the same role, among others. Since then her operatic successes have been numerous and she has been acclaimed in the leading opera houses of Europe, in North America, and in Australia since moving there. Born, raised and educated on Merseyside, in 1992 she starred in Fanfare for a New World, a gala concert in Liverpool forming part of Merseyside's Columbus celebrations.

ANNE EVANS ▲

Associated with both English National Opera and Welsh National Opera in Britain, operatic singer Anne Evans is particularly well known for her performances in Wagnerian works. She has played Brunnhilde, from The Ring, four times at the Bayreuth Festival under Daniel Barenboim and in 1992 made a highly successful debut at the Metropolitan, New York, singing Elisabeth from Tannhauser. (The 1992 production of the final cycles of The Ring has been filmed for video releases and will also be issued on record.) This year she will sing her first Isolde with Sir Charles Mackerras and Welsh National. In addition to her operatic work, Anne Evans enjoys an extensive concert career both in Britain and abroad, and has worked with many leading conductors.

TASMIN LITTLE ▲

Thanks to her television appearances and her performances in every major city and at many important festivals, violinist Tasmin Little is a well-known figure in the UK. Since studying at the Yehudi Menuhin School of Music, the Guildhall School of Music and with Lorand Fenyves in Canada, she has also given numerous concerto and recital performances throughout Europe, Scandinavia, Canada, China, India and South America to much acclaim. (She has a wide-ranging repertoire of over 30 concertos and has given many world première performances.) Her recordings have been equally successful, her Lark Ascending (Vaughn Williams) and Delius Double Concerto being nominated for the 1992 Gramophone awards. 1990 saw her debut at the BBC Prom concerts, to which she has returned regularly since.

EVELYN GLENNIE ▼

Believed to be the only full-time solo percussionist in the world, Evelyn Glennie has established herself as a consummate musician in a very short space of time. Born in Aberdeen, she studied timpani and percussion from the age of 12 and in 1982 entered the Royal Academy of Music, where she won many prizes, including the Queen's Commendation Prize for all-round excellence. As well as her busy recital schedule in the UK, Evelyn regularly works with all the major symphony and chamber orchestras and often champions new works. Her many television appearances, including documentaries about her life, have given her a high public profile; her autobiography, Good Vibrations, was published by Century Hutchinson in 1990. Outside the UK she is equally in demand. She makes regular visits to Japan and is planning a third tour to Australia and New Zealand which will include visits to Singapore and Indonesia.

FELICITY LOTT ▲

With a formidable reputation as one of Britain's most successful sopranos, Felicity Lott has become an immensely popular concert artist. Awarded a CBE in 1990 in recognition of her achievements, she appears each year at the BBC Prom concerts, has given recitals throughout Europe, is a regular guest at the Paris Opera, the Chicago Lyric Opera and the Munich Opera, and performs regularly at the Royal Opera House, Covent Garden. For many years she was closely associated with the Glyndebourne Festival where she gave a number of memorable performances. In the 1990/91 season she made her debuts at the Vienna State Opera as Arabella and at the Metropolitan Opera, New York, as the Marshallin under Kleiber. In 1992 she made her debuts at La Scala, Milan (again as Arabella), and at the Salzburg Festival as Countess Almaviva. This year will see her first recitals in Vienna and at the Munich Festival.

NORMA WINSTONE

Jazz Journal International has said that "Norma Winstone's voice is one of the glories of contemporary jazz". Norma, a Londoner, has worked with groups led by Mike Westbrook, Neil Ardley, Mike Gibbs, Michael Garrick, John Dankworth, John Taylor and Kenny Wheeler, and extensively with German, Dutch and British radio big radio bands and orchestras. Although she began her career singing jazz standards, her diverse musical interests led to her involvement in free improvisation. She writes many of the lyrics for the songs she performs, and teaches at Summer Schools and jazz workshops.

Photograph by Caroline Forbes

CLEO LAINE

The range of Cleo Laine's career, now nearing four decades, most of it beside her husband, friend and mentor John Dankworth is, to say the least, formidable. Her contribution to theatre alone, on both sides of the Atlantic, has been so extensive that it could have been the sum total of her work. She has starred in A Midsummer Night's Dream, The Trojan Woman, Seven Deadly Sins, Showboat, The Merry Widow, A Little Night Music and Into The Woods, amongst others. Alongside this, however, she has managed to accomplish a concert and recording career which has taken her all over the world, where she has performed in all the greatest venues with all the greatest performers. What remains astonishing about Cleo Laine is her undiminished vocal talent and her unfaltering aura as a performer. As Dick Hughes of the Australian says: "At some concert someone must send on a crown for this Queen of Song".

CHERYL ALLEYNE

Cheryl Alleyne is probably Britain's best lady jazz drummer. Educated at the Newcastle College of Art & Technology, Cheryl received her first break on her return to London in 1987, when she was invited to join the big band, Loose Tubes. She went on to play with Jazz Warriors, and has toured Barbados, her mother's homeland, with saxophonist Steve Williamson. Cheryl has recently been awarded a scholarship to study at the Manhatten School of Music and, in 1992, Richard Aj'ley and Afro Bloc, the all drummer band, held a benefit for her at the Jazz Cafe to help with funds for this.

TINA MAY

Born in 1961, Tina May had vocal training from an early age and, while studying in Paris for her degree in French, sat in at various venues such as Le Slow Club and Caveau de la Huchette. She appeared in every Edinburgh Fringe Festival, 1981-86, as a singer and actress, and in 1984 began residence at Cardiff's Gibbs Jazz Club with her own Trio, where she worked with Slim Gaillard amongst others. She works constantly as a singer and actress, and in 1989 she married drummer Clark Tracey, son of the legendary jazz musician Stan Tracey.

Photograph by Eamonn McCabe

BARBARA THOMPSON

Barbara Thompson was born in Oxford and educated at the Royal College of Music, where she studied clarinet, piano, flute and composition. The College did not have a resident saxophone teacher, and so she studied this privately, and joined the New York Jazz Orchestra, whose drummer, Jon Hiseman, she subsequently married. Barbara returned, briefly, to her classical roots following commissions from the BBC for her to write and perform three 30 minute works orchestrated for jazz and classical players. She formed the first version of the band Paraphenalia in 1977, recording their first album in 1978. The band has recorded seven further albums, the most recent, Breathless, released in 1992 and promoted with an extensive and highly successful European tour. Barbara also runs a 19-piece big band, Moving Parts, for which she composes and arranges all the music. Some of her most interesting projects have tended to mix jazz with traditional music from East and West.

KATHY STOBART

Kathy Stobart is arguably the best female tenor sax player in Europe. She has built up a sizeable reputation as a jazz player, appearing with top bands and fronting a number of her own bands. She has also played with Johnnie Griffin, Marion MacPartland, Dick Hyman, Zoot Simms, Earl Hines, Bobby Rosengarten, Jim Galloway, Buddy Tate, Slam Stewart and many more. Her own bands have toured for several years, and played opposite Bill Evans, Art Pepper and Chet Baker. Benny Green says that he has never regretted his decision to sell his baritone sax to Kathy.

ANDREA VICARI

Pianist and composer Andrea Vicari was born in 1965 in Miami to British parents and was educated in music at Cardiff University and the Guildhall School of Music, where she attended the Jazz and Studio Music course. Since 1988 she has lived and worked in London, performing on the jazz circuit with a trio, quartet and quintet all under her name. Andrea's principal instrument is piano, although recently she has been more involved with electronic keyboards and with sequencing. She is currently writing music for a new ten-piece ensemble sponsored by the Arts Council.

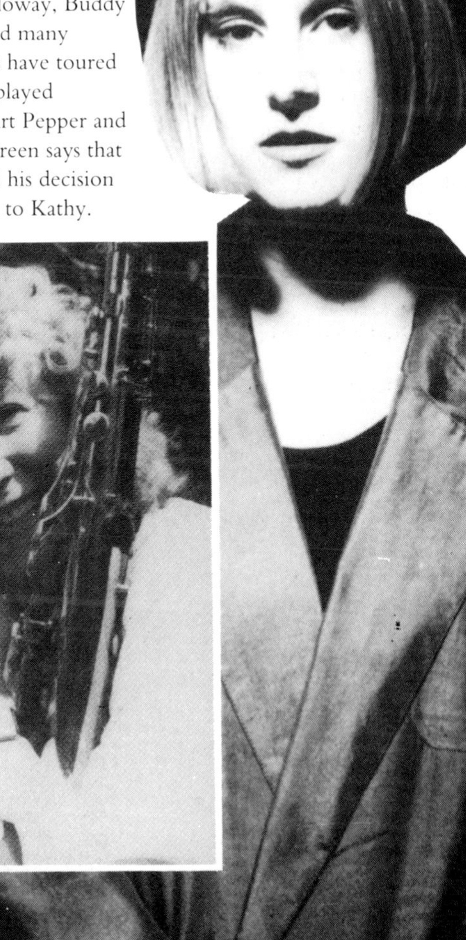

CATHY DENNIS

A Doc Marten's afficianado, with the looks of a 1950s screen goddess, Cathy Dennis is a newcomer making a lot of waves in the UK and the US. Once an insurance clerk in Norwich, she sang at holiday camps before joining D-Mob and singing on their hit C'mon and Get My Love. Touch Me went to No 1 in America, while more than a million copies of her debut album, Move To This, have been sold. All her singles releases in the US have gone Top 10 and she has had five singles in the UK charts. Seventh overall in Billboard's 1991 Top 10 Single's Artists, she left Madonna 17 places behind her and was the biggest UK act in the States that year; she was Billboard's Best New Female Artist in 1991. Cathy's second album, Into the Skyline, which she wrote and co-produced, was recorded with industry legend Shep Pettibone. She was Best International Newcomer in the World Music Awards and was recently nominated for two Best of Brits Awards.

SHAKESPEAR'S SISTER

Shakespear's Sister are Siobhan Fahey and Marcella Detroit. On their two albums to date, Sacret Heart and Hormonally Yours, they have been able to combine the rhythms of American R'n'B with something particularly dark and indefinably English: George Clinton meets The Smiths. Siobhan Fahey, ex-Bananarama – always known as the UK's most successful girl group ever – met Marcella Detroit in Los Angeles through a mutual friend; they have worked together since their first release: the double A-side Break My Heart/Heroine. Hits from the second album include the ballad Stay, which was at No 1 for a remarkable eight weeks, and Goodbye Cruel World. Shakespear's Sister released a further single from Hormonally Yours, Hello (Turn Your Radio On) late in 1992. The unusual lyrical imagery of Shakespear's Sister is complemented by the almost baroque sytle of Sophie Muller – who has worked on all their videos since You're History.

TASMIN ARCHER

A real example of patience being its own reward, Tasmin Archer's smash hit single, Sleeping Satellite, went to No 1 in the UK Singles Chart four years after it was written. Tasmin worked as a sewing machinist, as a clerk at a magistrates' court, and as a gofor at Flexible Response Studios, where she sang occasionally at recording sessions. Tasmin met her future partners at Flexible Response: guitarist John Hughes and keyboard player John Beck; they have been working together now for more than five years. Tasmin Archer signed to EMI in 1991. Great Expectations, written by Archer, Hughes and Beck, was released in 1992; it was a great critical and commercial success. The album deals intelligently with a number of complex social issues; from child abuse to inner-city poverty. Her live debut was at the Mean Fiddler in London; she has since performed with Squeeze and John Frey of the Eagles.

MICA PARIS

Mica Paris grew up in South London, was influenced by gospel groups like the Eddie Hawkins Singers, and sang in the church choir. A singer with the gospel quartet Spirit of Watts, Mica slowly moved from gospel to the rhythms of classic soul – listening to singers like Luther Vandross, Curtis Mayfield and Marvin Gaye. She signed to 4th and Broadway, a subsidiary label through Island Records in 1987. So Good, her platinum plus debut, went straight to No 5 in the UK album chart, going gold within a week of release. So Good featured many of Mica's later hits, like My One Temptation, Like Dreamers Do, Breathe Life Into Me and her duet will Will Downing, Where Is The Love? Contribution, her second album, features a song written for Mica by Prince, If I Love U 2 Nite, and contributions from rapper Rakim and funkster Nile Rodgers. Mica has been nominated for three BPI Awards and was voted Britain's No 1 soul singer at the DMC.

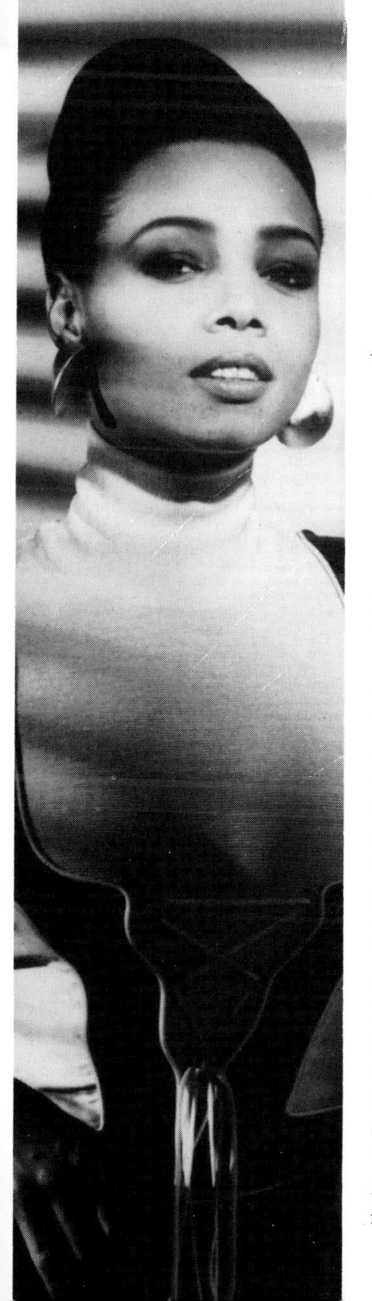

KIM APPLEBY

Kim Appleby was originally partnered by her sister Mel: they performed as Mel and Kim. Mel sadly died at a tragically early age in 1990. Mel and Kim had a number of hit singles in the mid and late 1980s, including Showing Out, Respectable and FLM. Kim released he debut solo album in 1990. It included two of the smash hit singles of the early 1990s: Don't Worry and Good Love And Devotion (GLAD) – both singles went Top 5 and the album soon went gold. Don't Worry is a concise expression of Kim's views about life: "It was such an 'up', positive record to return with, it was my way of saying 'Look, I'm back, and Life is jut great'." The song was nominated by the British Songwriter's Guild for Best Contemporary Song of 1990 at the Ivor Novello Awards. Kim feels that she made her comeback as much for her sister as herself: "To me it's like saying, 'Look Mel this is what we've done, this is what we've got."

NENEH CHERRY

Neneh Cherry produced her latest album in the converted schoolhouse in Stockholm where she lived as a child. Although she travelled widely with her father, jazz legend Don Cherry, her school years were in New York. In 1981 she sang with Rip Rig and Panic; they split in 1984, after recording three albums, to form Float Up CP which Neneh fronted. She went on to work with Matt Johnson, dueting with him on the single Slow Train To Dawn – from The The's album Infected. She has performed as a solo artist since 1989, debuting with the single Buffalo Stance – which she performed so memorably on television while eight months pregnant. Buffalo Stance was produced by Tim "Bomb the Bass" Simenon, who also produced Neneh's album

Raw Like Sushi – it has already sold more than two million copies worldwide. Further releases from the album, like Manchild, were bit hits in the UK and Europe. She recorded a version of Cole Porter's I've Got You Under My Skin for the Red Hot and Blue Aids benefit album. Neneh's second album, Homebrew, was released late in 1992 to great critical and commercial acclaim.

BETTY BOO

Still in her early 20s, singer, songwriter and now producer, Betty Boo was in her teens when she had her first hit with the Beatmasters. Hey DJ I Can't Dance was soon followed by solo recordings like Where Are You Baby?, Doin' The Do Are You Baby?, Doin' The Do and 24 Hours. Her first album, Boomania, sold more than 400,000 copies in the UK alone and soon went platinum. Betty Boo, the girl from Shepherd's Bush, was overwhelmed by her success: "I can remember it happening very quickly. Suddenly I couldn't even walk down the street – I know what that sounds like, but what else can you say – I couldn't." Not that her success has led to any compromises; she is still the numero uno of what is now the Betty Boo industry. For her latest album she has renewed a partnership with producer and writer John Coxon – established during the recording of Boomania. The first fruit of that working relationship is the eminently melodic Let Me Take You There – the first, of undoubtedly many, singles from Betty Boo's new album.

SADE

Sade was the torch singer of the late 1980s; her voice typifies all moodiness of the jazz chanteuse. Diamond Life was recorded in 1984 and won the British Phonographic Industry's Best Album Award and the band an American Grammy for Best Newcomer. The single, Smooth Operator, was released in 1985, soon followed by the album Promise. Sade appeared in the film Absolute Beginners, performing Killer Blow, a song she co-wrote. Sweetest Taboo, was the most played 45 on American radio between 1985 and 1986. After performing at the Live Aid and ANC benefits, Sade wrote, arranged, produced and recorded the album Stronger Than Pride in 1988. Sade released Love Deluxe in 1992, the fourth album.

ANNIE LENNOX

Annie Lennox is possessed of most singular and haunting voice; often deeply moving, it is crystalline in its clarity. With Dave Stewart, Anne fronted one of the music business's most influential and important acts of the 1980s: the Eurythmics. Eurythmics Greatest Hits, the 1991 compilation, has already sold in excess of five million copies. After the break-up of the group Anne Lennox remained, understandably, quiet for several years. Three years after the demise of the Eurythmics, she released her first solo single, Why, in 1992. It was taken from her album, Diva, for which he wrote all the songs. Of her latest recordings she has remarked: "In a sense I feel this is my very first album. And because of that it had to be something that represented me totally and exactly." Like her work with the Eurythmics, Diva has all the melody of pop, but includes a darker, inquiring lyrical sub-text; Annie is concerned with exploring the relation between her private self and her personna as a performer.

BEVERLY CRAVEN ↓

Beverly Craven had a normal upbringing in Hertfordshire, taking piano lessons as a child, encouraged by her mother, an accomplished classical violinst. After leaving school she played with various bands on the South London pub circuit and then did a brief stint touring with Bobby Womack. She recorded her first proper demo tape and soon hitched up with Go West manager John Glover, who got her a publishing deal. She signed to Epic soon after this and made her first recording with Stewart Levine of Simply Red fame. When the recording was finished, Beverly thought that it lacked the simplicity of her songwriting. So she went on to re-record with Paul Samwell Smith. Beverly's self-titled album wasn't an instant seller, and she had to build her own fan base by playing small clubs, like the Mean Fiddler and the Borderline. By the end of her first tour in February 1991 her showcase at the Duke of York Theatre in London had sold out. The album began to sell and by May the single Promise Me reached No 3 in the UK chart. The follow-up, Holding On, also reached the Top 5. She continued to have many sell-out shows all over the UK and she is now working on her second album.

ALISON MOYET ↑

"Female singer looking for rootsy blues band." This was the advert run in the back of Melody Maker in 1981. Having had a lot of previous experiences from punk bands to the R 'n' B scene, she was just starting to get known around town. It was at this point that the advert was spotted by Vince Clarke, who had just left Depeche Mode, and Yazoo was born. Clarke's brilliant electronic melodies and Alison's inspired soulful vocal made their first single, Only You, sell over 300,000 copies with two albums to follow Upstaris at Eric's and You and Me Both on Mute Records. In 1984 Alison left Clarke, and decided to pursue a solo career and signed to CBS Records. Her first solo album, Alf, sold three million copies and included the hits All Cried Out, Love Resurrection and Invisible. She then covered the Billie Holliday standard That Ole Devil Called Love which went to No 2 in the UK chart. This was also the year in which she performed at Live Aid and gave birth to her first child, Joe. From 1986 she recorded her second solo album called Raindancing which included such hits as Weak In The Presence Of Beauty and Is This Love. She then had a break of about three years from the world of pop to have her second child, Alex, and to write and record her third and most recent album Hoodoo.

LISA STANSFIELD ↑

Rochdale diva Lisa Stansfield released her debut solo album, Affection, in 1989; it went straight into the UK charts at No 2 and became a worldwide bestseller. Lisa's second album, Real Love, was released in 1991 and has already sold more than three and a half million copies worldwide. Her two albums have now sold more than eight million copies worldwide. Lisa Stansfield has made a significant contribution to the Aids awareness campaign; she recorded a version of Cole Porter's Down in the Depths for th Red Hot and Blue album and performed to a capacity crowd at the Freddie Mercury Memorial Concert at Wembley Arena. The concert was broadcast to a worldwide audience of more than 70 million and Lisa's duet with George Michael was one of its undoubted highspots. Lisa's 1992 world tour, which included Europe, North America, Japan and South East Asia, was a sell-out. Her latest recording, Someday (I'm Coming Back) released late in 1992 was written and performed especially for the blockbusting movie The Bodyguard.

TANITA TIKARAM

Singer and songwriter Tanita Tikaram wrote her first songs while revising for her A levels. Foregoing a place at Manchester University she signed to WEA Records in 1988 and had a massive hit in the same year with Good Traditin. That was followed by Twist in My Sobreity, a song that has been covered by 17 other artists. Tanita's first album, Ancient Heart, has sold 750,000 copies in the UK and a staggering three million worldwide; with Ancient Heart, her subsequent albums, The Sweet Keeper, Everybody's Angel and Eleven Kinds of Loneliness have sold ten million copies to date. Her most important musical influences are the writer/producer Phil Spectre, Nina Simone, The Beatles and Ry Cooder. She writes using a production by colour picture method: "When I'm starting to work on a song, I like to have a picture in my mind and fill the colours and the details of the picture with sound." Tanita has toured Europe and America extensively since 1989

MONIE LOVE

Queen of Hip Hop, Monie Love was born in London and raised in Brooklyn, New York. She has had a number of UK Top 20 hits with singles like I Can Do This and Grandpa's Party. Produced by Afrika Baby Bambaataa and the Jungle Brothers, Down to Earth, her 1990 debut album, featured the hits Monie in the Middle and It's a Shame. Monie has worked with De La Soul (Buddy), Queen Latifah (Ladies First), the Jungle Brothers (Doing Our Own Bang) and with Almond Joy (Back To the Black). Her second album , In A Word Or Two, released in 1993, includes the single Born to Breed. According to Monie: "Breed stands for build relationships where education and enlightenment dominate." In A Word Or Two, part produced by Prince and newcomers Marly Marl and Freedom Lyles, is notably harder than Monie's earlier work; Bullets Carry No Name, for example, which was co-written with Ice-T, is an examination of urban violence. With several other acts, like De La Soul and A Tribe Called Quest, Monie belongs to the positive and Afrocentric collective Native Tongues.

VIVIENNE McKONE

Vivienne McKone represents a move in modern dance music away from the sophistication of the studio and a return to the urgency of playing live. Something of a child prodigy, Vivienne has been dancing since the age of two. At nine, she was at the Royal Ballet School as a junior associate – while still a pupil at Barbara Speake's stage school. She was an actress in her early teens, with parts in The Water Babies and Bugsy Malone. Vivienne read Biology at Goldsmith's College and continued acting after graduation, while writing her own songs.

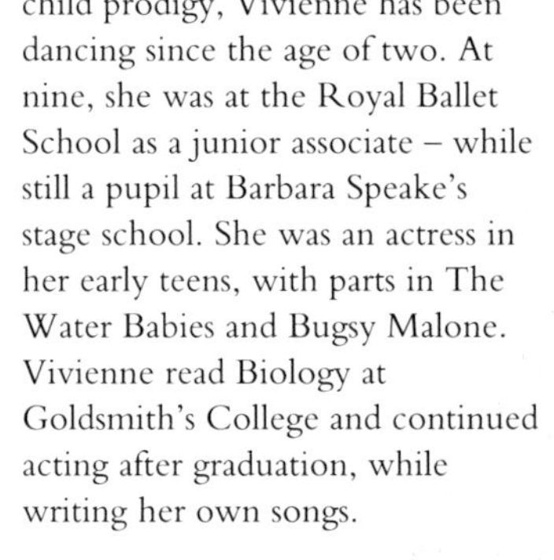

DES'REE

"No-one has ever stopped me doing what I do. No matter how big or small, it was me who always believed I would succeed." Des'ree is a new name to the pop industry; and her vocal style, although seen by many to be more that of a soul singer, is more in tune with Joni Mitchell than Tracy Chapman. She has been writing songs and poems since she was 14 years old and nearly opted for taking a psychology degree before deciding a mike was more therapeutic than a couch. She was quickly snapped up when Lincoln Elias heard her demo tape at Sony. Her single, Feel So High, reached No 13 in the UK chart followed by Mind Adventures which is also the title track of the album. Since then there has also been the release of a third single entitled Why Should I Love You.

CARON WHEELER

A self-taught singer, Caron Wheeler was surrounded by music from an early age. Her father was the bass player in a Jamaican band and her mother sang for a drama company. At 12 years old she was singing in a female reggae trio and by 16 had cornered the lover's rock market with four UK No 1 lover's rock singles. Strongly influenced by role models Stevie Wonder, Billie Holliday and Bob Marley to name but a few, she started to do sessions for the likes of Neneh Cherry, Aswad, Phil Collins, Elvis Costello and Erasure. After a rather hard time, struggling to make it in the business, she was recognised by Jazzie B of Soul To Soul fame. 1989 was an amazing year: singing, recording and co-writing Soul to Soul's best known songs such as Back To Life which won a grammy for Best Vocal Performance and Keep On Movin': these two songs were both platinum singles. Caron also received the Most Promising Newcomer UK award from DMC International. She now has her own company, Orange Tree Productions, which she started in 1991.

DINA CARROL

Dina Carrol is a girl in a hurry and she is clearly going to the top fast. With musical influences including The Isley Brothers, The Temptatoins and Aretha Franklin, it is not surprising that there is so much depth in Dina's singing and songwriting. A singer more by accident than design, she first sang on a number of dance records, notably Quartz's 1990 hit It's Too Late. On the break-up of Quartz Dina signed a solo deal with A&M Records. She writes with producer Nigel Lowis and works with master remixer CJ Mackintosh to create the ultimate garage music: modern dance meets classic soul. Her first single release Ain't No Man went straight to No 15 in the UK chart to be followed by two beautiful ballads, This time and You'll Never Know which wer both recorded in New York with the NY Philharmonic Orchestra. She also had a top 20 UK C+C Music Factory hit Special Kind of Love and an inspirational song recorded with Cissy Houston's New Hope Baptist Choir called Heaven. So Close is the most recent hit single and the title track to her debut album released in January 1993.

JULIA FORDHAM

Julia Fordham's signature is the great clarity of her voice and her thoughtful and often deeply emotional songs; although she claims that: "I am not the moody, sensitive type normally, but I can explore my vulnerabilities in my songs." Julia signed to Circa Records in 1987 and her first eponymous album went gold. within a few months of relase. Porcelain, her second album, was as successful and included the hits Happy Ever After, Lock and Key and Where Does the Time Go? Porcelain went to No 1 in the new Adult Contemporary Album Chart in America. Within only a few weeks of release, Swept, her third album, was also No 1 in the same chart. Julia wrote all the songs on the album and co-produced it with Hugh Padgham, Grant Mitchell and Dominc Miller. Julia's recent hit (Love Moves In) Mysterious Ways was used in the soundtrack of The Butcher's Wife.

MARY MACMASTER AND PATSY SEDDON

Harpists Mary Macmaster and Patsy Seddon met while studying at Edinburgh University for degrees in Celtic Studies and Scottish History. They both played for a seven-piece women's band called Sprangeen, which was formed for the Women Live festival in 1982. While with Sprangeen, they developed their playing to allow the harp to function both as a strong solo instrument and as a chordal, rhythmic back-up, adopting the role more usually played by the guitar in groups of today. When Sprangeen split up, Patsy and Mary continued playing together and took the name of a Gaelic poet, Sileas. Their repertoire now not only covers the breadth of Scottish music and Scots and Gaelic songs, but music from other countries, with a bias towards songs composed by or about women. They arrange all their own music, allowing their knowledge of classical, jazz and rock to influence their harmonic choices. They have appeared in festivals worldwide and tour extensively, both performing and teaching.

Photograph by Stoneyport

JUNE TABOR

June Tabor began her singing career in her teens as a traditional floor singer and soon became captivated by the highly ornamental vocal styles of Anne Briggs and Belle Stewart. Later, as a student in Oxford, she encountered a larger and more diverse folk community and a simpler approach began to appeal to her as she moved in the direction of the exquisitely controlled singing that is now her trademark. Her early music was almost always as an unaccompanied singer, but she often collaborated with Maddy Prior, as the Silly Sisters, and with guitarist Martin Simpson, drawing on whose interest in contemporary music she began to broaden her repertoire to include the work of contemporary songwriters.

MAGGIE HOLLAND

Hampshire-born Maggie Holland has performed as a solo singer, accompanying herself on acoustic guitar and five-string banjo, since the late 1970s. She started working as a musican by playing bass guitar and singing in the popular duo Hot Vultures with Ian Anderson from 1972 to 1981, touring round Britain and Northern Europe. Hot Vultures evolved into the English Country Blues Band, for which Maggie was the main singer and, later still, into the roots dance band Tiger Moth. For a short time she had her own band, Maggie's Farm, and has worked in other duos, notably with Jon Moore. It was Moore who encouraged her to expand her acknowledged talent for finding and interpreting other people's songs into writing her own, and her second solo album, Down to the Bone, released in 1992, is a showcase of her songwriting skills as well as her talents as a singer and musician.

FRANKIE ARMSTRONG

Born in Cumberland, Frankie Armstrong began singing when the skiffle boom hit Britain in 1957 and swiftly became involved with the folk revival. Since 1962 she has built up a repertoire of traditional British songs and ballads, which include industrial, rural and music hall songs, and contemporary songs, wirtten by herself, or by such songwriters as Sandra Kerr, Leon Rosselson and even Bertold Brecht. She selects and interprets songs which explore and express personal and social relationships, especially those which focus on the experiences of women. She has toured in the UK, Europe, the USA, Canada and Australia, singing in a variety of settings – folk clubs and festivals, community arts centres and theatres – and has frequently performed for anti-nuclear and women's organisations. Frankie was involved in the collecting and recording of 100 songs about women's lives, My Song is My Own and has collaborated on several other albums. She has, to date, six solo albums to her credit.

MADDY PRIOR

Maddy Prior enjoys many and various musical activities. She has been singing with Steeleye Span for more than 20 years, and continues to do so with undiminished enjoyment. She also works regularly with her husband, Rick Kemp, writing and performing their own compositions; their album Happy Families was released in 1990. She has done projects with June Tabor as Silly Sisters and has made numerous TV and radio appearances. She enjoys touring when family commitments allow. Maddy also collaborates with the Carnival Band, with whom she has made several broadcasts and albums of hymns and carols, both religious and secular. Her crowning achievement must, however, be in co-founding and providing the continuity for Steeleye Span, probably the most influential folk group in the world.

KATHRYN TICKELL

Born in 1967, in the North Tyne Valley of Northumberland, Kathryn Tickell has always been surrounded by music. She has played the piano since she was six years old and, in 1980, learned the Shetland fiddle style from Tom Anderson. As a result of this accomplishment, she was invited to play at the first Shetland Folk Festival in 1981, where she was so popular that she was invited back the following year. In 1983 she was a guest at the Edinburgh International Festival, the first time that traditional music had been included in the programme. Kathryn turned professional in 1985 and has since taken her unique music all round the world. At home she has performed to sell-out audiences at the Edinburgh Festival and the Purcell Room in London's South Bank Centre, besides her regular commitments to arts centres, folk clubs and music festivals nationwide. In 1987 she recorded a 60-minute documentary, The Long Tradition, for Channel 4, chronicling her musical development and background. In 1988 she was named Top Instrumentalist in the annual Folk Roots poll, and her album, Common Ground, was named as one of "Q" magazine's records of the year.

ALISON JOAN WENHAM

Alison Wenham is the current managing director of Conifer Records Ltd, a specialist A & R, marketing and distribution company within the record industry which is the largest independent of its kind. Since she took up her post seven years ago Alison's achievements for the company have been manifold, namely a 200 per cent increase in turnover and the creation of a dedicated team to develop ten brands (new labels) including The Royal Opera House Records, Classical Collection, Compact Selection, Conifer Classics, Saville, Movie Stars, Happy Days, Aspects, Classics and One To One, now accounting for over 45 per cent of turnover. She launched the Compact Selection, the first budget CD label in the UK in 1987 (it has sold 1,250,000 units to date), and instigated and produced, with the Boots Company Management, the Classical Collection, the first retail branded classical label.

SARA JOHN

Sara John read law at Oxford and then spent a year at the College of Law, Guildford, before doing her articles with the city firm of Theodore Goddard, where she qualified as a solicitor in October 1984 and got her first taste of the music business. For the first four and a half years after qualifying she worked as a solicitor in private practice, specialising in copyright law and contracts relating to general commercial and entertainment matters. In May 1989 she joined the BPI as their legal adviser and the following year was made director of legal affairs. She sees her most important achievement as helping to win the vitally important Copyright Tribunal mechanical royalty case against NCPS in 1991. The victory saved the recording industry some £10 million a year (and won Sara a holiday in the West Indies from her grateful employers). She has written articles for International Media Law, has spoken at MIDEM and is a regular speaker at London seminars on music industry matters.

LEE ELLEN NEWMAN

Lee Ellen started out in the music business in the New York office of PolyGram Records where she implemented campaigns for many artists on the Charisma and ECM labels. She was head of press at Charisma Records from 1985 to 1986, during which time she spearheaded campaigns with Malcolm McLaren, The Rocksteady Crew and Julian Lennon and also worked with Peter Gabriel and Genesis. In 1986 she became head of press at Virgin Records handling the press for the likes of Bryan Ferry, Donny Osmond, Killing Joke and Jimmy Nail. From 1987 to 1989 she was head of press for WEA Records, US Division, Warner Music UK. From 1989 she has been head of press for East West Records, Warner Music UK, handling the press for bands such as Simply Red and AC/DC and artists such as Chris Rea, Mick Jagger and Tori Amos.

JILL SINCLAIR

Jill Sinclair entered the music world in 1977 when her brother, John Sinclair, asked her to help him run his studio in the East End. Prior to this she had been working as a maths teacher in a comprehensive school. She met Trevor Horn in 1979, when he played her a demo tape of Video Killed The Radio Star, and married him a year later. She soon started managing him as a producer and working with Dollar, ABC, Malcolm McLaren and Grace Jones. In 1982 Chris Blackwell suggested Jill and Trevor start a record company and run the Island Recording Studio in Basing Street. A year later they signed Frankie Goes To Hollywood. Since then their company ZTT has signed bands such as 808 State, Shades of Rhythm, Switzerland and the singer Seal. Jill manages several leading producer/engineers and is managing director of SARM UK Ltd.

LISA ANDERSON

Lisa Anderson started out in the music industry as secretary to Chris Wright, managing director of Chrysalis Records. In 1973 she moved to Paris as PA to the managing director of A&M Records and was rapidly promoted to run their promotion department. In 1977 she returned to London and was hired by Richard Branson to run International Promotion at Virgin Records, before being poached by Polygram UK to head their International Marketing Division. Three years later she became the first female managing director of a major record company in the UK – BMG/RCA – a post she held for two years. She is currently a consultant within the record industry, working with Polygram, Mute and Sony, and is also executive producer of the Brit Awards for the BPI.

TINY FENNIMORE

A founder member of the independent record label Go! Discs, Tiny Fennimore first worked with the company as a press officer, promoting names such as Billy Bragg, The Housemartins and LAs. In 1986 she became a press officer and copywriter for the political pressure group Red Wedge, later becoming a consultant to the Labour Party's Communications Directorate, helping them in their efforts to gain the youth vote during the 1987 and 1992 elections. She left Go! Discs in 1988 to work with Billy Bragg's manager, Peter Jenner, at Sincere Management. Since her arrival the company has doubled its workforce and client roster to include a variety of highly regarded international artists such as Robyn Hitchcock, Baaba Maal and The Disposable Heroes of Hiphoprisy. At Sincere Tiny continues to work closely with Billy Bragg and has special responsibility for the press and marketing aspects of her clients' careers, both in the UK and internationally.

ANNIE ROSEBERRY

Annie Roseberry's first job in the record business was as a personal assistant to the head of A & R at United Artists. She left the company in 1979 to set up Genetic Records with producer Martin Rughent. In 1980 she was hired by Martin Davis, the managing director of Island Records, for the job of A & R manager. She was involved in the signing of U2 in 1980 and worked closely with the band on their first album. In 1981 she was hired by Muff Winwood as A & R manager at CBS and was promoted to the position of A & R director, Epic She signed Sade, Dead or Alive, The The and Beverley Craven before being hired by Bob Krashow, chairman of Elektra US as vice-president of A & R Elektra to run Elektra's London office in June 1989. She is currently senior vice-president of A & R Elektra Entertainment.

CLARE HENRY

Art critic, freelance exhibitions curator, lecturer and broadcaster on the visual arts, Clare Henry graduated from Reading University with a BA Hons in Fine ARts in 1964. After completing her degree she taught art and English. In 1972 she moved to Glasgow where she lectured in History of Fine Art at Glasgow University. At that time she was also working as an art historian and her first research was on the painter Whistler, she then worked for the Paul Mellon Foundation. Since 1980, Clare has been art critic for the Glasgow Herald, Scotland's leading quality newspaper, where she writes on a wide range of subjects which include contemporary painting and sculpture, Old Masters and the Culture of Germany, Hungary, Romania and Egypt. She also contributes to a selection of magazines and is currently an arts contributor to the BBC. As a curator she specialises in exhibitions of contemporary British art. In 1990 she was Commissioner for Scotland at the Venice Biennale; she curated The Vigorous Imagination for the Scottish National Gallery in 1987 and has curated various other exhibitions in London and New York.

MADELEINE PONSONBY

The New Art Centre was established by Madeleine Ponsonby in 1957, as a non-profit making company to help new artists. The original trustees of the gallery included Lord Clark, Sir John Rothenstein, the director of the Tate Gallery and Lord Sainsbury. Since 1976, the gallery has involved more established artists, because Madeleine Ponsonby came to believe that it was important to show several generations of artists together. In 1987 she opened a 60 acre sculpture garden in the grounds of a famous 18th century house in Wiltshire. Roche Court Sculpture Garden has proved a very important addition to the New Art Centre, presenting a comprehensive survey of British sculpture and attracting interest from artists, clients and the press. In addition to these activities, Madeleine Ponsonby organises the New Art Centre's annual participation in international art fairs throughout the world, from Basel and Madrid to Chicago and Hong Kong.

JO WALTON

The Atrium Bookshop in Cork Street, London, is the art book lover's idea of bliss, offering a mouth-watering range of current titles. Managing director and co-founder, Jo Walton has been a specialist bookseller for 18 years and has an astounding breadth of knowledge. She claims she can track down any in-print art title in the world and the selection of up-to-date international exhibition catalogues bears this out. Jo was born in Nottingham and gained Art History degrees at Leiceser and Oxford universities. She worked at St George's Gallery in Duke Street for 12 years after leaving university, before opening the Atrium Bookshop, with partners Sheenagh Henneage and Dasha Shenkman in November 1992. Given the high degree of expertise of the staff and the often highbrow nature of the books, one of Jo's major achievements at Atrium is that she has managed to render it completely unintimidating.

ANNA SOMERS COCKS

Born in Rome in 1950, Anna Somers Cocks graduated with an MA in History from Oxford University in 1971 and proceeded to the Courtauld Institute, where she graduated with another MA, in History of Art, in 1973. From 1973 until 1986 she was assistant keeper at The Victoria and Albert Museum, specialising in medieval and Renaissance goldsmiths' work and jewellery and, latterly, in ceramics. In 1986, Ann abecame editor of Apollo magazine, a post which she held until 1990, when she became founder/editor of The Art Newspaper. She has organised numerous exhibitions, including Princely Magnificence: Crown Jewels of the Renaissance 1500-1630 (1980) at the Victoria and Albert Museum and Treasures from the Hermitage, with the Hermitage at the Villa Favorita, Lugano. Anna's publications include The Victoria and Albert Museum, The Making of the Collection and, as co-author, Renaissance Jewels, Gold Boxes and Objets de Vertu in the Thyssen-Bornemisza Collection. She has lectured extensively at, inter alia, The National Gallery, Washington, The Metropolitan Museum of Art, The Carnegie Institute, Pittsburgh and The Los Angeles County Museum of Art. A Fellow of the Society of Antiquaries, she sits as a member of the Conservative Parliamentary Advisory Committee on the Arts and Heritage and on the Committee of Management of the Friends of the Courtaluld Institute.

ELIZABETH ESTEVE-COLL

Mrs Elizabeth Esteve-Coll was first appointed director fo the Victoria and Albert Museum, Britain's National Museum of Art and Design, in January 1988. She was re-appointed for a five-year second term in 1991. Born in 1938 she has a first class honours degree in History and Art History from the University of London, she is a Fellow of the Royal Society of Arts; a member of the council of the Royal College of Art and of the Craft Council and a governor of De Montfort University. In 1991 Elizabeth was awarded an honorary doctorate by the Council for National Academic Awards. A widow, she married a Spanish-born naval officer in 1959 and, before starting her career, travelled extensively with her husband. She speaks fluent Spanish, French and Italian. Between 1968 and 1977, she was a librarian with the London Borough of Merton, Kingston College of Art and Kingston Polytechnic. From 1977 until 1982 she was Head of Learning Resources at Kingston Polytechnic. Prior to joining the V&A, she was University Librarian at the University of Surrey, where she was also chairman of the Arts Committee, and is still a member of its Council. At the V&A Elizabeth has been responsible for wide-ranging management changes and has instituted an active programme of successful exhibitions and gallery developments. Born in Yorkshire, she now lives in West London; her interests include music, poetry, travel and French Romanesque sculpture.

BERYL COOK

Beryl Cook (née Lansley) left school at the age of 14 to work in an insurance office. She embarked on a short-lived stage career when the family moved to London and then did a stint as a model. It was these experiences which gave her a lifelong fascination with the way we dress and make ourselves up and how the reality often fails to live up to our intentions. From jobs managing a pub in the country to working for a fruiterers and an office equipment suppliers in Southern Rhodesia she moved to Cornwall with her husband and immediately began painting pictures for the walls, using, because they had no money, any material she could find. Today the flotsam and jetsam has been replaced by neatly cut plywood and their surfaces are coveted by collectors worldwide. Things took off when a friend persuaded her to let him sell some of her paintings. Exhibitions at the Whitechapel and Portal Galleries led to the publication of her first book of paintings, and greetings cards and limited edition prints soon followed. Serious critical appreciation was shown with her inclusion in the Peter Moores Exhibition at the Walker Art Gallery in Liverpool, alongside Bridget Riley and Victor Pasmore. Now a great-grandmother Beryl works all year round, travelling abroad for inspiration to Marseille, Barcelona and New Orleans.
Photograph by Robert Chapman

MAGGI HAMBLING

One of our most established painters Maggi Hambling studied with Lett Haines and Cedric Morris during the early 1960s and at Camberwell School of Art and the Slade. She received an Arts Council Award in 1977 and was artist in residence at the National Gallery in 1980. Her work is in numerous public collections including the Arts Council of Great Britain, the British Council, the British Museum, The Tate and the National Gallery and the National Portrait Gallery. She has appeared in numerous publications and her work has featured in several TV documentaries. In 1991 she exhibited at the Yale Center for British Art in Connecticut and in 1992 her work was on show at the Bernard Jacobson Gallery.
Photography by Tim Macpherson

ELSPETH LAMB

Elsepth Lamb studied at Glasgow School of Art and Manchester Polytechnic where she took a postgraduate degree in printmaking. She followed this with a course in stone lithography at the Ruskin School of Drawing. She has held a lecturer's post in etching at Glasgow School of Art, and in printmaking, drawing, and painting at Edinburgh College of Art and been a visiting lecturer at top art schools around the country. Among her many awards are a research bursary from Edinburgh College of Art to study at the Tamarind Institute of Lithography in New Mexico and a Scottish Arts Council Bursary to travel to the USA. In 1992 she won the Hope Scott Trust Award and the Scotland on Sunday Paper Boat Award. She has had 12 one-woman exhibitions and exhibited in some 32 mixed exhibitions since 1983. Her work has also appeared in nine international print biennials and is on permanent display at the British Council, the Scottish Arts Council, Glasgow museums and art galleries, the Hunterian Museum and the BBC. Her lithographs and screenprints have also appeared in several books.

ZSUZSI ROBOZ

Born in Budapest Zsuzsi Roboz came to London in 1947. She studied at the Royal Academy with Peter Greenham and Fleetwood Walker and then with the artist Pietro Annigoni, in Florence. Her first portrait commissions were for a series of portraits of Sir Alexander Korda's contract artists. Her sketches and lithographs of dancers, musicans and artists have been exhibited from Cork Street to New York, Los Angeles, Hong Kong and Budapest. Among her works on permanent display are a portrait of Dame Ninette de Valois in the National Portrait Gallery's Permanent Contemporary Collection, three life-size drawings of the ballet at the Royal Festival Hall and portraits of Sir Frederick Ashton and Lord Olivier in the V&A's Theatre Museum. Zsuzsi is currently putting the finishing touches to material for an exhibition and book, entitled British Artists Now – A Personal View. She is working on a new series of paintings on the theme The Spirit of Nature.

Agent: Michael Roosen Ent.

MARY FEDDEN

Mary Fedden studied at the Slade School of Art. She has taught painting at the Royal College of Art from 1958-64 and at the Yehudi Menuhin School from 1965-70. She is President of the Royal West of England Academy, has had major one-man exhibitions in top galleries in London and all over Britain and her paintings, watercolours and murals have been bought by, among others, the Queen for Windsor Castle, the Crown Prince of Jordan, the Chantrey Bequest for the Tate Gallery, the National Gallery of Victoria in Melbourne, the Contemporary Art Society, the Royal Scottish Academy and County Education Committees and city art galleries countrywide.

LAURA WHITE

Twenty-three year old Laura White is one of our most promising young sculptors. After graduating from Loughborough College of Art and Design with a first in sculpture she took time off to travel through Africa, India and America. She exhibits around the country, in 1992 at Global Village in Fulham, the Pearoom Gallery in Lincolnshire and at the Leicestershire Exhibition for schools and colleges.

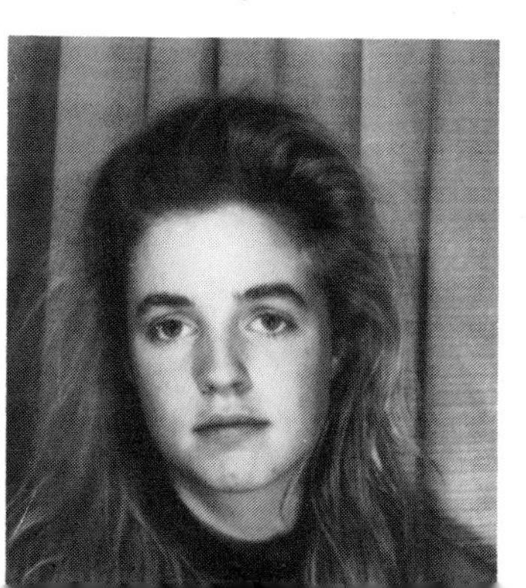

SUSIE ALLEN

Susie Allen studied at Croydon College of Art, Kingston Polytechnic and the Royal College of Art. Since 1976 she has been curating major exhibitions including British Art for the Festival Vienna Austria, Exhibition Road Painters at the Royal College of Art, a 150th anniversary survey exhibition for the RCA and 3 Ways Contemporary British Painting, a British Council touring exhibition for Eastern Europe. She has won an RCA Travelling Scholarship and a National Art Collections Fund Award for outstanding services to the Arts (1988-89). Her work is in public collections such as the British Council, the Scottish Council, the V&A Museum and South London Galleries. In 1992 she curated the exhibition In Sight at the Henry Moore Galleries and Off Sight, RCA painters exhibition at the Cooling Gallery. Last year she also set up a new company to develop fine art projects and corporate collections and commissions.

CAROLINE STACEY

Caroline Stacey trained with the Viennese sculptor Georg Ehrlich from 1942 until his death in 1966 after which she went to John Cass to study life modelling, anatomy and casting and the Beaux Arts in Paris for drawing. She managed to fit in all these studies while raising five children. Gallery artist at Alwin Gallery (now Art Scene) since 1975 and "artiste en permanence" at Galerie Bernheim-Jeune in Paris since 1982, she has undertaken portrait commissions in the UK and France, the US and Canada, and has done outside pieces in London and Sussex.

GILLIAN AYRES

Gillian Ayres' work is on permanent display in our most prestigious galleries and abroad in the Art Gallery of South Australia, Adelaide, the Gulbenkian Foundation in Lisbon, the Museum of Modern Art in New York, Olinda Museum in Sao Paulo and the Museum of Modern Art in Brasilia. Her awards include the Japan International Art Promotion Association Award (1963); an Arts Council of Great Britain bursary (1975); an Arts Council purchase award (1979). She won the Blackstone Prize (1988 and 1990), the Charles Wollaston Award (1989) and the Korn/Ferry Prize (1990) at the Royal Academy Summer Exhibition. In 1991 she took the gold medal at the Seventh Triennale in India.

Photograph by Mayotte Magnus

JUNE REDFERN

Born in Fife, Scotland, June Redfern studied drawing and painting at Edinburgh College of Art from 1968-72. She was awarded first prize in the Scottish Young Contemporaries in her leaving year. Since then she has had some 22 solo exhibitions and her work has been shown in public collections worldwide, from the Albertina Museum in Vienna to the Charlotte Eaglehart Foundation in Boston. In 1982 she received the Scottish Arts Council Award and became a part-time tutor in fine art at Preston Polytechnic. Elected a junior fellow in fine art at Cardiff College of Art in 1983 she was artist-in-residence at the National Gallery, London, in 1985. She has also been a guest artist at the University of Minnesota in Minneapolis (1986) and at Kunstagademie i Trondheim in Norway (1992).

Photograph by Andrew Sheriff

THERESE OULTON

Born in Shropshire Therese Oulton studied at St Martin's School of Art and the Royal College of Art. Her solo exhibitions include, since 1984, Fool's Gold: New Paintings, at Gimpel Fils (1984); Recent Paintings, Museum of Modern Art, Oxford (1985); Letters to Rose, Galerie Krinzinger, Vienna (1986); Skin Deep, Galerie Thomas, Munich (1986); Monoprints, Marlborough Graphics, London (1987); Lachrimae, Marlborough Fine Art, London (1988); Paintings and Prints, Pittsburgh Centre of the Arts (1990); Recent Paintings, Marlborough Fine Art; and Paintings and Works on Paper, LA Louver, Venice, California (1991).

WENDY TAYLOR

Born in Lincolnshire her roots are really in the East End of London where she now lives, with her family a few doors away. She enrolled at St Martin's School of Art when she was 16 years old and stayed there for six years, until 1967, teaching part-time at another college during her final year. In the 1970s she was one of the first artists to "take art out of the galleries and into the streets". Unlike other members of the same generation of sculptors, however, she wasn't interested in making impermanent work and meticulously engineered each piece to withstand the outdoors. Nowadays her works are familiar landmarks all over Britain. She probably has more major sculptures on permanent display in Britain than any other living artist. Among her awards are the Walter Neurath (1964), the Pratt (1965) and the Sainsbury (1966). She was awarded the CBE in 1988.

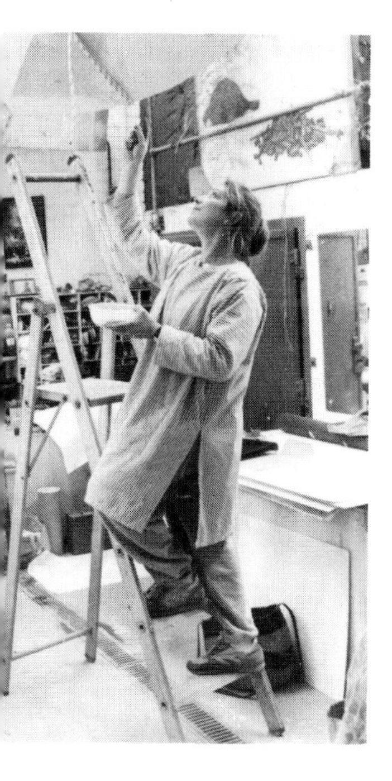

DAME ELISABETH FRINK

Born in 1930 in Suffolk Dame Elisabeth Frink studied at Guildford School of Art and Chelsea School of Art and later taught at Chelsea and St Martin's. She has exhibited throughout the UK as well as New York, Los Angeles, San Antonio, Washington, Montreal, Toronto, Sydney, Brisbane, Hong Kong and New Orleans. Her commissions include Eagle Lectern for Coventry Cathedral in 1962, Altar Cross for Liverpool Cathedral (1966); Horse and Rider, Dover Street (1974); Paternoster, Paternoster Square (1975); Horse, Goodwood Racecourse (1980); Christ's Head, All Saints Church, Basingstoke (1983); Standing Man, Walking Man and Running Man, WH Smith Headquarters, Swindon (1985); Water Buffaloes, Hong Kong (1986); and Desert Quartet, Worthing (1989). She was awarded the CBE in 1969 and the DBE in 1982, was elected a Royal Academician in 1977 and made CH in 1992.

ELIZABETH BLACKADDER

Elizabeth Blackadder studied at Einburgh University and Edinburgh College of Art. Her work is on permanent display in London at the Tate and the National Portrait Gallery and in America at the National Museum of Women In The Arts (Washington) and the McInay Art Museum (San Antonio). She was elected academician of the Royal Scottish Academy in 1972 and of the Royal Academy, London, in 1976. She is an honorary member of the Royal Incorporation of Architects in Scotland and of the Royal Watercolour Society, a member of the Royal Glasgow Institute of the Fine Arts, and a member of the Royal Scottish Society of Painters in Watercolours. She holds an honorary doctorate at Heriot Watt University and at the University of Edinburgh. She received the OBE in 1982.

Photograph by Antonia Reeve

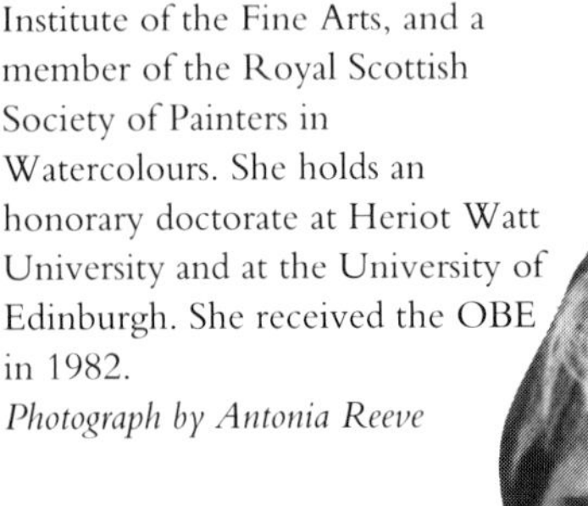

CATHERINE DENVIR

Catherine Denvir went to Chelsea School of Art from 1971-74. She has done posters for London Transport, the Royal Ballet, Bath Festival and World Wide Video Festival and book covers for Penguin, Grafton, Harper Collins, Random House USA and Faber. Her illustrations have appeared in the Sunday Times Magazine, Vogue, New Scientist, The Listener, GQ and the Sunday Independent Review and in advertisements for the Bank of America, WH Smith, Harrods and the Royal Mail. She is often a judge of illustration competitions including the Association of Illustrators Annual, Reader's Digest, Benson and Hedges, Elle and Laus '90 Barcelona.

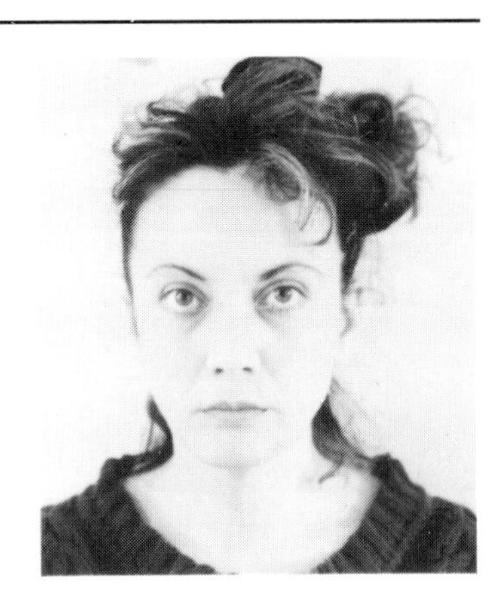

SANDRA BLOW

One of the most important British pioneers of abstract painting Sandra Blow studied at St Martin's School of Art and The Royal Academy Schools in London and L'Accademia di Belle Arti in Rome. Her work is in numerous public collections abroad, from the Felton Bequest in Melbourne to the Museum of Modern Art in New York, and in Britain at the British Council, the Arts Council of Great Britain, the Tate and the V&A. She has had some ten solo exhibitions since 1953 and participated in over 50 group exhibitions. A Royal Academician and an honorary fellow of the Royal College of Art one of her achievements last year was to win the Wollaston award for the most distinguished work at the Royal Academy Summer Exhibition.

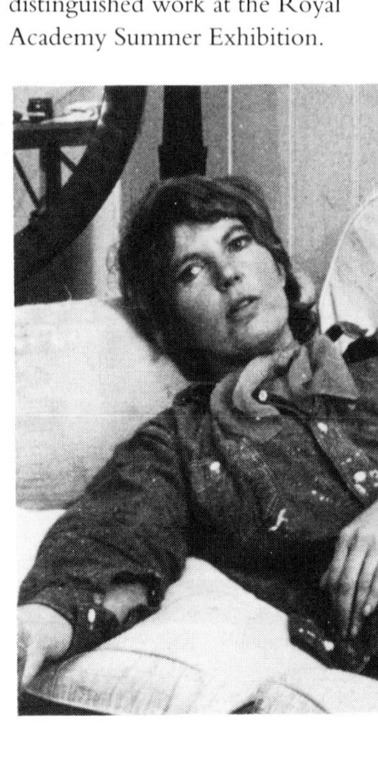

ROSE WARNOCK ↱

Rose Warnock studied for her foundation course at Watford School of Art and took her degree in fine art at Birmingham Polytechnic. She then studied painting at the Royal College of Art from where she graduated in 1989. She has been exhibiting since 1982 and has received a Welsh Arts Council Grant (in 1984) and a Darwin Scholarship (in 1988). Last year she exhibited at the 20th Century Art Fair and with Paul Storey in "Artistic Associations" at the Gillian Jason Gallery. In 1993 her work will be part of Art '93, also at the Gillian Jason Gallery.

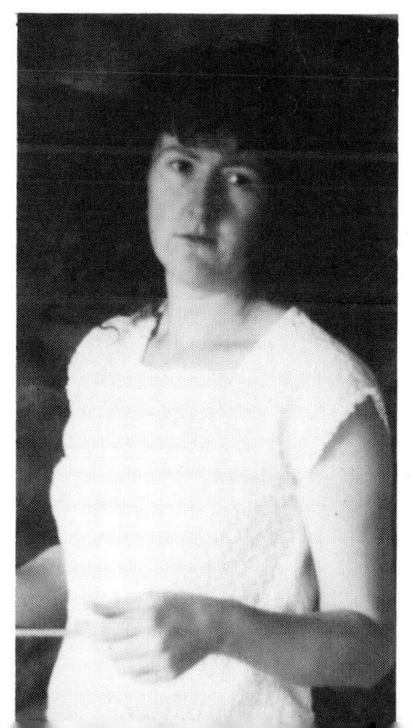

PAULA REGO ▲

Born and brought up in Portugal Paula Rego came to England in 1952 to study at the Slade for four years. She returned to Portugal on completing her course, with her husband, Victor Willing. Here she received a bursary from the Gulbenkian Foundation in Lisbon in 1962. for the next 13 years she divided her time between London and Portugal, settling permanently in London in 1976. She was a visiting lecturer in painting at the Slade in 1983 and was appointed the first National Gallery Associate Artist in 1990.

MARIANNE FORREST

Marianne Forrest makes clocks out of practically anything – glass, wood, silver, rubber, marble, even concrete; from miniature watches to huge sculptural clocks. A graduate of the Royal College of Art, where she studied silversmithing, she says it felt odd to be making little boxes with no function but a decorative one. Then a client asked for a clock and she realised she had found her metier. Today she makes timepieces for individuals as well as for offices, foyers and shops. Among commissions recently completed are a large sculptural clock for a Caribbean cruise liner and a 150kg clock of glass, steel and brass for the new-look Criterion restaurant in London, unveiled last September.

JANET LEACH

Born in Texas in 1918 Janet Leach has been a working potter for over 40 years. She studied sculpture in New York before establishing a pottery of her own near the city. In 1952 she met famous potters Bernard Leach (later to become her husband), Shoji Hamada and Soetsu Yanagi during their American tour. Under Hamada's invitation she studied pottery in Japan, the first foreign woman to do so, and learnt, among other things, Bizen firing techniques. In 1956 she got married, moved to England and became a partner in the Leach Pottery, which produced pots for export until Bernard's death in 1979. Since then she has exhibited extensively in four continents and her pots feature in permanent collections of public museums in both Europe and America.

VICKI AMBERY-SMITH

After leaving Hornsey College of Art Vicki Ambery-Smith was awarded a New Craftsman's Grant by the Craft Council to set up her own workshop. Inspired by the buildings of Tuscany, Venice and France and the Gothic spires of Oxford, where she grew up, Vicki has been making rings and brooches of silver, red gold and serpentine for some 11 years. Her credits include a gold and silver model of the Globe theatre, commissioned by the Duke and Duchess of York, but she can do any building, from the Art Deco Hoover factory to Florence's Duomo, or even a client's own house. Her work can be bought at the V&A shop and in shops in Oxford.

SARAH WALTON

Sarah Walton studied painting at Chelsea School of Art before training and working as a nurse for five years. She returned to the art world in 1971, studying on the Studio Pottery Course at Harrow School of Art and then working under David Leach and Zelda Mowat. She started working on her own as a potter in 1975, making thrown tableware and firing it in a salt-kiln. She quickly became known as one of the leading saltglaze potters in Britain – her work is now on permanent display in 13 museums in the British Isles. In the early 1980s she began to use methods other than throwing and started to make hand-built birdbaths on wooden bases. Last year, after 20 years of making domestic sealed pots, she decided to concentrate instead on developing her large pieces for outdoors. She began working in sections, re-assembling the pieces after firing with epoxy resin. She continues to use her salt-kiln, as always seeking to exploit and work with the haphazard effects that come from this way of firing.

MARY LITTLE

Born in Northern Ireland Mary Little studied furniture design at Ulster Polytechnic and then at the Royal College of Art. Since then she has exhibited worldwide and has permanent collections at the Vitra Design Museum in Basel and the Musée Des Arts Decoratifs in Paris. She has appeared in countless books on design, was designer in residence at Hooke Park College in Dorset, designing furniture using indigenous timbers and has tutored at this college and at Glasgow School of Art, Kingston Polytechnic and Ravensbourne College of Design and Communication in London. She has also taught Masters Degree course at Buckingham College and the Royal College of Art. She received a setting up grant from the Crafts Council last year. At the moment she is developing a collection of upholstered chairs for which she has been offered a one-woman show in Galerie Marzee, Holland, next autumn. She has also launched an edition of glass vases, developed at CIRVA, Marseille which were shown last autumn at The Cooling Gallery, London, and the 3rd International Ceramics Festival in Japan. Two of the vases were selected for inclusion in the Fonds National d'Art Contemporain in France.

ANNA LEVER

Born in Newbury Anna Lever is a self-taught ceramic sculptor concentrating on highly decorative earthenware figures. These show both a deep understanding of the ancient art of sculpture and an obvious fascination with the theatrical and idiosyncratic aspects of modern life. She has exhibited at, among other galleries, The Oxford Art Society, Luxters Fine Art and the Century Gallery at Henley-on-Thames and the Mall Galleries, where she won the 1990 Royal Society of British Artists Annual Sculpture Award. Her most recent exhibition was at Noott 20th Century Gallery in Broadway, Worcestershire.

JANICE TCHALENKO

Janice Tchalenko was the first British potter to abandon the Bernard Leach philosophy of craftsmanship, still much to the fore in the late 1970s, and to question the dominant Oriental aesthetic that had inspired so many "brown" pots. She proved that ceramics could be colourful, even funny, without being trivial. Her Persian-inspired windblown flowers, mosaic grids and cross-hatchings were a liberating alternative to the rustic appeal of most craft potters at the time. Janice worked in the Foreign Office and travelled throughout the Middle East before attending the Workshop Pottery Course at Harrow School of Art. She established a workshop with the aid of a Crafts Council grant in 1971 and since then has exhibited worldwide and been a tutor and fellow at the Royal College of Art. Her work is on permanent display at, among other collections, the V&A and the British Council. In 1988 she was awarded the Manchester Prize for Art in production for her Dart design and a Support for Design Bursary (Design Council) and she won the Radio 4 Enterprise Award Small Business of the Year; Dart Pottery. She was made curator of the British Council's Colours of the Earth Indian tour in 1991 and that year was consulting for Goa You porcelain factory in China to design new products.

Photograph by Caroline Forbes

JANE DILLON

Jane Dillon studied interior design at Manchester and furniture design at the Royal College of Art before working for Knoll International in London and then under Ettore Sottsass for Olivetti in Milan. She returned to London in 1972 and on setting up a studio with Charles Dillon worked as consultant to the Barcelona based companies Casas and Disform. Their collaboration of ten years produced many seminal pieces of work here and abroad including a nomination for the Delta de Plata for the Actis office chairs Casas collection in 1979. Since the death of Charles Dillon in 1982 she has continued to work internationally, collaborating with Peter Wheeler and Floris van den Broecke in the design of mass produced furniture, as well as working on experimental furniture projects and small batch production runs for architects. She is a visiting tutor at, among other institutions, the Royal College of Art where she is also an external assessor.

KATE MALONE

Kate Malone is one of Britain's leading ceramicists. A graduate of the Royal College of Art she built, owns and manages the Balls Pond Studios, housing 12 applied artists plus her huge kiln, the largest in London. She has received grants from the Crafts Council for glaze research and for equipment, has exhibited in Europe, Canada and Japan and has executed commissions for a lake sculpture for a London park, table tops and wall plaques for fish restaurants and, most recently, a bronze drinking fountain for her home town of Bristol, tiles for a swimming pool in Barbados and a lamp for Jean Muir.

LUCINDA LEECH

Lucinda Leech has designed furniture and run her own workshops in Oxford since 1977. She leads a team of skilled craftsmen producing individual custom-made pieces and is now a Fellow of the Society of Designer Craftsmen. Her clients range from private customers to colleges and churches, businesses and galleries. Recent work for private clients included a marquetry dining table to seat 16, inspired by Roman architecture. An award from the Worshipful Company of Furniture Makers took Lucinda to the Amazon and she has visited the forests in most other tropical areas to research sustainable projects and source her material directly. She feels her travels have added an extra dimension to her work. "Discovering new timbers is also an exciting design influence on my creation of original and individual furniture," she says.

JACQUELINE MINA

Jacqueline Mina studied silversmithing and embroidery before taking a degree at the Royal College of Art in jewellery. Since then her work has appeared in some 50 exhibitions, and been the subject of several TV programmes and books. She is a jury member of the Platinum Award, an external examiner for Edinburgh College of Art and Glasgow School of Art and a visiting lecturer at the Royal College of Art. Much of her inspiration comes directly from the metals as she works them. Her recent work incorporates platinum with other precious metals, a combination which, because of the unique physical properties of platinum, allows her to create a rich textile or embroidery effect with the surfaces. Among her commissions is a platinum filigree necklace for the V&A's permanent collection.

VENDY RAMSHAW

Vendy Ramshaw, FSIAD*, FRSA, s a Lady Liveryman of the Vorshipful Company of Goldsmiths. Her jewellery is on ermanent show at many museums nd public collections worldwide, ncluding the Royal Museum of cotland, the Philadelphia Museum f Art, the Stedlijk Museum, the chmuckmuseum Phorzheim, the National Gallery of Victoria and e Museum of Modern Art in Kyoto. Her first one-woman xhibition in 1970 confirmed her ommitment to a 20th century esthetic: in it she created turned pace-age forms in silver, namelled and embellished with emi-precious stones and small irrors. Two years later she eceived a Council of Industrial Design Award for innovative esign for a collection which ncluded sets of rings mounted on istinctive stands. A recent etrospective exhibition at the Royal Festival Hall contained riginal fold-out, 3-D 60s paper ewellery, designed with David Vatkins and ceramic and gold ewellery examples of her ollaboration with Wedgwood, rst exhibited in her solo show at e V&A. Her present on-going ork, Picasso's Ladies, is a ollection which celebrates the oncept of jewellery for personal xpression, creating individual ieces of jewellery which have een inspired by specific Picasso ortraits.

KAREN BEAUCHAMP

Karen Beauchamp trained as an architect and worked as a set designer for the BBC. After an exhausting stint as a Brixton nightclub owner she left London for the Isle of Man. Here she became interested in screen printing and the possibilities of wallpaper. Collaborating with Manx resident interior designer David Style, she began restoring old houses, mimicking the wallpaper using traditional methods. Instead of carving blocks the old way, Karen and her assistants cut screens which are individually painted by hand. The method produces results which no machine-roller can match. Sources for Karen's designs include a medieval book of hours and the drawings of Archibald Knox. Her company, Alexander Beauchamp, sells worldwide, with clients ranging from the State Treasury Building in Washington to Lenny Henry and Dawn French.

Photograph by Alexander Beauchamp

PAM LINTOTT AND ROSEMARY MILLER

Pam Lintott and Rosemary Miller little dreamed that their small quilt shop, The Quilt Room, would become so successful when they opened back in 1981. Nowadays people travel from all over Britain to buy supplies and attend their workshops. Pam's interest in quilts began in the 1970s when she was living in America and her passion grew through seeing different forms of patchworking and quilting on her travels abroad. Rosemary had always had a love of fabric and took up patchworking as a hobby. The shop is piled to the ceiling with over 1,200 bolts of fabric and there are countless books to buy on quilting, including Pam and Rosemary's own book, The Quilt Room Patchwork and Quilting Workshops which was published in 1992.

SUSAN BENJAMIN

Susan Benjamin founded the world famous antique shop Halcyon Days in 1950. Working with a manufacturer from Bilston, Staffordshire, she brought about the revival of enamelling in 1970 – it died out in the early 19th century – because he says she couldn't understand why everything she sold was still produced apart from enamels. In 1989 Susan introduced Halcyon Days Porcelain – superb animal sculptures and miniatures inspired by Chelsea porcelain. Halcyon Days has the distinction of being one of only 11 companies ever to have been appointed to four Royal warrants and the only company to be By Appointment suppliers of objects d'art.

Photograph by Prudence Cuming Associates Ltd

CLARE STREET

A designer, jeweller and hand engraver, specialising in seal engraving and classical diamond setting, Clare Street studied engraving and stone setting at Sir John Cass School of Art. Since leaving in 1971 she has won many commendations and prizes in the Goldsmiths competition and now exhibits her jewellery at the annual show and fair at Goldsmiths Hall and the Design Centre, London. Clare describes herself as "committed to realising the technique of seal engraving without compromise". She works to commission on precious metal signet rings, cufflinks, fob and desk seals, these last also in base metal.

SALLY HODGSON

Sally Hodson learnt dry stone walling as a child on the family farm. It has been her full-time occupation for the last four years. She began with field walls but these days specialises in more creative projects (she has a BA in textiles and fine art) such as walls, ponds and steps for landscaped gardens. She is a member of the Derbyshire branch of the Dry Stone Walling Association and is involved in their many sponsored walls and demonstrations. She also runs courses in her craft for children, adult education and women's and special needs groups. She is the best competitive female professional dry stone waller, having competed on equal terms with men in the DSWA Grand Prix. She has gained her intermediate certificate with the association and is working towards her Master Craftsman.

FAITH SHANNON

Faith Shannon has won practically every award there is for bookbinding including an MBE in 1977. Brought up in India and Ireland she studied at the Royal College of Art after Belfast School of Art and London University (where she gained a first). Some 40 exhibitions of her work have appeared since those days and her work is on permanent show at the British Library and the Crafts Council. Among her commissioned work is a Parker Pen presentation for the Prince and Princess of Wales' wedding. She teaches children and adults, was a lecturer at Brighton Polytechnic and lectures and gives demonstrations worldwide – in 1992 she was on a lecture/workshop tour to New Zealand.

Photograph by Shannon Tofts

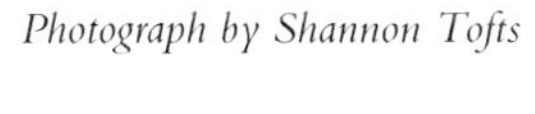

LOIS WALPOLE

Lois graduated in sculpture from St. Martin's School of Art in 1975. She then spent six years trying to work out what she wanted to do and finally went on a basketry course. She has never looked back. Her brightly coloured baskets made from cane, willow, recycled plastic and cardboard are now exhibited widely in Britain and Canada, the US, Japan and Norway. She featured on the Channel 4 documentary series Not Pots and is on the Crafts Council Select Index of Makers. Her book, Creative Basketing, was published in 1987 by Collins. She has her own design and production company called Rapid Eye Baskets which produces hand-made and very high quality "eye-catching" designs.

Photograph by John Brennan

JULIAN AKERS-DOUGLAS

Ten years ago Julian set up her company Specially For You, selling smocking from her 12ft long kitchen table. Today business is booming in the Sussex village of East Hoathly in Lewes. Her aim was to raise the profile of smocking, and encourage people to buy for themselves rather than just for their children. Traditional designs are ranged alongside the very contemporary, and each garment is made as it would have been many years ago.

VERNA BAILEY

Verna Bailey learnt to make corn dollies at evening classes back in 1976. She now teaches and demonstrates the craft herself. The tradition of corn dolly making dates back to pre-Christian times when early civilisations believed that the spirit of the crop or Corn Goddess lived in the corn fields and would die when the corn was harvested if some part of it was not preserved. To safeguard next year's crop the last sheaf to be cut was plaited into a dolly to provide a resting place for the spirit until next spring when it was returned to the soil. Verna ties the dollies with the traditional decorative ribbons: gold represents the harvest, red symbolises friendship and warmth. She collects her designs from farmers, and because modern farming methods produce corn with stalks that are too short for her purposes, she gets all her supplies from a traditional farm in Oxfordshire.

ISOBEL KENNETT

Isobel Kennett started making lace at a very young age – she began with nails and string when she was three. Today she is the only person in Britain selling this work worldwide, with the only market not yet cornered the Russian one! Isobel decided to try to revive the craft in the 1960s and started running evening classes. She now takes around eight a week and has some 100 pupils. Her work ranges from handkerchiefs to tablemats and paperweights and a wide variety of lace is made – among them Honiton, English point ground and Beds Maltese.

ELIZABETH CLIFFORD

Elizabeth Clifford has been weaving for over 20 years. She works alone, weaving fine dress fabrics in pure wool or wool and cashmere, many of them with an undulating warp-ways pattern resulting from tie-dying the warp prior to weaving. The subtle colours are obtained by careful blending of chemical dyes which have excellent light fastness. Her fabrics are available either as lengths or made up into simple clothes: these are designed to enhance the cloth by minimising cutting and seaming as far as possible without compromising comfort and wearability. Many of them are designed so that special details such as borders are woven in the right place according to the cutting plan.

CLARE McFARLANE

After completing a diploma course in ceramics at Croydon College of Art, where she concentrated on slip-casting and mould making, Clare McFarlane set up a small workshop. She started with large pieces but soon changed to smaller things when these proved unworkable – too time consuming and expensive. Domesticated animals, particularly cats, are today her most lucrative subjects. From a photograph she produces a clay model. While this is damp she makes a plaster of Paris mould. She uses semi-porcelain casting slip to cast with. Her pieces are bisques and hand-painted using underglaze colours and some brush-on glazes. A more natural finish is achieved when the pieces are first lustred and then smoked in sawdust.

Photograph by Sussex Express and County Herald

WENDY DOLAN

Artist Wendy Dolan embroiders textiles in the form of pictures, jewellery and fashion accessories. She took a BEd Degree in Art and Textiles and a Diploma in Creative Embroidery before setting up in business. Taking her inspiration from nature she paints, prints or dyes the backgrounds and then applies layers of fabrics and threads, gradually building up the surface texture of the design. A member of the Guild of Sussex Craftsmen, Janet was a founder member of CEATA Textile Artists and regularly teaches and lectures on the art and craft of embroidery.

JANET KAY

Janet trained in graphic design at Hornsey College of Art, specialising in illustration with a particular interest in animals and birds. She has been pebble painting since 1976, joining the Guild of Sussex Craftsmen in 1983. She chooses her pebbles carefully, allowing the shape to suggest the position of the animal, so that the finished painting complements the natural object. Painted in gouache watercolour and sealed with varnish, the pebbles are used as paperweights, doorstops or purely decorative objects. Orders are often taken for pets or favourite animals.

ANNE JONES

Anne Jones' fascination with gypsy things dates back to her early schooldays when she used to pass caravans on the way to school in Yorkshire. But she didn't get into the business of painting caravans herself until she met her husband in 1961. He owned a caravan which she set about restoring. Today she is one of our foremost caravan painters. Working in gold leaf scrollwork, line work and traditional gypsy, Anne uses traditional colours – dark green or red for the background with scarlet and bright green and cream for the lining. She gets her gold leaf from a British craftsman in his 80s whose product is far superior to the Italian and German machine made variety.

He is the only person left beating gold leaf in the old way. One caravan will probably take her 3,000 hours but she describes her work as a labour of love. The photograph shows the front of a bowtop waggon built c1910, decorated by Anne in gold leaf.

ANNE THOMSON AND REBECCA OWEN

Anne Thomson and Rebecca Owen are the formidable team at the Sue Rankin Gallery off the Portobello Road. Anne did her apprenticeship at Sotheby's and the Ruskin in Stratford before taking over the gallery from Sue Rankin in 1988. Her partner, Rebecca Owen, left Waddington to join her shortly after this. The gallery shows worldwide: New York, LA, Santa Monica and Manchester are planned for 1993. Last season Rebecca Owen and Anne Thomson showed Gordon Bryce, Joanna Carrington, Helen Napper, Michael Honnor and Joe Fan.

JANE HOULDSWORTH

A degree in geography and four years working as an editor for a map-making company aren't the most appropriate qualifications for a gallery owner. But Jane was probably following earlier influences (an artistic family on her mother's side and a businessman father) when she switched to the arts. She opened Flying Colours Gallery in Edinburgh in 1986, at a time when Scottish artists were enjoying new attention from the art world. She was then 29. As the name would suggest the gallery focuses on bright, vibrant painting and watercolouring and Jane's eye has picked some 100 Scottish artists for solo exhibitions in the past six years. The work ranges from the loosely representational to the near abstract, with unknowns given as much space as the most famous.

JESS WILDER

Jess Wilder joined Lionel Levy at the Portal Gallery in 1975, straight out of East Anglia University where she read fine art. After a stint in Paris working at the Galerie de Seine she returned to Portal and became a partner there in 1988. Portal has always aimed to provide a gateway for unknown artists into London's West End. The artists Portal represents are mainly British and many have no formal training. Their work often has a surreal quality. Beryl Cook, probably Britain's most popular painter, has exhibited at Portal since 1975 and Kit Williams (famous for his book Masquerade) has exhibited there since 1969.

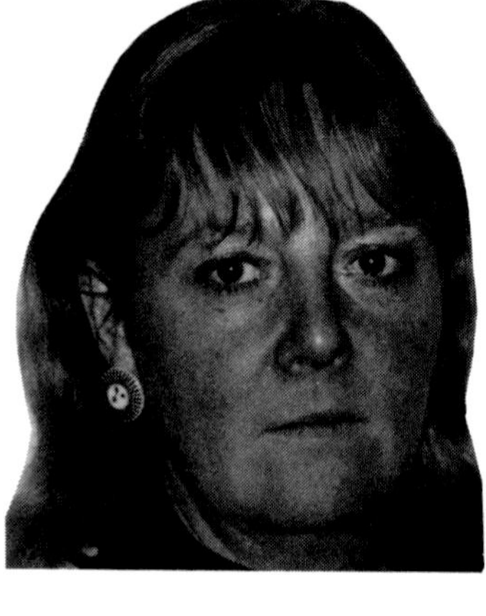

ANGELA FLOWERS

Angela Flowers' gallery, Flowers East, is probably the most prestigious gallery showing contemporary art in Britain. She opened her first venture in 1970 and the business has kept on expanding ever since. The present premises in the East End house five exhibition spaces with a new building opened in May 1992. Angela studied art and music in Paris before attending the Webber Douglas School of Singing and Dramatic Art. She then worked variously in advertising, film and photography. Flowers East represents a huge range of artists, from newcomers to the well established, among them Peter Howson, John Keane, John Kirby, Nicola Hicks, Boyd and Evans, Amanda Faulkner, Patrick Hughes, Alison Watt and Tai-Shan Schierenberg.

VALERIE STEWART, DEBORAH ELLIOTT, LINDSEY HOOLE, KRISTINA MASON

The Oxford Gallery has been showing the best of British applied art since its foundation in 1968. Its founder, Joan Crossley-Holland, was awarded an MBE for services to the crafts. Its present managing director, Valerie Stewart, has been with the gallery since its inception and was responsible for establishing it as the foremost retail outlet for contemporary jewellery in Britain. Other members of staff include Deborah Elliott, also a freelance photographer, who selects artists' prints for the gallery; Lindsey Hoole, who chooses the ceramics – she studied art history and ceramics and used to run a pottery exporting to the US and Japan; and Kristina Mason, a modern linguist who used to work for the Foreign Office and is currently studying for a post-graduate degree in history of art and design. She selects wood and glass for the gallery.

JILL GEORGE

Jill George is part of a small group of women who set up galleries in the early 1980s. Their aim was to take contemporary art out of its traditional home in Cork Street and bring it to a wider, less wealthy audience. George had a solid background in the arts. She began with the Old Masters, studying History of Art in Florence and went on to work at the V&A. But she had a passion for things more modern and, in 1977, aged 23, she joined the Thumb Gallery in Lexington Street, London. She became its director in 1981 and bought it outright just five years later. The gallery was renamed the Jill George. True to her original aims, Jill represents a wide range of British talent, with newcomers shown alongside our best known artists. These include Martin Kane, Harry Holland, David Hosie, David Leverett, Fraser Taylor, Mark Francis and Martyn Brewster.

MARY STEPHENSON

The only gallery dealing in solely bronze sculpture in London, Art Scene is managed by Robert Hooke and Mary Stephenson. Stephenson maintains she entered the business by default. A sculptor friend (Neil Lawson Baker) showed her round a foundry one day and through people there she met Robert Hooke. Art Scene's stated aim is to present sculpture in a "domestic" venue for collectors who are buying for their home or garden. The work of established international artists such as Ayrton, Frink, Hepworth and Moore is shown alongside British artists such as Robert Hooke, Eugene Ball, Maurice Blik, Ronald Cameron, Stephen Daniels, Philip Jackson, John Mills, David Norris, Sean Rice, Lyell Robinson, Caroline Stacey and Laura White.

GILLIAN JASON

One of London's leading lights in the contemporary art scene, Gillian Jason was trained in the classical tradition, first as a dancer (she attended the Royal Ballet School) and then as a singer and actress – she has appeared in numerous productions for film and TV. In 1973 she launched herself on the London art circuit, putting her considerable talents to use curating Campbell and Franks, the Fine Art Gallery in New Cavendish Street. Just five years later she opened her own gallery in Camden, her most successful venture to date, focusing on British artists with a vast range of styles.

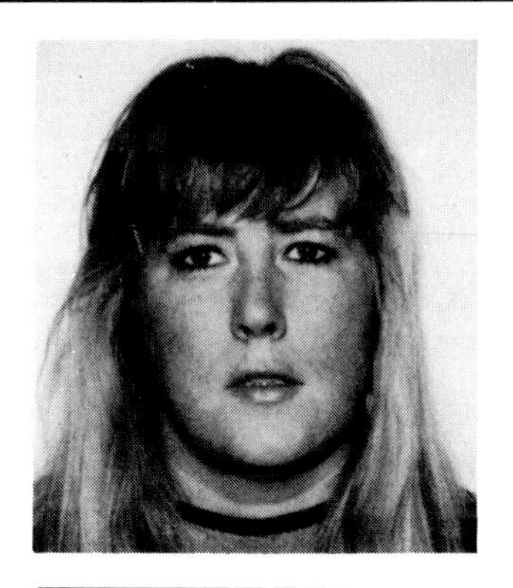

PATRICIA SPEIRS

Patricia Speirs set up Bohun Gallery in 1973 with her partner Ross Speirs. Their aim was to set up a gallery that would match anything in London and would show the best of British figurative art by living artists. This was at a time when abstract art was very much in fashion. To establish the gallery and survive in the early days needed both determination and courage. Recognition by press and public was hard won and the experience often painful. On the other hand, the gallery had strong encouragement from artists and others in the world of art. Soon they were showing the likes of John Piper and Dame Elizabeth Frink. This established their seriousness and gathered collectors from further and further afield. Twenty years on Bohun continues to exhibit both established and younger artists including Donald Hamilton Fraser, Lin Jammett, Mary Fedden, Harry Holland, June Redfern, David Remfry and the estate of Julian Trevelyan.

PAMELA KLABER

Brought up in a family of porcelain collectors, Pamela Klaber set up as an antique porcelain specialist in partnership with her mother in 1968. From modest premises on the Portobello Road, Klaber & Klaber moved to Knightsbridge and then to Kensington Church Street where they have been trading for the last 11 years. Pamela specialises in unusual pieces from English and Continental factories, especially the early French soft paste. She has been exhibiting at the Grosvenor Antiques Fair for the last ten years and lectures and writes widely on 18th century porcelain. She has many interests outside her work: currently she is restoring an old Cape Dutch house in the Western Cape with her husband, where they will soon be producing their own wine.
Photograph by Keith Wynn

DIANNE BRICK

The youngest daughter of a fine arts valuer and auctioneer, Dianne worked for many years in local government, primarily in education, becoming a careers officer in 1980. She set up her antiques business in 1986 and now divides her time between her shop in Sevenoaks and the antique fair circuit. She specialises in silver, porcelain and Tunbridge ware, the local souvenir marquetry produced primarily in the 19th century. She aims to provide for sale some 50 to 100 pieces representing some of the best of 19th century craftsmanship

ALEXANDRA RHODES

Alexandra Rhodes decided she wanted to work at Sotheby's when she visited the auction house in her mid teens. She started as jewellery department secretary in 1974 and progressed to cataloguing and valuing jewellery and auctioneering. In 1989 she was appointed director of the London jewellery department. She travels extensively in the UK and abroad, has written a book on hatpins and tiepins and lectures frequently in Europe and the US, principally on 19th and 20th century jewels. For several years she was a member of the London Philharmonic Choir, but had to give up professional singing because of her heavy travel schedule.

ELAINE PHILLIPS

Chairman of her own company, Elaine Phillips Antiques Ltd, and sole owner of Sarah Curran Elaine, Elaine Phillips specialises in English oak furniture from 1600 to 1800, a field in which she is widely recognised as one of Britain's foremost experts. She is a member of the British Antique Dealers Association and has a variety of interests, including early English glass and needlework, Arabic and the writings of Freya Stark.

SUE PEARSON

Sue Pearson's parents were keen collectors and she has collected dolls and toys since she was a child. She had always wanted to be a dancer and worked in TV, film and theatre until she caught polio and was forced to give up at the age of 21. After marriage and two children she rekindled her interest in dolls and toys and started a Saturday market stall. She took a unit in the market in Brighton specialising in old dolls and bears and doing restoration, and progressed from there to her own shop. She now receives enquiries from all over the country and abroad. She has written several books on dolls and bears and is currently writing another.

ANN LINGARD

Ann Lingard started in the antiques business with part of a stall in Rye market, which she ran in between working for a local pre-school playgroup. She began doing fairs and moved into the Bexhill Antique Centre for two years before opening her present shop, Rope Walk Antiques, in Rye in 1976. She started with linen and antique needlework accessories and moved on to kitchen, pine and country furniture, at the time an undiscovered area of the antiques trade. She now sells a wide range of antiques to mid 20th century collectable kitchen accessories, specialising in period pine furniture from all corners of the UK, with a large clientele in America, Australia and, most recently, Japan.

MARIA ANDIPA

One of Europe's leading experts on iconography, Maria Andipa began collecting at an early age, inspired by the paintings of the nuns on The Mount of Olives where she was born. When her family moved to Athens she studied with Stratoulis, the famous iconographer. She moved to London to study acting and launch her career as a folk singer but soon became involved with icons again. She opened a gallery displaying Byzantine art in Walton Street, part of which she designed as an old Greek church crypt. She has staged exhibitions in Westminster Abbey, Worcester Cathedral and the Metropolitan Museum in New York, and works as a fundraiser for several charities.

MEG ANDREWS

Meg Andrews established a costume and textile department for Sotheby's Belgravia in 1980 and for the past few years has been buying antique costumes and textiles and selling them to museums, collectors and individuals. She advises collectors on acquisitions and disposal and assists interior designers using decorative textiles in period and modern settings. She writes a regular saleroom column for Embroidery magazine and has written for Antique Collecting, Period Home, Interior Designers Handbook and Traditional Homes. In 1985 she went to Washington to lecture to the Associates of the Smithsonian Institute. She currently lectures to students on various Sotheby's Collecting Courses as well as to students at SOAS.

JOCELYN LUKINS

After 11 years as an assistant in an antique shop, Jocelyn Lukins set up her own business 15 years ago. Since then she has earned international acclaim for her expertise in Royal Doulton and is a successful dealer known to collectors throughout the world. She has written, designed and taken photographs for eight books on aspects of collecting Doulton, which she also publishes and distributes herself, with a new title annually. She specialises in Doulton Collectables – Doulton Figurines, Animal Models, Kingsware and Advertising Wares, an area which, despite the recession, is still doing extremely well. Originally a professional photographer Jocelyn also has an extensive library of Doulton subjects.

HILARY KAY

Senior director of Sotheby's, Hilary Kay's specialist knowledge includes toys, teddies, music boxes, talking machines, scientific instruments, sporting items, cameras and optical devices, domestic and office equipment, ephemera and rock 'n' roll memorabilia. She regularly appears on TV, on the Antiques Roadshow and Heirloom (Cable) and on antique phone-ins for LBC, Capital and the BBC. She is the author of Rock 'n' Roll Collectables, published last year by Pyramid.

VIVIENNE BECKER

Vivienne Becker started work in the antique jewellery trade when she was 18 years old. She left two years later to become a journalist and since 1977 has contributed articles as a jewellery historian to Antique Collector, Vogue, Harpers & Queen, Elle, and all the major broadsheets. She writes a regular saleroom report for Retail Jeweller and a fashion column for Jewellery International. Her books include Antique and Twentieth Century Jewellery (1980; 1987); Art Nouveau Jewellery (1985); Jewellery of Rene Lalique (1987); Fabulous Fakes: The History of Costume Jewellery (1988); and Rough Diamonds: The Butler & Wilson Story (1990). In 1987 she organised the exhibition The Jewellery of Rene Lalique at Goldsmith's Hall and in 1992 she curated Jewels of Fantasy, an exhibition of 20th century costume jewellery at the V&A. She launched her own collection, Classic Revivals, in 1990, based on classic jewels from past eras. Vivienne also works as a consultant to Christie's jewellery departments in London and Geneva and lectures widely in the UK and US.

CAROLE MILLER

Carole Miller set up an interior decoration business in Chelsea in 1968, having worked for Newsweek and Aims of Industry in Fleet Street. She then joined her husband Alan in his long established family antiques business – Millers of Chelsea in the Kings Road. She soon became involved in dealing on the Continent and was one of the first antique dealers to be involved with international antiques fairs in Europe. Millers of France SARL opened in 1978 to sell direct to Continental customers. When the company moved its head office to Ringwood in Hampshire, Carole began organising Antiques Weekends. With 25 exhibitors and over 2,000 visitors the annual event ran successfully for 15 years. Carole was one of the original members of LAPADA (London and Provincial Antiques Dealers' Association) and today she acts as adjudicator for the provision of customs certificates.

JULIA CLARKE

Julia Clarke started work on the front counter at Sotheby's in 1972, after graduating from Oxford and spending two years studying in Paris. She was soon moved to the exciting 19th century specialist branch at Belgravia. Since 1975 she has been Sotheby's expert on objects of vertu, specialising in gold boxes and English enamels. Recent triumphs in this field include two auction world records for gold boxes, one in 1989 and the other in November 1992 with a snuff box made for Frederick the Great which fetched over a million pounds. She has had several articles published in leading journals and is currently working on a study of Geneva gold box makers.

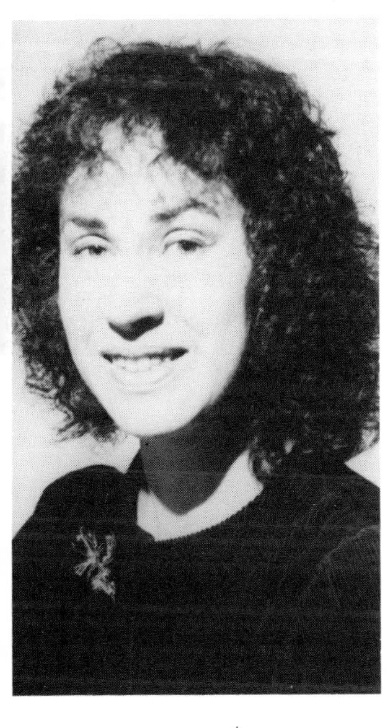

MAY SINCLAIR

Born in Lanarkshire, Scotland, May Sinclair decided to try her fortunes in London in the early 1970s. She managed to land a job as a secretary in the numismatic department of Spink & Son, despite having no idea what numismatic meant! A year later she became the receptionist in the coin department. She has been with Spink for 20 years and became an associate director of the company in 1987. Her knowledge ranges from British hammered coins of Anglo-Saxon times to Charles I and British Trade Tokens of the 17th, 18th and 19th centuries.

JOSIE MARSDEN

Josie Marsden set up Magic Lanterns at By George in St Albans in 1986. Here she restores and sells antique and period lighting including candle, gas and early electric fittings as well as unusual decorative pieces. Josie also advises clients on lighting schemes for pubs, restaurants and private homes from cottages to mansions and supplies period lights to TV, film and theatre companies. She writes for several leading publications and has written five books, the latest of which, entitled Lamps and Lighting, was published by Guinness Publishers in 1990.

W E L C O M E T

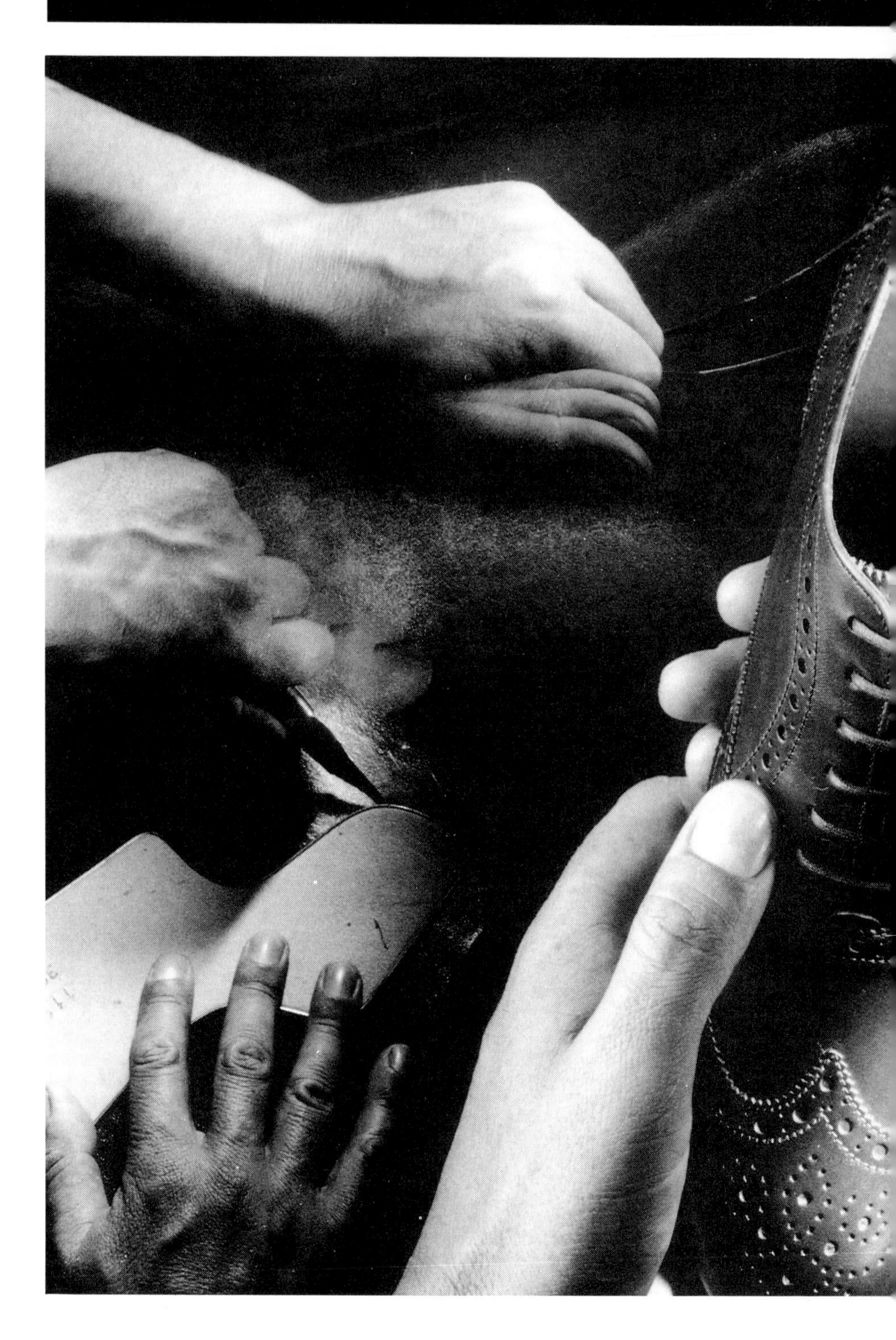

ANNE BRUH ("FRANK USHER" SPECIAL OCCASION DAY AND EVENING DESIGNER COLLECTIONS)

Anne Bruh arrived in England just before WWII alone, aged 15 and unable to speak English. After the war she joined her father's textile business and subsequently, with husband Max, acquired a textile company in liquidation called Frank Usher. This year, as managing director, she collected the first British Apparel Export Award. The style they sell is an essentially supranational version of the acceptably-glamorous occasion dress, or the perfect afternoon frock, or highly styled separates to be worn anywhere.

CATHERINE WALKER (COUTURE)

Born in Northern France, Catherine Walker came to London when she married an English lawyer. Tragically widowed, she threw herself into the design of her highly individual couture and ready-to-wear business. Holder of the British Fashion Council's Designer of the Year Award Coutre (1990/91) and Glamour (1991/92) she operates out of the Chelsea Design Co and the Bridal Shop.

FRANKA BARONESS STAËLVON HOLSTEIN (COUTURE)

Born in Croatia, Franka studied fashion design in Zagreb. She arrived in England in the early 1960s, and decided to stay. After a short spell with Norman Hartnell, she joined Mme Vernier as a junior partner, taking control of the business in 1975. She won designer of year in 1967, and designs for the Royal families of Britain, Norway and Sweden as well as films, film stars and the retail trade.

CORNELIA JAMES (GLOVES BY APPOINTMENT TO HRH)

Coming from Vienna on her way to the USA in WWII, Cornelia James paused to teach glove-making to injured servicemen. There she met her future husband, and has stayed in England, manufacturing leather and suede as well as fabric gloves and wonderful scarves ever since.

JUNE KENTON ("RIGBY AND PELLER" CORSETRY BY APPOINTMENT TO HRH)

June Kenton is grantee of the Royal Warrant and owner of Rigby and Peller, Corsetières to HM Queen Elizabeth II since 1960. Taking over the company in 1982, Mrs Kenton moved to Knightsbridge and, in 1988, launched their own label garments introducing them to Europe and the USA. Japan and the Far East followed, and manufacturing of the collection is in the UK.

CHRISTINE HAYTER ("S. LOCK AND COMPANY" EMBROIDERERS BY APPOINTMENT TO HRH)

Chris Hayter started as a trainee embroiderer at S. Lock Ltd, in the West End, in 1962 and, in 1991, assumed the mantle of director and embroiderer by appointment to HM Queen Elizabeth II. Complete dresses can be seen in the Court Dress Collection at Kensington Palace and at the V&A, as well as for sale in top couture houses.

ELIZABETH EMANUEL (COUTURE)

Born in 1953, daughter of American father and British mother, Elizabeth Emanuel's flair for design was quickly recognised and encouraged. Most famous, perhaps, for Lady Diana Spencer's wedding dress, designed with husband David. Since 1990 Elizabeth has been designing her dramatic and romantic couture from the Elizabeth Emanuel Studio Ltd in Mayfair, where she designs for the rich and famous, theatres, films, airlines and royalty.

GEORGINA VON ETZDORF (TEXTILE DESIGN AND DEVELOPMENT)

Georgina Von Etzdorf, with her partners, makes distinctive, hand printed accessories, fabric and clothing for a worldwide following (Princess of Wales, Lord Olivier, Mick Jagger, Kylie Minogue). Manufacturing in Salisbury and with outlets in London W1 and SW1, 70 per cent is exported with 290 accounts in 14 countries.

ZANDRA RHODES (COUTURE ART WORKS)

Born in Chatham in 1940, Zandra Rhodes is one of our most consistent and enduring designers. Awards include Designer of the Year 1972, Royal Designer for Industry 1974, Best Costume Award (Bafta) 1979, "Britain" Designer 1983, best Show of the Year, Saks Fifth Avenue 1985 and 1991, "Women of Distinction" Dallas, Texas, 1986, No. 1 Textile Designer (Observer Magazine) 1990. Her book "The Art of Zandra Rhodes" is published by Jonathan Cape.

PATRICIA LESTER (COUTURE)

With no formal training in fashion or textile design, Patricia Lester gave up her secretarial career and started designing full time in 1964. Husband Charles, expert in design, craft and technology, joined the comany full time in 1984. With totally individual fabrics as well as designs the company, in Abergavenny, has thrived. Patricia was nominated "Welsh Businesswoman of the Year" 1986 and appointed MBE in 1988.

EMMA HOPE ↑

In the past five years Emma Hope has become one of Britain's most influential shoe designers. Born in 1962, and brought up between Singapore and Surrey, Emma trained at the Cordwainers College from 1981-84. She has won five Design Council Awards, the 1988 Martini Style and 1989 Harpers and Queen Fashion Design Awards. She opened her first shop in the City of London in 1987.

GAYLE McVAY ↑

Gayle McVay started designing USU hats in 1983. The first customer was Harrods, and exclusive collections for Next, Jaeger, Mulberry, Laura Ashley, and others soon followed. In 1991 the company changed its name to A.M. Design, and Gayle continues to develop her ideas for the large groups as well as selling her own collections.

LULU GUINNESS ↓

A leading light on the international design circuit with her coutre quality day and evening bags, Lulu Guinness was born in 1960 and moved to Paris at 18 to study drama and design. She went on to become a successful model before starting designing in 1989. She introduced the wrist-strap to the UK. Coutre customers now include Hartnell, Caroline Charles, Bellville Sassoon.

TRACEY MOGARD, LUCY HODGES AND ROBYN ALLARDICE ↓

Tracy Mogard, Lucy Hodges and Robyn Allardice are the partners who make up Herald and Heart Hatters in London, SW8. Based very much on theatrical millinery, the shop is exactly as you hope a hat shop may be – antique blocks, shelves of ribbons and braids.

ANYA HINDMARCH ↑

In 1987, at the age of 19, Anya Hindmarch imported a handbag design she had seen in Florence to London where it was run as an offer in Harpers & Queen. The success of this led her to start designing handbags and she now sells in renowned shops throughout the world, and designs for the Princess of Wales.

ELIZABETH STUART-SMITH

Trained at Cordwainers College between 1981 and 1984, Elizabeth Stuart-Smith established a partnership which designed and produced shoes in London, designed for "Absolute Beginners" and opened a shop at Hyper Hyper. She produced her first collection in 1987. She now manufactures in Italy with a shop in Mayfair.

ANNE TOMLIN AND BRIDGET BAILEY ▲

Having both studied design at West Surrey College of Art, Anne Tomlin and Bridget Bailey formed Bailey Tomlin four years ago – Anne via the London College of Fashion and Bridget, Birmingham University. Their style is for traditional, hand finished hats using the best quality silk, velvet and furfelt. Their two annual collections are sold through prestigious stores throughout the world.

CAROLYN BROOKES-DAVIES AND ANITA EVAGORA ▼

Carolyn Brookes-Davis studied ceramics and Anita Evagora sculpture. After leaving college they travelled through Italy and, as a rebellion against "classic" Italian design, and fuelled by the fashion of the early 1980s, in 1983 they followed Fred Bare hats. Now, ten years on, Anita does the selling and Carolyn handles design. A first shop has been openec and a prime position achieved.

HELEN STOREY

Since launching her own label under the umbrella of Amalgamated Talent in 1984, Helen Storey has assembled an impressive clientele that includes Madonna, Prince, Kylie Minogue, Cher, Paula Yates and Greta Scacchi.

Nominated in 1989 for the Young Designer of the Year Award and as Best Evening Wear Designer, Helen went on to win, jointly with her then partner Karen Boyd, the British Apparel Export Award for that year.

The following year the first Helen Storey for Jigsaw collection reached Jigsaw stores throughout Britain, and the Helen Storey shop opened in London's Soho. Also in 1990, Helen launched "Rage", her first solo catwalk show, during London Fashion Week, and took the Most Innovative Designer of the Year Award.

In 1992 Helen opened her third London shop, in the King's Road, selling the main collection, classics and a new basics range.

Over the years, as well as designing her own collections, Helen has worked on freelance projects for a wide range of established clients, including Wrangler, Next, Empire Stores and Knickerbox, while her own creations continue to receive international acclaim and now sell to over 125 stores worldwide.

Photograph by Sophie Withers

ARABELLA POLLEN

Since the company's formation in 1981, the Arabella Pollen label has enjoyed notable success both at home and around the world. Its collection, in addition to being available in specialist and department stores throughout Britain, is exported to Europe, the USA, Japan, South America and Kuwait. The designs possess a strong, easily recognised signature that has won the loyalty of a host of celebrities from the international worlds of film and music.

In 1991 Courtaulds Textiles Ltd acquired a majority shareholding in Arabella Pollen Ltd, lending the company greater financial stability and more effective management. The international launch of Arabaella Pollen-branded collections and products is currently being planned and, with manufacturing now based in France, the quality of production is unsurpassed.

Arabella Pollen herself was nominated for the Designer of the Year and Classic Designer of the Year Awards in 1989, 1990 and 1991.

ALLY CAPELLINO

Before her first London show in 1986, Ally Capellino, who began her career in the late 1970s in Courtaulds' main design studio, had already been selling the Ally Capellino label internationally. Two years later she opened a shop in Soho, selling exclusively Ally Capellino menswear and womenswear. In 1990 her sportswear collection was born, and later that year Ally became design consultant to the industry giant Coats Viyella, developing jersey sportswear. Soon afterwards the London store was expanded to create an emporium selling childrenswear and lifestyle items, in addition to adult clothes.

The relationship with Coats Viyella plc blossomed in 1992 with a major investment by the company – a milestone in Ally's career as well as in British fashion.

AMANDA WAKELEY

Possessing a distinctive style that is at once glamorous and understated, Amanda Wakeley's clothes have made her one of Britain's leading young designers since she founded her own label in 1990. At the same time, her understanding of contemporary lifestyle dressing has

assured her of an ever-growing number of prestigious clients.

In her studio near London's Fulham Road, Amanda creates a range of garments embracing day wear as well as elegant evening wear, each designed to enhance the shape and beauty of the wearer. By mixing, for example, crèpe and velvet, cashmere and chiffon, she produces clothes with both texture and intrinsic style, so that they feel comfortable as well as look good.

SARA STURGEON

After seeing her degree show at the Royal College of Art, the retail group Michel of Hong Kong Ltd. offered Sara Sturgeon the opportunity to set up her own label. She saw her sales figures double each season over the five years from its launch in 1985, and now has offices in New York, Los Angeles and Paris, and an agent in Australia. But the nerve centre of her business remains the London showroom, with its international sales team. Throughout this period Sara has retained her manufacturing base with Michel of Hong Kong.

Sara's Clothes collection, launched at the British Designer Show in October 1992, was designed for a slightly younger, more middle market than previous collections. Already it has several dozen accounts in both Britain and the USA.

Sara has also developed a "suit" collection which is aimed at the slightly older "working" market. It retains the Sara Sturgeon feel, using beautiful fabrics but a more classic styling. This collection is complemented by a range of machine and hand knitwear in soft, neutral colours.

VIVIENNE WESTWOOD

Vivienne Westwood arrived in London from Derbyshire in her late teens, but didn't start designing until she was 30. Since then she has been pouring out inspirational ideas, like punk and the pirate look, that have had a decisive influence on youth culture and the international fashion scene alike. From 1971, for over a decade, Westwood and her partner, Malcolm McLaren, used their King's Road shop as a showcase for their radical experiments in street style.

In March 1983 she became the first British designer to show in Paris since Mary Quant, and the following year unveiled her new collection at the Best of Five show in Tokyo, alongside Hanae Mori, Calvin Klein, Montana and Ferre.

In her Davies Street, Mayfair, shop, opened in December 1990, Westwood promotes a more traditional approach to tailoring for both men and women. Having until then included menswear within her women's collection, that summer she had shown her first separate menswear collection in Florence.

Westwood appeared on ITV's South Bank Show in 1990 – the only designer ever to be featured on the programme. The following year she completed a two-year appointment as Professor of Fashion at Vienna's Academy of Applied Arts. In 1992 she captured the British Designer of the Year Award for the second year running – a distinction achieved by no other designer – and was awarded the OBE.

Photograph by Brad Branson

ANGELA HOLMES

Droopy & Browns is the creation of Angela Holmes, the sole designer of the company's day wear, occasion wear, ballgowns and wedding dresses, all of which are made in its Yorkshire workrooms. Among Angela's clients are opera singers, musicians, writers and professional women of all ages and nationalities – united by a shared love of the intricate cut and superb quality of her unique, highly feminine clothes.

After designing, making and selling clothes in London's street markets, Angela returned to her native north of England and, in 1972, opened the first Droopy & Browns shop in York. Inspired by the Hollywood movies that held her spellbound as a child, she designed and sold ballgowns and day dresses, attracting as one of her first customers the Theatre Royal Repertory Company. A second shop, in Edinburgh, followed in 1979. Her West End shop, opened in 1986, eventually relocated to St. Martin's Lane – appropriately enough, the heart of London's theatreland.

Photograph by Anthony Crickmay

CAROLINE CHARLES

Caroline Charles understands that for the modern woman it is all too easy to become absorbed in the practicalities of everyday life. So, in designing her clothes, she bears in mind the importance of keeping room in a busy lifestyle for luxury, craftsmanship and a little fantasy. Founded over 30 years ago and with headquarters in elegant Beauchamp Place, London SW3, the company offers a wide range of fashion items, including day wear, evening wear, knitwear, lingerie and accessories. As well as numbering members of the Royal Family and celebrities among her customers, Caroline Charles has a strong international profile, exporting to the USA, Canada and Japan. Manufactured in the UK, the company's collections are marketed nationwide through prestigious outlets, including its own flagship store in Knightsbridge.

BETTY JACKSON

In 1981, the year that Betty Jackson Ltd was launched, Betty Jackson won Woman magazine's Separates Designer of the Year Award. Two years later she captured the same award again, as well as being the magazine's Designer of the Year. The British Designer of the Year Award followed in 1985. That year Betty reached a licensing agreement with Seibu/Ellebis which included the opening of a designer shop and several in-store boutiques with distribution rights throughout Japan. Following the launch of Betty Jackson for Men in 1986, Betty has received further fashion industry awards and academic honours, including an Honorary Fellowship of the Royal College of Art. In 1987 she received the MBE for services to British industry and exports. Betty Jackson Accessories was launched the following year, and in 1991 the Betty Jackson flagship shop opened at London's exclusive Brompton Cross. The Spring/Summer 1993 collection is a reconciliation of opposites: masculine with feminine, soft with sharp, comfort with elegance, and natural with man-made fibres.

EDINA RONAY

Che unabashed glamour that
haracterises Edina Ronay's designs
s, in part, explained by her earlier
uccess as a RADA-trained film
ctress and model. It is this quality,
long with a feel for classic lines
nd a keen understanding of her
ustomers' needs, that has led her
o number among her clientele
ome of the world's most elegant
vomen, including the Princess of
Vales and Charlotte Rampling.

Introduced in the early 1980s,
dina's ethnic traditional style
roved a huge success, her sweaters
oon becoming highly prized
ollectables. By expanding the
nitwear into a full clothing
ollection in 1984, she laid the
oundations for an enviably steady
rowth in sales and influence. As a
esult, her designs are today
vailable in all the key UK outlets,
nd at the same time as enjoying a
rge following in the USA and
pan, Edina is busy strengthening
e company's profile in Europe.

MONICA ZIPPER

A highly talented designer who in 1991 won the "More Dash than Cash" award at the British Designer of the Year show, Monica Zipper of Monix has resolutely chosen to design clothes that are affordable with a wage packet rather than a bank loan.

KATHARINE HAMNETT

Katharine Hamnett's unmistakeable clothing is one of the best known success stories of the 1980s. After a fashion degree at St Martins Katharine freelanced as a designer until 1979 when she launched Katharine Hamnett Ltd. Three years on she won the International Institute for Cotton Designer of the Year Award and in 1984 she was made British Fashion Designer of the Year. Her Choose Life T-shirt collection came out in 1983, and was given nationwide coverage in the famous meeting with Mrs Thatcher at which she wore the 58% Don't Want Pershing slogan. Since then she has remained committed to environmental issues and people with collections themed to a new area of concern each season – spring/summer for 1992 was Green Cotton by the Year 2000.

PASCALE SMETS

After training at St. Martin's School of Art in London and gaining experience with Daniel Hechter and Jean Muir, Anglo-Belgian Pascale Smets formed her own company in 1989. Guided by the principle of "less is best", she designs pure, uncluttered clothes with a modern American feel. Her aim is to create styles that the working woman will find both beautiful and wearable.

LINDKA CIERACH

Lindka Cierach has been designing couture for the last 16 years. She rose to fame in 1986 with the Royal Commission for the Duchess of York's wedding dress. Since then her business, trading under Lindka Cierach, has gone from strength to strength and her designs are worn worldwide. She is known for her skills in cutting and use of luxurious French and Italian cloths. Her designing skills can be seen in wedding dresses, evening wear, day wear and sportswear.

CAROLINE ALEXANDER

Caroline Alexander worked in London for six years as a pattern cutter for a number of well known fashion houses before setting up her own business in 1989. From small beginnings, working from home as a freelance designer/pattern cutter she launched her first collection, debuted at the Harrogate Bridal Fair in 1990. It was an instant success, with coverage in the three main brides magazines. In 1991 she won You and Your Wedding Magazine's Bridal Designer of the Year.

GILLIAN SINCLAIR

Housewife Gillian Sinclair never thought, when she was asked to design a bouquet for someone's wedding a few years ago, that it would start her on a career in bridal headwear. The staggering success of her company, Florentina, is proof that it is still possible to beat recession. At its debut at the Harrogate Bridal Exhibition in 1989, Florentina attracted the attention of Harrods and she now sells to some 250 shops in Britain and Europe as well as all the top bridalwear designers.

CATHERINE RAYNER

Catherine Rayner formed her own company in 1987 and since then she has won many awards for individual dresses as well as the accolade of bridalwear Designer of the Year in both 1991 and 1992. Her dresses have been photographed by Norman Parkinson, Terence Donovan and Lord Snowdon and she exports to Japan, the US and Europe. Her success is due to an untiring perfectionism – she refuses to use anything but pure silk and natural fabrics and aims for an understated natural elegance.

HELEN RUSSELL

Helen Russell's Saturday job in a florist gave her the inspiration to try her hand at bridal headwear. She was training as a graphic artist at the time but decided to change direction and took a millinery course at the London School of Fashion. In 1986 she launched Silk Designers of Bridal Headwear. Helen won the prize for "headdress designer of the year 1991/92" with her shell design; she is also known for her gold and copper plated berries and flowers, porcelain orchids and roses.

MICHELE O'NEILL

A textile design and fashion degree (specialising in embroidery) at Trent Polytechnic in Nottingham gave Michele the talent and set up her company Fiorito in 1981. She was soon attracting big name buyers as well as individuals brought by word of mouth. She recently signed a three-year contract with Hardy Amies. Michele believes her success lies in the friendly and personal service offered by her staff.

BEVERLY SUMMERS

In the early days of her business, back in 1982, Beverly Summers started work cutting and finishing her dresses at 5.30 every morning. Today she has around 30 people working for her and operates out of a picturesque converted 19th century mill in Yorkshire, with Beverly Summers shops in Harrogate and Covent Garden. In 1988 she won two of the coveted bridal "Oscars", gold in the Best Short Dress and Extravaganza categories, and in 1990 she won the Innovative category.

DIANE HASSALL

At college Diane Hassall delved into everything from print to design to knitwear. She specialised in embroidery design, working on hats, bags and shoes. Shoes, however, were "her main passion". After a graduate enterprise programme in 1987 at Cranfield School of Management she set up in business and her shoes have been featured in all the major magazines. She opened her first shop (Hassall and Carlow) in 1992.

SHARON HARVEY

The experience of trying to find shoes (unsuccessfully) to match her wedding dress gave Sharon Harvey the idea to set up her own bridal shoe business (named Sharon Louise), providing brides-to-be with an alternative to the ubiquitous satin pump. Her efforts won her the Nat-West Enterprise Award for 1989/90 and Harrogate International Bridal Fair's Best Accessory Award in September 1991. Today her shoes range from Turkish slippers to Victorian boots, but the firm will make to virtually any specification. They also make hats and handbags, for evening wear as well as weddings. Sharon Louise sells to retailers all over Britain and recently opened a shop in Beverly Hills.

ELAINE GOSLING

Elaine Gosling trained at St Martin's College of Art in Fashion, Design and Tailoring. After a stint of illustration work for leading magazines she began to design coats and suits. In 1985 she set up her company Wizard of Goz with a view to making evening, cocktail and bridalwear to order. The bridalwear soon took over. She now supplies Harrods, Klein Feld in New York and select bridal houses in the UK. Her hallmark is clean lines and simple sophistication (no bows or frills) with the emphasis on making clothes that feel good to wear. Her most recent commission was Julie Walter's dress in the film "Just Like a Woman".

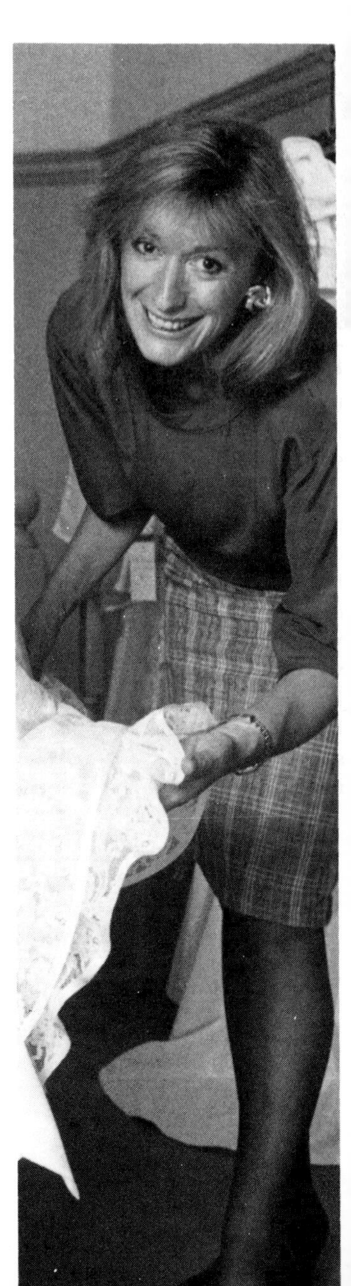

CATHERINE BUCKLEY

In a remarkable career spanning almost three decades, Catherine Buckley has achieved an enviable reputation for wedding wear. She has designed for, among others, Susannah York, Barbara Windsor and Elizabth Taylor, her creations have been photographed by Bailey, Donovan, Snowdon and Lichfield, and seen on TV in The New Avengers. They are now sold worldwide. Catherine Buckley Ltd is renowned for "a style that looks to the past for inspiration". This was apparent in the stunning wedding dress (trimmed with antique Brussels lace) at the Mountbatten wedding. Catherine also does a "total look" – hat, shoes, jewellery, and bag, all colour coordinated. *Photograph by Nigel Luckhurst*

LYN ASHWORTH

Unlike most fashion designers Lyn Ashworth had no formal training. She learnt the trade, she says, as she went along, "by the seat of my pants". She started a tiny dressmaking business trading under Lyn Ashworth in 1978 and began designing wedding dresses two years later. Nowadays she sells wedding dresses as far afield as Japan and the US and all over Europe. Her signature style is simplicity and elegance, a pure line in (almost always) silk fabrics.

ALLISON BLAKE

Allison Blake left Central St. Martins with a first in fashion and an MA in fashion and business. Since starting up her bridalwear business, Allison Blake Designs, in 1987 she has won six *Brides Magazine* awards. Four of these were for her embroidery and beadwork techniques. She describes her influences as classical – holidays to Greek and Pompeii constantly provide inspiration – but she takes ideas from every period of history as well as the modern world.

JENNY LESSIN

Jenny Lessin has been designing and making clothes with innovative beading and decorative work to order for ten years. Her company, Jenny Lessin Clothing and Textiles, use traditional techniques such as embroidery, beading, appliqué or rouleaux in an end product that has an entirely contemporary feel. Always innovative, never dull, Jenny's wedding wear designs range from a sinuous ivory linen column topped with a medieval wimple and a short red velvet dress with swinging crinoline and swirling satin decoration.

BOOTS SCOTT

Boots Scott's career began 20 years ago as a telephone receptionist in a film company. She progressed to PA to the head of an advertising agency TV department and back into a film company before going freelance as a wardrobe mistress. She specialised in commercials, as this allowed her the flexibility to raise a family. She commutes to London from Somerset and owns a remarkable collection of period clothing (hats, shoes, handbags, gloves, coats, dresses) as well as contemporary men's outfits. A fluent French speaker, Boots has diversified in the last three years into the world of food and publishing, writing four cookery/coffee table books and acting as a consultant food stylist.

DOMINIQUE CUSSEN

Born in England and educated in America and Ireland, where she acquired a degree in civil law at University College, Dublin, before embarking on a career in advertising which brought her to London in 1980. Having always bought her clothes secondhand, she harboured an ambition to open an up-market boutique specialising in designer clothes and accessories which were virtually unworn. She realised this ambition when Design opened its doors in Hampstead in 1982. The business grew rapidly and dramatically and now boasts over 6,000 clients, who leave their garments for sale. Dominique works on a small profit margin (two thirds to the vendor, one third to the shop) and attracts only top quality merchandise. Purchasers come from all over the world and Dominique has done more than most to take any of the residual stigma out of secondhand.

BERTIE GOLIGHTLY ↑

During her long career as a stunt woman, Bertie Golightly, was once flown over the Thames in a convertible car dangling from a helicopter and dropped in. When an ankle injury forced her to give up stunting, her leap into high fashion ten years ago caused as big a splash. Bertie Golightly, the shop, at Bradford on Avon, Wiltshire, is an Aladdin's cave of nearly new and sample designer clothes packed into two converted cottages. Clients travel from all over England, drawn by the headiness of the range and the experience of a day at Bertie's. Among the first clothes to go on show were those she wore while stunting for films like The Great Gatsby and TV series such as Morecambe and Wise, alongside nearly new clothes belonging to well-dressed friends from stage and screen. Her search for exclusivity takes her through some notable doors, although she strictly never names names, and sometimes she comes down from London laden with clothes only to see a clutch of them being bought the next day and disappear back up there again.

SEKA BAJIC ↑

Born in Bradford in 1965, Seka Bajic set up a market stall when she was 16 years old, selling 1950s American clothing. In 1983 she moved into mainstream fashion, firstly at the Pineapple Dance Studios, where she worked in retail and wholesale at Covent Garden and South Molton Street. She progressed from there to Museum Clothing and thence to The Costume Studio in 1987, where her knowledge of fashion, period clothing and styling was invaluable, her work involving television and video as well as theatre and film. Now managing director of The Costume Studio, Seka's interest in period fashion spills over into her private life, where her enthusiams are for vintage British motorbikes and classic American cars and her favourite haunt is Gaz's, the 1940-50s club in Soho.

ANDREA GALER →

Andrea Galer started out in her professional career as a costume designer on films such as Don't Look Now (1973), where she so impressed star, Julie Christie, that she not only still buys her clothes from Andrea but, more unusually, has posed in them for photographic sessions. While Andrea still designs for film, television, advertising shorts and promotions, the dwindling number of British films and the impending TV franchise wars led her to look elsewhere for a living. Realising how difficult it is for women to find exactly what they want to wear at reasonable prices, in 1991 she opened her own costume house in Hampstead, offering a unique, three-tiered service. Firstly, she sells her own collection of designer wear, specialising in suits; secondly, she hires to the public and the film industry and, thirdly, she provides a cost-effective, made-to-measure service for costume designers and stylists, based on her knowledge as a costume designer, with access to a wide range of other manufacturers, fabrics and tailors.

The companion volume to Best of British Women is also available either direct from Best of British Publications or from any good bookseller.

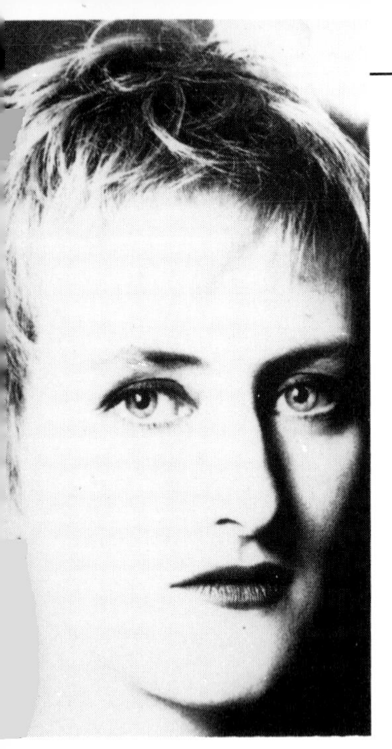

MARION FOALE

One of the most stylish of Carnaby Street's boutiques in the 1960s was Foale and Tuffin, thanks to the young, extrovert clothes of Marion Foale and Sally Tuffin. In the 1980s, after taking time out to start a family, Marion re-emerged with an innovative knitted sweatshirt pattern whose success persuaded her to resume her career. In designing her knitwear Marion brings into play her strong interest in three-dimensional structure and uses a jersey toile to produce the original pattern, giving each garment a highly tailored look. Marion's business is centred at her Warwicishire farmhouse, while the Marylebone showroom, opened in 1988, is increasingly the focus for marketing her collections, of which she produces two a year. Recently added to the Marion Foale range are collections of cruisewear and cotton designs.

GEORGINA GODLEY

Trained in painting and sculpture, Georgina Godley designed modern English menswear under Derek Morten for Browns at South Molton Street before opening Crolla of Dover Street with Scott Crolla in 1981. This inspired partnership pioneered the Dandy look, rejuvenating British tailoring in the early 1980s by creating a neo-traditional style that combined craftsmanship with the finest fabrics in unexpected qualities, textures and patterns. Georgina left Crolla in1985 and launched her own label, specialising first in womenswear and then children's clothes. In addition to working for a variety of manufacturers, she keeps in touch with her roots by designing and realising tailoring for male and female clients in collaboration with Anthony Hewitt of Savile Row.

SERENA KELSEY

Serena Kelsey specialises in bespoke tailoring for men, individually crafting suits at an affordable price, in styles ranging from classic to Avante Garde. Formerly a dancer, Serena switched to tailoring in the mid-1980s and now heads a London SW8-based company with 2,000 clients.

Photograph by Express Newspapers

PENNY MEACHIN AND KERRY HUGHES

A shared interest in hand embroidery detail and beading makes Penny Meachin and Kerry Hughes London's Christian Lacroix. Their company, Idol, was formed in 1989, the year after Kerry graduated from St. Martin's. Penny had previously had a stall at Kensington market and run two successful independent retail fashion labels.

JANET REGER

In the late 1960s, when women were supposedly burning their bras, Janet Reger saw things differently. She recognised that many women wanted to dress in beautiful lingerie while their men wanted to buy it for them. Within a decade she had a Bond Street shop and numbered rock and film stars, aristocrats and royalty among her customers. However, disaster struck in1983, when the business Janet had built with her husband Peter, the driving force behind the Janet Reger concept, went into liquidation. But Janet fought back, buying back the Beauchamp Place shop and the factory and, in 1986 after Peter's death, the Janet Reger trademark. Since then the company has expanded rapidly and as well as retaining the laurels for glamorous lingerie, Janet has diversified, bringing her exclusive style and sophistication to household textiles, bedlinen, swimwear and outerwear.

SUE SPILLER

In her 11 years with Slix Swimwear Sue Spiller's stylish designs have lent the company a more distinctive and fashionable image. Design director since 1989, the designer who turned down the chance of a place at the Royal College of Art to start work instead, has made Slix the UK's leading swimwear design company.
Photograph by Ian Macaulay

HARRIET ANSTRUTHER

For her textile designs Harriet Anstruther draws inspiration from neo-classical painters such as Carlo Maratta and Jean-Pierre Saint-Ours. Using the technique of cross-hatching.

JANE AND PATRICK GOTTELIER

Producers of knitwear coveted all over the world, Jane and Patrick Gottelier founded their company Artwork in 1977. Ever innovators, the husband and wife team were the first knitwear designers to revive print on knitwear and to use indigo-dyed yarn and trompe l'oeil techniques. In recent years they set up an extensive stretch jersey range and Artwork Blue, a diffusion label specialising in indigo-dyed yarn stretch jersey and knitwear. In addition, the comprehensive George Trowark menswear range, sold at the St. Christopher's Place shop Geo Trowark, and a childrenswear range, Minor Artwork, were launched. Artwork and Artwork Blue exhibit in London, Paris and New York, and agents sell the collections in France, Sweden, Belgium, the USA and Japan, Geo Trowark exhibits in London and Paris.

HELEN LITTMAN

Helen Littman founded English Eccentrics in 1982, a tiny set-up specialising inhand-printed clothing for sale in London's street markets. With her sister Judy and Claire Angel, Helen went on to create a series of high-fashion collections that were shown on London's catwalks to great acclaim between 1985 and 1988. English Eccentrics then began to focus exclusively on print design, securing the global status the label enjoys today, with a client list that includes Paul McCartney, Prince, Mick jagger, Toyah Wilcox, Belinda Carlisle and Selina Scott. Rich trompe l'oeil shirts and scarves, hand printed on silk in stunning colours, are Helen's distinctive hallmark.
Photograph by Robin Kiashely

ANNABEL JONES (LADY ASTOR)

Annabel Jones was just 18 when she opened her first shop in Brompton Arcade, Knightsbridge. She had managed to persuade a friend of her father's that she had a solid business venture in hand and he lent her £25,000. From retailing she soon turned to designing her own jewellery. These became instantly popular with London's jeunesse doree. Success, Jones says, was literally overnight. From an article in the Evening Standard featuring her gold rope rings she received 60 orders. She only had six in stock! Now based in Beauchamp Place her clientele includes British and European royalty and aristocracy and overseas dignitaries

VERONICA MANUSSIS AND TANIA HUNTER (COBRA & BELLAMY)

Dynamic duo Veronica Manussis and Tania Hunter joined forces 12 years ago when they opened Cobra & Bellamy in Sloane Street. Both women had worked as actresses but turned to the world of decorative arts to find more stable work. Their shop was an instant success, and they were soon designing their own jewellery and furniture; Ephestos, Manussis' own glass and steel furniture was designed for the Conran Shop, one of the tables now stands in the Design Museum.

DINNY HALL

It was something of a coup for a jewellery designer to win the accolade Accessory Designer of the Year for 1989. Accessories, after all, include everything from bags to belts. But it showed how far Dinny Hall has come since getting expelled from her convent. People believe she creates jewellery that lasts and also makes a strong fashion statement. And the Dinny Hall style is instantly recognisable – delicate wrought iron scrolls and twists and smooth shiny metal and wood domes. She is now feted by dozens of top fashion designers – Bruce Oldfield and Rifat Ozbek credit her with a level of professionalism and talent which is unique in jewellery designers. All this is even more staggering considering that she only opened her first shop in March this year.

JENNIFER CORKER

Jennifer Corker studied fashion and textiles at Middlesex Poly before launching herself in the jewellery business. Despite much critical acclaim for her inspired collections in those first years she decided to brush up on her technique and accepted a place at the Royal College of Art. Three years later she was back designing for the catwalk collections of Bruce Oldfield and Bodymap as well as Harrods and Liberty. She is now the market leader in a related field – designing beautiful haute couture dog collars in brass and leather as well as jewellery.

RA HILL (ERIC BEAMON)

ackground in painting and
drobe design – she designed
tumes for the ballet Rambert in
don and the Met opera house
New York – taught Sara Hill the
e of glamour. She decided to
tch from clothes to jewellery in
8 when she joined dynamic
erican design team, Eric
mon. She is now the
pany's head of design in
don. Hill and her colleagues
ught a new style to costume
ellery in London which was
k on diamante and small, subtle
es. Hill's work harks back to
r in the 1940s and 1950s,
vels for the woman who is not
id to make a statement, but
sn't take herself too seriously".
company is known worldwide
their high quality one offs and
r reputation has reached as far
audi Arabia, now a major
er.

RAH JORDAN

eputation for bold, original
rk, backed by a thorough
hnical understanding have
ught Sarah Jordan her present
own in the world of jewellery
ign. After her silversmithing
gree she taught for six months
l then set up her own company
years ago. Her work has been
ticularly successful in New York
l Tokyo; in fact she impressed
kyo's cognoscenti so much that
recently had a documentary
de on her for Japanese TV.

LOUISE SANT

Traditional jeweller Louise Sant went straight from Middlesex Poly where she won a platinum design award, to a job working for goldsmith David Thomas. Exhibitions in all the major centres in Britain and America quickly brought her worldwide recognition. People were entranced by her love of natural forms and dexterity with semi-precious stones such as pyrite and agate. As well as witty designs for English Eccentrics, Sant now works on collections for Wedgwood and the V&A.

LAURA LEE

Laura Lee took an honours degree in visual art, majoring in photography, back in 1982. She has brought these interests to her work in costume jewellery, finding that she often chooses beads and stones primarily for their colour. She launched herself in 1985 and now sells to Harrods and Liberty in London, Bergdorf Goodman in New York and as far afield as Singapore and Japan. Her work has also appeared on TV – remember the blonde covered in baubles eating Philadelphia cream cheese – the jewels are Lee's!

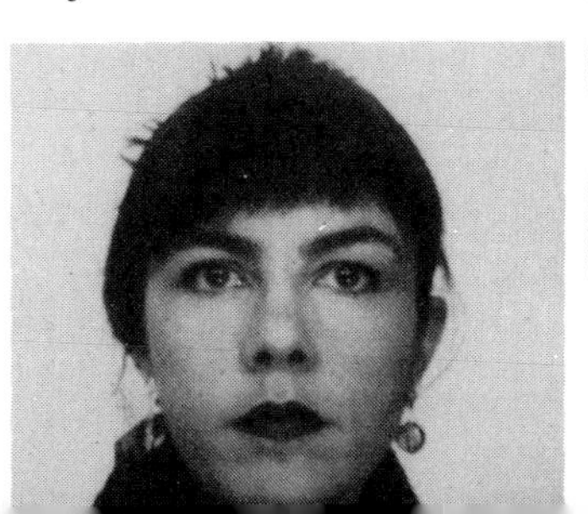

LINDA VAN PETERSON

Linda and her husband Eric Van Peterson were partially responsible for bringing jewellery back into the limelight in the 1980s. Instead of an afterthought their pieces became fashion items in their own right. They began with a stall in Camden market, selling 1930s clothing and specialist jewellery, but success quickly led them to Walton Street where they now stock some of the world's most covetable jewellery. The range is vast – from the leading names in jewellery design to the work of the American Indians to their own highly successful pieces.

ELIZABETH GAGE

Elizabeth Gage could certainly have been described as precocious. She had her first collection commissioned by Cartier soon after leaving art college. That was in 1968. Today most of her works are still one offs, and each is designed by Gage herself, who takes baroque pearls, Sumerian amulets and 19th century intaglios to create her pieces. Three years ago she was awarded Britain's top industry accolade, the Queen's Award for Export Achievement. Now based in Bond Street, Gage exhibits annually in America; this year she held her first exhibition in Dallas; it was a resounding success.

tec ni WAVE
The perfect, long-lasting foundation for today's softer, natural styles.
New from L'Oréal Technique Professionnelle, Tec Ni Wave Foundation Perm System.
For soft open curls with natural movement. For long lasting body and volume. Tec Ni Wave will leave your hair looking shiny, and in beautiful condition.
Tec Ni Wave, the perfect foundation for today's more natural styles. Exclusive to your L'Oréal Technique Professionnelle hairdresser.
For further information and advice visit your nearest L'Oréal Technique Professionnelle salon or contact L'Oréal Coiffure on 071-938 5990.
L'ORÉAL TECHNIQUE PROFESSIONNELLE
PARIS

RITA RUSK

Three years after she qualified as a hairdresser in the 1960s, Scot Rita Rusk and her husband Irvine set up a salon in Hamilton that was to prove truly innovative. Nowadays she still runs a salon in the centre of Glasgow which she started some 15 years ago. The largest salon in western Scotland, it has many clients from television, radio and showbusiness. In 1990 Rita opened Rita Rusk – The School, a Glasgow-based hairdressing academy which offers a comprehensive range of courses and attracts students from Britain and abroad. She also produces educational videos for use in Britain, Europe and the Far East and, with her team, has staged shows and seminars all over the world. During the 1980s Rita invented highly successful weaving scissors and electric tongs, and in 1987 she and Irvine were voted British Hairdressers of the Year, while in 1992 the French Ministry of Culture presented her with an award for her contribution to hairdressing.

DENISE McADAM

Denise McAdam started her hairdressing career in 1974 on her home ground of Edinburgh, where two years later Princess Grace of Monaco became her first prestigious client. In 1979 she settled in London as part of the artistic team of the leading Mayfair salon Michaeljohn. Before long she was in demand for session work for magazines like Vogue and Brides, as well as styling for the Royal Family. She was a partner in the Carey Temple McAdam salon before having a daughter in 1989. Three years later she picked up where she left off, but this time as sole owner of the Mayfair salon.

ELAINE HILL

At the age of 14 Elaine Hill had a Saturday job in a hairdressing salon, leaving school two years later to train in a salon in Edinburgh. In 1987, equipped with managerial experience gained in Glasgow, she set up the Alan Edwards Salon in the city, along with her business partner of that name. Having been nominated twice for the title of Scottish Hairdresser of the Year since the salon opened, Elaine eventually took the award in 1992. Although raised on a farm, Elaine denies spending her childhood shearing sheep in preparation for her present career. Her speciality is photographic fashion work, requiring as it does a subtle interaction between the stylist and photographer. She is also interested in the creative challenge posed by hair extensions and wigs. Elaine's philosophy for running a successful salon remains simple: the stylist needs to be open-minded and ready to learn from others, as well as letting them learn from her.

JOY AGAR

Originally from New Zealand, Joy Agar settled in Britain in 1980, since when she has built up a reputation as a hair artist whose imagination matches her outstanding technical and commercial skills. At her Northampton shop, she blends an understanding of individual needs with an open-minded approach and a firm grasp of new product developments. At the same time as creating new fashions in hair, Joy's dedication to her work leads her to share knowledge with fellow stylists, to teach and to motivate younger members of the industry.

JENNIFER CHEYNE

Jennifer Cheyne has built up a reputation as a hairdresser of international stature over many years of top-class salon, show, seminar and photographic work. With her husband Stewart, Paul Adamczuk and William Howarth, she is a director of five salons and a hairdressing school in Edinburgh. Perfectly at ease with long hair, and with both commercial and *avant garde* hairdressing, she still spends two days a week working on the salon floor, providing inspiration and motivation for everyone in the organisation. Heavily involved in Cheynes Education, the Edinburgh school to which student hairdressers come from all over the world, Jennifer also travels widely in Britain, Europe and the USA with the Cheynes Show Team. As well as numbering the Duchess of York among the prestigious Cheynes client list, Jennifer was recently chosen to create a new image for American singer Paula Abdul.

CARON BANFIELD

On graduating from the London College of Fashion, Caron Banfield won the prestigious Silver Scissors Award. As a result, she was commissioned by L'Oréal to demonstrate her skills to a packed Royal Albert Hall and was soon signed up for session work by the top hair and make-up agencies. Completely independent since 1989, London-based Caron numbers among her clients L'Oréal, Braun, Timotei, Sunsilk, Head and Shoulders, Wella, Finesse Pantène, Max Factor and Gucci, as well as the Pirelli calendar, Vogue, Tatler and Elle. She works with leading photographers such as John Swannell, David Bailey, Lester Bookbinder and Barry Lategan and has done hair shots with celebrities like Tina Turner, Sarah Brightman, Jane Seymour and Princess Michael of Kent. In addition to consultancy work and developing her own hair products, Caron has made videos on how to shoot hair commercials and on working as a hairdresser.

THERESE HAYNES

The owner since 1981 of the Pacific Hair Salon in Knightsbridge, Thérèse Haynes qualified as a stylist in the nearby Cadogan Club. In the 1980s she went on to work for the Root Salon and Profile Hair Designs before becoming manageress in 1987 of the salon she now owns. Thérèse, whose work has been featured in a string of influential magazines including Vogue, Tatler, Root, Hairdressers Journal, Chic, Black Beauty & Hair and Proline International, has given demonstrations of her skill in Britain, Europe, the USA and Africa, as well as judging hairdressing contests. A regular competitor herself, in 1989, 1990 and 1991 Thérèse was a finalist in the Afro Hair Stylist of the Year contest organised by Schwarzkopf and the Hairdressers Journal, eventually scooping the title in 1992.

ANNIE HUMPHREYS

For over 30 years Annie Humphreys has been responsible for recreating innovative colouring and perming techniques that are integral parts of the world-renowned Vidal Sassoon look. Annie and Vidal began their careers in England in the 1950s, when Vidal bought the salon in which Annie had begun her apprenticeship. Staying with Vidal, Annie went on to manage various salons in Britain and to consistently make major advances in her special area. In 1979 the Vidal Sassoon products company became independent of the schools and salons. Together with Phillip Rogers, Annie became a director of all the European schools and salons and, in 1983, of their US and Canadian counterparts. Despite her executive status within London-based Haircare Limited, Annie is seldom seen behind a desk, preferring to spend her days in the salons, tinting, perming, experimenting and teaching.

CAROLINE COLLIS

As the founder in 1972 of Molton Brown, and now co-owner with Leonard and Michael Warshaw, Caroline Collis is the creator of a collection of beauty and grooming products that pioneered the use of natural-based ingredients in modern cosmetics. Already highly successful among a discerning clientele in the late 1970s, Molton Brown supplemented its hair and bath care ranges with new ranges for skin care, colour cosmetics and men's grooming, and now manufactures over 200 items. The company's products are particularly well known in Britain, Canada and the USA, as well as in major cities worldwide, with distribution restricted to famous department stores, specialist boutiques, selected five-star luxury hotels and the first-class airline business.

EVE LOM

Eve Lom, regarded as one of Europe's finest beauticians, uses her hands as tools for therapy, diagnosis and human warmth. She offers an approach to skin care that deals with the texture of the skin rather than wrinkles, with glow rather than glamour and with cleanliness rather than beauty. Czech-born, trained in Paris and now based in London's West End, Eve explains that deep cleansing is her speciality, a task to which she brings a remarkable thoroughness. Believing that we cannot improve on nature, she uses natural extracts to emulate, rather than superficially imitate it.

JO MALONE

Since setting up in business in 1990, Jo Malone has become one of Britain's most sought-after skin-care specialists. International models, actresses and media personalities regularly visit her Sloane Square clinic, but enquiries about who exactly is on her client list are met with a polite but veiled response. Fascinated by skin-care preparations as a child, Jo was encouraged by an elderly family friend who had, many years earlier, worked in the leading French perfume houses in Paris. Nowadays, still under 30 years old, she has influenced hundreds of people with her unique massage techniques. Among her products, which will soon be available throughout the world, are a range of exquisite bath oils.

Photograph by Deborah Hood

MARY GREENWELL

Mary Greenwell has been a freelance make-up artist since 1982, and has worked all over the world for the leading publications, advertising campaigns, designers and photographers. Based in London, Mary has created make-up images for collections by major designers including Romeo Gigli, Rifat Ozbek and Jean-Paul Gaultier, and her clientele of celebrities ranges from Hollywood actresses, through pop stars male and female, to Baroness Thatcher. She has also been asked on several occasions to apply make-up for the Princess of Wales.

MAGGIE HUNT

After eight successful years as a model, Maggie Hunt became a make-up artist in 1977 and today works with the world's top photographers, creative directors and glossy magazines, as well as designing "looks" for the most influential cosmetic houses. Dismissing the "one look suits all" approach, she emphasises the individual's needs in every case, attracting an impressive catalogue of clients from all over the world. Leading celebrities who have consistently valued Maggie's talent and professionalism include David Bowie, Paul and Linda McCartney, Bryan Ferry, Tina Turner, John and Norma Major, Joan Collins, Meryl Streep and Geta Scaachi. Based in London and represented by the Joy Goodman agency, she also numbers royalty and aristocrats among her most prestigious clients, including the Princess of Wales, the Duchess of York and Princess Michael of Kent.

CHRISTINA STEWART AND LYNNE SANDERS

Cosmetics à la Carte was founded in 1973 by Christina Stewart and Lynne Sanders to produce the most comprehensive range of make-up, carefully blended to suit the individual look, and to provide professional guidance on its application. The company has since grown to be the leading British make-up supplier to the Royal Family and to the worlds of fashion television and film. The factory, which is on the same site as the company's headquarters in Battersea, uses ingredients of the purest quality and none which have been tested on animals. The first shop, in Motcomb Street, London SW1, is the site of the Studio and the School of Makeup Design, and there are two other London shops. Sales are supplemented by stockists in Exeter, Bristol and Glasgow and a thriving mail-order service run from Battersea.

CHARLIE GREEN

Charlie Green combines her influential role as a leading make-up artist in the fashion photography industry with work as a television presenter on BBC 1's Going Live! and ITV's This Morning. After leaving school with A levels, Charlie's work in fashn buying and then marketing brought her into contact with the world of international models, inspiring in her a keen interest in make-up. Before long she was taking her own bookings as a make-up artist, one of her earliest clients being Kylie Minogue. Nowadays, as well as working with top photographers for Vogue, Elle and Tatler, and writing for Arena and the Sunday supplements, Charlie powders the noses of many a pop and media personality. Among her current clients are Jason Donovan, INXS, Eric Clapton, Bryan Ferry, Pavarotti, Ivana Trump, Charlotte Rampling, Joanna Lumley and supermodels Linda Evangelista, Naomi Campbell and Claudia Schiffer.

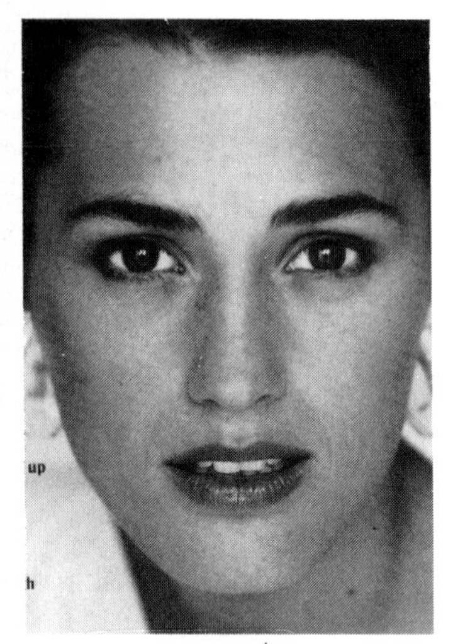

YASMIN LE BON

Super model, wife of singer Simon Le Bon and mother of two daugthers, Yasmin as worked all over the world. Currently she is with Models One, and her punishing schedule leaves her little time for anything but looking after her girls, but she is seriously committed to saving the environment and does whatever she can for green causes.

JANE MARCH

Jane March made her film debut in 1992 in Jean Jaques Annaud's highly acclaimed adaptation of the Marguerite Duras novel The Lover. Chosen by British Elle as one of Britain's most beautiful women, Jane was spotted by Annaud on the cover of a teenage fashion magazine. Her agency, Storm, arranged acting classes, and she made the part her own. The film was released in October 1992 in the USA, and Jane is now based in Hollywood.

Photograph by Patrick de Marcellier, courtesy of Harpers & Queen

SUSIE BICK

Susie Bick has been modelling since she was 15 years old. She is famous for being the Dior Cosmetics Girl, and for being Vivienne Westwood's muse. She has achieved cult status in the modelling industry, renowned for her jet-black hair and snow-white looks. She is now in all major editorials, including both Italian and French Vogue.

Photograph by CA Style

LOUISE GANDER

Sixteen years old and 5ft 11in, Louise Gander comes from Kentish Town in North London. She began modelling in September 1992 and, within a month of joining Storm, at the suggestion of a friend, was booked for Sky magazine, Harpers & Queen and featured in the British Fashion Awards catwalk show, which was shown on BBC TV. She is hailed as the face of 1993.

Photograph by Craig Fordham

NAOMI CAMPBELL

Naomi Campbell is Britain's supermodel, and one of the highest paid models in the world. She started at the tender age of 14 while at dance school. She joined Syncro after being discovered in Covent Garden by Beth Boldt. Her rise to stardom has been consistent with being the muse for various designers – Ozbek at 16, Jasper Conran, Karl Largerfield and now Versace's Elite group. Naomi was the first black Vogue cover girl. Now firmly set at the top, she is working on her singing career.

RACHEL BOSS

Rachel Boss started modelling at the age of 16. She has travelled to Australia to appear in Australian Vogue, and has been based in Paris. Featured in magazine editorials worldwide, she is widely renowned as an elegant showgirl, recognised by many top designers including Nicole Farhi, Charles Thomas and Chloe and Karl Largerfield.
Photograph by Shane Martin

SAFFRON BURROWS

Known professionally just as Saffron, Saffron Burrows comes from Islington, where both her parents are teachers. She was scouted at Covent Garden when she was 14 years old by Elite Premier, and by the age of 16 was doing Runway work for Chanel, and being photographed for editorial in Paris and Milan. Now pursuing an acting career alongside her modelling, she has recently completed a short film for Channel 4.
Photograph by Sacha Rens

LISA BUTCHER

Now aged 21, Lisa Butcher was born in Singapore, where her father was working as an executive for British/American Tobacco. In 1987, at the age of 15, she won Elle magazine's Elle's Angels competition as the Face of 87. Part of her prize was a modelling contract with Larraine Ashton – IMG, and Lisa's career as an international model took off from there. She has now been modelling for more than five years, and has graced the most prestigious catwalks and magazines in the world, wearing the most exclusive clothes. Lisa may currently be seen in every High Street in connection with the Lancaster Sun product range. Although she has lived in London for the past three years, Lisa is a country girl at heart. She loves riding and collects animals; she has, she says ". . . two horses, two dogs, two cats and a husband".

MERCY JEAN PATRICIA MARTIN

Scottish Jean Patricia Martin refused to join her mother and 90 per cent of the local workforce in the Chrysler car factory. She bought herself a one-way ticket to London, broke into a squat, signed on and went looking for work. She was 25 years old when she was taken on by a model agency and soon she was on the catwalk with the best of them. At the age of 32 she was the first woman to be taken on by the So Dam tuFF model agency.
Photograph by Adrian Wilson

CECILIA CHANCELLOR

Dark blonde, 5ft 10½in tall, blue eyed and with a perfect size eight figure, Cecilia Chancellor is an international model who is rapidly attaining the dizziest heights of the fashion business. When not making her living on the catwalk, in the studio or on location, Cecilia indulges her talent as an artist.
Photograph by Conde Naste Publications courtesy of Models One

SHARRON FISHER

Sharron joined Select three years ago and immediately worked for some of the best magazines including French, Dutch and American Elle and Harpers Bazaar. She was also the first cover girl on Arena magazine. During her career Sharron has worked with photographers such as Neil Kirk, Fabrizio Ferri and Tyen.
Photograph by Friedmann Hauss

ANGELA DUNN

Born in New Zealand, Angela left school with no career ideas so she went to university and studied history of art. An interest in fashion lead to a modelling course and offers for work took her to Tokyo and then Paris. After several more overseas trips for the designer collections, Angela decided to move to Sydney, Australia. One year and a book full of tear sheets and covers later, she moved to London where she has built up a client list including Yves Saint Laurent, Christian Lacroix and Jean Paul Gaultier.
Photograph by Ulli Weber

AMANDA WATERLOW

Amanda Waterlow was spotted four years ago in the Kings Road. She was photo tested by Willi Campden, which led to her first major editorial with English Elle. Her career snowballed, introducing her to many international magazines including Harpers Bazaar, Vogue and French Elle. This led to the worldwide make-up campaign for Givenchy, and the contract as the Armani girl.
Photograph by Dominique Isserman

LORRAINE-PASCALE WOODWARD

Nineteen year old Lorraine is topped to become this year's new supermodel. She has appeared in American and Italian Vogue and has worked with Bruce Weber and Patrick Demarchelier as well as for Chanel and Karl Largerfield. Lorraine loves dancing but avoids the club scene, preferring to spend her free time on quieter pursuits such as reading.

KATE MOSS

Acclaimed as the new supermodel, Kate Moss's career has soared during the past year or so. She has captured the imagination of some of the most influential fashion figures in the world, including Steven Meisel, Patrick Demarchelier and Calvin Klein as the look of the 1990s. Discovered by Sarah Doukas of Storm at the age of 14, in a queue at JFK Airport, Kate started working immediately for the Face and British Elle. Now aged 18, Kate is representing the Best of British all over the world.

Photograph by Bruce Weber for Banana Republic

PATRINA MORRIS

Very few Asian models have succeeded in Britain, but Anglo-Indian Patrina Morris has regularly appeared on TV and been featured in the press about her success. She is represented by Laraine Ashton-IMG, and is about to launch her singing career, with her first record to be released this year.

Photograph by Reiner Leizgen

JENNIFER JONES

Jennifer Jones has been a model with Select for four years. She has appeared in Dutch and English Elle, Sky, The Face, Harpers & Queen and Cosmopolitan, and has done worldwide campaigns for Mexx and Peter Styvesant. Currently she is based in New York.

Photograph by Keith Henderson

CAROLE WHITE

Carole White trained as a model at Lucie Clayton but says she "wasn't very good" so she got a job at Alfred Marks booking girls for exhibitions. She went back to Lucie Clayton to become a booker. At 30 she set up Premier, her own model agency. It was extremely successful and in 1991 the company merged with Elite. Elite Premier is unique in that it represents girls from independent agencies as well as their own. They have more famous models than any other agency, from Linda Evangelista to Naomi Campbell. Despite 20 years in the business Carole says she "still loves it".

TANDY ANDERSON

Tandy Anderson became a booker at Askews when she was 17, having modelled since the age of 13. At Askews she met Clare and Chrissie Castagnetti – the women with whom she was to form Select in 1977. Tandy went on to open Select Men. She was still only 27. On her books are, among others, Scott Denoit, John Francis and Giancarlo, as well as Mario Sorrenti, famous for the Levi ads, whom Tandy discovered two years ago.

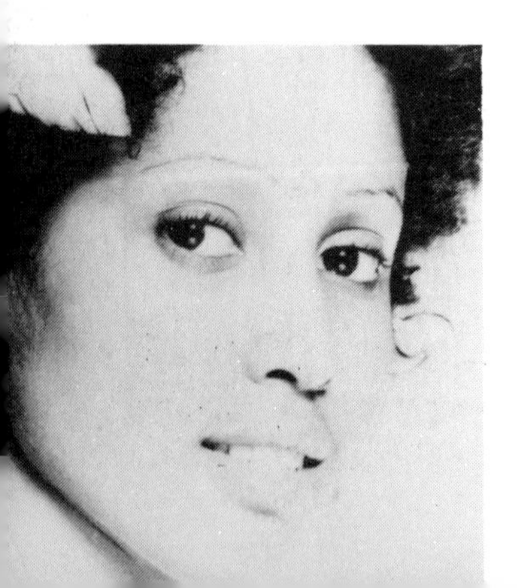

SARAH DOUKAS

Sarah Doukas managed a punk band and ran an antique stall at the Marche aux Puces in Paris and Antiquarius in the Kings Road before joining Laraine Ashton. She soon became the agency's head booker and five years later left to set up Storm, the models and actors agency in 1987, backed by Richard Branson, a 50 per cent partner in the company. Her first models were all found by her, scouting the streets. She discovered rising star Kate Moss in JFK airport four years ago, and signed Jane March on a hunch (the actress who played the lead in The Lover) despite the fact that, at 5ft 3in, she hardly fitted the brief for a model. Storm also represent Shana, Calvin Klein's Escape girl, as well as Rod Stewart's wife Rachel Hunter, and Monica Bellucci, the new Italian movie siren, Michiel, Levis and Gap and the internationally famous Albert.

LARAINE ASHTON

Laraine Ashton was born in London in 1946. She left school with no academic qualifications, and states she has since won no awards or titles. She became a model, briefly, in the 1960s, but "hated every minute of it". Despite these setbacks Laraine has risen to become one of our most respected model agents, well known for her forward thinking and for championing causes in the model industry. She founded Laraine Ashton in 1975 with Mark McCormack. They have represented Marie Helvin, Jerry Hall and Janice Dickinson; Laraine discovered Rachel Ward, Catherine Oxenberg and Lisa Butcher, and she recently signed supermodel Niki Taylor. Laraine has one son, Claude McCullin, aged five, whom she lists as her "pleasure and her hobby", and they live quietly in Little Venice with Terry O'Neill and the builders.

APRIL DUCKSBURY

April Ducksbury worked in film production in Europe and then for the United Nations in Paris, Rome and Geneva before assisting a top fashion photographer for 18 months. This job brought her into the modelling world and in 1968 she set up Models One with Jose Fonseca. Model agencies at the time were more versatile than they are now; most representing a wide range of people. April and Jose decided they wanted their agency to represent solely prestige international models. They started with just 20. "Everyone thought we were mad", says April, but Models One was an instant success and the agency was soon representing the likes of Yasmin Le Bon, Greta Scaachi, Jerry Hall and Cecilia Chancellor.

E. J. STEELE

E. J. Steele worked as a cordon bleu cook in Italy and Greece and a PA to the chief executive of the SDP when it was first launched before becoming involved in the model world. She worked for a few agencies before being headhunted for a job as a booker at Models One. She launched Profile Models Agency with her partner Roy A. Stevens in 1986. They now represent around 70 girls of international status including Clare Mulholland, one of Elle magazine's "new faces for 1993" who has just done a Katharine Hamnett campaign. Other new finds include 18 year old Mette, Patrick Demarchellier's girl Aga Marie, Albert Watson's new find and Bruce Weber's girl, Louise Hargreaves.

JOSE FONSECA

Jose Fonseca was working in one of the first boutiques in the King's Road back in the 1960s when Sir Mark Palmer asked her to run the model agency he owned with friends. He didn't seem to mind the fact that she had had no experience. The agency represented stars such as Brian Jones and James Fox as well as Christine Keeler. Two years later the agency was taken over and Jose decided to start up her own outfit. She chose April Ducksbury as her partner and together they set up Models One, representing prestige models of international stature.

ANNETTE RUSSELL

Annette Russell left school at 16 to do a secretarial course. She worked and modelled until she was 18 when she moved to London. It took her four years more of modelling to realise she was in the wrong job! She became a junior booker on the Nevs agency men's table in 1985 and rose to become head booker. In 1989 she decided to go into business on her own and opened the highly successful and innovative men's agency So Dam tUFF Ltd. Among the top models on her books are Robbie, Cassius, Moose and Roger Cook.
Photograph by Katy Baggott

SPORTING WOMEN

The changing face of Britain in the last two decades has introduced into our society a new meaning to the word "leisure". Alongside every Southfork influenced supermarket that has sprung up in and around our towns and cities in the 1980s and 90s, there has almost always been a leisure centre, equally architecturally challenged and equally welcomed by the populace. The purpose that the leisure centre has served so well is in making sport accessible to everyone and in providing world class facilities for sports which had hitherto been "games", played in church halls, or had been available only to the privileged few. The greatest impact of the rise of the leisure industry and of the government's Sport for All campaign has been on British sporting women, as the following pages seek to show. Although many of our greatest sports men and women are still having to leave our shores in order to receive the best training available, the immense improvement in facilities will surely change this and we hope that our champions of today will create the champions of tomorrow at home. One of the principal differences between men's and women's sport at the highest level is the enormous contrast in the money to be earned. With very few exceptions, the women who appear in the Best of British are amateurs and the extra dedication required to reach the top of the tree deserves the widest recognition. Even in one of the more lucrative sports, golf, the earnings of a top woman player compared with those of her male counterpart are risible – in an identical game played on the same course. We have included many of the sports which are more often overlooked in this, the first issue of the book, so bid welcome to the martial artists, the rugby players, the cricketers, the yachtswomen and, particularly, our indomitable paralympians as well as their more regularly feted colleagues.

DEBBIE SOUTHWICK

Debbie Southwick, the rhythmic gymnast, was born in Widnes in 1976, and is coached by Russian, Irena Viner. She was British overall silver medallist in 1992, and is British champion in hoop and ball. She has competed for Great Britain in all major championships since a broken wrist ended her career as an artistic gymnast in 1987. In 1992 she attained the highest place ever by a Briton at the Olympic Games, won a Dance Award for Achievement, and received two major SAF grants, as well as a Tampax Sports Award.

Photograph by Alan Edwards

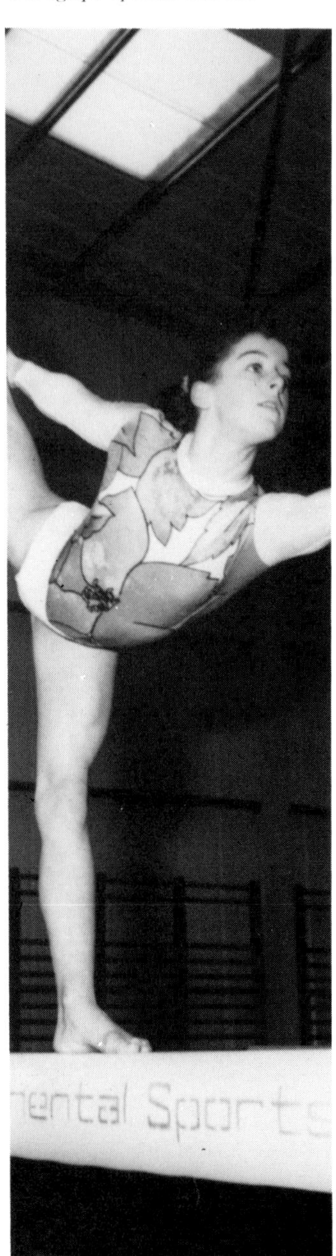

ROWENA ROBERTS

Rowena Roberts was born in Kingston, Surrey, in 1977. At the age of five she started gymnastics classes and, at nine, was a member of the National Under 12 squad. Under the direction of her coach, Gareth Davies, Rowena became the youngest ever British champion at only 14 and, in 1992, was Britain's youngest Olympic team member at 15.

KAREN ALMOND

Saracens, England and Great Britain flyhalf, 29 year old Karen Almond has been involved in rugby for 11 years, and has won 20 international caps. Captain of both England and Great Britain, she led her country to the first ever women's World Cup final, where they were narrowly defeated by the USA. Known for her prodigious acceleration and tactical awareness, Karen grew up supporting Rugby League, but switched her allegiances at university. A PE instructor, her ambition is to lead England to victory in the 1994 World Cup.

DEBBIE FRANCIS

Wing three-quarter Debbie Francis was the first woman ever to score a try at Cardiff Arms Park. She did not miss an international for England until impending motherhood somewhat affected her natural swerve and sidestep. "Debbie-Mac" nearly caused an international incident when playing against Wales, for sneaking on an embryonic 16th player, who turned out to be male!

JACQUIE EDWARDS

One of the rising stars of women's rugby, centre Jacquie Edwards is well known in the game for her devastating strength and speed. A canoeist, trampolinist and basketball player, Jacquie started to play rugby eight years ago, plays for Blackheath, and was part of England's World Cup squad.

LIZA BURGESS

Twenty-eight year old Liza Burgess is a second row forward for Saracens, Wales and Great Britain. She captains Wales and holds Britain's record for international caps. Known throughout the rugby world as "Bird", Liza has been involved in rugby for nine years, and her proudest moment was leading Wales out against England at Cardiff Arms Park. An ex-hockey player and head of PE, Bird is admired for her total commitment, which once generated so much heat that the tape protecting her ears melted!

GILL BURNS

The Waterloo, England and Great Britain No. 8, 28 year old Gill Burns ("Burnsey") has amassed 17 international caps in only five years of rugby. A PE teacher, she has played representative basketball, athletics and hockey, and has the distinction of being the first woman to referee at Twickenham, in an under 12 mini game.

KIM STRONGMAN

Kim Strongman was born in Nottingham, where her father, Les, had been a professional ice hockey player. She joined Peterborough Ravens in the 1984/85 season, when they won the league, a feat which they repeated in the following season, when Kim was top scorer in the league, as she was the next year. She was selected for the England team in 1987/88. In 1988/89 she joined Oxford City Rockets, won the league, was top scorer again and played with them in a tournament in Canada where they won the gold medal. In 1990/91 she was appointed captain of the newly formed Great Britain team. Oxford Rockets have won the league for four years in succession, and Kim has been top point scorer. During all this frenetic activity, usually involving extensive train travel, Kim has graduated, BA(Hons), from Cardiff University in human studies. Her dissertation was entitled, "the Relationship between Body Composition, Skill Levels and Physique in Ice Hockey Players".

CHARLENE VON SAHER

Charlene von Saher is the 1992 British figure skating champion. Born in Wimbledon in 1974, Charlene moved with her family to the United States and began skating at the Greenwich Skating Club. She entered her first competition at the age of nine, and at 14 moved to Boston to train with stronger competition. She was British silver medallist in 1991, and in 1992 was ranked 15th in the world.

CAROLINE WALKER AND TINA VAUX

When Caroline Walker learned to drive a bobsleigh in 1990, and asked Tina Vaux to be her brakeman, British women's bobsleighing was born. They went on to win the first international women's race held at Winterberg in 1991. For the 1991/92 season, with seven nations now competing, a three race international circuit was put together at Winterberg, Igls and Calgary, and Caroline and Tina were placed second overall. In 1992/93 there are ten competing nations, and their goal is to break down male domination of the sport, and see women's bobsleighing in the Winter Olympics.

LAURA URQUHART

Laura Urquhart is 28 and team manager of the Guildford Flames men's ice hockey team. A founder member of the Oxford City Rockets, she went on to found and coach the Chelmsford Cobras. Laura is assistant captain and top goal scorer for the Great Britain team.

JOANNE CONWAY OWERS

Britain's top skater for several years, the lovely Joanne Conway married Sunderland footballer Gary Owers in 1992, and now lives in Washington, near her training rink in Sunderland. Joanne entered her first international competition at 12, in Poland, and came second. A year later she won Junior Vienna. At 14 she was invited to train in America by Carlo Fassi, the world's top coach. In 1985 she won the British Championship for the first time – the youngest to do so for 32 years – and has since won it a record further five times. In 1991 she was placed fourth in Europe and seventh in the world. Injury kept her largely out of competition during 1992, but great things are expected this year and at the next Olympics. Her ambition on retirement from competition is to train a world champion.

Photograph by Kimberley Haggis

CLAIRE DE POURTALES

Born in Paris in 1969, and educated in Winchester, Claire de Pourtales turned down a place at university to join the British Development Ski team in 1987. She had started her racing career with the Downhill Only Ski Club, becoming British junior champion at 16. Claire joined the senior team in 1989, and is currently British No. 1, having won all four titles at the 1991 British Championships – a unique achievement. She was beset by injury at the Albertville Olympics, but aims to achieve excellent results for Britain in 1994.

JULIA SNELL

Julia Snell, 29, learnt to ski on the artificial ski slope in Southampton in 1979, but soon became bored, and decided to branch out into ballet skiing, a combination of gymnastics, skating and dance on skis. She was selected for the British World Cup team in 1986, and has won one gold (1992), two silver (1989, 1990) and two bronze (1989, 1992) medals. She won the bronze in the 1990 European Championships, and was placed fourth in the 1989 and 1990 World Championships. In the 1992 Olympics, Julia was placed fourth, the highest placing in the British team. She has been five times British ladies ballet skiing champion.

Photograph by British Ski Federation

EMMA BOWLES

Emma Bowles is the net-minder for the Oxford City Rockets, England and Great Britain. A founder member of the Rockets, she admits that the net-minder position originally became hers as a result of drawing the short straw; however, she has minded for men's teams as well as women's, and her skill and tenacity have helped the Rockets to be national champions for four consecutive years.

JANE SIXSMITH

Jane Sixsmith, whose red hair landed her with the nickname "Jasper" (after comedian Jasper Carrott) was called up for the 1988 Olympics when she was still in England's Under-21 hockey team. She was a member of the Great Britain squad which came fourth in the Seoul Olympics and of England's 1991 European gold medal-winning side. In Birmingham in 1992 she scored the only goal of the match in which England defeated the new Olympic champions, Spain. Scoring twice in the final game against Korea, "Jasper" put up a fine performance in the 1992 Barcelona Olympics, where Britain won the bronze medal. Also in 1992 she captained the First Personnel Sutton Coldfield Club, who won a gold medal in the European Cup Winners Cup that year. "Jasper" is the Great Britain squad's top striker, with 33 goals in 79 appearances. She has 61 England caps.

Photograph by Pat Ward

JANE BURRELL

It was the inspiration of Bobbie Trafford, who later became the England team coach, that set Jane Burrell on the path to her first England international cap. In 1992, at the age of 25, she played for her sixth season in the England team – a career which has taken on her two US tours and to Australia for the 1989 World Cup.

ALISON RAMSAY

The most capped women's hockey player in the world, with 214 international caps (107 for Scotland and 107 for Great Britain), Alison Ramsay was vice-captain of Great Britain's bronze medal-winning team at the 1992 Barcelona Olympics. In 1988 she had played in the British team which came fourth at Seoul. Alison, a defensive midfield player, belongs to the Western Klick Photopoint Club, winners for ten consecutive years of the Scottish National League, and the most successful British club side in Europe.

Photograph by Pat Ward

MARY NEVILL

Mary Nevill, captain of the Great Britain team which took the bronze medal in the Barcelona Olympics in 1992, holds a total of 180 international caps, 79 for England and 101 for Great Britain. Mary, a striker, has scored 26 goals for Britain. She captained the Olympic squad qualifying at a tournament in New Zealand and was a member of the British team which came fourth in the Seoul Olympics in 1988. The holder of a PhD in Exercise Physiology, Mary has seen her expertise in this field put to valuable use in Britain's Olympic fitness training programme.

Photograph by Pat Ward

JANET GUILBRIDE

Having gained a full blue in lacrosse at Cambridge and represented the British Universities team on three occasions, Janet Guilbride was first selected to play for England in 1979. Since then she has played for the side every year except 1987, her "retirement" year, and captained the team in 1983-86 and 1992. She was picked for the World Cups in 1982, 1986 and 1989, but missed 1982 through injury. Jan toured the USA in 1976, 1980, 1988 and 1991 and, as co-captain with Lois Richardson, toured Australia in 1985, becoming GB Player of the Series. Primarily a defender strong in team play, Jan has played every position but two at international level. In 1990 she won the Player of the Home Internationals title while playing in attack. She is an All-England senior coach.

SARAH RICHARDSON

Selected for the Junior England lacrosse team in 1985, Sarah Richardson went on to play in both the West and England Under-21 teams and then, in 1987, to represent England for the first time. In 1990 and 1991 she was England's vice-captain and in 1992 the co-captain. Sarah toured the USA in 1988 and 1991, and went to Australia in 1989 for the World Cup, in which England had its chance of a gold medal snatched away in a sudden-death showdown with the Americans. Highlights of Sarah's career include the victory for England in the decisive Test against the USA on the 1988 tour and winning the Territorial Championship with the West team in 1991. As well as being a full-time physical education teacher, Sarah coaches the Junior Berkshire, Junior West, Junior England and Senior West teams.

LOIS RICHARDSON

When Lois Richardson represented England at lacrosse in 1992 it was the tenth year she had done so and the fifth consecutive year of her captaincy. She has 52 international caps and has played in all three World Cups including the 1989 tournament when she captained England to a silver medal after a sudden-death play-off against the USA. In 1985 she was co-captain of the British team which toured Australia. Back in England, Lois has represented the West Territory since 1977 and currently both captains and coaches the team. She is also captain of the Hertfordshire County team and a Junior England coach.

SANDRA LISTER

Captain of England's gold medal-winning side in the 1991 European Cup and captain in over 50 of her 103 appearances for England, midfield player Sandra Lister also appeared for her country in the World Cups of 1983, 1986 and 1990. In the 1992 Barcelona Olympics she was an important factor in Great Britain's performance in each of its five matches. She has 43 international caps for Great Britain, and has scored twice for the team. Sandra is a member of Ipswich Ladies' Hockey Club.

Photograph by Pat Ward

JO DURIE

Jo Durie has been the British No. 1 tennis player on and off since 1983, and has never in that time been out of the top two. Six foot tall and hard hitting, on her day it is obvious that she has been able to beat anyone in the world, a fact that the partisan home crowd at Wimbledon has often found a source of frustration. Semi-finalist in the US and French Opens in 1983 at 23, an age when many of the American "Superbrats" were already burnt out, she reached the last 16 at Forest Hills again in 1991. Apart from her singles achievements, Jo has had tremendous success in the doubles, particularly the mixed doubles, Wimbledon champion in 1987, Australian champion in 1991 and Australian Open quarter finalist in 1992, to name only the Grand Slam tournaments. Now 32, Jo Durie continues to win tournaments and respect around the tennis world, and for the past decade has been a fine ambassador for Britain.

Photograph courtesy of Advantage International

MONIQUE JAVER

Born in California in 1967, Monique Javer is a member of the British Federation Cup team, and represented Britain at the Barcelona Olympic Games in 1992. Also in 1992 she reached the semi-finals of tournaments in Wellington and Kuala Lumpur, and quarter finals in Auckland and Tokyo. She won her first professional title in Singapore in 1988, and her career winnings top $200,000.

GILLIAN CLARK

Born in Baghdad in 1961, Gillian Clark now lives and trains in Wimbledon. She has been playing for England since 1981, and has won team gold medals playing badminton at the Commonwealth Games in 1982, 1986 and 1990, where she also won a silver in the ladies doubles, and a bronze in the mixed. In 1992 she won the All England Open Championship (with Julie Bradbury), and represented Britain at the Olympics. Gillian is the players' representative on the Council of the International Badminton Federation. She loves art and history and is a frequenter of the auction houses.

Photograph by Peter Richardson

LISA LOMAS

Aged 25, from Luton, Lisa is now firmly established as England No. 1 table tennis player. Her first major international success came in the European Youth Championships in 1985, when she collected gold, silver and two bronze medals. Less than 12 months later she made her mark at senior level, taking the bronze in the European Championships. 1992 was an excellent year, with a silver in the Olympic qualifying event, her ninth English National Championship and a silver in the European Championships, followed by leading her team to fifth place in the Olympics. After two seasons of club playing in Sweden, Lisa has now returned to England.

Photograph by English Table Tennis Association

CASSIE JACKMAN

Cassie Jackman is the British No. 1 and the world's No. 4 squash player. From her early teens, Cassie moved inexorably towards winning the world junior title, which she accomplished in 1991 in Norway. Whilst still a junior, Cassie was already becoming a force in senior squash, and her powerful style, excellent shot-making and superb temperament have enabled her to reach the semi-finals of the British Open and World Open Championships in 1992, only to be beaten in both events by World No. 1 Sue Devoy.

Photograph by Stephen Line

GILLIAN GOWERS

Gillian Gowers was born in 1964 and first played badminton for England in 1983. She plays at county level for Hertfordshire. Gillian represented England in the Commonwealth Games in 1986, winning a team gold medal and a ladies' doubles gold medal (with Gillian Clark) and, in 1990, winning the team gold and doubles silver. She represented Britain in the Barcelona Olympics. Her hobbies are squash and her dogs.

Photograph by Peter Richardson

ALISON GORDON

Alison Gordon is the current English national singles table tennis champion, and champion for the third time. Aged 29, Alison is the most experienced player in Europe, having played in all European Championships since 1984. She was English International Champion in the women's and mixed doubles in 1986. Alison now lives in Glasgow where she is studying sports therapy.

Photograph by English Table Tennis Association

SUE WRIGHT

Twenty-two-year-old Sue Wright shot to prominence in world squash in 1991, when she reached the final of the British Open, defeating both the world ranked Nos. 1 and 2 on her way. In 1992 she went on to win the national title. A real tiger on the court, Sue is currently ranked No. 6 in the world and, along with Cassie Jackman, will provide the hub of the British squad for the coming years.

Photograph by Stephen Line

PHYLIS SMITH

Phylis Smith (nee Watt) was born in Birmingham in 1965 at the hospital where she subsequently returned to work. Within three months of taking up athletics seriously in 1985 she won her first England vest, while working as a social worker. She won the UK Championship at 200m (in 1990 and 1992). Also in 1992 she was unbeaten by a British athlete at 100, 200 and 400 metres and won an Olympic bronze in the 4 x 400 metres relay.

DIANE MODAHL

Born Diane Edwards in 1966 in Manchester, Diane comes from a sporting family – her cousin is a former boxing champion. She won the silver medal in 1986 and took the Commonwealth in 1990. Now ranked first in Britain at both the indoor and outdoor 800 metres she was the only woman to cover this distance in less than two minutes. She made the semi-finals at the 1992 Olympics. She is married to her agent, a Norwegian.

ANN WILLIAMS

Born in Merseyside 27 year old Ann Williams was coached by her father through her first international when she was 16. But her real breakthrough came when she won the 800 metres in the UK Championships. She is the sixth fastest British woman of all time over 800 metres. She describes her greatest achievement as coming seventh in the World Championships in Tokyo in 1991. In 1992 she was a member of the British team in Barcelona, won the Rome Grand Prix and came second in the New York Games in the metric mile, her new event.

TESSA SANDERSON

One of our foremost sports personalities Tessa Sanderson holds the MBE for services to sport. She has competed in five Olympics, won the gold at the Commonwealth Games three times and has held numerous records for javelin as well as one for heptathlon. She is actively involved in many charity organisations and is often on TV, most recently with Cilla Black, co-presenting Surprise, Surprise. In 1992 she won the Europa Cup and came fourth at the Barcelona Olympics.

GOWRY RETCHAKAN

Ranked fourth in British athletics behind Sally Gunnell, Liz McColgan and Yvonne Murray, Gowry Retchakan began training seriously for the 400 metre hurdles in 1989. She had previously been 100 metre champion for Sri Lanka. Over the past three seasons she has won the WAAA title three times and in 1992 she took the UK crown. Now 32 she is married to her coach and the couple have a four year old son.

LIZ McCOLGAN

Born Elizabeth Lynch in 1964 in Dundee, Liz was our heroine in the 1991 Tokyo World Championships. She took the 10,000m gold medal and was voted BBC Sports Personality of the Year. She also won the silver medal in the 1988 Olympics and came fifth in the final of the 10,000 metres at the 1992 Olympics. She currently holds the world record at 5,000m. Trained by husband Peter, the couple live in Arbroath in Scotland. They have a daughter named Eilish, eight weeks after whose birth Liz won a 5,000m road race in Florida!

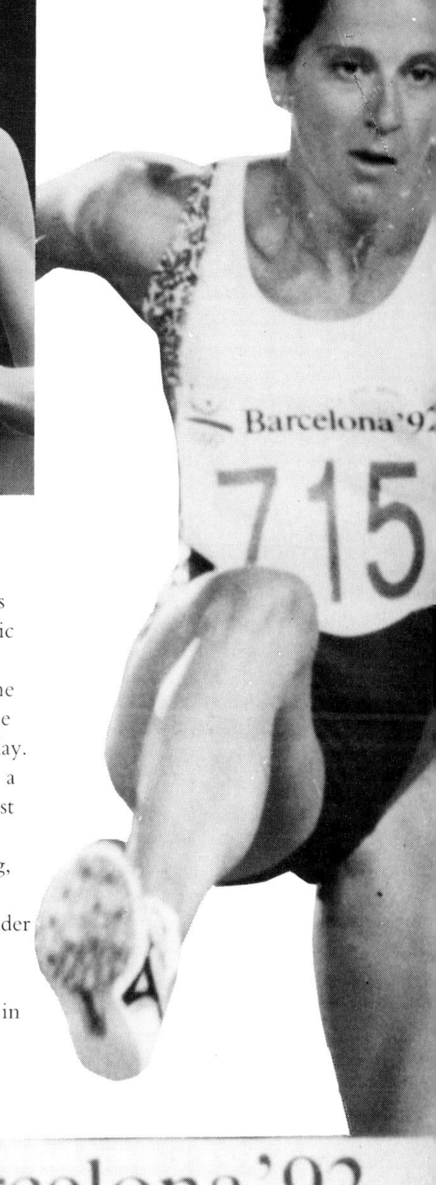

SALLY GUNNELL

Born in 1966, Sally Gunnell was our heroine in the 1992 Olympic Games, captaining the women's team and winning the gold in the 400 metres hurdles, as well as the bronze in the 4 x 400 metres relay. She began her athletics career as a long jumper, and was ranked best in England at 13. Sally lives in Brighton with husband Jon Bigg, the former international 800m runner, and is British record holder in the 100m and 400m hurdles, Commonwealth champion at 400m and won the silver medal in the 1991 world championships over that distance.

YVONNE MURRAY

Twenty-eight year old Yvonne Murray started competing when she was 15. By the time she was 18 she was the record holder for her age group at 3,000 metres. Now coached by Tommy Boyle she is the current British champion at 1,500 metres. She holds the distinction of being the first woman to win track golds in the World Cup and the European Championships. She has several silver and bronze medals to her credit, took the gold at the European Indoor Championships in 1987, the 1989 World Cup and the 1990 European Championships. She was a finalist in the 3,000 metres at the 1992 Olympc Games.

Barcelona'92

DEBBIE MARTI

Britain's best high jumper Debbie started athletics at the age of 11 and showed instant promise by achieving an age 11 best for the high jump. Four years later she achieved the world record, a bronze at the European Championship and second place at her first GB international. She gave up the sport for a while in the 1980s but returned with a vengeance in 1991 equalling the UK indoor record of 1.94 metres and coming fifth in the World Indoors in Seville. In 1992 she took the WAAA title, was the UK Champion and came ninth in Barcelona.

CAROLE HODGES

Carole Hodges is the captain of England's ladies cricket team. She has captained England at Under 19 and Under 25 levels as well as at full international level from 1982. She has made 1,164 runs for England in 18 Tests (av. 40) and taken 23 wickets. She holds the record for Test catches (25). Carole was born in 1959, and educated in Fleetwood, Lancs. She has worked for a bank for 14 years, enjoys reading and travel, and is an active member of Christians in Sport.

LISA NYE

Born in 1966, Lisa Nye is a policewoman, and England's wicketkeeper. Lisa began playing cricket in 1983, and was selected for Junior England. In 1988 she was selected for England to tour Australia for the World Cup. She has played in 25 one-day internationals, three 4-day Tests and one 5-day Test, and in 1992, secured a record eight dismissals in the final Test against New Zealand.

ENID BAKEWELL

Enid Bakewell is a cricketer of terrific ability who, now in her 50s, is still playing at club, area and territorial level. A left-arm spinner, and opening bat, her first full international tour was to Australia and New Zealand in 1968, when she scored over 1,000 runs and took 118 wickets at an incredible 9.2 average. In the first Women's World Cup in 1973, she shared in a record opening stand of 257, with Lynne Thomas, against an International XI. Enid was the first woman to be included in Wisden, in 1981, and is a member of the England Selection Committee.

VIVIEN SAUNDERS

Amongst her other many and various accomplishments, Vivien Saunders is the pioneer of Women's Professional Golf in Europe. She became a professional in 1969 and won the British Ladies Open Championship in 1977, and many other tournaments worldwide. She was founder and first chairperson of the WPGA. Twice winner of the British Sports Coach of the Year, for 18 years Vivien was the National Coach to the English Ladies Golf Association. A qualified solicitor, for several years she practised as a partner in a firm, before resuming full time golfing activities in 1986. She is now the owner of Abbotsley Golf Hotel and Golf Club.

CAROLINE HALL

Caroline Hall started to play golf competitively at 13, and at 14 was an English Girls' International. In 1990, at 16, she became the English Girls' Amateur Champion, and won the South-West Ladies Championship, the Cotswold Gold Vase and the Fulford Heath Scratch title. In 1991, Caroline was a member of the victorious English Ladies team in the European Championships, and the Great Britain and Ireland team that beat Europe to win the Vagliano Trophy. She retained the Cotswol Gold Vase, and was County Champion. Caroline Hall is the reigning English Amateur Ladies Champion, South-Western Ladies Champion and County Champion She played in the Curtis Cup in 1992, and won three out of four points. Caroline is thinking about turning professional in 1993, and if she does, some professionals will have to look to their laurels.

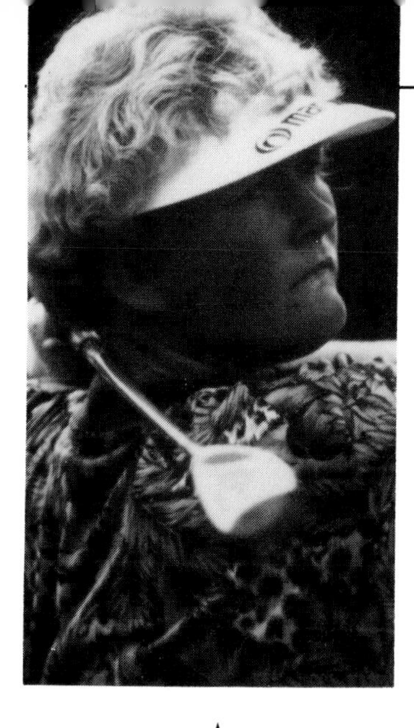

LAURA DAVIES

Laura Davies is unarguably Britain's finest lady professional golfer, and arguably the most talented in the world. After a successful amateur career, Laura turned professional in 1985, and announced her arrival by winning her first Open, the Belgian, and finishing top in the Order of Merit. The next year she repeated this feat, and won the British and Spanish Opens and, in 1987, she won the US Open, becoming the first woman ever to hold the two premier titles simultaneously. In 1988 she won tournaments on three continents, and her success has continued unabated. 1992 was a good year, even by Laura Davies' standards, with wins in the European, English and Italian Opens, and her indispensable contribution to winning the Solheim Cup for Europe.

Photograph by Jamie Lawson Johnston

MICKEY WALKER

Mickey Walker was the non-playing captain of the victorious European Solheim Cup golf team in 1992. After a distinguished amateur career, in which she won two British, the English, Spanish and Portuguese Opens, was Golfer of the Year, and awarded the Golf Writers Association Trophy, Mickey turned professional in 1973. She played on the USLPGA Tour for five years, and in 1979 won the Carlsberg Tournament and was runner-up in the British Open. In 1980 she won the Lambert & Butler Matchplay Championship. A further Carlsberg Tournament followed in 1981, when she was White Horse Golf Personality. Many other honours accrued, and from 1981-85 she was chairman of the WPGA. Mickey is head professional at the Warren Golf Club.

JAN BRITTIN

Jan Brittin made her cricket debut for Tadking Ladies at the age of 11. She quickly made the Surrey Junior and Senior XIs and is now Surrey vice-captain. She made her England debut in 1979, at the age of 19, and her maiden century for Young England vs India in 1981. Her 148 not out in the 1982 World Cup, against the International XI broke the world record for one-day scoring. During the 1984 New Zealand tour of England, Jan achieved a test average of 112.67, and featured on the front cover of the Cricketer magazine, as Player of the Month, a first for women's cricket. A consistently high run scorer, Jan is now second only to Rachael Heyhoe-Flint in all-time England scoring, and is currently training for the forthcoming World Cup.

JOANNE HOCKLEY

Now just 20 years old, amateur Joanne Hockley is the British Ladies Stroke Play Champion and was a finalist in the English Ladies Championship, where she only lost by one hole. As a result of this, she was selected to play for Great Britain and Ireland in the Espirito Santo, the World Amateur Team Championship, in Vancouver, where her team won the silver, losing out to Spain by one shot.

JOY HAWKEN

Joy Hawken studied at the Northampton School of Art and the Leicester College of Art, where she obtained a BA(Hons). She went on to win the David Murray Scholarship for landscape painting from the Royal Academy. She showed her independence as a student when she did not conform to contemporary trends, but sketched and studied the English countryside, its architecture and racing and rural scene. Among the well-known horses she has painted are Touching Wood, Oh So Sharp, Sharastani, Blakeney, Petoski, Jalmwood, Celtic Shot, Aldaniti, Osric, Norton's Coin, Kooyonga and Desert Orchid. She has been commissioned to paint Christmas cards for the Injured Jcokey's in 1987, 1990 and 1992, and the 1988 and 1989 Bob Champion Cancer Trust Christmas cards. Joy hunts with the Pytchly and rides out regularly for trainers when her work takes her to Middleton, Newmarket and Lambourne.

ANTHEA FARRELL

Born in 1962, Anthea Farrell couldn't wait for her 16th birthday so that she could start point-to-pointing. She had a distinguished show-jumping career as a junior and spent two summers teaching riding and travelling in America, a summer riding out for Peter Easterby and one riding out for Jonathan Pease, gaining invaluable experience in training flat-racing horses. She has won the Yorkshire Area Point-to-Point Lady Riders Championships in 1984, 1985, 1991 and 1992, and has ridden over 50 point-to-point winners. She rode her first winner under National Hunt rules in March 1984, and has ridden 36 winners since. She has also ridden three winners on the flat. Her biggest win so far was in the John Hughes Memorial Chase at Aintree in April 1991, on J. J. Henry, trained by her father Peter Beaumont.

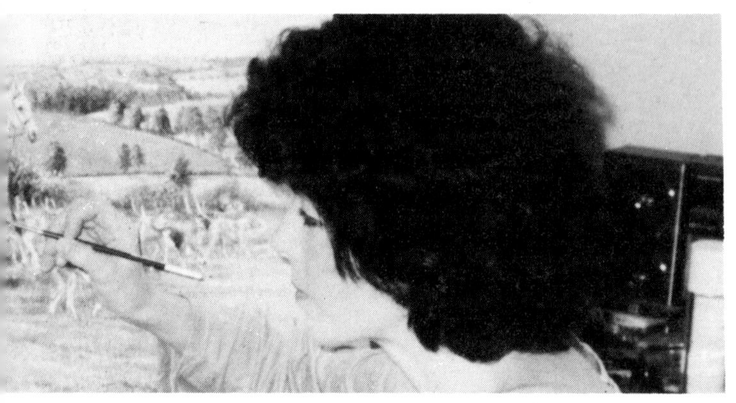

LYDIA PEARCE

Now aged 38, Lydia Pearce combines being Britain's champion amateur lady jockey with being a full time mother and partner in her husband's training business. In 1992 she won 13 races in 39 starts to secure the championship. She holds the record for the number of wins in a season by a woman amateur. The winning habit really started for Lydia, ironically, with the greatest disappointment of her career. First past the post on If Memory Serves in the Diamond Stakes at Ascot in July 1990, she was disqualified in an infringement judgement that appalled many. However, the quality of her riding had been noted by the people who mattered and success resulted including the Diamond Stakes for the last two years.

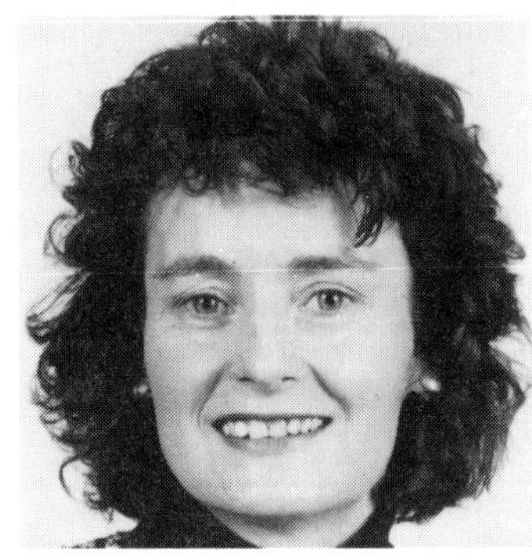

AMY OXENBOULD

Born in 1921, Amy Oxenbould studied at the Liverpool College of Art. She taught art until 1974, when she started sculpting: specialising in equine subjects – racing and polo groups and studies of Arabs and native breeds. The Sladmore Gallery cast and showed her first bronzes and she has exhibited in the Klausner Gallery in Louisville, Kentucky, and the Tryon Gallery in London. Her action studies have included Arkle, Troy, Mill Reef, Sea Pigeon and Brigadier Gerrard. Her racing pieces have been chosen as trophies by sponsors including Guinness, Lambert & Butler, Colt Cars and Goodwood Racecourse, and examples of her work are in the collections of owners and connoisseurs throughout the world.

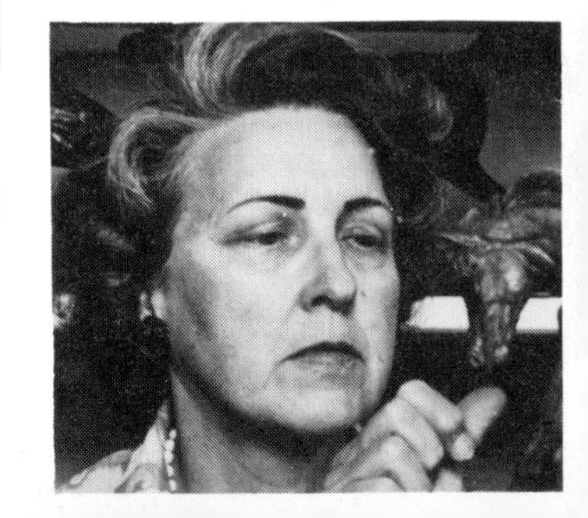

HENRIETTA KNIGHT

A lifetime's fascination with horses led Henrietta Knight to begin training in her own establishment in the 1989-90 season. At one stage it looked as though teaching children rather than horses might be her life. In 1970 she graduated from Teacher Training College, and for four years taught history and biology at St Mary's School, Wantage, before realising that she preferred horses to children. She started her own livery yard, breaking in young horses for other trainers, including Tim Foster, Oliver Sherwood, Fred Winter, Nicky Henderson and Michael Dickinson, and reschooling those with jumping problems. An internationally respected judge and selector, Henrietta sat for eight years on the Horse Trials Senior Selection Committee, as chairman for the last four.

MARY REVELEY

Dairy farmer's wife Mary Reveley started training under rules in 1981, after a lifetime spent with horses. She has become one of the country's most successful yet least known trainers, sending out 99 National Hunt winners in the 1991/92 season for nearly £240,000 in prize money, putting her seventh in the trainers' table. She has also recorded the highest ratio on winners to runners of any trainer, and has been voted National Hunt Trainer of the Year 1991/92. In 1992 she became the first woman to train more than 50 winners on the flat. Mary Reveley has become the small owners champion, with her ability to make the most of every horse's potential and place them in the right races.

JENNIE LORISTON-CLARKE

Jennie Loriston-Clarke comes from one of the most famous equestrian families in Britain, the Bullens. Her brother rode in two Olympics and her sister won a gold medal in the Mexico Olympics. She began amassing awards in 1964 when she was 21 with the Duke of Edinburgh's Gold Award. The highlight of her dressage career was to win the World Dressage Bronze Medal at Goodwood in 1978, the only Briton to have ever won a medal in this competition. She has won the Dressage Horse of the Year nine times including 1992 and she holds an MBE for services to equestrianism, presented to her in 1979.

LILLA WALL

Lilla Wall took up endurance riding 20 years ago when she was 40. At the time she ran a dairy farm with her husband – the business is still going. In 1989 she came second in the Goodwood 100 mile international with her new cob Alfie, now almost as famous as she is, which led to her being selected to represent Britain at Condrox in Belgium where she attained third place. At the first World Equestrian Games in Stockholm in 1990 at which the British team won gold, Lilla and Alfie came sixth, also obtaining the "best condition" award after the gruelling 160km ride. In 1991 she won at Fontwell Park and in 1992 she became the first British rider to finish in the World Endurance Championships at Barcelona.

TINA CASSAN

Tina Cassan has ridden since the age of four. Now 27 she got her first break when she landed a job working for Fred Welch. At his stable she got the chance to try out many different horses. She had a successful season in 1990, winning the Olympic Star Spotters Final at the Horse of the Year Show, but 1991 was really her year. She came second in the Hickstead Derby with one of only two clear rounds, and with the British team on the North American circuit she came second in the New York Grand Prix, won the Winner of the World Qualifier and earned herself $33,000 for winning the Masters Class, both in Toronto. In 1992 Tina was shortlisted for the Olympics. She was a member of three Nations Cup teams, including the winning team at Hickstead. She also won the Queen Elizabeth II Cup at the Royal International Horse Show and came second in the Spillers International Cup at the Horse of the Year Show.

CLAIRE TOMLINSON

Claire Tomlinson has held the highest rating ever awarded to a lady polo player (five goals). Born into a polo playing family Tomlinson began playing in earnest at Oxford University. But she also had other sporting interests; she won a Blue for fencing and squash, refusing the chance to train for the Olympics with the English fencing team. After University she worked in Argentina researching fertiliser uses (her degree was in agricultural economics) and gained much good polo experience. Back in England she set up her own polo team with her husband and fought hard for the relaxation of the rule prohibiting women from competing in the highest polo grade. In 1978 her effort paid off and she became the first woman to compete in English high-goal polo. The following year her team won the coveted Queen's Cup. In 1991 she captained the ladies team which won the International Tournament and in 1992 her team won the Warwickshire and the Challenge Cup.

JILL HOLAH

Born in Sheffield Jill Holah grew up surrounded by horses but she did not get seriously interested in competing until her early 20s when she took up driving. She has since won the National Driving Trials Championships nine times with pony singles and pairs and has remained unbeaten in international competitions with her pony pair, winning the Harrods International Driving Grand Prix for the last three years. Her most successful pony has been the Welsh Section B gelding Coed Coch Pippin. A keen driver of many vehicles Jill also holds a Class I HGV licence and drives her own lorry to competitions.

Photograph by Alf Baker

MARY THOMSON

Since 1984 when she won the Boekelo CCI on Divers Rock, thought to be a "horse who would never jump" Mary Thomson has won an astonishing number of titles. She started out in the yard of the famous event rider, Sheila Willcox, and became her cheif rider and groom. In 1986 Mary came first and second at Bramham and first at Osberton. In 1991 she was first in the Osberton Three Day Event, the British Open Championships and Loughanmore CCI. Her team also won the gold in the European Championships. Still on top form in 1992 she won at Bicton, Badminton and Windsor and came ninth on King William, probably her most famous horse, in the Olympic Games, having been in third place for much of the competition.

IRENE BENJAMIN

Irene Benjamin's motto is "have saddle, will travel". She is the best known side-saddle rider in the world. Following a serious accident some years ago Irene was told to prepare herself for paralysis. She refused to submit to this diagnosis and used riding to bring back her muscle strength. She has won countless competitions including in 1991 the prestigious Concurso de la Elegencia at the Championships of Horses of Pure Spanish Race in Seville. She is a professional entertainer on horseback, an instructor and clinician of high calibre. She also finds time to judge, lecture and write on all aspects of side saddle riding and on her specialisation – Iberian breeds.

SHIRLEY ROBERTSON

Shirley Robertson's introduction to sailing at national level came in 1983 when she was invited to join the Scottish Laser squad. By 1986 she was to finish runner-up in the Laser European Championships. In 1988 she realised that she would have to sail a Europe Dinghy in order to compete in the 1992 Olympics and, since there was no history of Europe sailing in the UK, she was forced to do most of her training on the continent, spending many months of each year travelling. Shirley worked her way up through the ranks, finishing fourth in the European rankings at the end of 1991. She qualifed for the British Olympic team, and finished a creditable ninth in Barcelona. Shirley is 24, has a BA(Hons) in recreation and was selected to represent the UK in the World Youth Championships, where she came sixth. Her immediate ambition is to take her Europe dinghy to the 1996 Olympics.

SUE CARR AND DEBBIE JARVIS

Debbie Jarvis (helm) and Sue Carr (crew) started sailing a 470 seriously in 1987. They finished as first British boat in their first international event together, and determined to qualify for the 1988 Olympics. In early 1988 they competed in the Women's World Championships in Brazil, and finished sixth, and subsequently won the Olympic trials in Weymouth. The Seoul Olympics were a bit disappointing, but the "buzz" was there, and they promised themselves they would be there in Barcelona 92. In the intervening years they went their separate ways, but teamed up again in 1992 for regattas in France, Spain, Italy, Holland and Belgium before going to the Games. At Barcelona, the winds refused to blow. Next stop Atlanta!

Photograph by Roger Leon Vercoe

PENNY WAY

Penny Way is the triple World and European Champion in Women's Olympic Windsurfing. She started windsurfing in 1980 and entered her first competition six weeks later, winning her first national title in the following year, and finishing second in Europe. She has since competed in most countries and won World Championships in 1986, 1990 and 1991, and European Championships in 1984 and 1988. Penny has won many awards – she is the current holder of the Yachtsperson of the Year Award and the Sports Aid Foundation Sir John Cohen Memorial Award, awarded "for being an outstanding competitor and ambassador for Britain" throughout sport. She was 1990 Helmsman of the Year, and Windsurfing Personality of the Year 1989, 1990 and 1991. She has been awarded the Most Outstanding Personality of the Year Award by the BJC. Penny entered the 1992 Olympics as the assured favourite, but the equipment (supplied by the organisers) broke up on her, and she came an agonising sixth. She has written three successful books, and made a video for beginners. Penny is coached by husband Rod Andrews, the Olympic sailing coach.

PENNY TYLER

Penny Tyler is Britain's and the RYA's No. 2 ranked lady windsurfer, 1992. Her first experience of windsurfing was on holiday in 1982, she bought her first board in 1986, and entered her first competition in 1988. By 1989 she had won her first national title, the RYA Ladies National Championship. In 1990 she retained that title, and also won the British Funboard Association National Series. In 1991 she retained both of these and added the UK Boardsailing Association National Raceboard Series Championship. She turned to

international competition, and came second in the European Championships and third in the World Raceboard Championships in 1991, and third in 1992.

PENNY MOUNTFORD

Penny Mountford is 17, and at school in Stourbridge studying for A levels in physics, chemistry, pure maths and applied maths. She is also the British Girls Youth Single Handed Dinghy Sailor. She started sailing at the age of six in an Optimist, and at the age of nine captured her first British title. At 12, she moved into the Topper class, and won many Opens and titles, including Topper Ladies Champion, which she has held for a number of years, and the RYA Women's Champion. On her 15th birthday, she borrowed her father's Laser and entered the British Youth Regatta, where she won the girls' single handed title,

Photograph by Peter Bentley

TITCH BLACHFORD

Titch Blachford has won the British Ladies Keelboat Championship seven times, five times in J24s and twice, in 1991 and 1992, in the Channel Handicap Division. During 1990 she was invited to compete in the Royal Lymington Cup, the British match racing event on the World Grand Prix circuit. Titch is currently First Class 8 Ladies European Champion. She has been shortlisted for the Silk Cut Nautical Awards Helmsman of the Year twice and, in 1992, was a finalist in the Cosmopolitan Magazine Achievement Awards. Also during 1992, she was tactician and second helmsman for "Sunstripper", a 47ft yacht selected for the English team in the RORC's Commodore's Cup.

Photograph by Max

EMILY SAUNDERSON AND ALISON HAKES

Emily and Alison teamed up in the 420 class in 1990. In September 1991, they were placed fourth in the RYA's National Championships, and gained selection for the UK team for the 1992 Youth World Championships in Portugal. They came seventh overall, winning race seven. They were then selected, with Amy Burgess, to represent England in the UK SSA Nations Cup, in a Sonata. They won the Endeavour Cup, and England won the overall competition.

CORDELIA EGLIN

Cordelia Eglin was born in London in 1968 and is an architectural student. She started sailing at four, on her parents' boat, and graduated to crewing and then helming Cadets, on the Thames and at Frensham Pond. She sailed Cadets internationally and with the British youth squad, and progressed into the British Women's sailing team in 420s and 470s. She won the British Women's Keelboat Championships in 1988, was runner-up in 1989, and was the first British woman in 1992 in her J24.

ALISON WILLIAMSON

Twenty-year old Alison Williamson had a head start in the world of archery. Both her parents were coaches in the sport and she picked up her first bow at the age of seven. She was representing her country at 13 and to date she has broken over 30 British records in junior and senior categories. She picked up a silver medal at the European Championships in Malta earlier this year, a good warm-up for the Olympics, where she finished seventh with two new British records.

Photograph by Miriam Stuart

FIONA McINTOSH

Fiona McIntosh manages to juggle a career as a teacher – she has a job as Head of Geography at a London college – and a life of National and Open fencing tournaments. She won her first British title at 15, the day before becoming the youngest ever winner of the Scottish Open Championships. She is the current Commonwealth Women's Foil Champion and is presently ranked eighth in the world following the Barcelona Olympics where she was the first British woman since 1956 to make the final.

GAIL CURRY

Gail Curry discovered croquet by accident in 1987 when she bought a cheap garden set and unravelled its Chinese rules. She soon abandoned it when she joined a local croquet club. Since then she has competed in tournaments countrywide and has won six major titles. She was the Barlow Bowl winner for three years running, in 1990, 1991 and 1992, the British Women's Champion in1991 and 1992 and the British Mixed Doubles Champion in 1992. She now works as a child care residential officer at a special school in Newcastle, where her Chinese set is still in use and much loved.

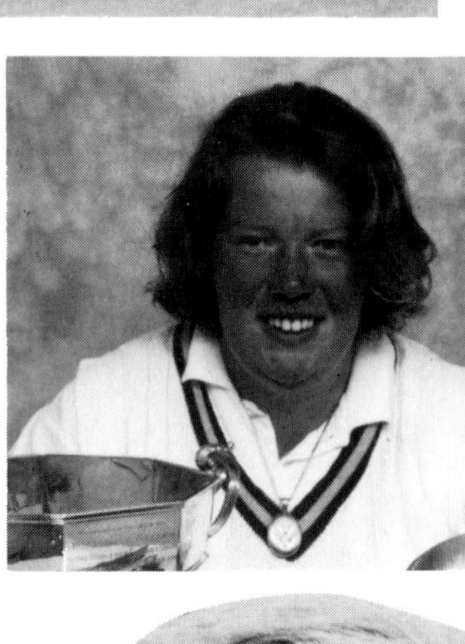

MARGARET JOHNSTON, MBE

The pinnacle of Margaret Johnston's bowling career was being presented with the MBE in 1991 for services to bowls for Northern Ireland. Her first taste of the sport was at a short mat bowls club organised by her local church in Northern Ireland some 30 years ago. This very popular Irish game gave her a sound foundation for indoor and outdoor bowling. She has won a glut of awards including, most recently, the Outdoor Singles and Pairs Gold Medals in the World Bowls in Scotland for 1992.

ANN SHEPHERD

Ann Shepherd is a library assistant for Cheshire County Council who took up archery 11 years ago at the age of 24. She still works for the library but has managed to fit in numerous tournaments at home and abroad. Five times British champion she has qualified as Grand Master bowman every year since 1986 and was made the first ever Ladies Compound World Champion in 1990.

Photograph by Alan Taylor

KAREN JOHNSTONE

Karen Johnstone got into crown green bowling through her parents, who played for a local club team. She achieved her first major win at Linthwaite Hall in Huddersfield when she was 16. One year later she was presented with the Ladies Waterloo Trophy, the premier event in ladies bowls. She repeated that success in 1992, the only woman to do so. Her ambition is to win this trophy a third time next year.

PAT DAVIES

Pat Davies is an outstanding crown green bowls player. She is the only woman to have won the British Parks All England Championships three times. She is also the only woman to have won the Capstan Challenge Cup in Colwyn Bay, held by a man for some 50 years. In 1990 she won 14 tournaments and in 1991 she won ten. 1992 found her winning nine tournaments including three of the major titles – the Spen Victoria Spring Classic, the Bass Talbot Trophy and the Scarisbrick Hotel Southport Flower Show.

SARAH GOURLAY

A part-time secretary from Scotland, Sarah Gourlay started bowling when she was 27. Only four years after taking up the game she won the Scottish Outdoor National Pairs Championship and since then she has won an amazing number of titles in both indoor and outdoor bowling. She has represented Scotland in three World Championships (in 1984, 1988 and 1992) and won the Team Gold Medal and World Indoor Singles in 1992.

HAYLEY ALLEN

Hayley Allen's international diving career started four years ago when she was 13. In 1989 she won the silver medal in the World Age Group Games on the springboard and the bronze on the highboard. In the following year, at 14, she was selected for the England senior team. She became national highboard champion in 1991, and was selected for the Barcelona Olympic Games, largely for experience, but her performance on the highboard exceeded all expectations, when she became the first Briton to qualify for the final for 28 years. She is a serious medal prospect for Atlanta.

SHARRON DAVIES

Britain's most successful all round female swimmer, Sharron Davies was born in Plymouth in 1962. At 13 she was the youngest member of the 1976 Olympic team, and was a double gold medallist in the 1978 Commonwealth Games. In 1980 she won the silver medal at the Moscow Olympics in the individual medley then retired. She returned to international swimming in 1989, after a nine year break, and won the silver and bronze at the Commonwealth Games in 1990, where she was ladies' captain. She was placed third, fifth and sixth in the World Cup in 1992, and broke and re-broke twice the 200m individual medley record and broke her own 12-year-old 400m record. In all, Sharon has held over 200 British records, been British champion 28 times and Sportswoman of the Year twice. She now works in media, fashion and business, as well as training three to four hours a day.

LINDA SHARP

Reigning British surfing champion, a title which she has held nine times since 1975, Linda Sharp has a background of competitive swimming (Welsh age group champion) and competitive life-saving (British surf live-saving champion). She has been surfing competitively for 21 years, and first won the Welsh title in 1971 – she has won it 17 times since – and won the European Championships in 1975 and 1979. She was appointed secretary general of the European Surfing Federation in 1992, and has been secretary of the Welsh Federation since 1981. A physical education teacher, Linda will be happy to be still surfing when she retires.

SUE KEY

Sue Key started rowing in 1983 as a pleasant way of spending time on the river, and for the social life. Nine years later she is still hooked on what turned out to be one of the hardest all round sports, and the social life has gone out of the window. She has competed in America, Australia, Canada and Europe, taken part in four World Rowing Championships, and won the silver medal in the lightweight (under 59kg) women's coxless four in 1989 and the silver medal in 1992 in the lightweight women's single skull in Montreal. The rigorous training involved in maintaining this standard of excellence is fitted in between her career as a senior economic development officer at Wandsworth Borough Council.

WENDY NOTT-BOWER

Wendy Nott-Bower is Britain's jet-ski champion 1991-92. She was the only British woman to qualify for the 1992 World Championships by coming fourth in the Europeans, and came an historic second place having led for five of the ten laps. Now aged 33 Wendy is a community staff nurse and lives in Dorset.

PHILIPPA ROBERTS

There is not room to list the titles won by Philippa Roberts since she started waterskiing in 1974 at the age of 14 but, in 1992, she won the European Slalom, and was overall champion; the French Masters Slalom; the Italian Masters Overall Championship; the European Tour Slalem Championship; the British Jump and Overall Championship (for the tenth time). She won the silver medal in the European Slalom Championship; the British bronze in the Jump Championships. As the record of a full-time professional this would be impressive; for a full time doctor and accomplished musician, it is astounding.

Photograph by Simon Roberts

KERRY SHACKLOCK

Kerry Shacklock is the national solo, duet and team synchronised swimming champion. Born in 1971 she first represented England in 1986, and Great Britain in 1987, when she became national junior champion. In 1988 she was Scandinavian solo, duet and team champion, and bronze medallist in the Junior Olympic Games. She first won the national title in 1989, and in 1990 won silver medals in solo and duet. She competed in the European Championships in 1991, and the Olympics in 1992, when she also came second in the Europa Cup, and became French Open champion.

SHELLEY NUTT

Shelley Nutt's father, John Doherty, is in the Guinness Book of Records for the British record for barefoot waterskiing endurance, and it seemed natural for Shelley to follow him into the sport. In 1977, at the age of 13, she was picked for the British team, and won the European Championship that year, and again in 1979. A knee injury kept her out of action for five years, but in 1984 she won the National Championship, and has retained it ever since. She won the European Challenge series in 1985, and held it for five years, and in 1986 won the gold medal for jump at the World Championships. Shelley holds the European record for slalom and tricks, and has joined her father in the Guinness Book of Records for breaking the forward and backward ladies speed record.

Photograph by Steve Wheeler

DEBBIE CAPENER

Debbie Capener was born in Widnes in 1968, and has always been a keen sportswoman. She took up Aikido at the age of 17 as a method of keep-fit as well as self-defence, but quickly found the competitive element addictive. Within four years, she had become national champion. She gained her 1st Dan at 21, and her 2nd Dan at 24, and has been European champion for the last three years. In 1992 she entered the World International in Cardiff, and won the silver medal. In 1993 she will be travelling to Japan, as part of the British squad, for the next World International. Debbie lives in Widnes and works as PA to the managing director of a design engineering company.

"BEAUTIFUL" PRINCESS PAULA

Princess Paula was born in the Carribean, but is now based in Manchester. She was introduced to wrestling by Cowboy Jack Cassidy, who trained her. She has wrestled all over the world, and is famous for her TV appearance as the very vociferous manager of husband Fit Finlay. Paula is a great showperson, always entering the ring in a head-dress and silver sequined dressing gown, but is also a fine wrestler, having won both the British and European Championships.

SANDRA MOORE

Sandra Moore is the youngest ever woman to be rated No. 1 in the world by the international Muay Thai Association, the governing body for Thai boxing. In 1984, at the age of nine, she was the youngest person ever to be awarded the Mongkon (sacred Headband). At the age of 11 she was the youngest to achieve the red armband and, in 1990, she was Britain's youngest champion. Sandra is a student and lives in Manchester.

VANDA FAIRCHILD

Vanda Fairchild, 3rd Dan, is one of the British Aikido Association's top women performers. Based at the Elephant and Castle Club, she has practised Aikido since the age of 11, and has been British individual champion three times. Now 26, Vanda is ranked third in the world, behind team-mate Debbie Capener, and is a vital member of the British team.

NICOLA FAIRBROTHER

Nik Fairbrother started at the Pinewood Judo Club at the age of eight. She progressed under the guidance of coach, Don Werner, until finally making the British squad in 1985, in fourth position. It was then she decided that she wanted to be World Champion, an ambition which she is still training towards. 1992 was a great year for Nik. She won the European Championship and then the Olympic silver medal in Barcelona, something she will remember for ever. However, her ultimate ambition will have to wait for Atlanta, Georgia, 1996. Nik lives in Surrey and works as a journalist in Reading.

Photograph by Bob Willingham

MOLLY SAMUEL

Molly Samuel was born in 1961 and is indisputably the best Karate fighter that Britain has ever produced. She currently holds the English, British, Commonwealth, European and World Cup titles. She has held the European title for four years and the World Cup for two. In addition to these individual achievements, Molly is the Women's National Coach, the only female coach in Europe. The team is currently champion of Europe for the second year. In 1989 Mollie was voted Sunday Times International Sportswoman of the Year. Molly is a full-time athlete.

MARY PUGSLEY

Target rifle shooter Mary Pugsley was educated at Imperial College, London, where she gained an honours degree in Zoology. She went on to take her PhD at the London Hospital Medical College and, until 1989, was a senior lecturer in medical microbiology at University College, London. She started shooting at University and shot for Surrey through the 1980s. Following an "eventful" tour of Australia in 1988 with the Great Britain Ladies' Rifle Team, when she met John Pugsley, whom she married in 1990, now shoots for Devon. She has represented England in the National and Mackinnon matches at Bisley, and, in 1991, shot for Great Britain in Canada when seven months pregnant. In 1990, she was the first woman to win a major prize at Bisley, the Donegall, since the war. She won the Grand Aggregate at Bisley in 1992 and, with husband John, the Fulton Pairs. Now aged 40, Mary enjoys game shooting and stalking as well as target rifle shooting. She and John rely on each other for baby-sitting and, at Bisley in 1992, there was much time spent swapping baby for rifle and vice-versa.

JEANETTE FORD

Having always fished as a child, Jeanette Ford was taught fly fishing and tying by her husband, Richard, 16 years ago. She learned on what she considers to be the best still waters in England, Chew and Blagdon Lake. The only lady ever to qualify for the England National competition, she had now done so seven times. She has fished for the Ladies International team since its foundation five years ago and, last year, won the Ladies National at Draycote, with 13 fish caught on dry fly. Jeanette's favourite fishing is riverbank fishing for wild brown trout or grayling.

ANN OLIVER

Farmer's wife Ann Oliver is the English Ladies Fishing Team captain for 1993. She started fishing some 12 years ago on a small lake at Skegness and, since then, has fished many reservoirs, including Rutland, Grafham, Draycote and Bewl, in England, and also many in Scotland, Ireland and Wales. She has been in the English team since its inception and her favourite style of fishing is the floating line. The most fish Ann has caught in a season is 758.

DENISE EYRE

Denise Eyre started shooting in 1980, at the age of 20. She changed from skeet and English sporting to Fitasc sporting in 1984, the year she married and, whilst on honeymoon, won the World Championship. Since then, she has added an extraordinary number of trophies amongst them: 1985, European Championship bronze medal; 1986, European Champion, English Open Champion, British Fitasc Champion; 1987, World Champion, British Fitasc Champion; 1989, World Champion, European Champion, EEC Grand Prix; 1990, French Champion, Belgian Champion, World Cup and World Championship silver medal.

JEANETTE TAYLOR

Jeanette Taylor, 42, started fly fishing some 12 years ago and her own fly tying business three years ago. She has fished for the Ladies International Team for the five years of its existence and is chairman of the Ladies' Fly Fishing Association. Jeanette has fished for several years in European matches and last year was a member of the team which won the French leg of the championship and came fourth overall; she came sixth as an indivudual. Teamed with Nicola Church, she came third in the Leeda Pairs event in 1992, out of 120 anglers, and won the individual prize. She led the team which won the Ladies International trophy at Rutland, in 1992, and won the individual there as well. Jeanette's heaviest fish to date is a 10lb rainbow trout.

ANTHEA HILLYER

Born in Somerset in 1951, Anthea Hillyer left school in 1968 and worked for a bank for 12 years. She took clay pigeon shooting lessons at the Blandford & Dorchester Gun Club in the early 1970s and, since then, her shooting career has been success all the way. Her first major title was the Ladies' English Open Sporting Championship, which she has now won eight times. She has also been Ladies' British Open Sporting Champion five times, All Round Shot of Great Britain three times, European Fitasc Champion twice, World Fitasc Champion six times and Beretta World Champion three times. In 1983, she won eight major world, European, British and English titles, and set the record score of 88/100 in the English Open Sporting Championship. She has been a member of the Great Britain Fitasc Sporting Team since 1980.

DEANNA COATES

Crackshot Di Coates started shooting in 1981, when she joined Rushmore Mallards. She won two silver medals and a bronze at the 1988 Paralympics in Seoul and had a particularly good games in Barcelona 1992, when she won the gold medal in the 40 shot standing event and came fourth in the 4 x 40. Di's favoured weapon is a Feinwerkbau .177 air rifle. A great all-rounder and incredibly fit, Di coaches young shooters and sets up tournaments to encourage new people to enter the sport. Restricted to a wheelchair, Di lives in Camberley and works as a VDU operator.

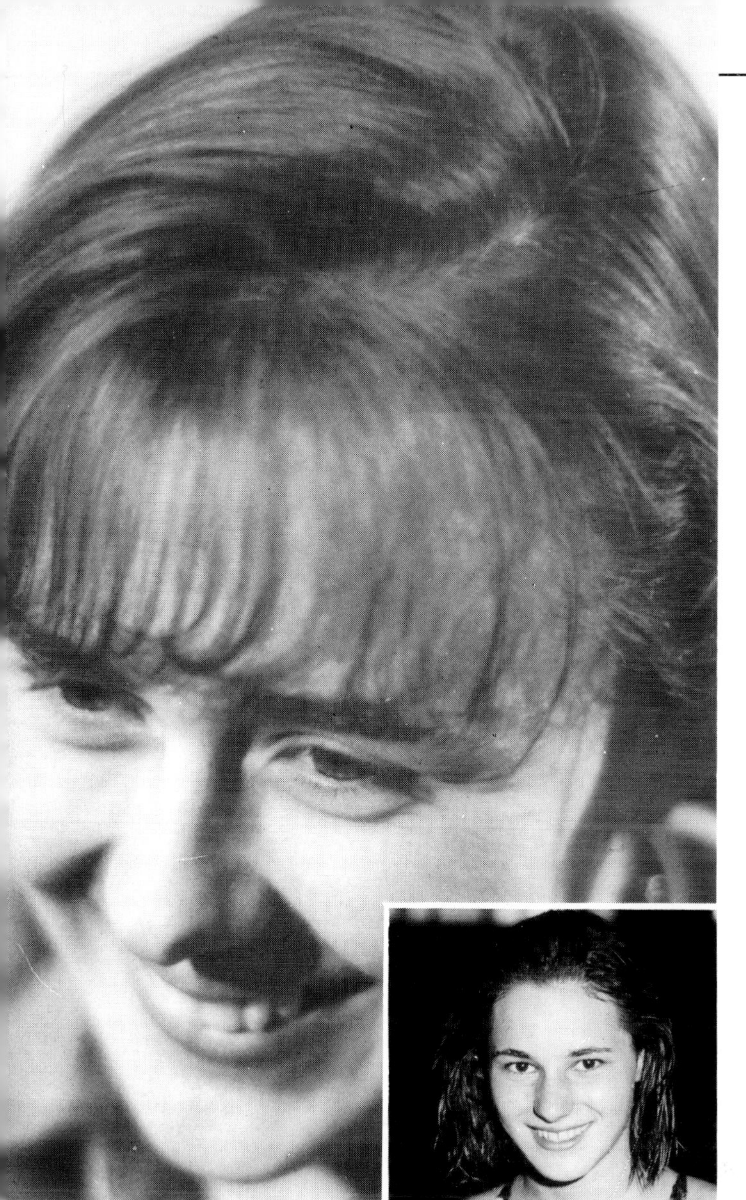

TANNI GREY

Ranked as the fastest wheelchair athlete in the world, within her classification, 23 year old Tanni Grey's achievements are outstanding. In the 1992 Paralympic Games in Barcelona she won gold medals in all her events, the 100, 200, 400 and 800 metres, setting a new world record in the 100m. In 1991 she won the Yardley Gold & Daily Express Award, competing alongside able-bodied men and women, which reflected her earlier successes, including her two gold medals in the World Wheelchair Games in the same year. She has twice competed in the London Marathon, but makes no secret of her preference for the track. Tanni now feels that her level of dedication to sport is beginning to be recognised.

SARAH BAILEY

Born in 1977, swimmer Sarah Bailey took part in her first Paralympic Games, in the "les autres" category, in Barcelona 1992. She won gold medals in both the 100m backstroke and the 200m medley, both in new world record times, silver in the 400m freestyle and the 4 x 100 medley and bronze in the 100m freestyle. A pupil at Poynton High School, Cheshire, her passion for swimming started when she was four years old and she trains, on average, 15 hours a week. Sarah competes at top able-bodied meetings with outstanding success and is surely destined for a brilliant career on the international swimming circuit.

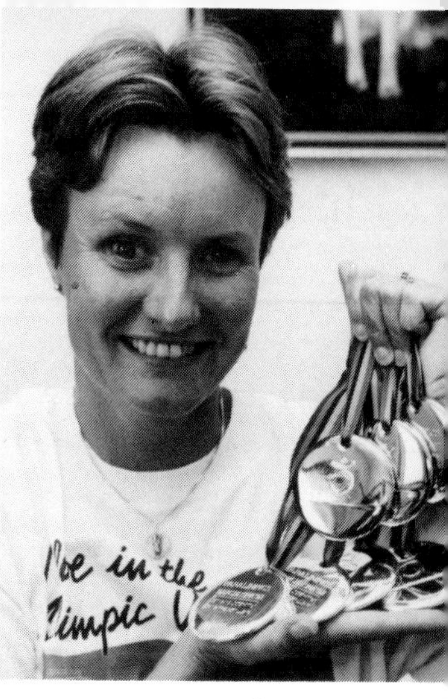

JANICE BURTON

An outstanding all-round athlete, 34 year old Paralympic swimmer Janice Burton is totally blind. Before going to Barcelona for the 1992 games, she already had accumulated 39 international medals and 11 Paralympic medals, including gold in 1984 and 1988. In Barcelona Janice won three golds, in the 100m backstroke, 200m medley and 50m freestyle and four silver medals. In addition to her unparalleled achievements in the swimming pool, Janice has a RDA gold for horsemanship and completed the 1989 Potteries Marathon. An exceptional cook, Janice lives in Stoke-on-Trent, where she is a housewife.

TARA FLOOD

Always an animated spokesperson for Paralympic sport, Tara Flood had already won a bronze medal at the Seoul Paralympics when she went to Barcelona in 1992. She came home from Barcelona with a gold medal for the 50m breast stroke, a silver for the 100m freestyle and bronze for the 50m freestyle. Affected by Thalidomide at birth, Tara works as a security officer, and her hobbies include skydiving, diving, travel, sub-aqua diving and dancing.

CAROLINE INNES

Eighteen year old athlete Caroline Innes suffers from cerebral palsy. Before the 1992 Paralympics, sprinter Caroline had already notched up five gold and two silver medals in international competition. Her performances in Barcelona were truly inspirational. In the 200m her class was combined and so she found herself competing against people of lesser disability. Nevertheless, Caroline managed to produce a personal best time. In the 100m she set the track alight and proved herself the fastest woman in the world, taking the gold medal. Caroline, whose hobbies include music, reading and swimming, is a student and voluntary worker with special needs children.

SHARON BOLTON

Sharon Bolton is an exceptionally talented and disciplined athlete and a key member of Highgate Harriers Athletics Club, where she is a high point scorer in able-bodied league events despite her partial sight. She won gold medals in the 100m and 200m events in both the 1990 World Championships and the 1991 European Championships, and in her first Paralympic Games in 1992, she won bronze in both these events and silver in the 400m with a personal best time. Twenty-seven year old Sharon has to be favourite for at least one gold at Aspen in 1996.

BEVERLEY GULL

Swimmer Beverley Gull was the holder of three Paralympic gold medals from Seoul and five from the 1991 World Wheelchair Games, when she went to Barcelona 1992, at the age of 39, and won four silver medals and a bronze. During a long and distinguished career, Beverley has won the Thames TV and National Sports Writers Association Sports Personality of the Year Award four times. A wife and mother of two, Beverley works as an administration officer and finds time to coach mentally handicapped swimmers, as well as fit in her own gruelling training.

CLARE BISHOP

At the age of 15, swimmer Clare Bishop is one of the most promising newcomers to Paralympic sport. Despite being an amputee her natural ability to streak through the water astounds her coach, Len Bell, at the Hillingdon Borough Swimming Club and has inspired other young Paralympians who swim with her. In her first Paralympic Games in 1992, Clare won the 50m freestyle and set a new world record, and won silver in the 100m backstroke, 100m freestyle, 4 x 100 medley and 4 x 100 freestyle. "She never complains about getting ready for training. She is totally committed to doing her very best for Britain and I just can't tell you how proud I am of her," says Clare's father.

ESTHER CRUICE

Now just 16 years old, cerebral palsy sufferer Esther Cruice was one of Britain's top sprinters at the 1992 Paralympic Games when she stormed home to win the gold in the 400m, in a new world record time. She also took silver in the 100m and 200m. She had previously won gold at all these distances in the CP Sport National Games and the BSAD Junior Games. A lively personality, whose hobbies include riding, netball, umpiring and hockey, Esther is poised to win many more sporting accolades.

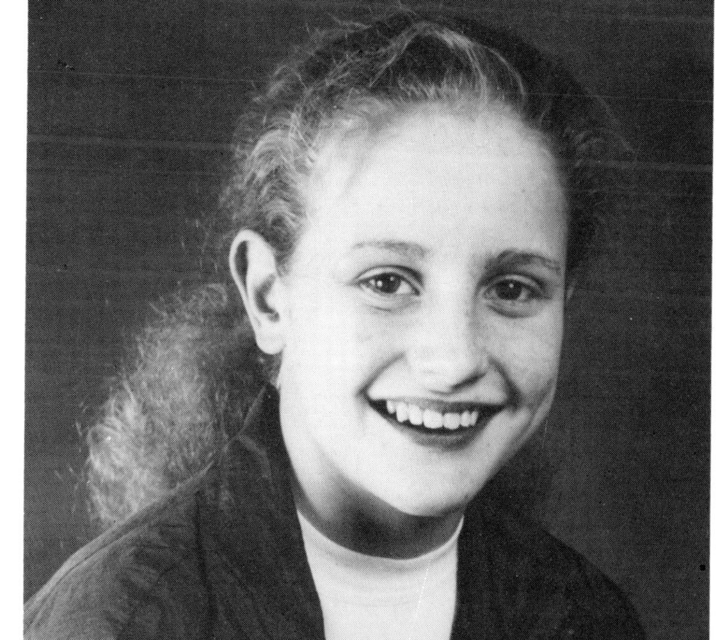

JULIE HILL

Julie Hill is the current director of Green Alliance, an organisation she joined, as administrator in 1985 after a period with the World Food Assembly. She is a member of the Government's Advisory Committee on Release to the Environment (of genetically modified organisms), a member of the board of the Pesticides Trust and of the Advisory Committee of the Environmental Law Foundation. In 1990 she co-authored Ethics, Environment and the Company, and in 1992 a follow-up report entitled Towards Good Environmental Practice.

FIONA REYNOLDS

Fiona Reynolds was educated at Rugby School for Girls and Cambridge University, where she was awarded an MPhil in Land Economy. In 1987, after seven years with the Council for National Parks, she was appointed Assistant Policy Director to the Council for the Protection of Rural England, becoming Director in 1992. The recipient of the United Nations Environment Programme's Global 500 award for outstanding achievement in protection and improvement of the environment, Ms Reynolds is respected in Whitehall and at Westminster. Her other interests include reading, music and opera.

VIRGINIA McKENNA

Virginia McKenna's initial love was acting, and she gained her first professional experience immediately after leaving drama school in 1949 with the Dundee Repertory Theatre. Her television debut came in 1951 and has continued ever since, with appearances far too numerous to mention. Her roles in animal films such as Ring of Bright Water and Born Free reflected a passion for animals and the environment that led, in 1984, to the formation of Zoo Check, a charitable trust dedicated to preventing abuse of captive wild animals which she co-founded with her husband, Bill Travers. In the last three years she has led a number of safaris to India and Africa helping to promote Zoo Check's work in protecting threatened habitats and species.

SARA PARKIN

A trained nurse who has practised in Scotland, England and France, Sara Parkin joined the Green Party in 1977. She was International Liaison Secretary from 1983 to 1990 and from 1985 to 1990 was co-secretary of the European Greens, a coordinating body for Greens from 24 countries. She is an advisor to the Engineering Council's Working Party on the Environment and speaks frequently on various aspects of green politics on television and radio both here and abroad. She was co-author of the Green Party's 1987 and 1989 manifesto and has written several books on ecological issues.

Photograph by Georges Mollon

FIONA McCONNELL, CBE

Following an early career as a scriptwriter and editor in the film and TV business, Fiona McConnell joined the newly formed Department of the Environment in 1971 where she worked on inner city policy, regional planning and international transport. She was head of the department's International Division for ten years, during which time she headed the British negotiations for the Montreal Protocol (which she signed for the UK in 1987) and for the Biodiversity Convention. She has served on numerous EC and UN environmental bodies, was chair of the OECD Environment Committee from 1986 to 1989 and is a member of the United Nations Environmental Programme's Senior Women's Advisory Group. She was appointed CBE in 1990. Ms McConnell is also an advisor to the Natural History Museum and a lecturer on international environmental negotiations at Imperial College.

TESSA TENNANT ↓

Since 1981 Tessa Tennant has progressed from voluntary work for The Green Alliance to her present position as head of the Merlin Research Unit and director of the investment management company, Jupiter Tyndall Merlin. She founded the UK's first environmental unit trust in 1988 following experience of socially responsible investment in the United States. She is a member of numerous environmental organisations and is a trustee to the Calvert World Values Fund, one of America's first socially responsible investment funds. In 1992 she was awarded an Honorary Fellowship by the University of Dundee for her work in the field of green investment.

JEAN LAMBERT ↑

After gaining a degree in Modern Languages from University College, Cardiff, Jean Lambert trained as a secondary school teacher, a profession which she practised for the next 15 years in various schools around East London. Convinced that ecological problems required political solutions, she joined the Green Party in 1977 and held a number of positions, including co-chair, her current role being that of principal female speaker. She has been a candidate at local, national and European elections, was a member of the Hansard Commission on Election Guidelines in 1992 and is a founder member of the Ecology Building society. Ms Lambert is an avid reader of detective fiction and loathes housework.

JANET BARBER ↑

Janet Barber was born and brought up on a farm in the Cotswolds. She worked for the BBC, Vogue and The Times before joining the World Wide Fund for Nature in 1972 and receiving a fellowship to explore the impact of the population increase on natural resources in Central America. In 1989 she was awarded the Order of the Golden Ark for services to conservation. She is on the council of the Government's advisory body on nature conservation, English Nature, and is currently director of UK Programmes at the World Wide Fund as well as a contributor to the organisation's international policy.

JULIE HAILES

As co-author of the best-selling Green Consumer guide, Julie Hailes was instrumental in the launch of green consumerism during the late 1980s. The author of several other books including Holidays that Don't Cost the Earth and The Green Business Guide, Ms Hailes is also active in environmental auditing, management briefing and environmental strategy and communications. She sits on the UK Eco-Labelling board, the UK United Nations Environmental Programme Committee and the UK Packaging Committee. A regular speaker at conferences, she has also made numerous radio and television appearances both in Britain and abroad, including a weekly series of programmes about the environment for British network television. Ms Hailes is currently joint founder/director of the environmental consultants, SustainAbility. In 1989 she received a United Nations Global 500 Roll of Honour award and in 1992 was elected to their Inaugural Council.

BERNADETTE VALLELY

Bernadette Vallely is the director and co-founder of the Women's Environmental Network, an organisation that works to empower women who are concerned about the environment, and which has mounted innovative and successful campaigns against, amongst other things, bleached paper and excess packaging. A consultant for many environmental organisations, including Greenpeace, Bernadette has also worked for Friends of the Earth and the Anti-Apartheid Movement. She is the author of several books including, 1001 Ways to Save the Planet and has made numerous television and radio appearances speaking on a wide range of environmental issues.

DIANA SCHUMACHER

After reading history at Oxford, Diana Schumacher worked for the British Council and for the University of Chicago, developing her interest in the four Es: energy, economics, education and environment; the basics of a holistic approach to ecology. She has been involved in the national and international environmental movement since the early 1970s and as well as being a prolific writer on the subject, is a founder member, trustee, or on the steering committee of over 20 environmental organisations. She is currently a partner in Schumacher Projects, a management consultancy specialising in work restructuring.

DIANNA MELROSE

Born in Zimbabwe and educated at St Catherine's School, Bramley, Dianna Melrose went on to take a degree in modern languages and an MA in Latin Ameican studies at London University. After a spell working in the City and for the British Council she joined Oxfam in 1980 where she is currently Public Policy Director. Her publications include The Great Health Robbery; Nicaragua – the Threat of a Good Example; Bitter Pills – Medicines and the Third World Poor. Her work at Oxfam embraces a wide range of North/South and international development issues including environment and development, trade, debt, aid and geopolitical issues relating to the horn of Africa, Namibia and Southern Africa. Ms Melrose is also a member of Oxfam's Overseas Programme Senior Management Team.

FIONA JACOBS

Born into a Suffolk farming family, Fiona Jacobs began a chiropractic course in Bournemouth when she was 19 years old. She graduated as Best Student four years later and started her own private practice in Bury St Edmunds. Further experience was gained at a practice in Peterborough. In 1991, aged 30, she moved her own practice to larger premises and the Bury St Edmunds Chiropractic Clinic now employs two other professionals. She has always been keen on sport and attended the International Triathlon in Canterbury in 1987, Women's World Weightlifting Championships in Manchester in 1989 and the fifth All-African Games in Cairo in 1991 (as part of medical support teams). In 1991 she qualified as a certified chiropractic sports physican and has chaired the British Association's sports committee since 1990. She remains active in local sporting events and is married with a young son.

MARY CLEGG

For 35 years Mary Clegg has been working with children who have a neurological deficit and who are delayed in their development, most with cerebral pasly. She is the co-author of Cerebral Palsy Problems and Practice, published in 1988 with a second edition due in 1993. She is Course Director of the University of Central England in Birmingham and was closely involved in the development of the course which leads to the advanced certificate in paediatric phsyiotherapy, the first of its kind to hold an academic qualification. She is also Head of the Paediatric Phsyiotherapy service for Leicestershire Health Authority, working in hospitals and in the community. She was National Chairman of the Association of Paediatric Chartered Phsyiotherapy from 1990-92 and was elected President of the Leicestershire branch of Chartered Phsysiotherapists in 1992. Mary is married with two sons and lives in a farmhouse in Shropshire.

VIVIAN GRISOGONO

In the world of sporting physiotherapy, no name is better known that Vivian Grisogono's. Her work with athletes and her widely-read books and magazine articles have guaranteed her prominence within the profession. When war broke out in the former Yugoslavia, she became involved in humanitarian work, producing a report on victim priorities on behalf of the United Nations. After qualifying as a chartered physiotherapist, she specialised in sports injuries and in 1978 set up the first full-time clinic within a national sports centre – at Crystal Palace, London. She was the British team physio at the 1977 World Student Games, 1978 Commonwealth Games and 1980 Olympics. She lectures on sports injuries, writes for the Sports Council publication Sport and Leisure, and often appears on TV. Her books, which include Sports Injuries: A Self-Help Guide and Children And Sport, are essential reading. She has been in private practice since 1978 and is currently head of the physiothrapy department at the Royal Masonic Hospital.

Photograph by Andrew Sceats

LORRAINE de SOUZA

It was Lorraine de Souza's interest in neurological disabilities that led her to train as a chartered physiotherapist (at Newcastle-upon-Tyne). Most of her research work has been in the field of disability and rehabilitation in multiple sclerosis. She is author of several publications in this area. Born in 1955 she gained a Bsc(Hons) in anatomy at Bristol University and later an MSc in neurophysiology. She has been closely involved with the charity Action and Research for Multiple Sclerosis (ARMS), developing and co-ordinating phsyiotherapy services through the national branch network. She was manager of the interdisciplinary research and clinical team at the MS unit during the time it was funded by ARMS. She is now Director of Postgraduate Physiotherapy Studies at the West London Institute in Isleworth, Middlesex. In 1991 she was awarded a Fellowship of the Chartered Society of Physiotherapy in recognition of her work. She includes horticulture, travel and the Arts among her interests.

FIONA WALSH

Fiona Walsh is a member of a London group practice with a special interest in dance injuries. She has been consultant osteopath to the Central School of Ballet and travelled with London Festival Ballet (now English National Ballet) on provincial tours. Unlike her sporting counterparts who can run on to the field of play when a mishap occurs, she has to work on a "running repairs" basis, treating dancers between scenes. The most difficult aspect of her job – rare, thankfully – is having to persuade an enthusiastic young dancer that their body is just not suited to the rigours of professional ballet. Born in 1953 Fiona graduated from the British School of Osteopathy and became a member of the General Council and Register of Osteopaths in 1977. She is Principal Clinic Tutor at the BSO and a member of the Polytechnic of Central London (now University of Westminster) Degree Validation panel. Her leisure interests include ballet (of course), opera, golf, skiing and good wines.

AUDREY SMITH (LADY PERCIVAL)

It would not be amiss to call Audrey Smith an elder stateswoman among osteopaths. Now well past the age at which women officially retire in other professions, she continues to lead the field. In fact, she took on a new lease of life as recently as 1990 when she married businessman and one-time Under Secretary at the Board of Trade Sir Anthony Percival and became Lady Percival. Born in 1929 Audrey was educated at Bromley County Grammar School for Girls and the British School of Osteopathy where she qualified with the Dorothy Wood Gold Medal in 1951. She was personal assistant to the principal from 1959-62 and became vice-principal and Head of Faculty from 1962-86. She was the school's Director from 1968-86 and in private practice since then. She was Designer of a BSc course for Victoria, Australia, in 1979 and this was accepted by Philip Institute of Technology, Melbourne. She was President of the British Osteopathic Association of Great Britain from 1964-65 and given the J. M. Littlejohn award for services to the profession in 1980. She is an Honorary Life Member of the Australian Osteopathic Association and Honorary Fellow of the British School of Osteopathy. She is the author of ten papers in British journals. Her hobbies include walking her dog, gardening, fundraising and music.

DR CATHERINE GEISSLER

After qualifying and working as a dentist in her native Edinburgh, Dr Catherine Geissler undertook dental and nutrition research at the University of California at Berkeley, where she later gained her PhD. Having developed an interest in the nutrition problems of developing countries, she worked in Africa, the Caribbean, the Middle East and Asia. In 1976 she joined the Department of Nutrition and Dietetics of Queen Elizabeth College, now King's College, University of London, becoming Head of Department in 1990 after a year as Visiting Professor at the USA's Cornell University. Her studies include individual variations in energy expenditure related to obesity, leanness and energy requirements, and aspects of nutrition policy in developing countries throughout the world. She is a consultant to the FAO, World Bank, British Council and French and Iranian development consultancy companies.

CAROLE MIDDLETON

Carole Middleton, who graduated with an honours degree in food science and physiology from Leeds University in 1975, has been Chief Dietitian at the city's St. James's University Hospital since 1988, before which she was the hospital's Senior Dietitian, Renal Disease from 1985 to 1988. Her current interests are nutrition and dietetics related to liver disease, particularly post liver transplantation and intensive care. She has been actively involved in the British Dietetic Association since 1978, and among her current offices is Honorary Chairmanship of the Association.

ANN PRENTICE

Ann Prentice is Senior Scientist and Head of the Micronutrient Group at the Medical Research Council's Dunn Nutrition Unit at Cambridge. Educated at the Universities of Oxford, Surrey and Cambridge, she worked for the Dunn Nutrition Unit in the Gambia from 1978 to 1983, and since 1984 has been based at Cambridge. Her research interests are human bone and mineral metabolism; nutrient requirements for human growth, pregnancy and lactation, and old age; human lactational physiology and breast-milk composition; and developing world nutrition. She is a member of many organisations in her field, including the Register of Accredited Nutritionists, the British Nutrition Society, the American Society of Clinical Nutrition and the Society for International Nutrition Research.

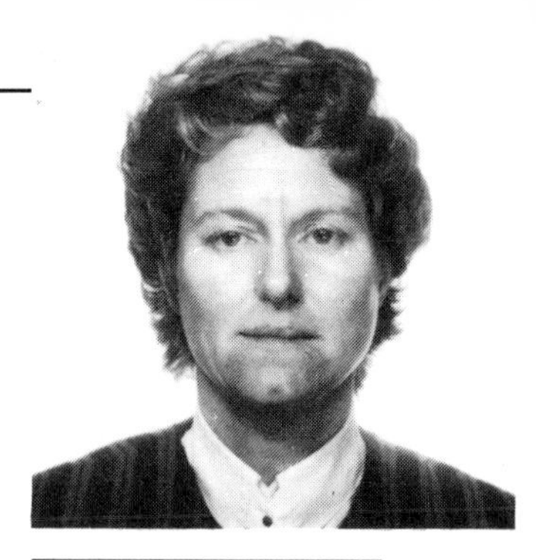

ELSIE WIDDOWSON

Elsie Widdowson studied at London's Imperial College from 1925 to 1931, gaining a BSc in chemistry and a PhD in plant physiology. From 1931 until 1988 she worked at many important research centres, including the Middlesex Hospital's Courtauld Institute of Biochemistry, King's College Hospital, London, and Addenbrooke's Hospital, Cambridge. Her fields of research are the composition of foods; food and nutrient intake of individuals; mineral metabolism; composition of body (human and animal) during development; under-nutrition in man and animals; nutrition and growth; the physiology of newborn infants and animals; and the effect of early nutrition on later development. Currently the Honorary President of the British Nutrition Foundation, she has received numerous professional honours including, in 1981, the James Spence Medal of the British Paediatric Association, in 1983 the first European Nutrition Award of the Federation of European Nutrition Societies, and in 1992 the first Edna and Robert Langholz International Award for Nutrition, from the American Dietetic Association.

PROFFESSOR MARIAN HICKS

Professor Marian Hicks, OBE, is Director, Food Issues, in the Research and Development Centre of UB (UK) Ltd, a major group of food manufacturing companies. She provides the group with scientific support and advice on food safety and nutrition, and is responsible for interacting with national and international independent scientists to ensure that her employer keeps abreast of current thinking and best practice in these areas. She has been closely involved in the development of new ranges of nutritionally modified food products by UB Group. A Fellow of University College, London, from which she graduated in physiology, later gaining a PhD and a DSc. She is Chairman of the South West Thames Regional Health Authority and is involved in implementing the *Health of the Nation* White Paper. Her administrative roles include membership of the Council and Executive Committee of the British Nutrition Foundation.

DR SHEILA BINGHAM

Dr Sheila Bingham is Senior Scientist at the Medical Research Council's Dunn Clinical Nutrition Centre in Cambridge, with particular interest in dietary modulating factors and carcinogenesis. She is a principal investigator, with Professors Day and Kay-Tee Khaw, in the European Prospective Investigation into Cancer (EPIC) in Britain.

SUSAN FAIRWEATHER-TAIT

Susan Fairweather-Tait obtained a BSc in food sciences at King's College, London (formerly Queen Elizabeth College) in 1973 and an MSc (with distinction) in nutrition the following year. After gaining her PhD, on the chemical and biological availability of iron in foods, she worked briefly for Beecham Products before, in 1979, joining the AFRC Insitute of Food Research in Norwich. She is currently head of the Mineral Nutritional Group, an honorary lecturer in the University of East Anglia's School of Chemical Sciences and a member of the council of the Nutrition Society.

In 1991 she was elected to the American Society of Clinical Nutrition. Her main interests are in mineral requirements and the use of stable isotopes to study mineral metabolism.

DR MARGARET ASHWELL

After gaining a first-class honours degree in physiology and biochemistry from Southampton University in 1967, Dr Margaret Ashwell obtained her PhD at the Medical Research Council's National Institute for Medical Research. Having worked briefly for the Consumers Association, she returned to the MRC, working at its Clinical Research Centre at Harrow and then at the Dunn Nutrition Unit in Cambridge from 1986 until 1988. Since that time she has been Science Director of the British Nutrition Foundation, where she has responsibility for the Foundation's publications and initiatives such as the Human Nutrition Research Forum. She was Honorary Secretary of the Nutrition Society from 1984 to 1988. Dr Ashwell's particular interests are the links between diet and heart disease, the causes of obesity and nutritional labelling.

The companion volume to Best of British Women is also available either direct from Best of British Publications or from any good bookseller.

The area of medicine is a difficult one to research, because of the strictures imposed by the General Medical Council. We feel, however, that there is no reason why the consumer should not be told who is at the top of this or any other field. The people who appear on these pages are not indisputably the best, but their names have been put forward by a broad cross-section of their peers as having achieved a pinnacle of excellence in their chosen areas.
The medical profession seems to come in for more and more criticism in the press and in television "insight" programmes, forever pointing out the horrors of medical mistakes and the supposed cover-ups which follow. It is only necessary to look across the Atlantic to see which way this path leads. American medicine is rapidly reaching the stage where every doctor is terrified of taking the smallest risk or performing any experiment for fear of the massive law suit which will inevitably follow and he spends as much of his earnings on professional indemnity insurance as he does with the IRS.
Fortunately, we have not yet reached this point in Britain and we hope that common sense will continue to prevail.
There is no doubt, however, that in this as in any other field of endeavour, some people are better than others and here we are pleased to introduced you to some of the best.

OPHTHALMIC SURGEONS (eyes)

Prof Susan Lightman
Moorfields Eye Hospital
Tel: 071-253 3411

RHEUMATOLOGISTS

Dr Barbara Ansell
Northwick Park Hospital
Tel: 081-869 3025

ENDOCRINOLOGISTS (glands (pituitary)/ hormones)

Prof Leslie Rees
Dean – St Bartholomew's Hospital
Tel: 071- 601 8888

PAEDIATRICS (children)

Dame June Lloyd
Institute of Child Health
Tel: 071-404 6454

CARDIOLOGISTS

Prof Celia Oakley
Hammersmith Hospital
Tel: 081-7453 2030

GYNAECOLOGISTS

Prof Wendy Savage
Royal London Hospital
Tel: 071-377 7000
(Obstetrician)

Mrs Ursula Lloyd
Portland Hospital
Tel: 071-580 4400
(Gynaecologist/Obstetric Surgeon)

NEUROLOGISTS (brain doctors)

Prof Anita Harding
National Hospital of Neurology
Tel: 071-837 3611

BRAIN SURGEONS

Miss Carys Bannister
North Manchester General
Tel: 061-795 4567

LIVER SPECIALISTS

Dame Sheila Sherlock
Royal Free Hospital
Tel: 071-794 0500

PSYCHIATRISTS

Dr Julie Hollyman
Springfield Hospital
Tel: 081-672 9911

VASCULAR SURGEONS (veins and arterys)

Miss Avril Mansfield
St Mary's Hospital
Tel: 071-725 6666

DERMATOLOGISTS (skin)

Dr Irene Leigh
Royal London Hospital
Tel: 071-377 7000

AIDS

Dr Margaret Johnson
Royal Free Hospital
Tel: 071-794 0500

ENT (ear, nose and throat)

Ms Valerie Lund
Ear, Nose and Throat Hospital
Tel: 071-837 8855
(Rhinologist: Nose Reconstruction)

ORTHOPAEDICS (joints)

Ms Clare Marx
St Mary's Hospital
Tel: 071-725 6666
(Knees and Hips)

RE-HAB CLINICS (alcohol and drug addiction)

Margaret McCann
Castle Craig Centre
Tel: (0721) 52625

THORACIC MEDICINE (chest and lungs)

Dame Margaret Turner-Warwick
Royal Brompton Hospital
Tel: 071-352 8121

TROPICAL DISEASES

Prof Jenny Blackwell
Addenbrooks Hospital
Tel: (0223) 336700

KIDNEYS

Prof Mary McGeown
Belfast City Hospital
Tel: (0232) 329241 ext 2786

MISCELLANEOUS

Prof Kay Davis
Institute of Molecular Medicine
Tel: (0865) 741166
(Molecular Biologist)

Margaret Hodson
Brompton Hospital
Tel: 071-352 8121
(Physician in Cystic Fibrosis, Heart and Lung)

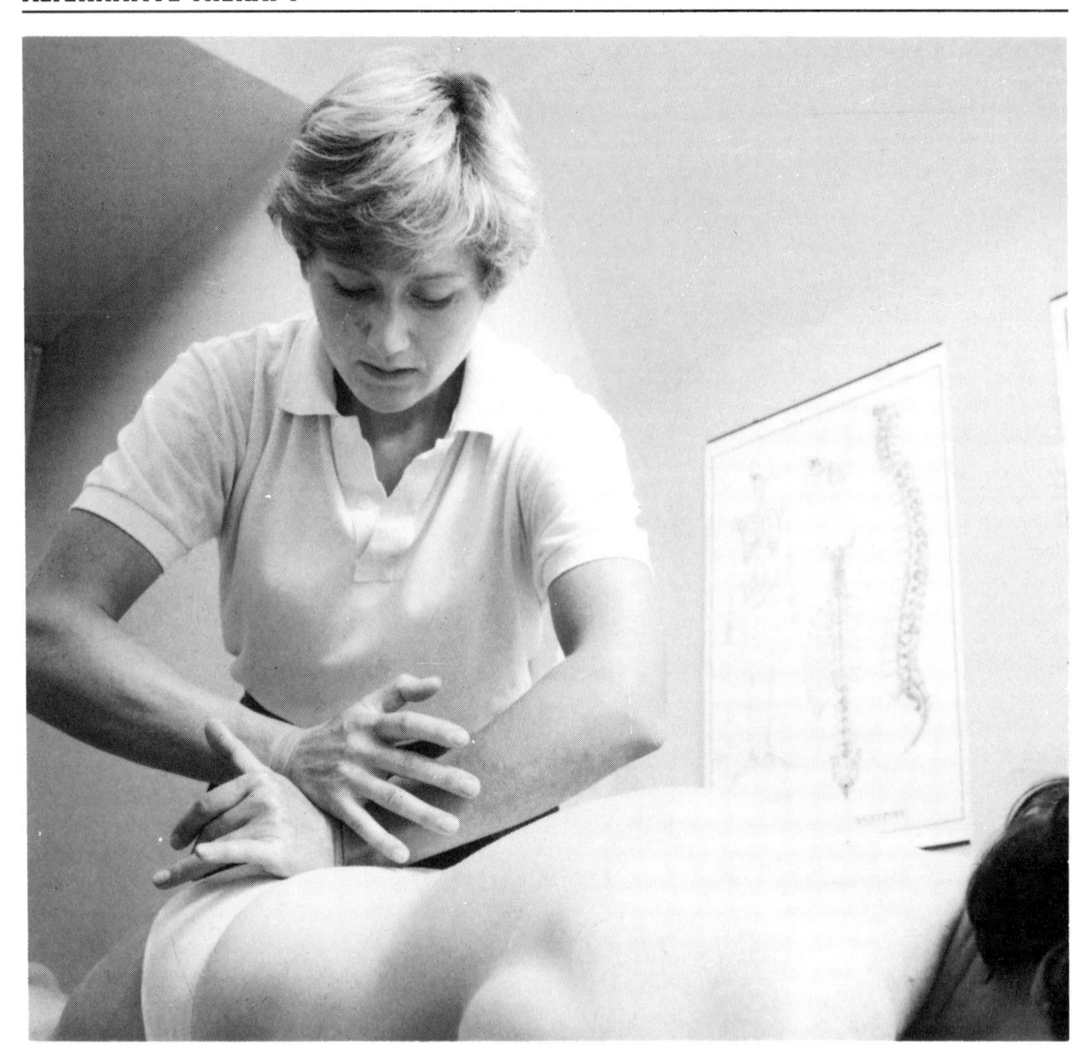

JANE McWHIRTER

Having survived countless spectacular accidents on ski slopes, Jane McWhirter imagined herself virtually indestructable until one day when her back went as she was walking down Verbier High Street. Nine months of pain and endless visits to specialists followed, all to no avail. Jane was abandoning hope of ever being able to ski again when she came across a McTimoney chiropracter. She was so impressed with the methods of chiropractic, which aims gently to realign the entire structure of the body, that she decided to train as a McTimoney chiropracter. She set up All Hallows House with 18 dedicated practitioners in 1990. The site, a magnificent Wren spire in the city of London, is a sanctuary of calm that provides a lifeline to people suffering from stressful and unhealthy lifestyles. The centre won its first corporate contract in July 1991.

MARYON STEWART

Maryon Stewart studied preventive dentristry and nutrition at the Royal Dental Hospital in London and then worked as a counsellor with nutritional doctors in England for four years. She was responsible for setting up the PMT Advisory Service which has subsequently provided help to thousands of women all over the world. In 1987 she launched the Women's Nutritional Advisory Service. She is author of the best selling books Beat PMT Through Diet, Beat Sugar Craving, The Vitality Diet and is the co-author of The PMT Cookbook. She has a weekly radio programme on Health and Nutrition, has co-written several medical papers and has written articles for many women's magazines. She has appeared on The Miriam Stoppard Health & Beauty Show, TV-am, This Morning and Pebble Mill.

CAROL DAGLISH

When Carol Daglish was cured of illness by acupuncture and herbal treatment. She knew she wanted to work in the alternative medicine field and works part-time for three organisations. Carol joined the Register of Traditional Chinese Medicine in 1982 (a register of qualified acupuncturists) while still at university. Three years ago she took up a part-time position at the Council for Complementary and Alternative Medicine, which comprises seven professional organisations representing acupuncture, homoeopathy, medical herbalism and osteopathy and provides lists of qualified practitioners. She began working for the British Acupuncture Accreditation Board a year ago and is currently developing her own practice as a therapist of shiatsu and therapeutic massage.

TERESA HALE

Teresa Hale trained as an economist and then taught stress management before opening the Hale Clinic five years ago. She has recently developed the Hale Corporate Health Programme and a new medical insurance policy that covers both conventional and complementary medicine with the primary focus of investing in the future good health of employees rather than just waiting for ill health to occur. Teresa has lectured extensively in the UK, Europe and America on health economics and complementary medicine. She formed the Hale Foundation in 1992 to fund research, training and treatment in complementary medicine.

JANET BALASKAS

Born in Johannesburg, Janet emigrated to England in 1968 where she trained with the National Childbirth Trust. She is known internationally for her pioneering work as a lecturer, author, childbirth educator and activist. In the late 1970s she introduced a new approach to pre-natal preparation with yoga and the concept of active birth which focuses on women's self-empowerment in pregnancy and freedom and autonomy in birthing. Her work has furthered our understanding of physiological childbirth and helped bring about change in maternity practices in many countries. She is the founder of the International Active Birth Movement and the International Active Birth Teacher Training course. With Beverley Beech and Melody Weig she organised the first International Home Birth Conference in London in 1987. She is co-director, with her husband Keith Brainin, of the International Active Birth Centre in London, a resource centre for Active Birth and Water Birth, and produces a range of Water Birth pools for use at home and in hospital. She has written several books on pregnancy and birth, the latest, Preparing For Birth With Yoga, will be published this spring.

PAT PILKINGTON

Before helping to set up The Cancer Help Centre in Bristol, Pat Pilkington worked as a radio reporter for the BBC while her husband, Canon Christopher Pilkington, served in parishes in Worcestershire and at Bristol City Parish Church. With the collaboration of Penny Brohn, The Cancer Centre opened its doors in the autumn of 1980 and soon became known throughout the world for its holistic and complementary help for cancer sufferers. It is fully staffed by doctors, nurses and therapists and helps patients from all over the world in day and residential courses. Penny has now retired from The Cancer Centre to further her career in writing and teaching but Pat and Christopher are still there full-time, working in an honorary capacity. The couple have lectured in many countries around the world and similar centres now exist abroad as a result of their tours.

DR SHEILA GIBSON

Sheila Gibson graduated from Glasgow University with a BSc Hons in biochemistry in 1959, and Hons MBChB in 1962. She was Brunton Medallist (top student of her year). After qualifying she researched lead poisoning in the University Department of Medicine, Western Infirmary, Glasgow, and obtained her MD degree in 1969, with a thesis entitled The Medical Effects of Lead Poisoning. After a four-year break, she took up the post of lecturer in medical genetics at Glasgow University. She joined the staff of the Glasgow Homoeopathic Hospital in 1976 as a research physician to conduct research into homoeopathy. She has collaborated in homoeopathic research in both arthritis and allergy; the use of the New Zealand green lipped mussel in arthritis; diets, especially in relation to pesticide contamination of wheat; neural therapy with particular reference to multiple sclerosis; posture and muscle relaxing techniques; and the post-viral fatigue syndrome. Her homoeopathic reserach is both laboratory based and clinical. Her work with diets led to an interest in environmental pollution and laboratory research showing adverse effects of low levels of fluoride on immune system function.

Photograph by Jim Cordiner

DR ROSY DANIEL

Dr Rosy Daniel opened the Pulse Alternative Therapy Centre in Cardiff during he fourth year at medical school. After qualifying in 1983 she began working at The Cancer Help Centre in Bristol where she still works as doctor and therapy development officer. As well as working holistically with cancer patients she also works with patients using self-help healing and complementary therapy at her own centre, the Observatory in Lothary. During the ten years since qualifying she has trained as a general practitioner, written Loving Medicine (published by Gateway Books) – a series of course studies from The Cancer Help Centre in Bristol – and organised holistic conferences for the British Holistic Medical Association. She has also served on the executive boards of the BHMA and the NCC ACM and pursued a passion for singing with her acappella group The Sweet Soul Sisters.

DR ALICE MARY GREENE

After graduating in medicine from Trinity College, Dublin in 1977, Alice completed a three year vocational training scheme in general practice, gaining her MRCGP in 1980. Alarmed at the high rate of drug prescribing, she left Ireland to study homoeopathy at the Royal London Homoeopathic Hospital and became a registrar there in 1982. She then entered general practice in the NHS and in 1984 opened private practice in Hampstead. She has studied Ayruvedic medicine, taken courses in counselling, acupuncture and autogenic training. In 1989 she set up a Harley Street practice, where she offers a holistic, non-drug approach to therapy. She lectures for the London Faculty of Homoeopathy, The Oxford Homoeopathic Physicians Group and The British Association for Autogenic Training and Therapy. She is presently completing a three year professional training in counselling and psycotherapy with the Psychosynthesis Education Trust.

DR ANNE CLOVER

After qualifying for medicine in 1963 Anne worked in psychiatry with appointments in training posts and then as a senior rigistrar. Her work concerned all aspects of acute psychiatry for adults and specialist training in psycotherapy. She then decided to pursue her interest in holistic medicine in general practice and worked in Manchester for a year-and-a-half. During this time she started attending postgraduate courses in homeopathic medicine which led to a training post for homoeopathy at the Liverpool Homoeopathic Hospital and then to a four year appointment at the Manchester Homeopathic Clinic. During this period she passed an examination for membership of the Faculty of Homoeopathy. In 1979 she moved to London and began working at the Royal London Homoeopathic Hospital. Later that year she was appointed as a consultant in homoeopathic medicine in the Tunbridge Wells Homoeopathic Hospital. Since then she has continued working in these two hospitals as a consultant with most of her time committed to NHS homoepathic services. In recent years, while seeing patients with diverse medical needs, she has also pursued a specialist role in advising on homoeopathic therapy for patients with cancer.

CAROLA BERESFORD-COOKE

Carola Beresford-Cooke spent her early childhood in the Far East. On returning to England she completed her education at St. Paul's Girls School and St. Anne's College, Oxford. As well as practising shiatsu, which she began studying in 1978, she has qualified as an acupuncturist and gained a diploma in herbal medicine. She co-authored the best-selling Book of Massage (Ebury Press, 1984), writing the section on shiatsu, and presented a six-part series on massage for Thames TV in 1986, with an accompanying book which reached the best seller lists that summer. She has produced and presented a popular video, Shiatsu – An Introduction, and is currently working on a shiatsu textbook synthesising classical and modern shiatsu theory. She has been teaching shiatsu since 1981 and currently teaches at the Shiatsu College in London, while running her own shiatsu practice. She was a founder member of the Shiatsu Society, sat on its Ethics Committee and served on its Assessment Panel from 1986 to 1992.

PEGGY WILLIAMS

One of the most experienced exponents of the Alexander Technique – she has taught extensively both in the UK and abroad for over 40 years – Peggy Williams was trained by the founder of the Technique, F M Alexander. She became interested in the Technique in the 1940s when her husband had lessons to overcome his stammer. In 1946 she began training with Alexander and stayed with him until his death in 1955. Peggy is a member of The Society of the Teachers of the Alexander Technique.

MIRA MEHTA

Born in India, Mira was sent to yoga classes run by BKS Iyengar in Bombay from the age of three. She started to teach yoga while at university abroad, returning to India after graduating to attend an intensive course at Iyengar's newly opened institute in Pune. She has attended courses there every year since. Her interest in yoga led her to study for a master's degree at Oxford in Sanskrit and Indian Religion, after which time the popularity of the Iyengar method of yoga was widespread throughout the UK. Pupils and teachers in the south east grouped together to purchase a building for an institute in London, run initially by the voluntary efforts of Mira and other teachers. In 1989 Mira and her family wrote Yoga: The Iyengar Way.

CLARE MAXWELL-HUDSON

A major international figure in health, massage, beauty therapy and education, Clare Maxwell-Hudson is director of The Institute of Health Sciences in London, principal of the Clare Maxwell-Hudson School of Massage, London and company director of Clare Maxwell-Hudson Ltd. She went to school in Kenya and studied at the Sorbonne and in London where she trained as a beauty therapist and took a course in cosmetic studies at the Society of Cosmetic Chemists of Great Britain. She went on to travel in the Near East, the Far East and Africa, collecting traditional beauty lore. She is a registered massage therapist for the Riverside Health Authority, teaches doctors at the British Post Graduate Medical Association and runs courses for nurses at several hospitals in London. She is also a consultant to industry and adviser to film companies. Her publications include Kaleidoscope of Beauty (Octagon), The Natural Beauty Book (MacDonald), Your Health & Beauty Book (MacDonald) and The Complete Book of Massage (Dorling Kindersley).

Photograph by Sandra Lousada

DIANA KENDALL

Chair of The British Wheel of Yoga, Diana Kendall has been teaching yoga for over 20 years, to classes of mixed ability and special needs students. She has worked in various capacities over the last 12 years on the British Wheel of Yoga committees. A registered charity, The Wheel is one of the largest yoga organisations in the country. Its nationwide teacher training syllabus is approved and accepted by all local education authorities and by the European Union of Yoga, of which it is a member. The Wheel is currently engaged in standardising the provision of yoga qualifications throughout Europe.

LINDA ODELL

Linda Odell trained at Sussex University and the Laban Art of Movement Studio. Having been trained in teaching, she was asked by parents at her school to arrange "Keep Fit" classes. On the first day she had 400 people, and the business was born. Pinks Dance Centre was created in 1982 in Winchester, and opened in 1983 at the YMCA. It relocated to a custom-built studio in 1988. Linda has organised and taught at numerous workshops, charity events and seminars worldwide and is now the UK step Reebok choreographic consultant, a European aerobic championship judge and a member of the Way Ahead workshops team. She has won awards as the ASSET Instructor of the Year 1991 and Fitnes Professionals Business Person of the Year 1992. She holds numerous appointments, and has made many keynote speeches. In 1991 she took the decision to make the Pinks Dance Centre business concept available on franchise.

KIM TURNER

Born in 1956, Kim Turner is the founder and owner of The Mill Health Club in Loughborough. She qualified as a physical education and biology teacher in 1977 and went to work in a large comprehensive, which she found rather restricting. Kim discovered aerobics while spending a year in San Francisco, and on her return to the UK began work in three different gyms, before opening The Mill in 1985. The Mill was listed as one of the top ten health clubs in Britain in the Daily Express in 1991, and continues to thrive.

LOTTE BERK

It is hard to believe that Lotte Berk celebrated her 80th birthday in January. For more than 40 years she has dominated her profession with a dedicated authority that has provided the foundation for many of the popular exercise systems of today. She still regularly subjects pupils to her energy and wit during classes at one of her studios.

A dancer, Lotte arrived in London as a Jewish refugee in 1935, and continued a successful career for several years before opening her first exercise studio. She has enriched the lives of thousands of women who have become her devoted following, and who travel from all over the world, just to be taught by her.

YVONNE HARPER-WAKE

Yvonne Harper-Wake was born in 1952, and has been 20 years in the fitness industry. A competitive swimmer at school, she always felt a desperate need to teach people how to live longer, enjoy life and stay healthy, and she must have been right because, 20 years on, she says that she is still doing most of what she did in the beginning. Yvonne runs her own company in Covent Garden called the Gym at The Sanctuary, and has been doing so for two very successful years. She teaches ten fitness classes per week, and runs programmes for "Over Forty Fatties", started in 1980 for a huge fat friend, and still very popular. In addition to her work at the Gym, Yvonne also teaches at Montessori nursery schools – French and PE, and teaches in a church hall near her home in Barnes, which she enjoys enormously.

PAULA BELL

Paula Bell, 41, began her career as a nurse. In 1976, after the birth of her daughter, Paula began to take an interest in exercise, and found that the dance oriented classes available were rather hard for customers to follow. After a great deal of research and experimentation, she opened Bodytalk in 1984, the first fitness centre of its kind in Edinburgh. Success was instant and enduring and she is currently seeking larger premises.

PAULA TATTERS

Paula Tatters is the founder and co-owner of Fitness 'N Fun in Morayshire, Scotland. She trained as a PE instructor and remedial therapist in the WRAF, but left to become an air hostess, during which career she met her husband who is in the RAF. Paula next became a games and aerobics instructor at Gordonstoun School. She started Fitness 'N Fun with her sister, and with great support from their "long suffering, supportive husbands" they now have 900 members, from ten months to 77 years.

VALERIE VICKERSTAFF

Forty-five year old Valerie Vickerstaff's career in health and fitness started by accident. After losing five stone in 1983, she took up jogging to tone herself up, and caught the bug. Jogging led to the London marathon and, after suffering through poor training, Valerie decided to take the job seriously, acquired her RSA qualification and founded the highly successful Lorrens Health Hydro in Torquay. Valerie has pioneered specialist training for ladies combining healthy eating with exercise for life.

GLENYS CARTER

Born and educated in Lancashire, Glenys Carter qualified as a teacher of 11 to 18 year olds, and gained teaching experience in grammar and comprehensive schools. Whilst a young mother, she became involved in the Federation of Children's Book Groups and served as national chairwoman. She served as a member of the Government's Child Health Services Committee, set up in 1973, to investigate the provision of health services for children. She was Area Voluntary Liaison Officer for Somerset Social Services Department from 1976 to 1984. In June 1984 Glenys Carter was appointed Director of Play Matters/The National Toy Libraries Association. She is currently the International Secretary of the International Toy Libraries Association.

SARAH BRADLEY

Born in 1959, Sarah Bradley graduated BA(Hons) from Exeter University, and did post-graduate training in the teaching of 8-14 year olds. She taught from 1982 to 1988, principally at Hill House School in Knightsbridge, London. In 1983 she began running Adventure and Computer Holidays. In 1985 she bought The Manor House near Wadebridge in Cornwall to form her own adventure holiday centre. She runs residential adventure holidays and day camps during every school holiday and half-term and, during term time, takes school groups to Cornwall, runs weekly clubs and organises children's parties. Adventure and Computer Holidays Ltd provides children with the opportunity to learn about and explore the outside world, as well as to move from keyboard innocents to expert hackers.

PIPPA DEAKIN

Twenty-seven year old Pippa Deakin founded and opened Pippa Pop-ins, the world's first hotel for children in January 1992. She spent six years researching the project, which also involves a nursery school, a "school run" service with tea and holiday excursions, parties and skiing trips. In November 1992, the England for Excellence Awards Committee on behalf of the English Tourist Board, presented Pippa Pop-ins with an award for its "special commendation for innovation". Pippa Pop-ins has established an occupancy rate of 86 per cent, and is opening in New York in the immediate future.

TERESA SCIBOR-KAMINSKA

Born in London of Polish origin and brought up in a bi-lingual environment, Teresa Scibor qualified with an honours degree in French and a Certificate of Education from the University of London. She has considerable experience in teaching a wide cross-section of age groups, from "tots" at Woodentops Nursery School through common entrance applicants to adults at the Kingsway College of Further Education. Aside from her teaching posts, she set up Le Club Tricolore in 1988, where children as young as four learn French, solely through fun and play, and make astounding progress. The club's membership has grown rapidly over the years, largely as a result of recommendation. Teresa has recently created The Adventures of Zozo, a bi-lingual storybook and cassette which teaches children French without their realising it and has been working on FrenchStart, an activity pack commissioned by Living and Learning, available in 1993.
Photograph by Tom Stoddart

ALICE LEWES

Alice Lewes set up her organisation, Maternal Instincts, in 1989 to combat the general ignorance of safety and first aid for children. A qualified Norland nanny, her idea originated when she was in partnership running a mother's help agency, and was horrified by the lack of quality of the applicants. She now runs courses designed to educate against every eventuality, divided into three sections: accident prevention; general areas of safety and the chief causes of accidental death, including how to administer correct first aid. A unique aspect of the Maternal Instincts training session is that it includes stages of a child's play development to illustrate the importance of certain preventative measures at certain stages.

BARBARA HALL

For years Barbara Hall had been complaining about the fees charged by agencies for employing mothers' helps and nannies. Since she was working in the computer world anyway, she and a colleague designed a programme tailor-made for the purpose. ComputaNanny is a new concept in registered employment agencies, providing a quick, efficient low cost service dealing with nannies and mothers' helps and special needs carers. Using its unique programme, ComputaNanny matches employers' requirements with the skills and abilities of candidates. The service operates nationwide.

SUZIE WOOD-ROBERTS

Suzie Wood-Roberts opened Nipper Snippers in 1990, having conceived the idea when she found that there was no salon in central London catering for children in a totally stress free atmosphere. She has created a fun environment where children can sit on alligator and hippo chairs, watch videos and play with toys while having their hair cut by top stylists. All first haircuts are remembered with a certificate with a lock of hair attached. There is a crèche facility and music and French workshops running throughout the day. Other activities include interior design, cookery, deportment and art lessons. Suzie can also supply nannies and babysitters and has information on anything connected with children at her fingertips.

GEORGINA HOOD

Having trained at the Montesori St Nicholas Centre and the Central Academy of Film Art and Drama, Georgina Hood introduced art and music classes for children at the Pineapple Dance Studios in South Kensington in 1986. In 1987 she opened Paint Pots Chelsea, a workshop for children from the age of 18 months to five years. Six months later, she opened the Paint Pots Montessori School in Bayswater. Both schools have a name for their innovative, stimulating and happy approach to learning. Using face paints, puppets, music, theatre and plenty of imagination, Georgina emphasises the development of each child's creativity as they learn.

NUTZ (FIONA ROOME)

A combination of artist's block and the gift of a secondhand camera gave Nutz the excuse to abandon an art foundation course for life behind the camera lens. Having worked as an assistant to an established photographer, mastering developing and printing, she turned her eye to capturing the innocence and spontaneity of children on film. Armed with a natural rapport with children and a name that made them laugh, she has never looked back. Initially, Nutz supplemented her income working as a model but, ten years later, the catwalk has been left far behind. Based in London, Nutz spends a great deal of her time on location in Britain and the Far East.

ROSEMARY FISHER

Born Rosemary Giles in 1945, Rose married Mark Fisher in 1963. In 1976, after having had four children, she started trading in East Sussex as an antique dealer. She introduced a range of hand-painted children's furniture which has grown into the well established and highly regarded Chelsea business, Dragons of Walton Street Ltd. Rose has written three books on hand-painting furniture: Rooms to Grow Up In (1986); Painting Furniture (1988) and Decorating Children's Rooms (1989). She has developed a wide clientele from all walks of life, and regularly exports to the USA, Norway, Sweden, Germany, Belgium and Saudi Arabia.

NORRIE CARR

Norrie Carr started the Norrie Carr Model Agency 28 years ago when she became pregnant with her second child. She was determined to specialise in children and family modelling, and with her husband, Julian Crader, has built the business up to be one of the most successful in the country, with over 500 models on its books. An ex-model, Norrie now commutes to London from the New Forest, where her spare time is spent riding and driving horses.

OLIVIA STIRLING

Olivia Stirling is the co-founder and a director of Nursery Window, an exclusive, top of the market firm which specialises in children's furnishings of all kinds. The company was started seven years ago to fill a gap in the market identified by the founding partners when they sought to furnish their own children's rooms. Prior to starting Nursery Window, Olivia ran her own soft furnishing business in London, supplying the decorating trade for several years.

FELICITY "FLISS" TEMPLETON

Born in 1947 into a medical family, Fliss Templeton left school in 1964 and took a year off to travel before returning to attend Bath Academy of Art for a four year art and design course. After acquiring her diploma, she took a year long post-graduate course in art therapy at St Albans College of Art. In 1976 she left England to pursue a life of art and travel and, in 1978, settled in Spain, where she could give more time to her painting, selling her work through exhibitions. She returned to England in 1983 and has been working as a portrait artist specialising in children since then, with most of her clients from London and Sussex.

RUTH KOHNER

Born in Czechoslovakia, Ruth Kohner grew up in Belfast and after art school entered the fashion industry, learning all about the business by working her way through the factory processes. She eventually became a designer before being appointed to control the purchasing, design and production of the Belart brand. Sold in outlets such as Harrods and Selfridges, the range is also exported around the world and, with her fluency in several languages, Ruth is particularly well equipped to boost the Ulster-based company's export drive.

PAULA FINNERTY

While still at college Paula Finnerty was headhunted by a successful menswear company. But, keen to design clothes of quality, it was not long before she set up her own company. Little Darlings, formed in 1989 and located in Northampton, produces clothes exclusively for girls aged from three months to eight years. Mainly based on Paula's own furnishing-like prints, the hats, berets, socks, bootees and coats represent a break with more traditional childrenswear and sell in exclusive stores and boutiques all over the world.

IRENE DEE

Irene Dee studied art and design for four years before working for major British companies, designing clothes for mass-market outlets. In her spare time she designed more adventurous clothes and soon built up enough of a reputation as a freelancer to open her own shop in Biddenham, Bedfordshire, where she sold garments designed by herself and made up by machinists she employed. The shop's huge success led to Irene being invited to manufacture her own range of Irene Renee children's clothes. Ten years later the company, whose philosophy is price and quality in perfect harmony, sells its products all over the world and is one of the success stories of the childrenswear industry.

SARAH BARKER

After graduating in Classical Studies from Hull University, Sarah Barker yielded to her lifelong passion for footwear and spent two years studying shoe design at Cordwainers College in Hackney, London. Then, with a mere six months' experience as a buyer for Next and eight more as a designer and cutter in a small shoe factory, she turned one room of her flat into a studio and took to the road to promote her first design venture – brightly coloured children's slippers. Four years later Sarah's priorities are still originality of design and fine workmanship. Furthermore, despite keen demand for her products, all of which are designed and made in her North London premises, her commercial sense, along with the dedication of her small band of employees, has so far ensured that every deadline has been met.

ANDREA TYRER AND JULIE BRODIE

Formed in April 1990 by Andrea Tyrer and Julie Brodie, 123 GO has grown steadily to become a supplier to over 100 top independent retail outlets for children's clothes. Andrea and Julie had both worked in London before moving to Ayrshire – Andrea for five years after graduating from St Martin's College of Art, and Julie teaching teenagers in the East End for ten of her 16 years in the capital. Attributing 123 GO's success to sheer hard work, the partners are quick to stress the dedication of their team as much as their own efforts.

ANGELA McLEAN

A graduate in Communication Studies, Angela McLean worked in sales and marketing before starting in business in 1986, manufacturing racing colours and riding-hat covers. Her quest to find attractive and yet practical rainwear for her daughters led Angela to come up with a novel solution. With her friend and colleague Barbara Condliffe, she developed fun, fashionable wet-weather clothing that folds neatly into its own attached bag. Set up with very little equity to make Baggers products, Angela and Barbara's company in Tyne and Wear has grown from a sewing-machine on the kitchen table to a portakabin-based operation on a farm. At the same time, the range of products has expanded to embrace other items of children's clothing, including stylish, baggable swimwear.

SYLVIA WILLCOX

Before she was in her teens Sylvia Willcox began adapting clothes to make them more stylish and individual. Later, as a mother, she became interested in designing clothes for both boys and girls, above all in garments that appealed to children and their parents alike. Syliva and a friend began trading as Little Monkeez in 1989, in time progressing from selling children's clothes through party planning and making clothes to order to selling a collection to London's Harvey Nichols department store. Soon after, they showed their spring and summer 1991 collection at the Junior Fashion Show, held in London's Docklands, and in August that year Little Monkeez Limited was formed. Based in Wandsworth, the company supplies independent retailers all over the country as well as exporting to Scandinavia and the Middle East.

SALLY MEEKIN

Winner of Nurse '92, Sally Meekin from Belfast has pioneered the specialism of Occupational Health Nursing among police services in Europe and is the first British nurse to have taken on the role of post-trauma counsellor. She was honoured for her work with trauma victims in Ulster together with her innovation in a wide range of health-promotion programmes and research work. Norah Casey, editor of Nursing Standard, said of her: "Sally is an exceptional nurse . . . the epitome of the mix of art and science which expresses nursing at its best." Sally originally trained at the Royal Victoria Hospital in Belfast and spent many years in Brazil. She has held a number of posts in Northern Ireland in Occupational Health, and for the past six years has been Chief Nursing Adviser in the NI Civil Service. She is presently working in a senior post with the Royal College of Nursing.

ANNE SHEPHERD

Anne Shepherd's prize money for the Motor Show's Community Service Award for 1992 (£1,000) has gone straight into launching a new campaign – to buy an ambulance for £32,000. Anne runs the Attleborough volunteer ambulance, a project she started 14 years ago to give weekly outings to the old and people who are terminally ill, blind or mentally handicapped. Apart from organising pleasure trips, Anne also ensures that those who need it are taken on hospital visits to relatives, shopping, and to the doctor and dentist. A 14-year-old girl with cancer was taken by ambulance from Norwich to the airport for a trip to Amsterdam, a place she had always wanted to visit.

SIAN WORGAN

For her "skill, fortitude, and judgement", 25-year-old Sian Worgan, a nurse from Hampshire, was last year awarded the 1992 Silk Cut Seamanship Award. Sailing with her skipper and two other crew off the north coast of New Zealand under gale force 8 winds, they had an accident in which the mizen mast landed on the skipper, killing him and breaking the arm of one of the other men. Sian succeeded in navigating the boat under severe conditions for 21 hours. She dived twice inside the boat to find bolt cutters, eventually giving up and lashing the remnants of the mast to the deck. As daylight broke for the second time, the two men were helicoptered off while Sian stayed with the boat and was towed back to shore. Sian's nominators, the Royal Southampton Yacht Club, said: "Not a single mistake of seamanship was made by her in 21 hours and this resulted in the saving of three lives."

DEBORAH ORCHARD

A former cross-channel swimmer, 30-year-old Deborah Orchard received the 1992 Silk Cut Individual Rescue Award. While on holiday in Wales, she came to the aid of a swimmer, swept out to sea by a freak wave. She dived into the surf with a small torpedo float. Battling against the huge waves, she eventually managed to reach the man, who was totally exhausted. Deborah held on to the rope attached to the float which he managed to grasp, reassuring him constantly that the rescue services would be with them soon. She swam with him to shore, managing to avoid the rocks. One witness, former police sergeant John Watkins, said: "It was the highest act of bravery I have ever seen."

HANNAH KELLY ↓

Hannah, 10, and her 12-year-old brother Ross Kelly won the public bravery category at the Motor Show Awards for 1992. Their quick thinking saved their father's and their own lives when he had an epileptic fit while driving on the M1. With the car travelling at about 70mph, Ross jumped into the front to steer. Since Ross's legs were not long enough to reach the pedals, things might have been very different had Hannah not had the presence of mind to slow the car down with the handbrake.

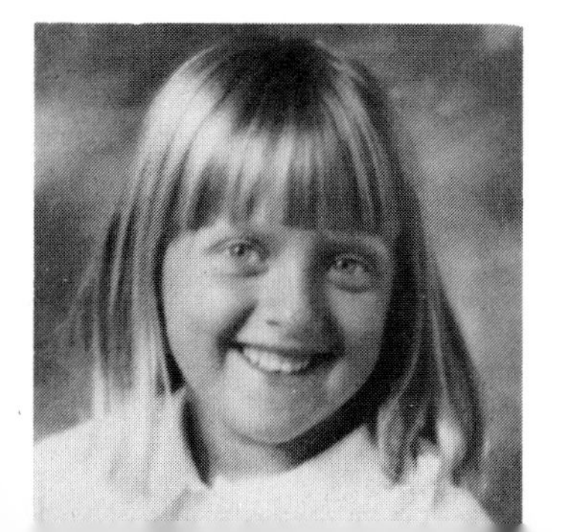

VERA CATTON ↑

Chosen from some 3,500 nominations as Londoner of the Year for 1992, 73-year-old Vera Catton won her Brightening Up London Award (organised by London Electricity in association with LBC News Talk) for her tireless work for Cancer Research. Vera formed the Wandsworth Committee of the Cancer Research Campaign in 1971. In 1991 she raised £250,000 through organising sponsored swims, greyhound meetings, flag days, coffee mornings, balls and barn dances. Her winnings as Londoner of the Year (£5,000) went straight to the Wandsworth Committee.
Photograph by London Electricity

JUDY CROSS ↑

Postie of the Year for 1992, Judy Cross has always done more in her 13 years as a postwoman than deliver letters. Her good deeds include delivery packages and parcels on to the laps of wheelchair-bound customers, collecting prescriptions and groceries and styling the hair of some of her elderly housebound customers. Judy, of Foulden, near Thetford, Norfolk, also operates her own neighbourhood watch and last year won an award from the police for helping to catch two robbers. Seeing two men acting suspiciously, she took down their car number and telephoned the police when she heard a house had been burgled that night. Thanks to Judy, the police were able to catch the men who were later jailed.
Photograph by David Napthens

ERICA DE'ATH

Currently Director of National STEPFAMILY Association, member of the National Children's Bureau Board of Management, and Chair of the Thames Telethon Children's Panel, Erica De'Ath has worked in the voluntary sector concerned with the needs of children, their parents and family crises for 20 years. She has written widely both for the popular press and television and for academic and professional journals, her most recent publications being Changing Families (1991), Parenting Threads (1992) and Stepfamilies (1992). As Head of the Children's Society Social Policy Unit she has also prepared various briefing papers and reports on social issues concerning juvenile delinquency, youth homelessness and family support.

BARBARA YOUNG

In 1991 Barbara Young was appointed Chief Executive of the Royal Society for the Protection of Birds. This marks a change in direction as, educated at Edinburgh and Strathclyde universities, her previous posts have been within the health service. She has been a member of the BBC General Advisory Committee and the King's Fund Institute Committee and an International Fellow of King Edward VII Hospital Fund College.

VALERIE PAKENHAM KEADY

Consultant to the Globe Centre, Valerie Pakenham Keady has worked in the charitable sector since 1977. Following a degree in Fine Arts, her early career was varied: she worked as a technical artist, an art and occupational therapist, a jewellery designer, and ran her own catering company. Since then she has held directorships, VSO and SSAFA, and latterly has been Chair of Charity Forum, Editor of Fundraising Magazine, and served as a member of the Charity Advertising Committee to the IBA and Trustee Kosova Aid. She has also lectured on a wide variety of topics, although her particular interests lie in the fields of strategic planning, marketing and use of the media to shape the future of non-profit-making organisations.

JUDY WELEMINSKY

Director of the National Council for Voluntary Organisations since 1991, July Weleminsky was previously Director of the National Schizophrenia Fellowship (1985-90) and the National Federation of Community Organisations (1982-85). Her posts prior to that have been with NACRO as Employment Development Officer, with the London Borough of Wandsworth as Equal Opportunities Officer and with the London Council for Community Relations as Community Relations Officer. She read psychology at Birmingham University and organisational psychology at Lancaster and has worked in a voluntary capacity with numerous voluntary organisations. From 1980 to 1988 Judy was a JP. She is currently a Fellow of the Royal Society of Arts and a Trustee of Charities Aid Foundation.

Photograph by John Whitfield

SU SAYER

Su Sayer, co-founder in 1973 and Chief Executive of United Response, began her career as a management trainee with ICI Fibres after reading chemical physics at university. Her expertise in health and safety matters is widely recognised: in 1987 she won the RoSPA Safety Officer of the Year Award for her work in producing guidelines and procedures for residential care homes, and her recent publications (she has written extensively on the subject) include a book on safety for children and a comprehensive manual for residential care homes. Currently Chair of ACENVO (the Association of Chief Executives of National Voluntary Organisations), Sue has also served as a Director of the Lifecare Charitable Trust and of the Association of Residential Care. *Photograph by Carol Matheson*

SYLVIA DARLEY

Having joined Sir Malcolm Sargent as a temporary secretary after leaving the Wrens in 1946, Sylvia Darley founded the Malcolm Sargent Cancer Fund for Children in 1967 in memory of the conductor who died that year of cancer. Since those early days when Sylvia worked at the kitchen table, over £25,000,000 has been raised, and as it enters its Silver Jubilee Year the Fund now distributes £2 million annually to young people suffering from cancer. Sylvia, at one time an aspiring concert pianist, received an OBE in 1987 in recognition for her work with the Fund. She sees significant landmarks in the history of the Fund as being the appointment of the first Malcolm Sargent Social Worker in 1976, royal patronage by HRH The Princess of Wales, establishment of the Fund in Australia, the opening of holiday homes and the staging of the first international Paediatric Oncolofy Seminar in 1992.

ELIZABETH MILLS

Elizabeth Mills, Director of Research Into Ageing, joined the charity as Administrator in 1985 when it was still known as the British Foundation for Age Research. Brought up in Farnham, Surrey, and educated at the local girls' grammar school, she later worked as a secretary to economist and inventor Patrick de Laszlo. An interest in politics led her to join the Conservatives as a trainee party agent in 1976, the year she married. The following year, her husband's work took them to Hong Kong for a seven year stint during which Elizabeth worked for a dental practice and a medical supplies distributor, rising to managing director of the latter. The couple returned to the UK in 1984. Elizabeth is on the National Executive of Age Concern England and the Association of Medical Research Charities. In 1987 she was elected to the General Synod of the Church of England and her position on at least one contentious issue is clear – she is on the National Executive of Women Against the Ordination of Women!

SHEILA McKECHNIE

Director of Shelter since 1985, Sheila McKechnie has seen the organisation's profile rise significantly in that period. Its turnover of £7.5 million in 1992 is a significant improvement on the figure of just over £1 million seven years ago. The charity has extended its network of services outside London and brought a number of independently-managed centres under its umbrella. Born in 1948 in Falkirk, Stirlingshire, Sheila graduated from Edinburgh University and later got an MA in Industrial Relations from Warwick. She made her mark as Health and Safety Officer of the Assocation of Scientific, Technical and Management Staffs, achieving a major improvement in laboratory safety in both the public and private sectors. She represented the TUC on a number of major committees from the oil industry to the NHS. Since joining Shelter, she has been at the forefront of developing strategies to integrate young people into society, helping to identify housing problems and find a solution for them. She is a member of the National Housing Forum, the Advisory Board of Warwick Business School and the Joseph Rowntree Building Standards Committee.

JANE TEWSON

Jane Tewson set up Charity Projects in1984 to raise "new money" for charity and to give grants in Africa and the UK, covering all fundraising costs by sponsorship and attempting to bring a smile along the way. The greatest triumph of the organisation is Comic Relief with its celebrated Red Nose Days. They anything-goes approach, and the involvement of TV's new breed of comedians like Lenny Henry, caught the public imagination. Through sales of records, books and various spin-offs like Teacher Relief in schools, the charity has raised more than £75 million to date. In 1992, Comic Relief produced Behind The Nose, a two hour TV programme examining some of the causes of poverty in Africa and the UK, which was seen by more than 7 million viewers. Despite the charity's high profile, 33-year-old Jane tries to avoid the spotlight and lets her achievements speak for themselves.

TINA FUNNELL

The National Eczema Society is the only charity in Europe solely concerned with the needs of sufferers and their carers. Christina (Tina) Funnell is the Society's Director and has helped to develop it from a small organisation with an income of £74,000 a year to one that takes in some £½ million annually. Born in 1947, Tina took a secretarial course before studying for a degree in Social Administration, Sociology, Psychology and Social Structures. From 1971-74 she was organising secretary of the Greater London Standing Conference of Voluntary Youth Organisations and representative on the British Youth Council. She was elected first President of the European Federation of Asthma and Allergy Associations in 1992.

ALISON THORNE

As Founding Director of the British Liver Trust, Alison Thorne has succeeded in achieving a high profile for this important new medical charity and is currently in demand as a charity consultant specialising in "start-up" situations. After training as a state-registered nurse at Guy's Hospital in London, she left "just for a year to experience a world beyond life and death". The move changed the course of her life and in the 1980s she spent five years in the Far East, setting up a company's Hong Kong offices and lecturing in People's Republic of China. She later studied Mandarin at the Chinese University of Hong Kong. She is active in the Association of Chief Executives of National Volunteer Organisations, the Institute of Charity Fundraising Managers and the Institute of Directors.

SARAH LANGTON-LOCKTON

As Director of the Centre for Accessible Environments since 1979, Sarah Langton-Lockton admits that its work – promoting the provision of accessibility for everyone, including disabled people – was not well-known in those early years. Today, thanks to the Centre's training courses and information services, the problem of accessibility is much more widely recognised and understood. Born in 1942, Sarah was educated at Northampton High School for Girls and Lady Margaret Hall at Oxford University, graduating with a BA Hons in Modern Languages, Spanish and French. Her first job was as Simpsons of Piccadilly's first graduate management trainee. She then spent several years living in Paris and Brussels. Chief Executive of the International Council of Societies of Industrial Design and joined the CAE in 1977.

ROSEMARY BROOK

A graduate of Cambridge University, Rosemary Brook is a specialist in developing communications strategies for industry; notably for the food, farming, pharmaceutical and paper industries. She specialised in industrial marketing, advertising and public relations at Wiggins Teape and at McCann Erikson before joining Edleman Public Relations Worldwide in 1982. Appointed UK General Manager of Edleman in 1989, she was made chairman of Daniel J Edleman Ltd. and managing director of Edleman Europe in 1992. Rosemary Brook is a fellow of the Institute of Public Relations, a member of the Public Relations Consultants' Association Board of Management, a Trustee of the Public Relations Education Trust and chairman of the PRCA's International Committee. Rosemary is an Associate of Newnham College, Cambridge and a Freeman of the City of London.

ANN BRUNTON

Ann Brunton is the managing director of the Covent Garden public relations consultancy Wellbeck Golin/Harris Communications Ltd. The consultancy, which has won several industry awards, has corporate clients including Elida Gibbs, Kensitas, Wilkinson Sword, Rotring and Story. A founder director of Wellbeck in 1968, Ann is now responsible for much of the consultancy's business. A specialist in consumer marketing public relations, Ann has also co-ordinated numerous international campaigns and is an expert on crisis management. She spent several years as a publicist in the fashion industry and two years at the showbusiness consultancy Deane and Phillips before becoming a director of Wellbeck Public Relations.

SARA PEARSON

Before starting her own highly-successful PR consultancy in 1980, Sara Pearson worked in the Sports Editor's office at the Sunday Telegraph and in the Jockey Club's public relations department – "primarily', she avows, "for the free racing". In 1973 she joined the David Wynne-Morgan agency Partnerplan. Two agencies later, by which time she had succeeded to board level, she formed her own consultancy: SPA, which is "focused on developing marketing strategies and delivering substantial supporting media coverage", has corporate clients including MFI, Mercury Communications, Tupperware, Barclays Bank and Hasbro. Now an independent consultancy, SPA was briefly acquired in the late 1980s by Yellowhammer.

LYNNE FRANKS

Although already something of an institution in the PR industry, Lynne Franks will never be accused of being afraid of new ideas. In the mid-1960s she worked briefly in Petticoat magazine's editorial department before editing a magazine for the Freeman's Mail Order Group. It was only at a friend's insistence, however, that she decided to form her own PR agency; that friend, Katherine Hamnett, was her first client. Throughout the 1970s and 1980s Lynne Frank's agency repeated its earlier success with Katherine Hamnett, becoming a byword for fashion and style PR. Lynne has worked with Next and Amnesty International, co-ordinated Green Consumer Week and, with Harvey Goldsmith brought opera to the people with stadium performances of Carmen and Aida. The agency's clients now include Michael Jackson's Heal the World Foundation and Jean Paul Gaultier, as well as the Merseyside Development Corporation and Lloyds Bank. A Buddhist, Lynne is committed to the promotion of holistic medicine and personal growth.

MARY BARTHOLOMEW

A former researcher with the BBC, Mary Bartholomew is now director for International Quality Standards at Shandwick Plc and managing director of the Shandwick subsidiary Gibson Public Relations (Singapore) Ltd. Mary worked in television and then as a market researcher for an advertising agency before becoming a PR professional. A director of InterEurope Communications, she joined Shandwick in 1979 when the group acquired InterEurope. She became chief executive for Shandwick UK and later deputy chief executive for Shandwick Europe with responsibility for business development. Since 1990 she has worked in Singapore developing business for Shandwick in the Asia Pacific region. She took a brief sabbatical in 1992 to co-ordinate the news room for the Conservative Party for their Election campaign.

JULIA THORN

Lauded with many industry awards for excellence, Julia Thorn is chairman and chief executive of Paragon Communications (UK) Ltd. A graduate of the National Council for the Training of Journalists scheme, Julia was a reporter and feature writer for UK regional dailies before going on to specialise in industrial reporting. An authority on both corporate and employee communications, she has worked with numerous public relations consultancies and in-house with Marks and Spencer. Julia was a founder member of Paragon in 1981 and became a member of the Board in 1985. Appointed managing director of the principal operating company in 1987, she has been chairman and chief executive since 1990. Julia Thorn is co-author, with the Institute of Personnel Management, of The Communications Challenge – PR and Personnel Perspectives, published in 1989. She is a Member of the Institute of Public Relations.

ANNE DICKINSON

Anne Dickinson is director of Birkdale Group Plc and chairman of Leedex Cornerstone, Leedex Public Relations and CCP Ltd. She was an Account Executive with W S Crawford for four years, between 1960 and 1964, before moving into magazine publishing in the mid-1960s. Promotions director of Good Housekeeping, between 1964 and 1965, and of Harpers Bazaar for two years after that, she was appointed director in charge of magazine promotions at the National Magazine Company in 1969. Her work in public relations dates from the late 1960s when she joined Benson PR (latterly Kingsway Public Relations) as a director in 1968. Chairman and chief executive of Kingsway Rowland between 1969 and 1989, she was appointed chairman of the Rowland Company in 1989. A Fellow of the Institute of Public Relations, she was nominated PR Professional of the Year (1988-1989) by PR magazine. Anne is also chairman of the Family Welfare Association.

CHRISTINE WALKER

Christine Walker is one of the most powerful figures in the advertising jungle, notorious for her tenacity, sharp wit and even sharper tongue. She started at Benton & Bowles in 1976, less than a year out of Exeter University, at a time when the place was awash with what she calls "a group of outstandingly talented people". She joined Ray Morgan & Partners as one of the partners in 1985, some time after Benton & Bowles became DMB & B. When Saatchi & Saatchi turned up in 1988 with a fistful of cash and the idea for Zenith, Christine became the director of broadcast buying and later the company's chief executive. In 1989 she won the Advertising Woman of the Year Award. A self-confessed workaholic she is married with a five year old daughter, for whose delivery only one month was erased from her schedule.

ANNE WICKS

The first child in her large, extended working class family to even think of going to university, Anne studied sociology with the original intention of becoming a probation officer. She soon realised, however, that she was not cut out to be a social worker and transferred her interest in people's behaviour into market research. After obtaining a degree in sociology at London University she worked for ten years in research before moving into advertising. She has worked in almost every consumer market, from newspapers to shampoo and grocery retail, experience which, she says, has given her the "valuable ability to turn numbers into people with shopping baskets". A frequent contributor to marketing and advertising conferences she is a member of the Market Research Society, the Women's Advertising Club of London and the Marketing Group of Great Britain.

BARBARA NOKES

Before becoming a shareholder and founder member of Bartle Bogle Hegarty in 1982 Barbara worked as a copywriter at Boase Massimi Pollitt, Collett Dickinson Pearce and Doyle Dane Bernbach, where she was deputy creative director and a member of the Board for three years. She was appointed deputy creative director of Bartle Bogle Hegarty in 1987 and resigned in 1992 to take a three month break before joining CME KHBB as executive creative director in January 1993. Her awards include a Cannes TV Gold and Silver Lions (Levi's and Girobank); a New York One Show Gold (Volkswagen); D & AD Copywriting Silver (Dr White's); Campaign Poster Gold and Silvers (Volkswagen, Creda and Brewer's Society); BTAA Silvers and Bronze (Levi's and Girobank); and a Clio Statuette for Dr White's.

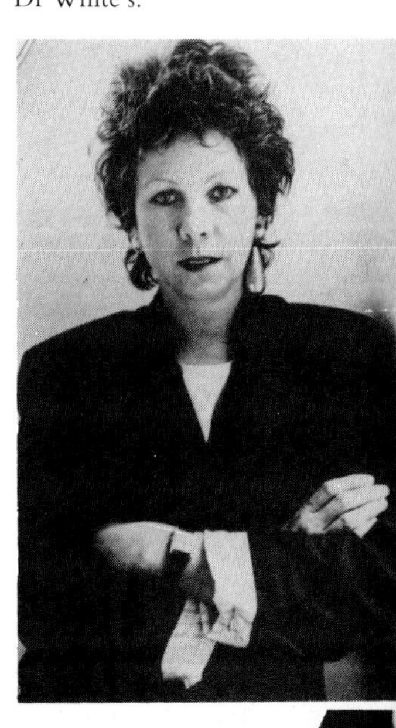

M T RAINEY

Scotland-born Mary Theresa, who goes by the name of M T, read psychology at Glasgow University. She left in 1976, having succeeded in getting her undergraduate thesis on Signal Detection Theory published by NATO. That same year she became an account manager at Davidson Pearce Advertising. She then spent two years at TBWA Advertising and another two at Gold Greenless Trott as senior account manager before joining Chiat/Day Advertising in San Francisco becoming vice-president, director of account planning for the West Coast (1983-87) and then senior vice-president, corporate head of planning in New York. Currently chief executive officer/managing director in London she was made Adweek's Adwoman of the Year in 1991. In America she is an Effie Award judge, a member of the Advertising Research Foundation and the Management Association and an executive member of the Marketing Association. Here in Britain she is a member of Forum UK, the Marketing Society, the Women's Advertising Club of London and the Institute of Practitioners in Advertising.

CATHY HENG

The current head of art at DMB & B Cathy Heng arrived at the company in 1989 from Collett Dickenson Pearce and Partners. Aged 46, and educated at the Reigate College of Art, Cathy joined Grey Advertising in 1969 and her career thereafter reads like a Who's Who of agencies. Winner of numerous awards including the Campaign Gold (twice) for BMW Cathy's creative talents are in demand on both sides of the Atlantic.

ALEXANDRA TAYLOR

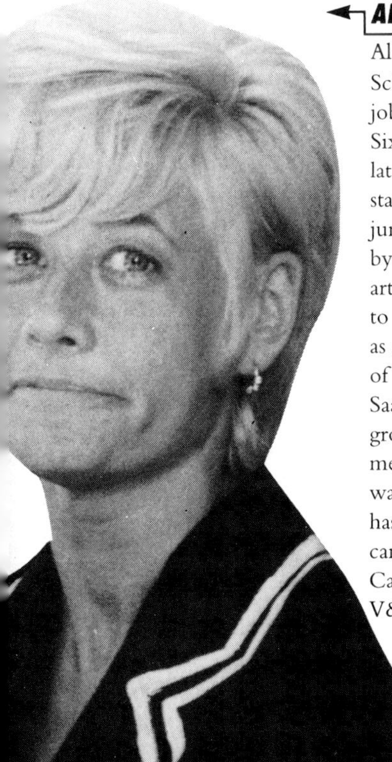

Alexandra Taylor left Newcastle School of Art in 1980 and landed a job on Cosmopolitan magazine. Six months later she joined BBDO, later to become SJIP, where she stayed for one and a half years as a junior art director. She was hired by Saatchi & Saatchi in 1982 as an art director. She moved from there to do a six month stint for WCRS as senior art director and member of the main board. Returning to Saatchis in 1988 she became a group head and was made a member of the board. In 1992 she was promoted to Head of Art. She has written award winning campaigns for InterCity, Castlemaine XXXX, Silk Cut, the V&A and Schweppes.

CAROL REAY

Carol graduated from Manchester University in English before working for short spells in sundry industries ranging from food to employment to engineering. Her advertising career began at Benton & Bowles on accounts such as Johnson Wax and General Foods. She later moved to Reeves Robertshaw Needham where she was promoted to the Board of Directors and worked on Weetabix, United Biscuits and Canada Dry. In 1984, with three partners, she set up Jenner Becker Reay and helped build the agency to annual billings of £27m and into a top 60 creative shop. Two years ago, as managing director of JKBR, she took the company into a merger with Newton & Godin to form a new agency, Reay Keating Hamer. Today the agency has billings of £62m, a staff of 55 and a list of blue chip clients ranging from Hitachi to TDK to Kleenex. Carol is considered to be the true expert on all things female – this even before the Kleenex launch which featured three women not leading totally subservient lifestyles – and she is constantly being interviewed and quoted on women's issues. This year she is a committee member of WACL (Women's Advertising Club of London), a charitable organisation which limits itself to 80 members.

BARBARA SMITH

Barbara Smith has held the post of PA to the chief executive of the Thomas Cook Group for three years. Previously she worked for the chairman of Vickers plc for four years and before that for the UK chairman of the Sedgwick Group plc. She is qualified as a secretarial linguist in English/Spanish. Barbara is the national chairman of the European Association of Professional Secretaries, an organisation with some 1,500 members across Europe.

PATRICIA SHADFORTH

Patricia Shadforth joined the engineering company NEI as secretary to a senior executive responsible for computer development. A number of senior secretarial positions followed, involving organising company open days, arranging travel for overseas customers and even climbing offshore cranes.
In 1988 she was appointed "supernumerary" secretary to the main board of NEI plc. Since 1990 Patricia has been secretary to a main board director at NEI plc. She is a member of the European Association of Secretaries and a committee member of the Institute of Travel Management.

DOROTHY FLEETWOOD

Training as a legal secretary, followed by a lengthy period in local government at director level, equipped Dorothy Fleetwood to enter industry when she joined Tarmac as secretary to the managing director of Roadstone and, later, to the chairman of Construction. After 17 years she joined Birmingham Heartlands Development Corporation where she works for the chairman and the chief executive. She sums up her job as "ambassador, diplomat and adivser, directing internal and external intelligence networks whilst continually creating secretarial order out of bosses' chaos". Dorothy is UK national membership secretary of the European Association of Secretaries, in which position she recruits PA/secretaries working for chairmen and chief executives. She is dedicated to making the Association the recognised voice of the secretarial profession throughout Europe.

SALLY PRATT

At the National Computing Centre, Manchester, Sally Pratt's work included the compiling, promoting and running of educational courses at home and abroad. She later joined an engineering company as executive secretary to the managing director. An opportunity arose to train in production planning and she was subsequently appointed production planner. Her present post is as personal assistant to the group director of education services at Cheshire County Council, where she is involved in a great variety of tasks, including the organisation of the North of England Education Conference, serving on a local commission for secondary education and business parternships with the Training and Enterprise Councils. National work has involved the Schools Curriculum Award, the Royal Society of Arts, City and Guilds and the Schools Examination Assessment Council. Sally believes that the PA function is becoming increasingly important as a vital part of management. She is also a member of EAPS.

ANN STODDART

Most of Ann Stoddart's working life has been spent in Scotland, although she worked for some years in Canada. From 1974 to 1980 she was senior personal secretary working for the chief executive and chairman of the Scottish Tourist Board in Edinburgh. From 1980 to 1983 she was personal assistant to the chairman of the Scottish Tourist Board, where her duties involved travelling in the UK and the USA. Since 1983 Ann has been personal assistant to Angus Grossart, chairman of Noble Grossart Limited, Scotland's leading merchant bank. Angus Grossart is also chairman of the Trustees of the National Galleries of Scotland. Ann is former president of the Edinburgh branch of the Association of Secretaries and is a member of the European Association of Secretaries, where she has been instrumental in the formation of the Scottish section.
Photograph by John Doyle Photography

JANIS NOWAK

Janis Nowak was born in Kent and graduated from the University of Bradford with a degree in French and German, having completed a secretarial course at Pitman's Secretarial College in Wimbledon. Whilst studying she spent a year in France and Germany working for Rowntree Mackintosh, consolidating her language and business skills. On leaving university in 1980 she took up the position of secretary to the retail trade director of Courage Ltd. After a year she joined Schroders plc where she has worked ever since, initially as secretary to a main board director and, since 1984, for the executive chairman of the group. A member of the European Association of Secretaries since 1986, Janis was UK membership secretary from 1987 to 1989 and is currently national public relations officer for the UK. She was runner-up for the Observer Career Secretary of the Year Award in 1988, and a finalist for Top PA in 1989.

WENDY SYER

During the 1970s Wendy Syer worked as a school administrator/secretary in Tunbridge Wells, while gaining her BA in mathematics and the humanities from the Open University. She has now worked for Abbey National plc for 12 years and is secretary/personal assistant to Sir Christopher Tugendhat, the chairman. During this time Wendy has been a member of the European Association of Professional Secretaries. She has served on the UK committee as public relations officer for four years and on the executive committee for two in the same capacity. She edits the Association's newsletters and publications and has overall responsibility for public relations and the sponsorship strategy.

JOAN MOSEY

Joan Mosey began her career as secretary to the principal of a college of further education, where her desire to teach secretarial skills was spawned. Since then she has alternated between teaching and secretarial roles, keeping up-to-date in both professions. She promotes protection of the secretarial heritage by close liaison with students and tutors in local colleges and collaboration with a strong network of colleagues in the secretarial profession. Joan is the secretary of the Yorkshire region of the European Association of Professional Secretaries. Her current position is as personal assistant to the chairman and managing director of Computer Services Consultants (UK) Ltd.

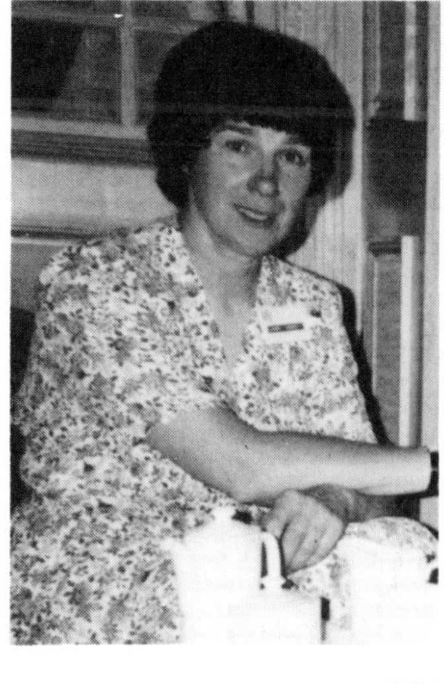

ALEXANDRA SHULMAN

Alexandra Shulman was educated at St. Paul's Girls School and read social anthropology at Sussex University. She began her career in journalism as a secretary on Over 21 magazine. In 1982 she joined Tatler on the strength of a freelance article she wrote for the then editor Tina Brown. She stayed at Tatler as a writer and commissioning editor for five years and became features editor under Marc Boxer. In 1987 she joined the Sunday Telegraph as editor of the women's pages and then moved to become deputy editor of Seven Days, their current affairs/reportage based tabloid section. She joined Vogue as features editor in 1988 and then moved to GQ as editor in February 1990. She was appointed editor of Vogue in January 1992.

KATHRYN FLETT

Kathryn Flett was educated at Notting Hill and Ealing High School For Girls, Hammersmith and West London College and Kings College, London. She was a staff writer at i-D magazine from 1984-87 before becoming Intro editor/fashion editor and then features editor on The Face. In 1991 she became a contributing editor for Arena and was appointed the magazine's editor in 1992. She has freelanced for most of the broadsheets as well as magazines such as Harper's Bazaar, Elle, Tatler and Details.

Photograph by Kevin Davies

GLENDA BAILEY

In 1987 Glenda devised Folio, a quarterly fashion magazine based on Marie Claire. The first issue was so successful that it sold 90,000 copies without any pre-launch publicity. The plan was to broaden its appeal to include features with the intention of launching the magazine as a monthly in the following year. However, when Glenda heard of the plan to launch her favourite magazine, Marie Claire, in Britain, she telephoned Evelyne Provoust-Berry, the managing editor of Marie Claire, France and told her she was determined to be editor. Despite the fact that another publishing group was involved in negotiations Glenda was so persuasive that she was offered the job without even producing a dummy. In 1988 British Marie Claire was launched. It is now the biggest selling upmarket fashion monthly in the UK and has just celebrated its fifth consecutive increase in sales with a year on year circulation rise of 38.8 per cent (Jan-June 1992). Last year Glenda won two awards, Editor of the Year, Women's Monthly Magazines, and Editor's Editor of the Year from the British Society of Magazine Editors.

ILSE CRAWFORD

Ilse Crawford became editor of Elle Decoration at the age of 29, when it was launched four years ago. Stylish, practical and a valuable source book, Elle Deco has become the interiors magazine for the 1990s. Prior to her editorship, Ilse was deputy editor of The World of Interiors, a sub-editor on The Architect's Journal and a checkout girl at Woolworths. She was brought up on a building site and "seems to have lived in them ever since". One day, she says, she would like to live in a finished house.

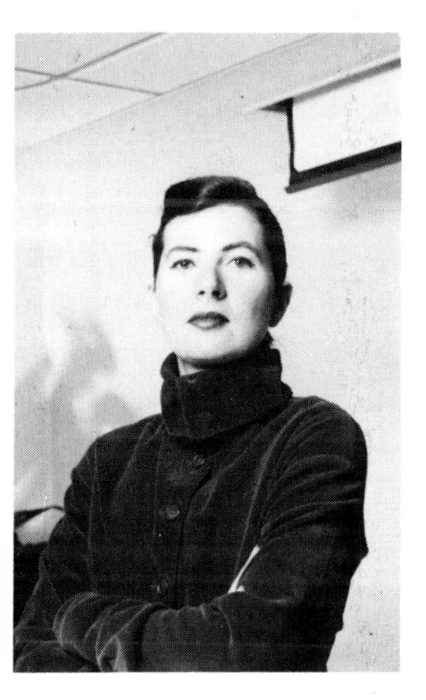

MAGGIE GOODMAN

Maggie Goodman was educated at Plymouth High School and at Birmingham University and College of Commerce. She worked as a secretary before getting her first job in publishing on a small educational magazine called The New Era with a staff of just two. She became acting editor of The New Era before landing a job on Honey as a sub-editor. In her four years with Honey she rose through the ranks to showbiz editor, features editor and finally assistant editor. In 1969 she transferred to Honey's sister magazine Petticoat as deputy editor and then editor. In 1970 she left Petticoat and worked as a freelance writer before being appointed deputy editor of Cosmopolitan. Six years later she became editor of Company magazine, a position she held for nine years before being made editor of Hello! in January 1988.

VICKI WOODS

Vicki Woods began her career as a sub-editor on Harpers & Queen in the early 1970s. She left the magazine to join Radio Times in 1973 but returned two years later as associate editor. In 1981 she joined Tatler and was soon promoted to deputy editor. She was named writer of the year by the Periodical Publishers Association in 1986. She edited the Daily Mail's Femail pages for two years between 1987 and 1989 and was editor of the Mail's Saturday magazine Male and Femail. She then joined Vogue (USA) as contributing editor, responsible for personality profiles and fashion features and became a contributing editor to The Spectator. She was appointed editor of Harpers & Queen in June 1991.

GAIL REBUCK

Born in London in 1952, Gail Rebuck was educated at the Lycee Français de Londres and took a degree in Intellectual History at the University of Sussex. She started her publishing career as production assistant with Grisewood & Dempsey, moving on to become editor of Robert Nicholson guidebooks. In 1979 she was taken on as non-fiction publisher by the Hamlyn Group to launch their new mass market paperback division. She became a founder director of Century in 1982 and, as publishing director of their non-fiction list, was instrumental in the rapid growth of the company, culminating in its merger with Hutchinson in 1985, and take over by Random House Inc in 1989. In 1991 Gail was appointed chairman and chief executive of Random House UK Ltd, with overall responsibility for the publishing group, its two distribution centres and its overseas subsidiaries in Australia, New Zealand and South Africa.

ALISON CATHIE

Educated at Cheltenham Ladies College and the University of Keele, where she acquired a joint honours degree in French and Law, Alison Cathie is the managing director of publishers Conran Octopus. She started her career as a management trainee at George Rainbird in 1970 and, in 1972, moved to Octopus Books Ltd as a junior editor. She became assistant publisher in 1978 and, later that year, publishing director of Orbis Publishing. Alison took up her current post in 1984, and launched her first list the following year. Conran Octopus now publishes about 30 new books per annum, all aimed at the international market. Alison is married to Paul Whitfield, deputy chairman of Bonhams, and they have two children.

LIZ ATTENBOROUGH

Liz Attenborough started working in children's publishing 21 years ago, as secretary to the children's editor of William Heinemann. After a brief spell at Pan Books she joined Kestrel, the hardback children's list within the Penguin Group, as commissioning editor and became chief editor in 1979. In 1983 Liz was appointed chief editor of Puffin Books and, in the following year, was made a director of Penguin Books UK. Liz is now publisher, children's books, for all children's imprints at Penguin, which include the Puffin, Fantail, Blackie, Hamish Hamilton, Ventura and Viking lists. She is a member of the board of the worldwide Penguin Books Company.

PHILIPPA HARRISON

Born in Lancaster in 1942 and educated at Bristol University, Philippa Harrison is managing director of Little, Brown & Co (UK) Ltd and of Macdonald & Co (Publishers) Ltd, which was taken over by Little, Brown & Co in 1992. Her publishing career started in 1963, as promotions organiser for Associated Book Publishers, a position which she held for three years until moving to Jonathon Cape, as reader and editor in 1967. She became editorial director of Hutchinson in 1974, joint editor-in-chief of Penguin in 1979 and editorial director of Michael Joseph in 1980. After two years as managing director and publisher of Macmillan London, she took a year's sabbatical in 1989, taking a post-graduate diploma in History of Art at the Courtauld Institute, before becoming managing director of V & A Enterprises in 1990. She took up her present position in October 1991. Philippa has served on numerous committees in the publishing world, the Book Marketing Council Board (1983-88), the Booker Management Committee (1987-89) and the Literature Panel of the Arts Council (1988-92) amongst them. She is a Companion of the British Institute of Management and a Fellow of the Royal Society for the encouragement of Arts, Manufacturers and Commerce.

CARMEN CALLIL

Chairman of Virago Press since 1972 and managing director of Hogarth Press since 1983, Carmen Callil was born in Australia in 1938 and educated at Melbourne University. She started her career as a buyer's assistant at Marks & Spencer in 1963 and moved into publishing two years later, as an editorial assistant for Hutchinson Publishing Co. Between 1967 and 1972 she worked for Panther Books and Virago Publishing and André Deutsch before founding the Carmen Callil Book Publicity Company and Virago Press in 1972. In addition to her publishing role, Carmen has been a director of Channel 4 since 1985.

ROSEMARY CHEETHAM

Rosemary Cheetham's first step on the publishing ladder was taken in 1973, the year after she left Cambridge, when she became secretary to the editorial director of Sphere Books. In the same year she moved to become editorial assistant at Futura Publications, where she stayed until 1978, rising to the position of editorial director. In a series of rapid moves, Rosemary progressed from publishing director at Hamlyn Paperbacks (1979) to senior fiction editor and director of Hutchinson General Books (1979-80), fiction publishing director at Macdonald and Company (1980-82), publishing director of Century Fiction (1982-91) and publisher, Century/Arrow (1991). In 1992, with husband Anthony Cheetham, Rosemary co-founded and became publisher of Orion Books Ltd. Rosemary Cheetham has experience of both paperback and hardcover fiction publishing. The Century Fiction list, which she created in 1982, became known for discovering and promoting new and unknown authors with best-seller potential, such as Maeve Binchy, Edward Rutherford and Penny Vincenzi. Other authors who joined her list were Joan Collins, Coleeen McCullough, Len Deighton and Michael Caine. Rosemary built the Century list from its inception to an annual turnover of £3 million, with a stable of internationally recognised authors.

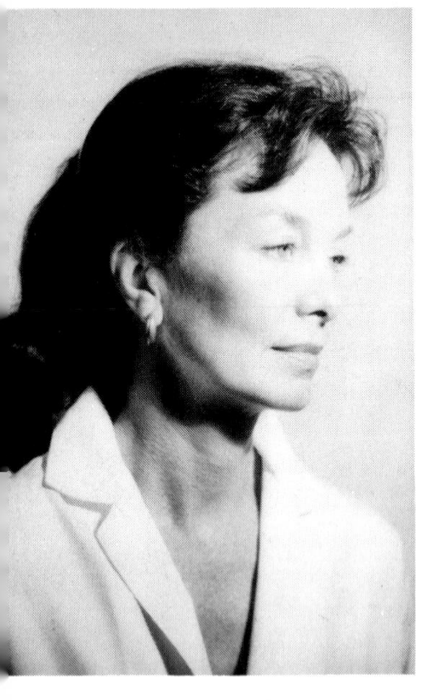

PAT KAVANAGH

Pat Kavanagh has been a literary agent with A. D. Peters (now Peters Fraser & Dunlop) since 1966.

Photograph by Jillian Edelstein

PIPPA MARKHAM

Pippa Markham trained and worked as an actress from 1966 to 1976. Her performances for theatre, TV and film include Eyeless in Gaza (a BBC series), The Ambassadors (also for the BBC), and Jenny Churchill (for Thames). She has also worked with Ken Russell, in The Music Lovers and The Devils, and toured North and South America with the RSC. She joined Plant and Froggatt as an assistant in 1976 and became a partner in 1980. When Cy Plant retired in 1989 the company name was changed to Markham and Froggatt.

JUDY DAISH

Born in 1947 Judy Daish trained with Jimmy Wax of ACTAC Ltd (theatrical and cinematic) in 1974. She formed Judy Daish Associates Ltd in 1978.

Photograph by Nicky Rushman

JENNE CASAROTTO

Jenne Casarotto dropped out of her "boring" British boarding school early in order to pursue her dream of working in America. She spent a year there in all, working in advertising at a Cincinati agency and taking a four-month Greyhound bus trip. Back in London she was saved from advertising by American novelist Leon Uris for whom she researched a book. This led to work at US agency CMA (now ICM) in their London literary department. After five years with the company and a brief spell with the Robert Stigwood Organisation, Jenne joined Douglas Rae to form an independent agency building an impressive roster of writer and director clients in film, television and publishing. Three years ago she formed her own writers, directors and producers agency, Casarotto Company, with her husband Georgio. In spring 1992 they formed Casarotto Ramsay with the famous Margaret Ramsay agency to represent the finest in theatrical writing. Casarotto Marsh was formed at the same time with US agent Sandra Marsh to represent "the best behind the camera talent".

Photograph by Mark Gerson

ANNE HUTTON

Anne Hutton's first job was a secretarial position in the entertainment industry, at MCA, in 1957. She left in 1960 to work abroad for a sports-loving screenwriter, becoming the first secretary to take notes on skis, horseback and surfboard. After two years she emigrated to America under the sponsorship of Volkswagen. She endured six months in a car plant before being rescued by the BBC's New York office and set to work liaising between the American TV networks and visiting BBC executives. Of these she found the men hopeless, interested only in bars, whereas the women were keen to learn everything the Americans could teach them about their way of doing things. She returned to England in 1965 to join Christopher Mann Ltd, a successful theatrical agency representing the top stars and directors of the 1960s. She started Hutton Management Ltd in 1974 and now represents some of the biggest British names in the film and theatre world.

Photograph by Ben Adam

SHEILA LEMON

Sheila Lemon worked for ATV abroad and at Elstree before setting up the script department of the actors' agency, Peter Crouch Ltd, which she ran for several years. She joined Curtis Brown in 1973, leaving to establish her own agency, Sheila Lemon Ltd, in 1978, and joined forces with Stephen Durbridge in 1986. She specialises in representing writers for theatre and television and has special experience with comedy. Formerly married to the writer, Hugh Whitemore, she has a teenage son, Tom.

CAROLE BLAKE

Carole Blake started in publishing with Rainbirds, the packagers. After eight years of progression through the company, she created a rights department for Michael Joseph selling an enviable list of authors through the early 1970s into paperback, book club and foreign markets. She was headhunted to start W. H. Allen's first rights department, then became marketing director of Sphere. After 14 years in publishing she started her own literary agency which then merged with Julian Friedmann's agency to become Blake Friedmann in 1983. She married Friedmann in the same year. An editorially based agency selling a wide range of rights for a limited client list, Blake Friedmann has a staff of 11 and represents 140 writers as well as several North American agencies and one of America's largest publishers. The agency is represented by associate agents throughout the world. Carole Blake is currently president of the Association of Authors' Agents.

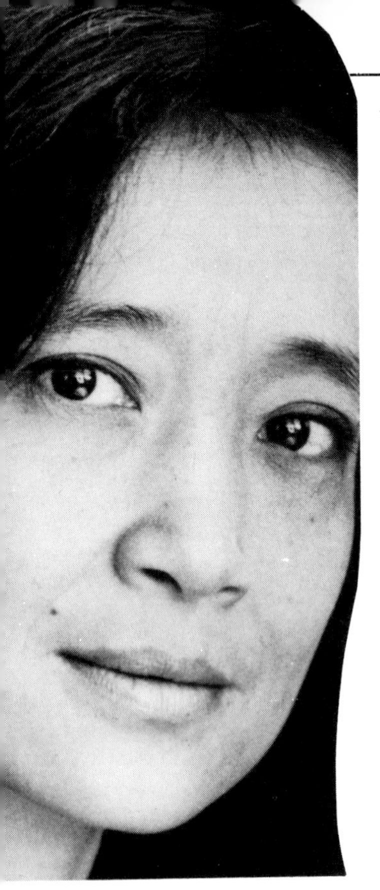

JUNG CHANG

Probably our most astute commentator on China, Dr Jung Chang recently won the 1992 NCR Award for Non-Fiction and the Writers' Guild of Great Britain Award for Non-Fiction for Wild Swans: Three Daughters of China (published by Harper Collins). She was brought up in China, where she was (briefly) a Red Guard at the age of 14, a peasant, a "barefoot doctor", a steel worker and an electrician, before becoming an English language student and an assistant lecturer at Sichuan University. She left China for England in 1978 and obtained a PhD in Linguistics at York University, thus becoming the first person from China to receive a doctorate from a British university. She has been working as a commentator and consultant on China for British television since 1982, and is the co-ordinator of Chinese Studies for the External Services of the School of Oriental and African Studies. She is currently working on a biography of Mao Zedong with her husband, the historian Jon Halliday.

Photograph by Peter Simpkin

LEE LANGLEY

Born in Calcutta of Scottish parents Lee travelled widely in India during her childhood. Two of her novels are set in India: the fifth Changes of Address was short-listed for the Hawthornden Prize, and the sixth Persistent Rumours won the Writers' Guild/Macallan Award for Best Fiction 1992 (presented in September). As well as books Lee has written screenplays, television scripts, poetry and a stage play. She is a member of PEN's Writers in Prison committee, a body concerned with the condition of writers persecuted or imprisoned by repressive regimes throughout the world, and has served on the Executive Committee of PEN for the last four years. Married to a writer, she lives in Richmond-upon-Thames where she is a member of the board of Richmond's Orange Tree Theatre.

Photograph by Theo Richmond

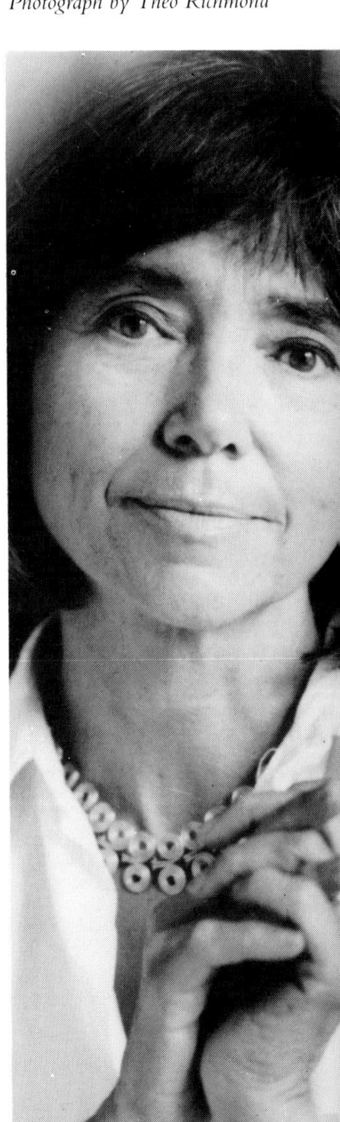

ELSPETH BARKER

Elspeth Barker had a remarkable debut with her first novel, "O Caledonia" (Hamish Hamilton and Penguin). It won the 1981 Winnifred Holtby Memorial Prize (awarded for the best regional novel of the year), presented in June 1992. It was short-listed for the Whitbread Prize and won the David Higham, the Scottish Spring Book Award and the Angel Fiction Prize. In the romantic and Gothic mode the book is set in Scotland (where Elspeth herself grew up) and tells the story of a girl brought up in a remote castle who, the author says, "manages to get herself murdered through her own naivety". Elspeth was educated in Scotland and at Oxford, and was married to the poet George Barker, with whom she had five children.

Photograph by Jane Brown

JACQUELINE BROWN

Jacqueline Brown began writing poetry eight years ago. She has been awarded both Yorkshire and East Midlands Bursaries and has had poems published in many magazines. She has given readings of her work at various venues as part of East Midlands Arts "New Voices" tour in 1990 and more recently as part of the "New Voices" series at the South Bank. She has won prizes in many competitions, notably the Leek Poetry Competition two years ago. Her sequence of poems, Thinking Egg, won the Avron/Observer competition in 1992.

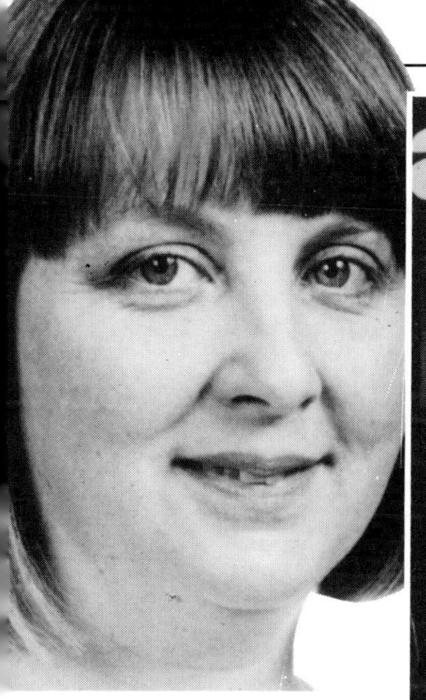

HILARY McKAY

Joint winner of The Guardian's Award for Children's Fiction in 1991, 32 year old Hilary McKay was born and grew up in Lincolnshire, the eldest of four girls in a family devoted to books – they had no TV. Their father was a great storyteller, so much so that the girls were often scared to go to bed. Hilary went to St Andrews University where she studied Botany and Zoology before switching to English, History of Art and Psychology) "because I got bored of dissecting things". The Exiles (Gollancz) is her first book. It draws on her childhood – there are four sisters who read a lot but here the similarity ends. The antics and misadventures of the girls "in exile" with their Big Grandma for the summer makes for extremely entertaining reading: "a bright new talent with a gentle comic gift . . . made me roar with laughter", said Gwen Grant.

RACHEL ANDERSON

Rachel Anderson (joint winner of the 1991 Guardian Children's Fiction Award, presented in March 1992) was born at Hampton Court, the second of five children of writer Verily Anderson. She began writing at 17 as a teenage correspondent for The Observer, and later worked for the BBC, in publishing and as a freelance journalist. Paper Faces is her ninth children's book. The Daily Telegraph said of her: "Rachel Anderson writes with observation and subtle humour". She contributes to journals and TV programmes, is a regular speaker on Woman's Hour and writes for Good Housekeeping on children and childcare and frequently reviews children's books. Married with four children, she lives mainly in Norfolk, with her extended family of four generations.

A. L. KENNEDY

A. L. Kennedy's first collection of short stories *Night Geometry and the Garscadden Trains* (Polygon) was described by the judges of the Mail on Sunday/John Llewellyn Rhys competition as a novel combining "a truly original poetic ear with a profound understanding of human motives and actions". The book also won an SAC Book Award and the Saltire Award for Best First Book. Born in Dundee in 1965, she studied English and Drama at Warwick University before becoming a community arts worker. She has directed youth theatre, performed at the Edinburgh Fringe – and even once sold brushes, for extra money. At present she is Project Ability's Creative Writing Coordinator and also Writer in Residence for Hamilton and East Kilbride Social Work Department. She is currently working on a novel.

MICHÈLE ROBERTS

One of Britain's most exciting contemporary writers, Michèle house in Normandy, *Daughters of the House*, published by Virago, has Booker prize. The saga of a family feud set in a prosperous farmer's house in Normandy *Daughters of the House*, published by Virago, has been compared to the writings of Colette in its minuteness and immediacy. Half-French and half-English, Michèle grew up in London. She has already published five novels,

LIANE JONES

Liane spent her early years in Wales and Bristol. A degree at Cambridge led to a series of journalistic jobs. Her first two books were non-fiction – *Flying High: The Woman's Way to the Top* and *A Quiet Courage: Women Agents of the French Resistance*. Her first novel, *The Dreamstone* (Heinemann), in which a story in the present is entwined with a story in the past – a 12th century Welsh prince who discovers America – won the Betty Trask Award for romantic fiction.

ANITA RODDICK

Born Anita Lucia Perella in 1942 in Littlehampton, life before The Body Shop for Anita Roddick included working in her mother's cafe, teacher training, work at the UN and extensive travel. With husband Gordon, she first set up in the hotel/restaurant trade. The Body Shop was born when Gordon went travelling and Anita had to find a means of support for herself and their two daughters. The Body Shop centred around what Anita, as a consumer, wanted and could not find – products made from natural ingredients, not tested on animals, simply packaged and at affordable prices. Anita opened and ran the first Body Shop in Brighton in 1976. There are now over 800 shops in 41 countries. Anita has won many awards, including the OBE, but makes it clear in her autobiography, Body and Soul (1991), that what matters more to her is learning first hand from other cultures and believing passionately in everything she does.

NICKI McCANN

Barton-on-Humber Industrial Estate is not the sort of exotic location which one would think of as a site for the manufacture of pasta, but this is where Nicki McCann and The Pasta Company have made their home. Nicki, 28, and her two partners were working in the Mars food division when they conceived the idea of setting up their own fresh pasta manufacturing company.
They went to Italy to study the art and the machinery and, on their return, found the site and raised £100,000 to get started. The Pasta Company makes fresh pasta for the British market and will flavour it, colour it and stuff it with whatever the market requires. Black pasta or pasta stuffed with baked beans may not be popular in Rome, but they are in Rotherham and, since its inception in 1987, the company's turnover has gone from £4,000 to £5 million – and rising. Nicki was a finalist for the Veuve Clicquot Business Woman of the Year Award 1992.

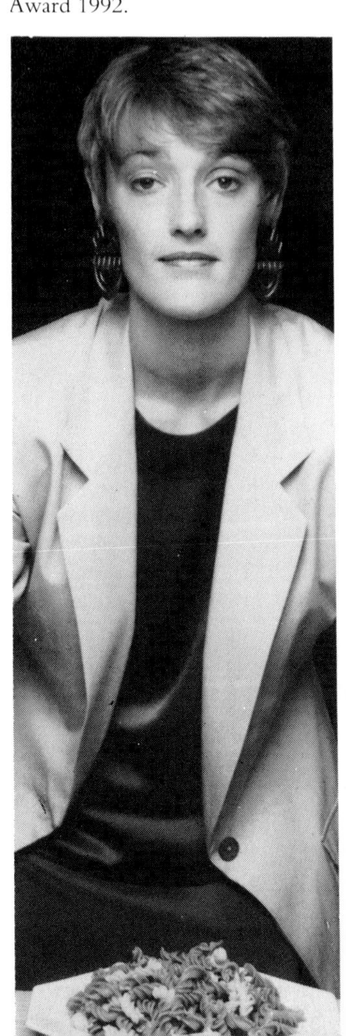

SOPHIE MIRMAN

Educated at the French Lycee in London, Sophie Mirman joined Marks & Spencer as a bi-lingual secretary. She rose from the typing pool to work for Lord Sieff and became a management trainee. In 1982, aged 24 and feeling the need for a change of direction, she started Tie Rack, where she rose from general manager to becoming managing director, responsible for a chain of 15 shops. As the chain grew, Sophie decided that she wanted to start something that was all her own. Having established the success potential of small, specialist outlets selling single product lines, a concept which was later to be enlarged by many other retailers, Sophie embarked on her new project. She conceived the idea of Sock Shop, selling socks, tights and stockings. The first branch opened in Knightsbridge in 1983 and a further 135 soon followed. In 1990 Sophie created another new concept, Trotters, a children's mini-emporium selling clothing, footwear, gifts and hairdressing. Named Business Woman of the Year in 1987, Sophie Mirman was named Motivator of the Year in 1991.

DEBBIE MOORE

Having left school with no academic qualifications, Debbie Moore won Honey magazine's model competition in 1964, which launched her, at the age of 15, on an international modelling career. Towards the end of 1978, Debbie learned that the dance centre which she attended in Covent Garden was to close, leaving several teachers and 2,000 dancers with nowhere to go. Spotting a ready-made business opportunity, she grabbed it with both hands and, in 1979, opened the first Pineapple dance centre in an old warehouse in Covent Garden. Two more dances centres in London followed and in 1982 Debbie launched the company on the USM, becoming the first woman chairman to walk on to teh floor of the London Stock Exchange. She published The Pineapple Dance Book in 1983 and, in 1985, was voted Business woman chairman to walk on to the pioneered fashion in the 1980s with stretch cotton Lycra with her Survival of the Fittest range of clothing, which now has 33 retail outlets.

JENNIFER d'ABO

Born in 1945, Jennifer d'Abo has two children who are successful entrepreneurs in their own right. Jennifer's first love is design, which she has incorporated into all her diverse business ventures. She also loves flowers, which led her to buy Moyses Stevens, the florist, in 1989. She has built on the tradition for quality for which Moyses Stevens is renowed by instituting a product development service for a large range of different product types, including baskets and china. She has travelled to trade fairs throughout the world, seeking out new and unusual products for the retail market. During her time as chairman of Ryman, she was the first retailer of matching office accessories – even pink filing cabinets! Jennifer enjoys cooking, and likes nothing better than an informal supper around her kitchen table with good food and good company.

THE HON MRS SARA MORRISON

Sara Morrison is a director of GEC plc and a non-executive director of The Abbey national plc and of Carlton Television Ltd. Until she retired in 1981, she was chairman of the National Council for Voluntary Organisations. She was a member of the 1976 Annan Committee of Enquiry into Broadcasting, a director of Channel 4 from its inception until 1985 and for the last 18 months of the Imperial Tobacco Company. Other roles over the years have included the National Consumer Council, the National Association of Youth Clubs and the Volunteer Centre. She was vice-chairman of the Conservative Party from 1971 to 1975 and , from 1981 until 1984, she was appointed by the Secretary of State for Employment to chair the National Council for the employment of Disabled People. Sara Morrison is a member of the Video Appeals Committee, a Fellow of the Royal Society of Arts, a Companion of the British Institute of Management, a member of the governing body of Imperial College and of the governing council of the Family Policies Studies Centre.

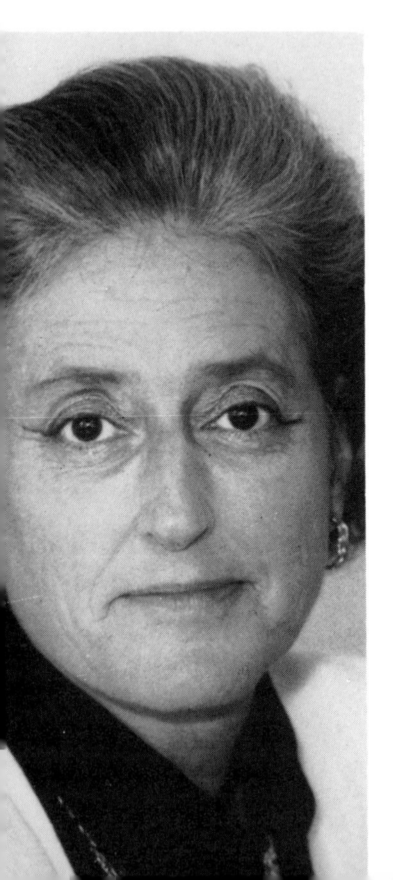

RHIANNON CHAPMAN

After serving as personnel director of the London Stock Exchange, Rhiannon Chapman ran her own business consultancy before joining The Industrial Society as director in July 1991. During her early career, Mrs. Chapman worked in a range of front-line and policy development roles in major engineering design and manufacturing companies. She has been a member of the Universities Funding Council since 1989 and has recently been appointed an independent governor of the City of London Polytechnic. She is a member of the Employment Appeal Tribunal. As leader of the UK's largest independent advisory and training organisation, Rhiannon Chapman is in frequent demand as a speaker, writer and broadcaster.

PENNY HUGHES

A graduate in Chemistry from Sheffield University, Penny Hughes was appointed president of Coca-Cola Great Britain and Ireland in July 1992, at the age of 33. She is also a vice-president of Coca-Cola International and serves on the company's European Operating Board. She joined the company in 1984 and was appointed marketing director of

Coca-Cola & Schweppes Beverages Ltd (CCSB) in 1987, moving on to the board as commercial director in 1989. Penny Hughes was a finalist for Business Woman of the Year in 1991.

PHYLLIS CUNNINGHAM

Phyllis Cunningham spent three years as administrative/research assistant to the medical director of the Geigy Pharmaceutical Company, before moving to the Roosevelt Hospital in New York. Returning to London in 1964, she became assistant house governor at the Royal Free Hospital and planning officer for its new 880 bed hospital. Here she found her true vocation – being involved in the construction of a brand new hospital facility from blue-print to admission of the first patient. In 1974 she was appointed deputy house governor of the Royal Marsden Hospital and in 1980, chief executive. Her business acumen is well demonstrated by her running of the £25 million 'hospital on two sites' appeal, launched in 1990. Phyllis convinced the board of governors to commence building work when one third of the appeal target was met. This was a splendid incentive for the money raising efforts, and the target was met in full at the beginning of 1993. Phyllis Cunningham was the winner of the Veuve Clicquot Business Woman of the Year Award for 1992.

COLLEEN RYAN

A finalist for the 1992 Business Woman of the Year Award, Colleen Ryan is chairman of the Research Business Group, the largest independent research company in the UK. Born in 1952, she co-founded the company ten years ago and her business acumen and managerial skills have seen revenues increase to £9.2 million in 1991, with a 200 per cent growth since 1990. Colleen is chairman of the Association of Market Survey Organisations and a frequent conference leader and speaker for the market research industry.

JUDITH DONOVAN

Judith Donovan is the chairman of Judith Donovan Associates, one of the UK's most successful direct marketing agencies. Born in 1951, Judith graduated from Hull University and worked in a series of advertising positions, culminating in joining Grattan, where she was advertising manager for five years. In 1982, she became a self-employed direct marketing consultant. She founded JDA, her Bradford based agency, in 1985, and now has a prestigious blue-chip client roster drawn from around the UK. The agency employs 50 people and is ranked in the UK's top 20. Judith is a high profile speaker within the industry and a key member of the Direct Marketing Association committee. In 1988, she was runner-up in the Women Mean Business competition and in 1989 she won the Yorkshire Enterprise Woman of Achievement Award. She is founder vice patron of Women Mean Business and the first woman patron of the Small Business Bureau. Chairman of the Bradford Training and Enterprise Council, Judith is a member of the Bradford Chamber of Commerce and patron of two prominent theatre companies.

GERALDINE BROWN

Geraldine Brown is the founder and managing director of The Domino Consultancy Limited. Apart from her acknowledged commercial expertise, she is highly regarded in the area of implementing equal opportunities. During the past two years, Geraldine has spoken at conferences and appeared on television, speaking on the subject of women returning to work and women managers. Geraldine is the president of the European Women's Management Development Network for women managers.

STEPHANIE (STEVE) SHIRLEY

In 1991, Steve Shirley, the founder director of the FI Group plc, became the eleventh person, and the first woman, to win the British Institute of Management's Gold Medal – BIM's highest award – in recognition of her outstanding management achievements. The medal citation praised her ability to motivate and inspire staff and gave recognition to the significant contribution she has made while president of the British Computer Society, raising the awareness of senior management on how information technology should be used as an integral part of strategic business planning. Steve graduated from London University in 1956 and founded FI in 1962. She was appointed a Freeman of the City of London in 1987 and a Fellow of the Royal Society of Arts in 1985. Amongst many various awards and appointments, she received the Recognition of Industry Technology Achievement Award in 1985. In 1980, Steve Shirley was awarded the OBE in recognition of her services to her industry.

SUSAN GOMPELS

After qualifying as a chartered accountant with BDO Binder Hamlyn in 1969, Susan Gompels spent a year at the University of Michigan Business Administration School. Since her return to the UK in 1971, she has been principal of her own chartered accountancy practice, which now has a largely professional client base. Susan is an elected member of the ruling council of the Institute of Chartered Accountants in England and Wales (ICAEW) and of its executive management committee, chairman of Women in Accountancy and vice-chairman of the General Practitioner Board of the ICAEW. She has been much involved in the fields of recruitment and training and, in 1989, was appointed to lead a team of experienced chartered accountants as the Recruitment Trends Study Group. The resulting report, Recruitment in the 1990s – A Seller's Market, was published in 1990, offering a clear agenda for action to the profession. Susan has lectured widely on the report and on technical and professional matters and is increasingly called upon as a consultant in relation to the recruitment and retention of professional women. She sits on the board of the Surrey Training & Enterprise Council and is a member of the Law Society's Women's Careers Working Party.
Photograph by Argentum

JANE BRADFORD

Banker Jane Bradford began her career in her home town of Derby in 1964 and gained experience in a wide range of banking roles in and around the East Midlands before moving to London in 1980 as NatWest's first Equal Opportunities manager. After a stint as lending manager at Westminster branch, she returned to Head Office as Loan Schemes manager and then undertook a number of marketing and planning relates roles, before taking up her current position as head of Small Business Services in April 1991. As head of SBS, Jane is responsible for developing and directing the bank's marketing activities for its million small business customers. She is a member of the CBI's Smaller Firms Council.

JANET COHEN

Janet Cohen graduated from Cambridge in 1962 with a 2:1 honours degree in Law, and qualified as a solicitor in 1965. She spent the next four years in the USA, designing war games, and in the UK, working for John Laing Construction. She worked for the DTI for 12 years, specialising in industrial reconstruction, before joining Charterhouse Bank in 1982, as an industrial and privatisation specialist. Janet, 52, is the author of four novels, the most recent of which, The Highest Bidder, concerns a management buy-out from government.

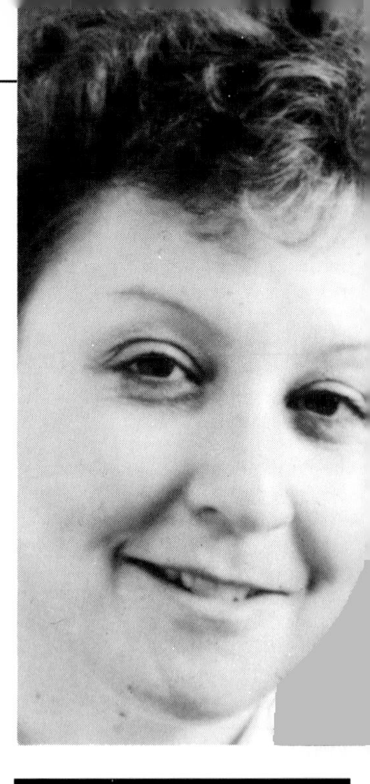

ROSALIND GILMORE

Rosalind Gilmore is First Commissioner of the Building Societies Commission, Chief Registrar of Friendly Societies and Industrial Assurance Commissioner. She is the head of the UK government department which supports these statutory authorities. She was educated at University College, London, where she is now a Fellow, and Newnham College, Cambridge, where she is an associate Fellow. She spent much of her career in HM Treasury, dealing mainly with domestic and international financial matters, including exchange rate and monetary policy. She was head of the Financial Institutions Division of the Treasury form 1977 to 1980. After leaving the Treasury in 1982, she became general manager of corporate planning at Dunlop Ltd and then executive director in charge of marketing and personal banking at Girobank plc. She was non-executive director of the London and Manchester Group plc and Mercantile Group plc and a member of the Financial Services Act Tribunal, before resigning these appointments on becoming full-time deputy of the Building Societies Commission in 1989, and chief executive in March 1991.

KAZIA KANTOR

Central Independent Television's group director of finance, Kazia Kantor is the most senior woman in the Central Group and one of the most senior in commercial television in Britain. Kazia, 42, was educated at Manchester University and began her working life at Price Waterhouse, where she was the first woman audit manager. She moved to Inchcape plc in 1970, where she became group financial controller, working some of the time in SE Asia, the Middle East and North and South America. She left Inchcape in 1987 and joined Grand Metropolitan plc as finance and business affairs director of the retailing and property sector in 1990, after spells at HMV Group, as finance director, and Aegis, where she was involved in restructuring the worldwide advertising group into an international media group. Prior to joining Central in September 1992, Kazia had been business development director at Grand Metropolitan. She is a non-executive director of British Rail.

LESLEY KNOX

Lesley Knox gained her MA in Law from Cambridge University in 1975 and joined Slaughter & May in the following year, where she qualified as a lawyer. In 1980 she joined Shearman & Sterling in New York, where she passed the New York State bar exams. She then joined Kleinwort Benson and became involved in all aspects of corporate finance, becoming a director in 1986, at the age of 33. In 1987 Lesley was a finalist for Business Woman of the Year. In 1991, as head of Institutional Fund Management, she became a director of Kleinwort Benson Investment Management Ltd. Lesley is also chairman of Kleinwort Benson International Investment Ltd, chairman of Langbourn Property Investment Services, director of Kleinwort Benson Investment Management Holdings Ltd and a non-executive director of Strong & Fisher plc.

SHEILA MASTERS

Law graduate and chartered accountant, Sheila Masters has been a partner in KPMG Peat Marwick since 1983. Sheila won first place in her examinations for both the ICA and the Institute of Taxation. Her particular expertise is in the public sector; she has been seconded to the government twice, to HM Treasury (1979-81) as accountancy and financial adviser, and as director of finance on the NHS Management Executive (1988-91). Her particular skill in crossing public/private sector boundaries was recognised in 1992, when she was appointed as one of the first private sector members of the Management Board of the Inland Revenue as a non-executive. Sheila, 43, is married to farmer Barry Noakes and is a member of Chartered Accountants in England and Wales.

JANET WALFORD

Starting in the personal finance industry in 1971, Janet Walford, 46, worked initially for three insurance companies and a national firm of insurance brokers in a technical support capacity. She joined Money Management magazine in 1978 as a staff writer, became assistant editor in 1979, and deputy editor in 1981. In 1985 she left to start up Pension Management magazine for the Financial Times, and returned to Money Management in December 1986 as editor. Janet has won six awards for journalism (plus three runner-up prizes) and, under her editorship, Money Management journalists have won five awards and six runner-up prizes. Janet has written for all the major newspapers, and is the author of the FT Handbook of Personal Pensions, now in its 13th year. She has made numerous radio and television appearances.

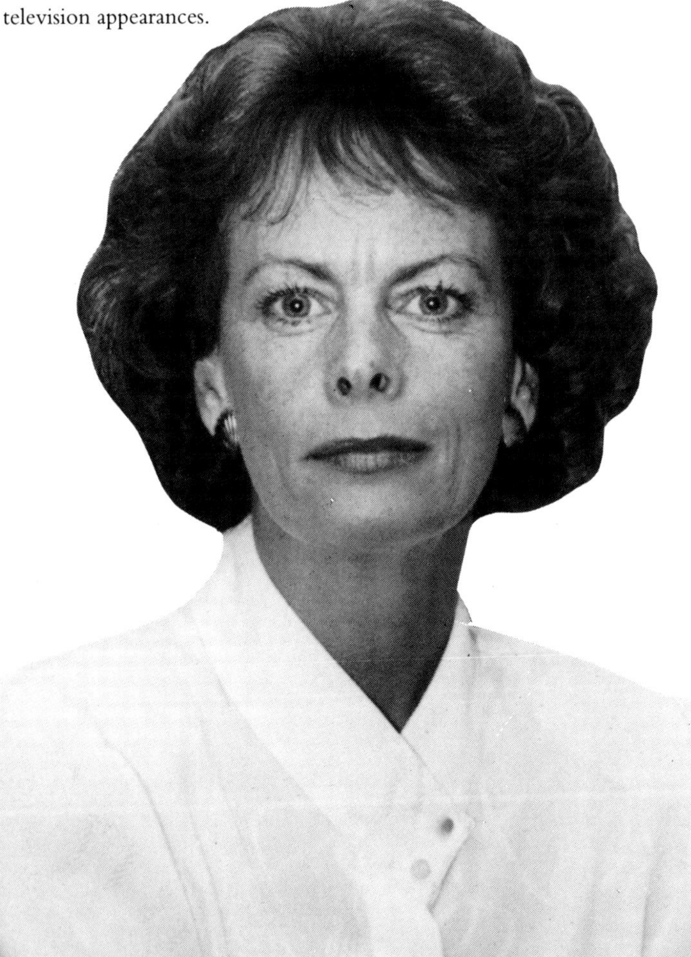

ANN BALDWIN

In 1972 Anne Baldwin joined Grant Thornton in Northamptonshire, having qualified as a chartered accountant in Middlesex. She became a partner in 1978 and from 1978 until 1985 she specialised as a tax partner. In 1985 she moved to Bristol, as group managing partner and staff partner of the Bristol and Bath offies. In 1989 she became part of Grant Thornton's national executive, responsible for recruitment and the development of the 2,700 staff, and for the firm's information technology. Ann lectures regularly on various topics and was a regular contributor to Channel 4's Moneyspinner programme. She is a member of the CBI's Smaller Firms Council. Now aged 46, Ann is married to a chartered accountant.

TERESA GRAHAM

Teresa Graham is a partner with Baker Tilly. She is the company's national staff partner, responsible for training, recruitment and all employment policy issues. Before joining Baker Tilly, she was a senior manager in the department of privatisation services of a large international firm based in London. Previously, she worked for the same company in Newcastle. Teresa is chairman of the London Practitioner Board of the London Society of Chartered Accountants, with some 25,000 members, and chairman of the Advisory Committee for Finance Education and Training for the RSA Examinations Board. She is a Fellow of the RSA. Teresa was business advisor to the Department of Employment team in the 1990-91 GEC National Business Game. She is a member of the Institute of Chartered Accountants for England and Wales' working party on small company audit relaxation.

Photograph by Monitor Photography Ltd

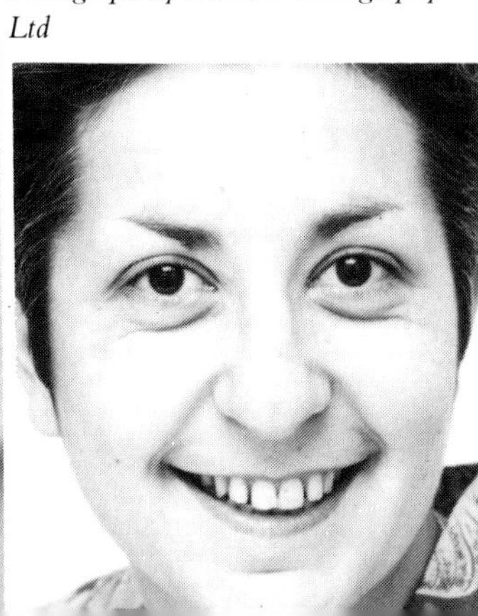

FIONA PRICE

The combination of chartered accountant and healer seems an unlikely one, but these are some of the qualifications of 33-year-old Fiona Price. Fiona gained a BA in Psychology from Exeter University and an MBA in Marketing from the City University. In 1991 she qualified as a Licentiate of the Radionics Association for healing. From 1983 to 1986 Fiona was a financial adviser with FPS (Management) Ltd, offering independent financial advice to private clients. She left FPS when it lost its independent status, and set up her own company, Modern Money Ltd, with a partner, who bought her share in 1988 when she founded Fiona Price & Partners. The company now has over 1,000 female clients and a number of corporate clients selected for their favourable attitude towards women. In 1989 Fiona Price was the winner of the Cosmopolitan Women of Tomorrow Award in the Entrepreneurship category. She is the founder of The Financial Exchange, a non-profit making organisation for women working in financial services and related professions and of the financial Services Woman of the Year Award, which she founded in 1991. Fiona appears frequently in the press, on radio and on television and has been a money columnist for Company magazine.

ANNE McMEEHAN

Anne McMeehan is managing director of Framlingham Unit Management and group marketing director of Framlingham Group plc. She joined the company in 1985, having previously worked at Allied Dunbar (1976-81) and Arbuthnot Latham (1981-85). She studied for her degree in Economics, Politics, French and German at Loughborough University, her earlier education having been at Portsmouth High School for Girls.

MARY BAKER

President of Women in Management, Mary Baker joined the board of Barclays Bank UK in 1983, while she was chairman of the London Tourist Board. She was appointed to the group board of Barclays in 1988 and to the board of the Prudential Corporation in the same year. She is a director of Avon Cosmetics Ltd and the MFI Furniture Group plc and was a member of the board of Thames Television from 1975 to 1990. A Scot, and a graduate of St Andrew's University, Mary Baker taught in London for eight years and has worked on a number of publications on education, metrication and legislation and taxation affecting women. She was elected to the Women's National Commission from 1976 to 1978 and is part-author of Macmillan's Days of Decision – Women. From 1986 she chaired the national charity, the Holiday Care Service and, currently, heads up the Tourism for All campaign. She is an honorary Fellow of Nene College, a trustee of the Independent Broadcasting Telethon Trust and a Freeman of the City of London.

Photograph by Dr Nicholas Posner

ALLWYNNE McDONALD

Pawnbroking was the family business for young Allwynne. Her grandfather, James Greenwood, had established it at the beginning of the century in Middlesbrough and her parents continued to run the business from 1946. But Allwynne, born in 1929, did not become involved until the age of 40, having left school at 16 to work as a trainee librarian at Middlesbrough Public Library. Marriage followed three years later and she raised two sons and a daughter before taking over the shop. Her brother John, a lecturer and Head of Mathematics, takes care of the firm's accounts. Together they have introduced many changes to the business, giving it a contemporary profile – or, as Allwynne herself put its, "placing the jewel of traditional pawnbroking into a modern setting".

MARGARET SMITH

A Geordie born and bred, Margaret Smith has been trading as a pawnbroker in North Shields, Tyne and Wear, since 1985. She had started out two years earlier simply selling jewellery but found that people wanted to sell her items, asking her to hold on to them until they could afford to buy them back. The National Pawnbrokers Association gave valuable advice in the early stages and 35-year-old Margaret is now firmly established in her profession. She will accept most goods but draws the line at clothes. One customer even tried to unload a collection of fancy-dress outfits, including police uniforms and clowns' costumes. She is happy to leave such things to other establishments. Margaret, who married in 1991 and lives locally, tries to help people to overcome the stigma which is still attached to visiting a pawnbroker's shop, comparing her business with running a pub – "it's friendly and I have my regulars". In the summer, she says, customers use her shop "like a safe – they bring in a watch or ring and take the cash for their holidays".

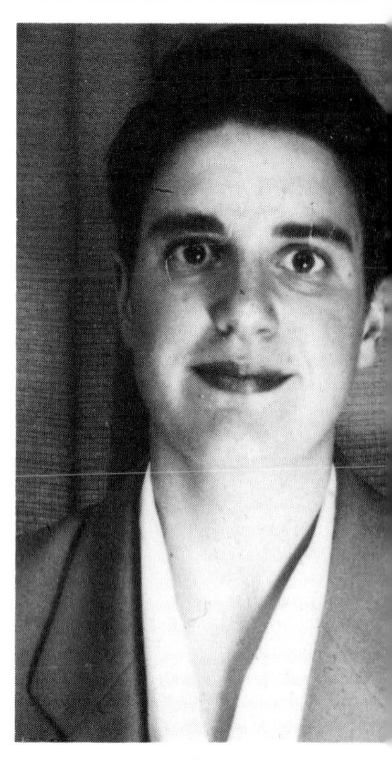

MARIE ATKIN

Marie Atkin's family owned a jewellers in Sheffield and she remembers her father showing her how to repair neck-chains when she was just a young girl. It was training that proved invaluable in later life, since her career has been spent in the jewellery and pawnbroking trade. Having gained an advanced City & Guilds qualification in jewellery manufacture and design in Manchester, she studied for an extra year to learn techniques of diamond setting. This led to a part-time job in a Birmingham jewellery workshop, where she learned "quick trade techniques". At the same time, she was helping to run the Sheffield shop, which she eventually took over with sister Lynne. In 1989 Marie decided to open her own pawnbroking business with the help of a bank overdraft. Happily, the service was in great demand and she ran it for two years before selling up and bringing her skills to London, where she now manages a busy shop. She is single and lives in Wood Green, North London.

NICOLA TEMPLETON

Still only 21 years old, Nicola Templeton runs the Sunderland branch of Albemarle and Bond Pawnbrokers Ltd. Leaving school at the age of 16 without any real idea of what she wanted to do for a living, Nicola took her interest in jewellery as a starting point and applied to the company for a junior position. She found the sheer variety of the work fascinating and her obvious enthusiasm led to her promotion to senior assistant. This allowed her to learn even more about the business, especially dealing with the public in occasionally difficult situations. In January 1992 the manager of the branch left to have a baby and Nicola, at the age of 20, got the job. She believes a friendly but professional manner is essential in her job and encourages it in the overall running of the branch, which is the busiest in the group.

CLAYRE BRYANS

A degree in philosophy is not essential for a pawnbroker but it has no doubt helped Clayre Bryans in her dealings with the public since she expanded her jewellers to include pawnbroking. Now established as the leading member of the profession in Croydon, Surrey, she takes both jewellery and non-jewellery pledges. Born in 1957, Clayre worked for oil giant Esso in its employee relations department before setting up Rio Jewellery as a concession within a Croydon department store in 1982. Two years later she acquired her own premises in the town and expanded into pawnbroking in 1987, moving to larger premises in 1989. She is a member of the National Association of Goldsmiths and the National Pawnbroking Association. Divorced, her leisure interests include travel and weight-training.

ANN SHOOSMITH

Ann Shoosmith was brought up, she says, as a boy by her father, Harry Rose. She was trying to tune his motorbike at the age of two and a half. Her first car was an Austin 7, when she was 17, and her first competitive motoring centred on the Bournemouth College and the West Hants and Dorset Car Club doing autocross, sprints, hill climbs, trials and rallies. Ann has driven all sorts of vintage cars, including a 1904 Talbot and an 1898 De Dion Tricycle, before moving to the ultimate, the 1928 Le Mans Bentley team car. She has been a member of the Bentley Drivers Club for 30 years, culminating in taking on the chairmanship. An enthusiastic member of the VSCC, she gains the most pleasure from driving a vintage Bentley up Prescott hill climb.

Photograph by Tom Threlfall

AVERIL SCOTT-MONCRIEFF

Averil Scott-Moncrieff was born 76 years ago, two miles away from where she lives now, in Staffordshire. She was hooked on cars from the age of 12, but took ages learning to drive one. In 1941 she married Bunty Scott-Moncrieff, of "horseless carriage" fame and first raced in 1950, in a 37a Bugatti. In 1951 she turned the Bugatti upside down in the "Rest-and-be-thankful" hill climb – her only accident. She raced a Lotus 6 in 1954, followed by a Cooper Climax, a Frazer Nash Meadows and, finally, the Type 57 Bugatti, originally modified by Twink Whincop in 1951. She is now retired and drives a 1933 Morgan Jap. Her racing epitaph is "Never First Never Last".

DI THRELFALL

Di Threlfall mainly races a 1930 Lancia, but also a Theophile Schneider, a chain-driven Bugatti, a Bristol engined Frazer Nash and is the works driver for the National Motor Museum's Prince Henry Vauxhall. She drives a Frazer Nash and an MGB in races for post-war cars. Di was the Vintage Sports Car Club Ladies' Champion 1981-84, and her husband, Tom, was VSCC President 1980-84. A member of the Waynfleet Singers, who take over from Winchester Cathedral Choir in busy periods, and plays the 'cello for a local orchestra. She is a professional tennis coach.

JO MOSS

Jo Moss was born in 1964 and lists her occupation as a vintage car restorer. Jo's first car was a 1948 Morris 8, and old cars have always fascinated her. When she was offered the opportunity of driving a 1930 4½ litre Invicta she jumped at it, despite a few pre-race nerves, and has now driven it on most of the British circuits and competed in sprints and hill climbs. Although the Invicta seems a heavy car, Jo says that she finds it light and responsive.

Photograph by Alan S. D. Cox

SOPHIE WALKER

Sophie was born in England and brought up in Southern Ireland where her first love was horses. After leaving school, she qualified as a Montessori teacher, set up her own school and married into a keen vintage motoring family. She took up racing in her 1929 chain-driven Frazer Nash in sprints run by the Vintage Sports Car Club, competing on equal terms with men, in the very competitive 1500cc sports car class and achieved a number of successes, culminating in taking the long-standing class record at Prescott in 1991. In 1992 she took a year off to start a family, but looks forward to breaking her own record in 1993.

ANNABEL JONES

An Oxford and Harvard educated management consultant, Annabel Jones started navigating vintage cars at the age of 14, and learned to drive with her mother's Austin 7, and her father's Vauxhall 30/98. She rebuilt the bare bones of the Austin 7 she received for her 17th birthday and, while at Harvard, rebuilt and made a competitive car out of a derelict Model A Ford. In 1992, in her own cars and her father's racing Frazer Nash, she competed in 25 events, in Britain and overseas, in all forms of racing, and she won the Lycett Memorial Trophy, the major award of the Vintage Sports Car Club, the first woman ever to do so.

JANET GILES

Janet Giles met her husband Freddie through their mutual hobby of vintage cars. Freddie is a director of the Vintage Sports Car Club. Janet owns a 1928 Anzani-engined Frazer Nash and has competed regularly in speed events and rallies both in this car and in single seater Frazer Nash racing cars. Janet is an active member of the Frazer Nash section, and has been secretary and editor. She assisted in the computerisation of the VSCC which runs 26 events a year, at which she either competes or marshalls.

Cameo photograph by P. Selwyn Smith. Car photograph by Roger Collings

VALERIE STOGDALE

An Oxford graduate with an MA in Human Sciences from Lady Margaret Hall, Valerie has had 11 of which were spent in the London office of a worldwide US firm, Russell Reynolds Associates Inc, latterly as executive director with a focus on the consumer and retail sectors. She joined Norman Broadbent (BNB Resources plc) in 1992 as Board director of NB Selection Ltd to work on increasing middle to senior management selection.

CAROL SPEED

Carol was born in Yorkshire and grew up in Hertfordshire. Following a grammar school education she spent her early career in publishing and then went into advertising where she worked for five years as a media planner/ buyer. She then moved into marketing within the petroleum and pharmaceutical industries before entering executive search in 1977 as search manager at Boyden's London office. In 1981 she started Kynaston, now one of the top independent search firms in London, became managing director in 1985 and masterminded a management buyout in 1988. To take on the world market she started up EMA Partners International Ltd in 1988. The company has grown within four years to be No 15 in the world in the search business. They now have offices throughout America, Asia and Europe, including Eastern Europe. Carol has now set her sights upon expansion into Japan and Australasia.

JILL LYE

Having graduated from Exeter University with a law degree (specialising in industrial law), Jill joined the Cadbury Schweppes Group. She started in personnel and progressed through training and industrial relations to management selection and became development manager for Cadbury Ltd. She then changed course and moved to Schweppes Ltd, taking up an appointment as trade marketing manager and moving into National Account Management. A return to Human Resource Management with Coca-Cola & Schweppes Beverages Ltd was the forerunner to her final move into consultancy – a long held ambition. She joined Illingworth & Associates five years ago and is now one of the senior partners. The company specialises in the recruitment, training and development of senior executives for major corporations. Jill is currently chairman of the Association of Search and Selection Consultants – a voluntary body aimed at raising standards within the search and selection industry.

KATE DONAGHY

A founding member of Whitehead Selection Ltd Kate Donaghy worked first as a nurse and then as a barrister. On leaving school (St Mary's, Ascot) she went home to Belfast to train as a nurse, specialising in casualty. After qualifying in midwifery she went to the Far East between 1981 and 1983, working and travelling through China and Indochina from a base in Hong Kong. In 1983 she returned to take up a place at the School of Oriental and African Studies at London University to read Law. The LLB with which she emerged equipped her with almost more knowledge of Chinese and Japanese than English law. In 1987 she was called to the Bar as a member of Gray's Inn. Deciding to have a commercial career as a headhunter in London rather than continue as a student in Beijing she joined Whitehead Mann as a trainee headhunter and researcher. She now works across almost every industry sector in all disciplines.

GILL CARRICK

Educated at Bradford Institute of Technology Gill spent the early part of her career as a translator with Cementation, the civil mining and technical engineers. She then spent eight years with Williams Hudson, the shipping, wharfaging and property dealing group. After a period of two years with the National Enterprise Board, at that time headed by Lord Ryder, she joined Rotaflex, an international public company involved in light engineering as Head of Personnel. She was appointed to the Main Board in 1980. She joined GKR in 1982 and since then has been involved in assignments across a wide range of disciplines and industry sectors in the UK, Europe, the US and the Far East. In 1986 she was appointed to the Board. In recent years she has been involved in developing GKR's expertise in the media and retail sectors.

FIONA HANNAN

Fiona Hannan studied English Literature at Westfield College, London, and took a PhD at LSE and Birkbeck College, covering industrial relations, personnel management and organisational behaviour. She then worked in industrial relations research and as a personnel manager for Allied Breweries. She moved to the City in 1987, initially working at Midland Montagu before being headhunted to UBS Phillips & Drew, where she was mainly involved with recruitment and on developing the graduate programme. A director of David Sheppard & Partners since 1991 her principal clients are in investment banking, the property sector and retailing. She also undertakes specialist advisory work in assessment and compensation.

KAREN MOONEY

Brought up in the Surrey countryside Karen Mooney was educated at a convent, stage school and sixth form college. She took a degree in Business Studies, specialising in personnel management, before joining the police force. She rose to become a manager with the Metropolitan Police, serving firstly at New Scotland Yard where she was responsible for a staff of 30 and then at Buckingham Palace where she was in charge of the civilian staff of the Royalty and Diplomatic Protection Department. She set up the Sara Eden Introduction Agency, specialising in business and professional people, in 1988 and has retained full responsibility for its management and day to day running ever since. She is the press officer for the Windsor, Ascot, Eton and District Chamber of Trade and Commerce and has been an active member of the Executive Committee since 1990.

SYLVIA LONGSTAFF

Widowed 23 years ago and left with two small boys to bring up Sylvia started organising parties and chat groups for other single people. Later, when her sons were older and didn't want a holiday with mum, she began to look around for somewhere to go to widen her circle of single friends. There was nothing on offer. Two years later she set up Longstaff Leisure Singles Holidays from a cottage in the Yorkshire Dales with the aim of bringing singles together in a relaxed atmosphere without any sexual connotations. Four years ago she moved into bigger premises, large enough to sleep 19 people. Activities at the hotel range from abseiling, pony-trekking and ballooning to swimming, long walks and even longer meals. Over the years Sylvia has met and entertained thousands of people and "never ceases to be amazed that she is the only person in the UK who has a holiday hotel where single people are warmly welcomed".

HEDI FISHER

Hedi Fisher was born in a small town near Budapest. One of five children whose father was a rabbi, her family were killed in Auschwitz, apart from one older brother. In 1944 she was imprisoned in an Austrian camp and in 1945 was hidden and saved by a Christian family in Vienna. She was brought to England in 1947 by an uncle and educated here. When he died she was forced to work in a dress factory and study by night. Later on she worked as a shorthand typist and in 1960 became a social worker, dealing with delinquents and adoption. She has been married twice, and has a daughter from her first marriage. She founded the Hedi Fisher Marriage Bureau in 1970 and in the past 22 years she and her partner Susan Sander (also ex-Hungarian) have brought together thousands of people and been responsible for countless marriages.

BARBARA BRADSHAW

Barbara Bradshaw gave up teaching biology in 1975 to be at home with her children. Once they were at school she decided to start work again and set up a home-based friendship agency, thinking this would be a good way to further her interest in people and the environment. Natural Friends was launched in 1985. It was designed for people, mostly non-smokers, with interests in many aspects of natural living, including complementary medicine, health-conscious eating, personal development and cultural pursuits. People are asked to write about themselves in a 100 word paragraph which goes into a bi-monthly newsletter. Members then write to each other through a box number system to ensure privacy and security. Finding friends with the same interests is the aim of most members; if anything romantic happens it is an added bonus.

MARY BALFOUR

Having always had a flair for matchmaking Mary Balfour paired off many of her friends before deciding to run her own introduction agency. Research showed that what was needed was an agency for graduates working in the business, professional and creative world. She bought Drawing Down the Moon in 1986 and quickly transformed it into the best known personal introduction agency in Britain. Clients include lawyers, doctors, business people, musicians, teachers and people in the media. Drawing Down the Moon is known as the "thinking person's introduction agency" and utilises personal profiles to facilitate matching. Only 40 per cent of applicants who come in for interview are taken on as members. They are successful, positive people seeking committed relationships. Mary has worked as a photographer, a model, and in education as head of Centre in an adult education institute. She has made numerous radio and television appearances and also runs occasional seminars on how to meet people. She is married with two stepdaughters and lives in North Kensington.

CHRISTINA RHODES

Christina Rhodes met her photographer husband beneath the statue of Eros in Piccadilly and married him following a whirlwind romance. She went to Australia with him and returned alone and penniless three years later with her two year old daughter. After living in a series of B&Bs and half-way houses Christina obtained her divorce and set up a series of small businesses from home which enabled her to combine her work with the care of her daughter. Astrology had always been one of her interests and she conceived the idea of setting up Britain's first astrological introduction agency. It was an immediate success and attracted a great deal of publicity. It was while running this agency that she received repeated requests from British women wanting to meet American men. Curious to study the phenomenon further she went to live in California for a while. Back in Britain she set up the English Rose Anglo-American Introduction agency. Its sister agency, the English Connection, which specialises in introducing American women to British men grew out of this. The agencies' enormous success has earned Christina publicity on several TV programmes including Wogan.

FRANCES PYNE

After 25 years in public relations Frances Pyne joined Dateline International and started working as a press officer for the Association of British Introduction Agencies. ABIA was formed in 1981 by 80 per cent of the leading introduction agencies and marriage bureaux within the UK, at a time when people contemplating joining agencies needed someone they "could talk to". Having studied at The Lincoln Clinic & Institute of Psychotherapy, Frances speaks with authority to people from all walks of life and from all age groups, advising them on any problems they may have in forming a successful relationship. She is a regular contributor to newspaper and magazines and has become a celebrity on both radio and television.

FRANCES PENROSE HALSON

From a family of university lecturers, missionaries and craftsmen Frances went to many schools, ending with Millfield, before taking a London BA. She then combined teaching French and Spanish with writing for The Guardian and Punch and writing and editing educational and children's magazines, multi-media packs and books (over 50 titles). She became headmistress of a small private ballet school, highly eccentric but approved by the Department of Education and Science and ILEA and then did a stint as a lowest-grade French teacher at an ailing grammar school. Before meeting her husband Bill, she had used various marriage bureaux. Bill is a management consultant and executive counsellor, very skilled at placing people in the right job and in 1986 they bought the Katharine Allen Marriage Bureau, of which Frances had been a client. She had been very impressed by the bureau's work and knew that many professional people needed such a service – and Bill was right in predicting that the work would suit her very well.

SUMAN BHARGAVA

Suman Bhargava was a teacher in India before coming to the UK in 1965. She worked in Slough teaching Hindi to children born in Britain before setting up Suman Marriage Bureau in 1972. Since those days she has arranged over 5,000 marriages and saved hundreds of others. For these skills she received the Mother India Award from NRI, New Delhi in 1989 and the Mahila Shrimoni Award in 1990 from the Institute of Sikh Studies, New Delhi in 1990. She is married with a son (26) and daughter (19).

HILLIE MARSHALL

Hillie Marshall used to be a radiographer at Westminster Hospital until she decided to leave X-rays behind her and pursue her interest in music and theatre. She took a course at the Guildhall School of Music and then worked for many years as a singer and actress, starring in numerous TV and theatre productions. In 1980 she formed Edwardians Unlimited, which became Britain's foremost Old Time Music Hall Company. In 1989 a conversation over dinner prompted Hillie to put one of her long held ideas into practice, and in so doing change the face of the singles dating service in Britain. She founded Dinner Dates, the first organisation of its kind to enable large groups of single people to meet together in a relaxed atmosphere over dinner. Since then over 4,000 people have dined with Dinner Dates in restaurants and nightclubs all over London and the parties have resulted in numerous marriages, engagements and friendships.

PATRICIA WARREN

Brought up in the Worcestershire countryside Patricia Warren did her SRN training at Worcester Royal Infirmary and then set off on a world tour before deciding that only a farming way of life would really suit her. She retrained as a farm secretary at Agricultural College and ten years ago started the highly successful Farmers and Country Friendship and Marriage Bureau. Having been told she could not have children naturally she and her husband decided to adopt. They have two children and live on a farm.

Getting there is always
more exciting

Being there is always
more challenging

ADELAIDE "DELLA" CLYNE

Della Clyne read economics and international law at University College, London, where she met her husband. They lived all over Europe and while in Rome Della ran an Oxfam shop, raising funds for Mother Theresa and became a trustee for the Overseas School of Rome, with special responsibilities for fundraising. Returning to the UK she started Elizabeth Hunt Recruitment Consultants Ltd in 1978, in a small office in Grosvenor Street. Today, the company has offices in the City and the West End, with a turnover of several million pounds. Della Clyne is a Governor of the Institute of Employment Consultants and is chairman of the London Group of the FRES, amongst her other appointments. She has three children and six grandchildren, and lives in London.

JUDY FARQUHARSON

Having started in recruitment in 1966, Judy Farquharson soon realised that women at the time needed help to break into the male dominated management areas. With this in mind, in 1968 she established the first specialist recruitment bureau for women graduates, opening up hitherto forbidden areas to them in, for example, banks and stockbroking companies. By 1972, attitudes had changed and she set up her present eponymous company, concentrating on placing men and women in communications, publishing and market research in particular, filling the gap at a level above high street employment agencies and below director-level headhunters. With the company's increasing reputation, she is now placing people in senior management posts, but would still like to see more women at board level and involved in the planning stages of new products and services.

ANGELA MORTIMER

Angela Mortimer gained a distinction in her teaching practice and graduated from London University with a Bachelor of Education. She worked for two years as a teacher, largely in deprived areas of inner London. She then spent two years in a secretarial recruitment agency before setting up Angela Mortimer Ltd in 1976 with her husband John. The success of Angela Mortimer Ltd has been largely due to her personal charisma, her effectiveness in direct assignment work and the encouragement which she gives members of the company. Now a mother of two Angela is chairman of the company and concentrates her efforts on the secretarial recruitment division where she maintains a close watch over client relationships.

SUSAN HAMILTON

Born in 1948 and educated at the local grammar school in Wiltshire, Susan Hamilton established Susan Hamilton Personnel Services in late 1974 as a personalised professional recruitment service to clients from across a broad spectrum. She has offices in the West End, Knightsbridge and at the Palace of Westminster. Her particular aims are to raise the profile of women in business and to instill effective communications and counselling skills. Her other businesses include two training colleges in London, offering courses for private and corporate clients and higher skills training for the local Tec. Susan is a member of the Institute of Employment Consultants, the Institute of Management and the Kensington and Chelsea Chamber of Commerce.

LYN CECIL

Born in 1947 in Essex, Lyn Cecil began her career in the personnel department of a large insurance company, before gaining five years experience in the recruitment industry. In 1975 she started Secretaries Plus, specialising in the top end of the secretarial market, followed by LJC Banking Appointments in 1978 which provides a recruitment service to City institutions. Farn Williams followed in 1992, which handles executive search for qualified accountants in the UK and Europe, all coming under the LJC Group umbrella. A Fellow of the Institute of Employment Consultants, the training body for the industry, she was a governor and vice-president from 1981, and president in 1984-85. She is currently a national member of the executive committee for the Federation of Recruitment and Employment Services. Lyn is a great supporter of the Lady Taverners and a Ferrari enthusiast.

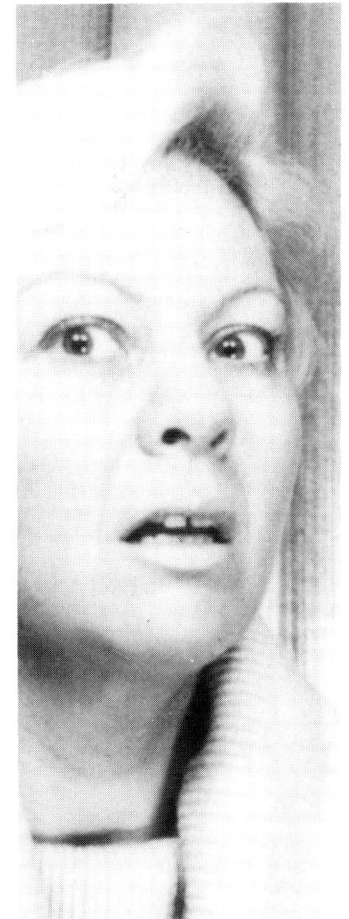

IRENE MARVIN

The managing director of the new Blue Arrow Group, Irene Marvin was born in Lincolnshire in 1952. She started her career at the plastics company, Plysu, where her ability to influence people led her into recruitment. She joined Blue Arrow Personnel Services in 1976 and moved from managing a branch to controlling a region. She became a director in 1984 and managing director in 1986. In 1991 Irene headed a management buy-out team in a successful £34 million bid to acquire Blue Arrow from the parent group. She is a Fellow of the Institute of Employment Consultants and Blue Arrow is an active member of the Federation of Recruitment and Employment Services, the legislative body of the recruitment industry.

JUDY FISHER

Judy Fisher started her working career as secretary to Peter Cook and Dudley Moore in their Beyond the Fringe days. Having been asked to find various impossible props, she realised that she enjoyed the challenge and decided to move into recruitment. Starting in the mid 1960s, she was with one company for many years, working her way up from trainee to managing director. In 1986 she set up Judy Fisher Associates, to fill a gap in the market recruiting intelligent, well qualified secretarial and support staff for the media. Specialising in supplying staff for the arts, television, films, music and publishing, JFA works with most of the major companies within the media and has placed many staff at junior levels who are now well on their way to the boardroom. Now aged 49, Judy Fisher is the undisputed leader in placing staff within her specialised industry.

MAUREEN MIFFLING

As managing director of Manpower plc, Maureen Miffling heads the UK's leading employment company, with an annual turnover of £150 million. She joined the Bristol branch of the company in 1969 and rose steadily through the ranks, having previously worked in secretarial training. From supervisor at Bristol, Maureen became branch manager at Cardiff and then area manager for the West and Midlands, a strategic area accounting for 25 per cent of the company's turnover. In the 1980s she took over as regional manager for the West and for Central and Outer London. She joined the board in 1988, as operations director, and took up her present appointment in 1990. Throughout Maureen's career with Manpower, her commitment to the development and maintenance of a quality service has been paramount. As a testament to this, Manpower's 150 branches now hold the accreditation BS 5750 from the British Standards Institute, the largest service network ever to have achieved.

CLARE CAMPBELL-LAMBERTON

Clare Campbell-Lamberton, 31, was educated in Spain and England. Having completed a one year secretarial training course in Oxford, she found employment in the public relations sector and took up appointments in Hong Kong and Madrid. On her return from Spain, she joined a successful PR company in London, where her specialist understanding of the media industries resulted in her role developing into more of a human resource/personnel function. In 1989 she joined a multinational firm of accountants as graduate recruitment officer and, in November 1990, she joined the recruitment consultants, Grosvenor Bureau, as manager.

STELLA WALKER

Stella Walker first went into recruitment in the early 1960s, developing a small, private consultancy over ten years. When she left the company to start a family, she had been largely responsible for its expansion into a 15 branch business. In 1978, in her late 30s, she set up Handle Recruitment, under the umbrella of her brother, David Walker's Handle Group, specifically to provide a recruitment service to the communications – and particularly the music – industry. The music industry is dynamic and experimental by nature, and Stella enjoys the challenge of introducing new blood, from all over the world, as well as retaining a reservoir of temporary and permanent applicants, enabling her to provide a continuity of experienced personnel for her clients. She is very proud of Handle Recruitment and has always resisted the temptation to expand for fear of losing the quality of personal service which she provides.

TRICIA GUILD

Tricia Guild founded Designers Guild in London in 1970. The company is now a market leader for furnishing fabrics and wallcoverings in Europe with distribution throughout the UK and in over 40 countries worldwide. Her ongoing support of British artists and craftspeople is reflected in the Designers Guild showrooms where one-off ceramics, glassware, limited edition prints and hand woven throws are sold. She is a member of the Crafts Council and has tutored ceramic students at the Royal College of Art. Her awards include the Textile Institute Gold Medal for her outstanding contribution to international textiles (1989), the Queen's Award for Export Achievement (1991), and the Export Award for Smaller Businesses (1992). Her books include Designing With flowers, Deisgn and Detail, Design A Garden, Tricia Guild's New Soft Furnishings and Tricia Guild On Colour (1992).

Photograph by David Montgomery

KATE AINSLIE WILLIAMS

After graduating with a diploma of interior design from the Inchbald School in 1978 Kate Ainslie-Williams joined Charles Hammond, the internationally renowned interior design company founded in 1907. Appointed a design director in 1989 Kate's commissions include the interiors of the head offices of the Crown Estate Commissioners, Grand Metropolitan and Merrill Lynch Europe and numerous spacious town and country residences for private clients. She is highly respected within the business for her detailed knowledge of historical period restoration and decoration and is often involved with overall refurbishments of listed buildings. She is a member of the Interior Decorators and Designers Association and the International Society of Interior Designers.

TESSA KENNEDY

Tessa Kennedy has built up her London based interior design practice over the last 25 years. Her clients include King Hussein of Jordan, Stavros Niarchos (on his yacht Atlantis), Candice Bergen and Stanley Kubrick. She has worked on Claridge's, the De Beer offices in London, the Waterside Inn at Bray. Her current projects include Henley House for George Harrison, the London offices of Rothschild's Bank and Ascot House for King Hussein. Last year Tessa was elected as president for the International Society of Interior Designers.

EMILY TODHUNTER

Emily began her decorating career while still at school as an apprentice for the master painter Jim Smart. She started her own small company at Bristol University where she studied philosophy and psychology. After graduating she went to Saint Louis, Missouri, to paint for a decorator. Her big break came in New York when she was commissioned to decorate Howard Stein's new night club, Au Bar, at the age of 24. New Yorkers loved it and Emily appeared in countless American magazines as a result. Since then her commissions have included Taki Theodoracopulos's flat in London, the private wing at Sissinghurst Castle and Christopher's restaurant in Covent Garden. Her flat was photographed for House & Garden in 1990; the photographs of her drawing room are still used as the advertisement for the magazine. Last year she and her team completed a suite at the Berkeley Hotel in Knightsbridge, the new stand at Newbury racecourse and a house in Bel Air, LA, a Japanese restaurant in Athens and a refit of the restaurant Daphne's off Walton Street.

CLARE FERRABY

Clare trained as a painter at Sheffield College of Art, specialised in textiles at Manchester, and then became a freelance designer and consultant. Her first job for the theatre was designing the carpets at the Crucible Theatre in Sheffield. She went on to refurbish the Victorian Theatre Royal in Nottingham. Her success there led to a commission for the Palace Theatre, Manchester, and the Grand Theatre, Leeds. She became a consultant to RHWL for a wide range of arts buildings and today her unique specialised work can be seen at some 30 completed auditoria in Britain. These include the Old Vic and the Duke of York theatres in London, the Bradford Alhambra, Newcastle's Theatre Royal, the New Theatre, Cardiff, and the Lyceum in Sheffield. She worked closely with Cameron Mackintosh on the 1930s style musical theatre, the Prince Edward in Soho, which reopened in February.

MELISSA WYNDHAM

Melissa Wyndham comes from a family of well known decorators. She has been working in London for many years and set up her own company ten years ago, decorating for private clients all over Britain. Together with Vincent Dané she has started a range of materials, the latest collection being inspired by English Gothic architecture.

JO ROBINSON

Born in Cornwall Jo went to Cranbourne Chase School in Dorset before emigrating to South Africa where she went to art school in Cape Town. After graduating she married and had two daughters. In the early 1970s she joined Mrs Monro Ltd (Jean Monro is her godmother), and by 1976 she was ready to start her own company, Jo Robinson Design. She returned to Mrs Monro Ltd as a director and then left to set up own company with Guy Wilkins. Based in Yeomans Row Jo Robinson Ltd combines a retail shop with a full interior design service. The company work on both domestic and commercial projects and recent projects have included the Chewton Glen Hotel, a Victorian Gothic rectory in Devonshire, a boat on The Thames and various houses and apartments in London and abroad.

LYNNE LAWRENCE

Lynne started out in the flower business at the age of 23 when a friend asked her to help out in her busy new shop in King's Lynn. A few years later she moved to London after her early marriage ended and worked for the Inn On The Park. A year in the hotel business proved enough, however, and she decided to set up in business with her sister, dealing mostly in event decorating, weddings and other moveable feasts. She sold the business when her daughter was two years old, wanting to spend more time with her and do some travelling. Around this time she met her flower partner of the 1980s, Sally Aspinall, and began doing the flowers for John Aspinall's casino. From her present premises in Elystan Street she fulfills a huge variety of commissions: Bond Film premieres, Rocco Forte's 40th birthday party, John Aspinall's Feast of Torgamba, The Cartier Million at Phoenix Park, Dublin, and the gardens at Port Lympne.

CAROLINE ALEXANDER

After leaving Cambridge in 1972 Caroline Alexander decided to pursue her interest in the countryside by studying landscape management at Wye College, Kent. After several years of landscaped advisory work she married and moved to the Alexander family farm. In 1987 the couple began a new business venture – growing and drying hops, flowers and grasses. Under the name The Hop Shop the enterprise achieved widespread acclaim. Over 70 home-grown varieties are now sold from the farm shop and distributed nationwide. Dried flower enthusiasts can attend lectures and demonstrations or read Caroline's book Dried Flower Gardening, published in 1991, which describes each stage of growing, harvesting and drying. At the Royal Horticultural Society Shows in Westminster her stands received the first gold medals awarded to dried flower displays by the Society.

JENNIFER RIMELL

Having been asked for many years to provide flower arrangements for charity events, Jennifer Rimell decided to make a business of it. Her work today ranges from decorating parties for pop groups to arranging flowers for dinner parties for the Royal Family. She designs and puts colours together in surroundings as diverse as Westminster Abbey and the crypt of the House of Commons or a tent in a cottage garden.

KITTY ARDEN

Florist, artist, set designer and stylist Kitty Arden has done it all. In her work as a floral decorator for parties she is known for her imaginative wild and natural-looking arrangements, composed of a mass of greenery and aromatic flowers. She has done fashion shows for Victor Edelstein and worked for Vogue magazine and David Linley as well as numerous weddings, dances and chic soires. She is an expert at themed parties, creating fantastic arrangements for events dubbed Legendary Lovers, Cowboys and Injuns and Caribbean. As an artist she has had many exhibtions: her work (etchings and oil paintings) has appeared twice at the Royal Academy Summer Exhibition. She also designs cards and tapestry kits.
Photograph by Rory Carnegie

JOANNA SHEEN

Joanna Sheen took a diploma in floristry at the Constance Spry School before starting her own highly successful business. Her efforts earned her runner-up in the Women Mean Business Award run by Options magazine in 1983. Now a regular exhibitor at the Chelsea Flower Show and the Ideal Homes Exhibition, Joanna's work and courses on pressing and drying flowers and flower arranging have featured in many publications as well as on TV and radio programmes. She opened a shop in Torquay in 1990, and in the same year was invited to Japan to demonstrate her craft. She has since been invited back three times. She has published nine books describing her skills, from pressing flowers and dried flower gardening to decorating.

PAULA PRYKE

Paula Pryke began her working life as a teacher, having studied history at Leeds University and drama at the Royal Academy. Always passionate about flowers she decided to change direction and opened a shop in Islington. Today she is a leading New Wave Floral Artist creating arrangements for top interior designers and architects as well as private individuals and businesses. Her team will produce assembles to suit any occasion, providing a huge selection of flowers and greenery including Christmas trees and poinsettias in summer and peonies and sun flowers in winter. Paula is currently writing the definitive title on flower arranging, The New Flower Artist, to be published by Mitchell Beazley this year.

SOPHIE HANNA

Sophie Hanna has spent some 20 years working in floristry in the UK and Australia – she owned a florist's shop in Sydney for some 15 years before becoming a partner in a London business. Despite the business's great success Sophie wanted to "go it alone" and set up as a freelance designer. Since that time she has built up an impresive list of clients including top London hotels, the St James's Club, Estée Lauder and Pierre Cardin. She has also carried out commissions for the Royal Family. She describes herself as something of a traditionalist, preferring not to detract from the main ingredients in an arrangement with anything too busy. "Each flower should be given a context and each flower should be seen individually as a part of the whole."

JANE PACKER

Jane Packer's talents are much sought after as a consultant within the horticulture industry. She has lectured throughout Europe, the US and Japan, has written five books and released two videos which have sold worldwide. She has also developed successful flower arranging schools in London and Tokyo, attracting students from around the world. She opened her first retail outlet in 1981 in the West End. Her team of talented individuals are equally responsible for the continuing demand for her flowers, ranging from simple bouquets to corporate product launches and work for television.

SASHA WADDELL

Sasha Waddell has always loved "beautiful things". After a career in the theatre and having had children Sasha decided to rekindle her interest in visual things and go into design. She took a course at the Chelsea College of Art and, in 1985, opened her shop. In contrast to the ornate design of the mid-1980s she offered a spare style, influenced by Scotland and Sweden "cool and comfortable without being austere – pretty without being sentimental". Her commissions range from theCrown Prince's apartments of the Thai Embassy in London to a mostly yellow house for an Italian client and a tiny cupboardless cottage in Ireland.

JENNY ARMIT

Jenny Armit trained and worked in Madrid before setting up Jenny Armit Interiors in London four years ago, working on commercial and residential projects here and abroad. She soon established a reputation for a "comfortable contemporary look" which is not afraid to use bold contrasts, mixing Shaker with Santa Fe or baroque with the baronial. Spanish landscape colours are a prevalent theme, gleaned from her time in Spain. Jenny often commissions one off pieces from British craftsmen because, she says, "a piece on its own where you're not expecting it often has more power than the obvious pair".

Photograph by Richard Davies/ Elle Decoration

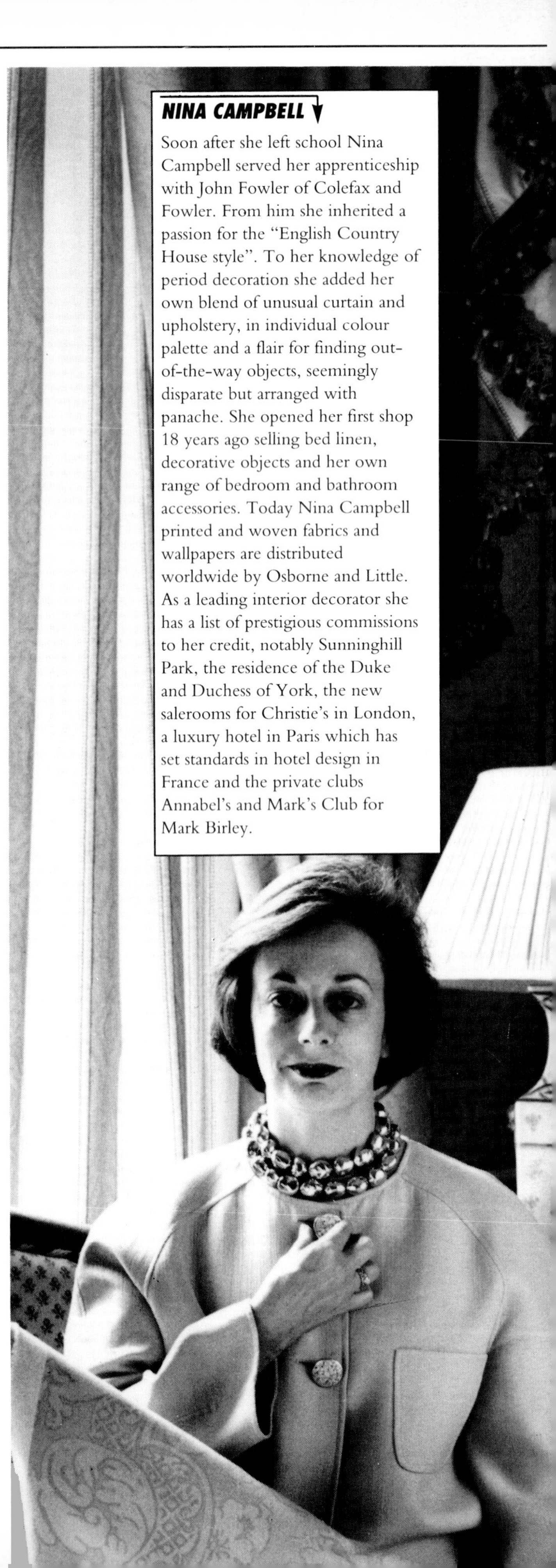

NINA CAMPBELL

Soon after she left school Nina Campbell served her apprenticeship with John Fowler of Colefax and Fowler. From him she inherited a passion for the "English Country House style". To her knowledge of period decoration she added her own blend of unusual curtain and upholstery, in individual colour palette and a flair for finding out-of-the-way objects, seemingly disparate but arranged with panache. She opened her first shop 18 years ago selling bed linen, decorative objects and her own range of bedroom and bathroom accessories. Today Nina Campbell printed and woven fabrics and wallpapers are distributed worldwide by Osborne and Little. As a leading interior decorator she has a list of prestigious commissions to her credit, notably Sunninghill Park, the residence of the Duke and Duchess of York, the new salerooms for Christie's in London, a luxury hotel in Paris which has set standards in hotel design in France and the private clubs Annabel's and Mark's Club for Mark Birley.

MARY FOX LINTON

Mary Fox Linton started out in the interior design business some 28 years ago. She began by buying furniture for foreigners but soon became known in England too for her impeccable eye. She pioneered the use of contemporary furniture and antiques, with the emphasis on creating a total look through collaboration with architects and craftsmen, often commissioning one-offs from fabric and furniture designers in order to achieve an effect. The mix of old and new has been highly successful internationally. Recent projects include a golf club in Japan, a palace in the Middle East, a country house in France and a house in Los Angeles. The simplicity and quality of her schemes is sure to prove as successful in the 1990s as it has been in the last two decades.

JOANNA WOOD

Joanna Wood worked for Alannah Dowling at Asprey's interior design department before setting up her own business, Joanna Trading, when she was 25. That was 12 years ago. Today she owns four companies and her work has been commissioned from as far afield as Norway, Japan, Europe and America. She has just opened a small office in Tokyo and another is planned for 1993 in Paris. Joanna Trading has five teams of decorators, able to cater to a wide variety of tastes and provide a total design service. A reputation for professionalism and sound project management, coupled with Joanna's own perfectionism, attracts commissions for specialist commercial work as well as individuals with castles in Castile or cottages in Scotland.

EVA JIRICNA

Czechoslovakian-born architect Eva Jiricna had never done interiors before she met Joseph Ettedgui but their collaboration on his shops, restaurants and bars brought her instant worldwide recognition. Her work is pervaded by a sense of order and restraint inherited from her Czech functionalist father and a love of ships and boats, sparked by her work on the Brighton Marina in the late 1960s. Her success in the retail world is partly due to the fact that she sees her job as producing a background. The finishes are, of course, stunning, but the design never swamps the goods. Her clients have included international shoe designers Joan and David, Lloyds of London, Le Caprice and nightclubs Legends and Browns.

LADY VICTORIA WAYMOUTH

Lady Victoria has been in the interior design and decorating business since 1965 when she began working with David Mlinaric, whose appointment to the National Trust led to his company undertaking design and restorative work on some of the finest country houses in England. In 1970 Lady Victoria travelled to South East Asia and worked on commissions all over the continent. On her return to England she started her own interior design company, Victoria Waymouth Interiors, launching a retail outlet eight years later. Commissions range from projects for hotels and company houses to private yachts and, of course, private houses. Sir Clive Sinclair and Chris Blackwell are just two of her well-known clients. In 1991 she won a prize from the World of Interiors magazine for the Best Room at the British Interior Design Exhibition.

SUE TIMNEY

Sue Timney was born in Libya of Scottish parents. She graduated from Newcastle-upon-Tyne College of Art with a first in Fine Art and from Heriot Watt University with a distinction in post-graduate textiles/tapestry. In 1975 she won the Washington Sculpture Prize. In 1977 she started her MA at the Royal college of Art. An RCA scholarship took her to New York in 1978 and the following year she went to Japan on an RCA Sanderson scholarship. She set up the Timney Fowler partnership with Grahame Fowler in 1979. They started by developing the Japanese market for print designs and consultancy, with clients such as Issey Miyake and Yohji Yamamato and created design concepts for major middle market clothing and accessory companies. In 1984 they produced their first range of interior fabrics in the UK, expanding their studio design services to haute couture houses and fashion houses in Paris and Italy. Today their range includes ceramics, accessories, jewellery and clothes and furnishing fabrics. In 1988 they set up five new showrooms in America to promote the TF furnishing fabrics and wallpaper, and in 1990 they won a contract from Wedgwood for table and gift ware and were included in the V&A's first travelling exhibition of contemporary design. Last year they had a retrospective exhibition in Tokyo where they opened a new shop and began their book on the company, to be published this year by Phaidon.

Photograph courtesy of International Textiles

HELENE MARKS

Before creating her highly successful company, Mark II Deisgns Ltd, Helene Marks organised an international art exhibition entitled Israel Observed in which artists immersed in the English tradition of landscapes went to paint those of Israel. The project, sponsored by the British Council and an international bank, was an outstanding success, and was later the subject of a TV documentary. Prior to the exhibition Helene had trained as an artist, specialising in portraiture and had been a consultant on the purchase of contemporary art. It was a natural progression from this to designing the environments in whch they would be hung.

Photograph by Mark Stenning

CAROLE ROBERTS

Carole Roberts studied textiles at Liverpool and Birmingham Colleges of Art. Her interest in historic textiles was fuelled by research for her final thesis, which she worked on in the textiles archives of the V&A. After graduating she ran an antiques shop and eventually decided to start her own interior design business. Eight years ago she set up No. Twelve Queen Street in Bath. She designs private houses as well as offices, commercial premises and hotels, for clients worldwide. Commissions in Britain include Stapleford Park Country House Hotel in Leicestershire and refurbishment of part of the National Trust stately home Cliveden, when it was converted into a hotel.

JEAN MONRO

A country house specialist with an interest in the 18th century Jean Monro's mother started her interior design business in 1926, when her husband was ill, at a time when it was very rare for a woman to go into business. Jean joined Mrs Monro Ltd in 1946 and took over the running of the company in 1960. Since then she has been a design consultant for many of the top British banks and industrial companies such as RTZ, BP and Lazards and, in particular, the British and Commonwealth Shipping Company for whom she designed and decorated the interior of three ships. Other commissions include decorating the country houses Arbury and Ston Easton Park, the state bedroom at Ickworth for the National Trust and the decorating and furnishing of the Museum at No 1 Royal Crescent, Bath, for the Bath Preservation Trust. Jean recently set up Jean Monro Design Ltd to market the firm's special chintzes worldwide. A new collection, for the National Trust, is due out this year. Jean's work has taken her to the US, Canada, Australia, South Africa and Jamaica, where she had an office for two years. In 1972 she held a much acclaimed exhibition, Le Style Anglais, in Paris. She is a fellow of the Royal Society of Arts and a founder member of the Interior Decorators' and Designers' Association. Now in her 70s Jean is still very much involved in her company as a consultant.

SUSAN LLEWELLYN

Susan Llewellyn established her company, Susan Llewellyn Associates, Private and Corporate Interior Design Services, almost 30 years ago. Over this period she has undertaken a wide variety of projects from advice on fabrics and furnishings for private homes to the refurbishment of corporate headquarters. She used to own shops dealing in antique furniture and paintings through which she began exporting antiques to the Far East, Europe and the US. She worked in Beirut, maintaining her business in the UK by commuting back and forth on a regular basis. She owned a company in Valetta, Malta, which was an import house for antique furniture and supplied design and decorating services. She holds the Richmond Society Award for the King's Observatory, Richmond Deer Park and a commendation from HRH Princess Margaret for restoration works undertaken to Leighton House Museum, London.

PAMELA LEWIS

Pamela Lewis worked as a theatre and film designer until she was 36 years old. She trained first as a scenic artist and property maker and worked at Sadler's Wells, assisting with the decor of West end plays, opera and ballet. Finding post-war London drab and dreary she decided to take a design job in Johannesburg. She lived and worked in South Africa for ten years where she was able to gain valuable experience handling large scale productions as a set and costume designer. She returned to Britain in 1967 and obtained an interior design diploma from the Brixton School of Building, having developed a deep interest in historic architectural work. Since 1970 she has worked as an interior designer and as an architectural paint expert with the Historic Buildings Directorate, DOE, and latterly with English Heritage, specialising in the presentation of historic interiors and their soft furnishings. Her lastest design work has been at Frogmore House, Windsor, and as a member of the project design team for the restoration of the King's Apartments at Hampton Court Palace.

CAROLINE GLEDHILL

In 1992 the Engineering Council awarded the title of Young Engineer for Britain to Caroline Gledhill. It was the first time that a girl had been declared overall winner. Nineteen year old Caroline, from Ringwood in Hampshire, won the award for her invention of a low-cost, high quality measuring device for all high speed tape recorders. She also won the WISE (Women Into Science and Engineering) award for the best project by a girl. Caroline worked on the invention while at Racal Recorders of Hythe, Southampton, as part of a Year in Industry work experience scheme, prior to taking up her university place at Cambridge. She sees her future at the head of a large electronics company.

CLAIRE STATON AND SARAH SKELTON

Claire Staton, 15, and Sarah Skelton, 14, are both students of Ridgewood Comprehensive School in Yorkshire. They are the inventors of the "One To Jack", an idea which combines the best properties of both the car ramp and the scissor jack whilst eliminating the inconvenience and inherent dangers of both. Their invention involves a low ramp with an indentation for the wheel, so that the driver knows when the car is correctly positioned. The scissor jack principal is then brought into play, raising the car to the required height by means of a crank winder. Safety locks clamp the framework, making collapse impossible. The jack may then be removed to allow the mechanic to work. Claire and Sarah are currently working on a lighter "One To Jack". As they say on their report, "another splendiferous project from the one and only Ridgewood School Technology Club".

PATSY BLOOM

After gaining her secretarial qualification, Patsy Bloom decided to make her career in advertising. She joined a large agency and quickly worked her way up to account manager. She left to work in-house on the launch of Mary Quant's new cosmetic range. In 1968 Patsy moved into publishing as promotions manager for Queen magazine and then publicity manager for a publishing company. She changed direction again to work for a major charity. Patsy first had the idea of a pet insurance scheme because of her own dog's growing vet's bills and, in 1977, she and David Simpson launched Pet Plan. The company has proved immensely successful, with 51 per cent of the small animal insurance market and over 325,000 pets currently under cover. There are successful franchise operations in Canada and Italy.

MAUREEN HIRON

Games, both physical and cerebral, have always been Maureen Hiron's principal interest. A former head of physical education at a London comprehensive, she has represented England and Great Britain at bridge. After giving up teaching, Maureen made the discovery that she could invent games. She formed a company, Hiron Games, and her first product, Continuo, became Britain's top seller within six weeks of production. Her Quadwrangle, Quizwrangle, Cavendish and Chip In also received international acclaim. An approach from a Swiss playing card company led to the formation of Rhino Games as an international vehicle for her range of card games, which include Duo, Croque, 77, Teddy's Party, Rhino's Word Game and The A Pack. With her husband Alan, a world bridge champion, she has written several best-selling books, including the Trivia Quiz series and Beginning Bridge. Maureen devises puzzles and questions for TV quiz shows and was herself the subject of a documentary, A Will to Win.

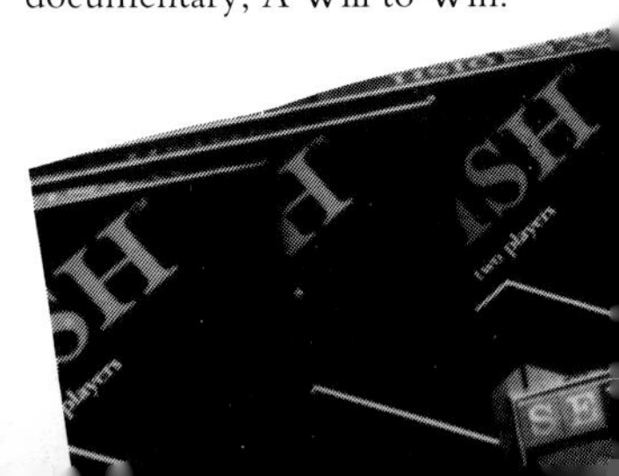

CHRISTINE HALL

Christine Hall, with husband Simon, is the founder of Five Halls Trading Company Ltd, a true family business. Hit particularly hard by the financial crash of 1987, they desperately sought a way out of their troubles which involved no financial input on their part and no banking assistance. An infuriating lost sock provided the answer – or, at least, the question – why not use "poppers" to hold socks together. They followed the trail of "popper" manufacturers in Britain, Italy and even Japan, fixing them by hand and by machine until they came up with the solution – ultrasonic welding. Now, she believes, the single sock should be a thing of the past. "Poppa Socks" keep socks in pairs in the laundry basket, the washing machine, the clothes line and the sock drawer. For the Halls, it looks as if the recession is over.

CINDY GEORGE

A Londoner born and bred, Cindy George started work as a junior in a City office and, over the years, worked in a number of offices, rising to be a legal secretary, which she thoroughly enjoyed. She had thought about starting a taxi service for women for some time, mainly because of her concern for the elderly being mugged for their pensions and women being uncomfortable travelling alone. Reading in the newspaper about yet another old lady being beaten up for the contents of her handbag put Cindy's thoughts into action and, ten years ago, she founded Ladycabs London Ltd. She now has five franchised offices around London, and innumerable lady drivers, full and part time, providing a service particularly for women, children, the elderly and the handicapped.

ROSIE BOYCOTT

The founder of the feminist magazine Spare Rib in 1972, Rosie Boycott later went on to establish Virago Books. She moved to the US and worked on New York's legendary Village Voice magazine. Further travels took her to Kuwait, where she edited an Arabic women's magazine. On her return to Britain, she became Features Editor of Honey and later Deputy Editor of the Daily Mail's Male and Femail pages. After a period of editing Discount Traveller, she became a Commissioning Editor at the Sunday Telegraph. Her next ventures were Harpers & Queen (Deputy Editor from 1989) and Esquire (Deputy and Features Editor as of June 1991, Editor six months later). She has written four books including the controversial A Nice Girl Like Me, and has appeared on radio's Any Questions and Start The Week, and on TV's Tonight With Jonathan Ross. She was brought up in Shropshire but now lives in London.

Photograph courtesy of Nat. Mag. Co. Corporate Comms.

MARCELLE D'ARGY SMITH

Marcelle D'Argy Smith began her association with Cosmopolitan when several of her poems were accepted for publication – a humble beginning for someone who was one day to edit the magazine. She was formerly publisher and editor of British Antiques Year Book and International Antiques Year Book. After a one-year creative writing course at Columbia University in New York, she became a contributing editor to Cosmopolitan before being appointed editor in 1989. She specialises in writing about relationships and her book, Men, Women And Me, was published 1987. She was named Women's Magazine Editor of the Year by British Society of Magazine Edit in 1991. Her numerous radio an TV contributions include Behinc The Headlines, This Morning, T Media Show, Today and Wome Hour. She was brought up in Ess and now lives in London.

Photograph courtesy of Nat. Mag. C Corporate Comms.

PAT ROBERTS

The Editor of House Beautiful since its launch in 1989, Northumberland-born Pat Roberts began her career as a reporter on an Essex newspaper. During the 1960s, she worked for IPC's Young Magazine Group and later wrote for leading women's weeklies. She then helped to launch London's first free magazine, Girl About Town. She joined the Daily Mail and wrote for the Femail section but returned to magazines, becoming Deputy Editor of the supermarket title Family Circle when it underwent an editorial re-vamp. She edited Over 21 magazine for five years. Joining the National Magazine Company as marketing editorial consultant in 1988, she introduced the concept of House Beautiful, offering a down-to-earth and economical approach to homemaking. She is in demand for radio programmes and has her own weekly slot on London's LBC. She has homes in London and Brighton.

SALLY O'SULLIVAN

After toiling as a freelance writer for eight years, Sally O'Sullivan joined Woman's World as Deputy Editor in 1977. After a spell in New York writing for various publications, she joined the Daily Record in Glasgow as Women's Editor, moving on in the same role to the Sunday Standard. She joined Carlton Magazines in 1982, becoming Editor of Options and Editorial Director of the company. In this period she launched Country Homes and Interiors and Options For Men. She was Launch Editor of Riva in 1988, joined She magazine in early 1989 and was appointed Editor of Harpers & Queen later that year. Since 1991 she has been Editor-in-Chief of Good Housekeeping. A frequent guest on radio programmes to discuss the role of women in the 1990s, she has clocked up stints on Any Questions? and Today, and has reviewed the newspapers on breakfast TV. Brought up in Harpenden, Hertfordshire, she is now married with two children and lives in London.

Photograph courtesy of Nat. Mag. Co. Corporate Comms.

JOAN BARRELL

Joan Barrell worked for IPC from 1959 to 1971, becoming the first woman advertising representative and the first woman advertising manager. She launched Honey in 1965, Fashion in 1967 and was appointed merchandising manager for all the group's women's magazines in 1970. She joined the National Magazine Company in 1971 as associate publisher of Vanity Fair and Cosmopolitan and was responsible for the launches of both Cosmopolitan and Company (her own brainchild) when she became publisher in 1978. She became a director of the company in 1981 and is still the only woman on the board. She became board director of magazine distributors Comag in 1984 and was appointed publishing director of Country Living in 1986. She assumed the same position on Good Housekeeping in 1990. She has been President of the Women's Advertising Club of Great Britain and recipient of the Adwoman Award. She was Chairman of the Publicity Club of London in 1989. The author of The Business of Women's Magazines, she has been a member of the panel of the radio programme Any Questions? She lives in Pimlico and Kent.

Photograph courtesy of Nat. Mag. Co. Corporate Comms.

JANE THYNNE

Jane Thynne was born in Venezuela and educated at Lady Eleanor Holles School in Middlesex, and at St. Anne's College, Oxford. After being a finalist in the Vogue talent contest, she joined the BBC as a production trainee. She moved to the Sunday Times in 1987 and on to the Daily Telegraph in 1988. She is now that paper's media correspondent and often appears on the BBC's Breakfast News reviewing the morning papers. She has also presented What The Papers Say. She has written for The Spectator and The Oldie among other publications. She married novelist Philip Kerr in 1991.

EVE POLLARD

A pioneer among the new breed of women newspaper editors, Eve Pollard has run the Sunday Express and its magazine since 1991, establishing a mini-dynasty there since her husband is Daily Express editor Sir Nicholas Lloyd. At the same time, she has established herself as part of the TV guest-panellist circuit, appearing on such popular shows as Through The Keyhole with David Frost. Her rise began in 1970 when she joined The Observer as Woman's Editor of their magazine, moving to the Mirror Group where she remained for the next ten years as Woman's Editor of the Sunday Mirror before being appointed Assistant Editor of the Sunday People. She left the Holborn-based group in 1983 and joined breakfast TV company TV-am as Features Editor and presenter before moving in 1985 to New York, where she freelanced for the Sunday Times and launched Elle (as Editor-in-Chief). She moved to the News of the World to edit its colour magazine, Sunday, in 1986, but the same year she was offered editorship of Associated Newspapers' high profile You Magazine (supplement of the Mail on Sunday) and ran it until late 1987, when Robert Maxwell made the inevitable offer that could not be refused. She edited his Sunday Mirror and launched its magazine section in 1988. The move to the Express Group came in May 1991.

Photograph courtesy of Sunday Express

BERYL VERTUE

Once a secretary to aspiring comedy writers Spike Milligan, Eric Sykes, Alan Simpson, Ray Galton and Johnny Speight, Beryl Vertue is now one of the most influential women in the world of films and TV. Having moved from secretary to literary agent (and adding performers like Frankie Howerd and Tony Hancock to her client list), she formed a film company to utilise their talents. It made The Spy with the Cold Nose, film versions of hit TV shows Steptoe and Son and Till Death Us Do Part, and the classic short The Plank. In 1968 the company became part of the Robert Stigwood Group and Beryl eventually became deputy chairman. She was the first British producer to make a series directly for a US network (Beacon Hill, based on the Upstairs, Downstairs format). In 1974 she produced the film of the rock opera Tommy. During the 1980s she formed her own independent company, Hartswood Films, which makes the TV series Men Behaving Badly, voted Best ITV Sitcom in the 1992 Comedy Awards.

LIZ FORGAN

Liz Forgan's career took a dramatic new turn at the end of 1992 when she was offered the No. 2 spot at the BBC by Director General John Birt. Born in Calcutta in 1944, she read Modern Languages at Oxford and was arts editor of the Tehran Journal from 1968-69. She joined the Hampstead and Highgate Express in 1970 as a reporter and was later promoted to news editor, moving in 1975 to the short-lived Inside London as political editor. She joined the Evening Standard in 1975 and rose to be its chief leader writer and feature writer, moving to the Guardian as women's editor and assistant features editor until 1981, when she joined Channel 4. After a stint as senior Commissioning Editor (News and Current Affairs), she became Director of Programmes in 1988 (having been both Assistant Controller and Deputy Controller). Her future as First Lady of Broadcasting now seems assured with her appointment to the rarefied heights of the BBC.

ANDREA WONFOR

Andrea Wonfor gained an honours degree in History from Cambridge University. She started in television as a production trainee at Granada, moving on to Tyne Tees in 1969 to be a researcher. In 1976 she was promoted to Head of the new Children's and Young People's Programmes and in 1982 became the company's Director of Programmes. She launched The Tube and, at the opposite end of the spectrum, the religious programme Highway. Andrea became Chairman of Regional Controllers in 1986. She joined Zenith Productions in 1987 as production executive and became managing director the following year. Since 1990 she has been Controller of Arts and Entertainment at Channel 4.

SALLY HEAD

Sally Head began her career in TV drama with Warner Brothers, where she worked first as European Story Editor and then as Script Executive. She moved to Thames Television as a Script Editor before joining the BBC. Her credits as a producer there include The Life and Loves of a She-Devil (winner of a BAFTA award for Best Series in 1986), First Born and Jumping the Queue. For the past three years she has been Head of Drama at Granada, where her credits include BAFTA winner Prime Suspect (she was Executive Producer) and its sequel, shown late last year. Other favourites for which she is responsible include Jeeves and Wooster, Maigret, Sherlock Holmes and Angels.

SOPHIE BALHETCHET

Sophie Balhetchet joined the film and TV industry in 1979 as Director of the Association of Independent Producers after gaining a double first at Oxford. In 1981 she left to produce documentaries and drama for Channel 4 (including Giro City with Glenda Jackson). In 1986 she set up ZED Ltd with partner Glenn Wilhide. Recent credits include The Manageress (with Cherie Lunghi as a football boss) and the acclaimed The Camomile Lawn. She was a founder member of the Independent Programme Producers Association and its chairman from 1986-89, leading the negotiations for 25 per cent access by independents to BBC and ITV output. She is a founding Board member of Women in Film and Television (UK) and a member of the British Screen Advisory Council.

JANET STREET-PORTER

Janet Street-Porter has been BBC TV's Head of Youth and Entertainment Features since 1991, having joined in 1988 as Head of Youth Programmes. Her department is responsible for over 40 series ranging from quiz shows like Mastermind and Going for Gold to factual programmes such as the sports magazine On the Line and youth series Reportage and Dance Energy. She produced The Vampyr, a 19th century German romantic opera relocated in contemporary London, for BBC 2 (shown last Christmas). Originally trained as an architect, she was a design writer and newspaper columnist before moving into TV in 1975. Her ground-breaking Network 7 was a BAFTA award winner. She is on the Board of Women in Film and Television and is the author of two books.

JANE WELLESLEY

It was in the art world that Jane Wellesley first made her mark. She worked for the magazine Apollo, then helped set up a 20th century department at Colnaghi's gallery in 1972, spending two years as a research assistant organising exhibitions. In 1975 she joined the BBC as a publicity officer responsible for drama and documentaries. She moved to Granada TV in 1981 as a researcher for their series The Spanish Civil War. After two years she returned to the BBC to oversee international co-productions for their Music and Arts department. She joined Antelope Films in 1984, becoming a fully-fledged producer, and in 1986 was made managing director. In late 1987 she joined Warner Sisters, setting up a new joint venture with Lavinia Warner. Born in 1951 she is on the Arts Films Production Committee of the Arts Council.

LAVINIA WARNER

Lavinia Warner joined the drama department of London Weekend Television direct from university and later moved on to work as a researcher for Thames. In 1978 she became a contract producer/ director at the BBC. After making Women In Captivity, an Omnibus documentary on women survivors of a Japanese prison camp, she created the drama series Tenko on the same subject. It ran to three series, collected major awards and was a huge international success.

She set up the cheekily-named Warner Sisters in 1984 and it is now one of the leading UK independent production companies, having made Jailed by the British, GI Brides (Broadcasting Press Guild award and BAFTA nomination), Lizzie, Wish Me Luck, Selling Hitler and Rides. Lavinia, who was born in 1950, was one of the original members of the 25 per cent Campaign for increased independent access to the BBC and ITV companies.

SUE MacGREGOR

Sue MacGregor has been a presenter of BBC Radio 4's Today programme since 1987. She was born in Oxford in 1941, and educated mainly in South Africa, where she gained some of her early broadcasting experience. Her first jobs for the BBC included reporting for The World At One, The World This Weekend and PM. She was presenter of Woman's Hour for 15 years from 1972. Sue has her own occasional Radio 4 series, Conversation Piece, in which she interviews people of her own choice. Amongst the many awards which she has received are the Broadcasting Press Guild's annual award for Outstanding Contribution to Radio (1979), the Sony award for Female Radio Pesonality of the Year (1983), Radio Personality of the Year (1990) and Woman Journalist of the Year (1990), awarded by the 300 Group. In November 1991 Sue was presented with the Network Award for Woman of the Decade and, in December of the same year, she was awarded the OBE in the New Year's Honours List.

Photograph by Jeff Overs

SALLY FELDMAN

Before joining the BBC in 1983, Sally Feldman had edited several magazines for teenagers, and the magazine Woman's World. She joined Radio 4's Woman's Hour in 1983 as a producer and was appointed deputy editor in 1987. In 1992 she was appointed joint editor. For a year she presented the compilation programme, Weekend Woman's Hour. She is also editor of Treasure Islands, Radio 4's programme devoted to children's books, which she launched in 1987.

SHARON BANOFF

In 1977, when Sharon Banoff was 30 years old, she received a call from a frantic Radio 4 producer, inviting her to replace a researcher who had suffered a nervous breakdown halfway through an investigative series with Roger Cook! Thrown in at the deep end, Sharon later moved to programmes such as Checkpoint and Reel Evidence. Three years on she became a producer, working initially on the daily You and Yours and Woman's Hour, before settling into the documentary features area. She took a year out to set up and co-produce Face the Facts, and then returned as chief producer to the Features Unit, where output includes The Radio Programme, The Village and The Locker Room. She initiated and still edits the Soundtrack series, Relative Values and Your Place or Mine? – the first radio collaboration with American documentary producers. Sharon won the Medical Journalists Gold Award in 1990 and 1991.

LIBBY PURVES

Libby Purves graduated from Oxford with a first class Honours degree in English in 1971, and joined the BBC as a trainee studio manager. Her broadcasting career began in 1975 as a reporter for Radio 4's Today; she became one of Today's presenters from 1978 until 1981 and has presented Midweek since 1983. Libby has also worked on Sunday, File on 4, Profile and other programmes. Radio documentaries include The Singing Bells, Holy Bones, Street Gospel and Seven about Seven. Since 1983 she has been a journalist and columnist for The Times and the Sunday Express and, formerly, for Punch and the Evening Standard. Libby is the author of several books: How Not To Be A Perfect Mother; How Not To Raise A Perfect Child; How Not To Be The Perfect Family; One Summer's Grace; Britain At Play; Where Did You Leave The Admiral? and The Sailing Weekend Book amongst them. She lives on a Suffolk farm with her husband, Paul Heiney.

ANNA RAEBURN

Born in 1944, in Middlesbrough, Anna Raeburn wanted to be an actress. Turned down for a grant by the local authority, she learned to type and went to London, where she spent ten years working as a secretary. She answered a rather ambiguous advertisement for a job and was selected as one of three young women to launch Forum, a sex magazine, in the USA. On her return, in 1971, she was offered a job by the British publication, where she spent her next three years. In 1974 Anna succeeded Evelyn Home as agony aunt at Woman magazine. During that time she co-presented a series for LWT, A Question of Sex, with Clive James; anchored a summer series of Songs of Praise; appeared many times on radio and television, including a guest appearance with David Frost; co-wrote and presented an hour's documentary for Man Alive and established the Capital Radio phone-in programme, affectionately known as Anna and the Doc. This began in 1975 and carried on until 1989. In 1978-79 she co-created and co-wrote the LWT sitcom Agony with Len Richmond. In 1979 Anna moved to Cosmopolitan, where she contributed a monthly column and for a year in 1986-87, she wrote a regular column for Punch on Men. Anna stands in for Anne Robinson on Radio 2, co-anchors the morning news programme on LBC and appears every two weeks on the Steve Wright Show on Radio 1. She has published three books, a memoir, Talking To Myself, a monograph on Joan Crawford and a novel, Keeper Of Dreams. She writes a column for The People and for Company magazine.

SUSANNAH SIMONS

Currently presenting her own daily programme on Classic FM, Susannah Simons, 44, is one of the foremost television and radio news presenters and journalists. She has an ever growing following in the financial and business world and is able to combine great authority with warmth and humour. Susannah can currently be seen presenting Channel 4's Answering Back and she has presented programmes for Radio 4: The World This Weekend; Today; PM; The World At One; Budget Special and Election Night. Her speciality is live broadcasting and, for the past 11 years, she has presented the Massed Bands of the Royal Marines for Radio 2. She performed Facade, with Richard Baker at the Crawley Festival and commentated on the Royal Wedding in 1981. Susannah piloted the new BBC TV Question Time to great acclaim in 1991. She has been keynote speaker for numerous conferences and presents company videos and training films for industry.

CAROLINE MILLINGTON

Head of Magazine Programmes, BBC Radio since 1988, Caroline Millington was born in Essex in 1949 and graduated in English Literature from the University of York in 1970. She joined the BBC as a journalist trainee and, from 1972 until 1978, was producer of The World Tonight and other current affairs programmes. She produced BBC TV's Nationwide in 1978-79 and, from 1980 to 1985, produced for Radio 4: The Week In Westminster; Talking Politics and In Business. She worked with Robert Carvel on various radio documentaries: The Usual Channels; The Odd Couple – Parliament and the BBC and Pandora's Box – a Critical Look at BBC Journalism. She produced Brass Tacks for BBC Manchester in 1986 and was appointed assistant head of Current Affairs Magazine Programmes for 1977-78 before taking up her current position. Programmes which come within her remit include: Woman's Hour; You and Yours; Start the Week; Midweek; Loose Ends; Desert Island Discs; Any Questions; Face the Facts; In Touch; Does He Take Sugar?; The Food Progamme and Call Nick Ross. Caroline was a member of the Charter Review Task Force on BBC and the Communities in 1991 and a founder member and first chair of the Radio Academy.

JENNY ABRAMSKY

Born in 1946 and a graduate in English from the University of East Anglia, Jenny Abramsky joined the BBC as a programmes operations assistant in 1969. She moved to The World At One as a producer in 1973 and was appointed editor of the relaunched PM programme in 1978. In 1981 she returned to The World At One as editor. After five years working with Sir Robin Day, Jenny took over the editorship of the Today programme. In 1987 she became editor, News and Current Affairs Radio, in charge of all news and current affairs programmes on all five BBC Radio networks. During the Gulf War, Jenny set up Radio 4 News FM, virtually overnight, providing continuous news and analysis for the duration of the war. In 1990 Jenny received the accolade of Woman of Distinction from Jewish Care, one of the country's major voluntary social welfare organisations. In October 1992 she was appointed to the Economic and Social Research Council.

JENNI MURRAY

Jenni Murray became presenter of Radio 4's Woman's Hour in 1987. In 1991 she was at the helm for the show's relaunch at 10.30am. Before joining Woman's Hour, Jenni presented the Today programme on Radio 4 and BBC 2's Newsnight. Her television documentaries include Everyman (No Great Trauma; Breaking The Chain; Here's Looking At You), The Duchy of Cornwall, with HRH The Prince of Wales and a major series for BBC 2, Women in Politics, in which she featured Benazir Bhutto, Cory Aquino, Eugenia Charles and Simone Weil. Jenni is a regular contributor to magazines and newspapers.

CLARE SELERIE

Clare Selerie joined the BBC in 1977 after beginning her career as a Russian translator and interpreter. She spent two years as a producer in the Russian section of the BBC Overseas Services before moving to the Radio 4 arts programme, Kaleidoscope, in 1980. In 1983 she started working on Woman's Hour and became the editor in 1987. After the birth of her daughter in 1991, she returned to work part-time and now shares the editorship with Sally Feldman.

SANDI TOKSVIG

Sandi Toksvig spent six years of her schooling in New York before going up to Cambridge, where she gained a first class honours degree in Law/Archaeology and Anthropology and won the Theresa Montefiori Memorial Award for outstanding academic achievement and the Raemakers Prize for Archaeology. Her professional theatre experience embraces the Nottingham Repertory Company and The New Shakespeare Company, The Orchard Theatre, Dartford, where she played the fairy godmother in Cinderella and Big Night Out, at Tunbridge Wells. She co-wrote and appeared in The Pocket Dream for the Nottingham Playhouse and the Albery Theatre in the West End. Her television appearances include: No 73, of which she was the co-author; BBC Sixty Minutes, six months as special correspondent; Happy Families; Saturday Starship; Points of View; Get Fresh; Toksvig; Motormouth; Gilbert's Fridge; Ghost Train; Whose Line Is It Anyway? and Behind The Headlines. Recently, she has co-starred in The Big One, with Mike McShane, which she wrote with Elly Brewer. Sandi is an original member of the Comedy Store Players.

BARBARA WINDSOR

Barbara Windsor was evacuated to Blackpool from her native Shoreditch in WWII. After the war, she won a scholarship to a convent and then attended the Aida Foster Stage School. Her first West End show was Love From Judy, when she was 14 years old, it ran for two years. The turning point in her career came in 1959, with Fings Ain't Wot They Used To Be, which ran for two and a half years at the Garrick Theatre. During that period, she also starred in the hit TV show, The Rag Trade, and took her first major role in a film, Sparrers Can't Sing, which was a hit on both sides of the Atlantic, in spite of having to be shown with subtitles in the USA! Her list of theatrical successes includes: Sing A Rude Song; The Threepenny Opera; Carry On London; Entertaining Mr Sloane and Guys And Dolls. Apart from the Carry On . . . films, she has starred in amongst others, Too Hot To Handle; Chitty Chitty Bang Bang and The Boyfriend. Barbara was delighted recently to be the subject of This Is Your Life.

JENNIFER SAUNDERS

In addition to her work with Dawn French and the Comic Strip, including the film, Supergrass and the 1991 Christmas Special, Little Pig Robinson, in which they played the sister pigs, Porcas and Dorcas, Jennifer Saunders, 34, has recently written and starred in the series Absolutely Fabulous, with Joanna Lumley for BBC 2. She is co-writer with Dawn of the series Girls On Top and French and Saunders. The bossy partner on things practical and the ignorant one on things sexual, particularly in the famous contraception sketch, Jennifer is married to Ade Edmondson of the Comic Strip, The Young Ones and Bottom fame.

DAWN FRENCH

Half of the comedy duo, French and Saunders, Dawn French, 35, is a founder member of the Comic Strip. Her work for the Comic Strip, for Channel 4, includes: Five Go Mad In Dorset; Five Go Mad On Mescalin; Slags; Summer School; Private Enterprise; Consuela; Mr Jolly Lives Next Door; Bad News Tour and Strike, which won the Golden Globe Award in Montreux in 1988; Happy Families, for BBC television; three series of French and Saunders, for BBC television and Sapsorrow, for TVS Films/Henson Organisation. Recently, she has been seen creating a different role for each of six individual films in the TV series, Murder Most Horrid. She is married to comedian Lenny Henry.

DORA BRYAN

Born in 1924 in Parbold, Lancashire, and brought up in Oldham, Dora Bryan has been one of the most enduring stars of British stage, screen and television since she first appeared at the Palace Theatre, Manchester, in 1936. She left school at the age of 14 and joined a local repertory theatre in Oldham and left there at 20 as the leading lady. Her first appearance in London was in Stage Door and the credits which have followed include: No Room At The Inn; Peace In Our Time; Accolade; Traveller's Joy; The Lyric Revue; The Globe Revue; Living For Pleasure; Simon And Laura; The Lovebirds; Gentlemen Prefer Blondes, in which she played Lorelei; Six Of One; Too Good To Be True and Hello Dolly, in which she played the title role at the Theatre Royal, Drury Lane. More recently, she has played Mistress Quickly in The Merry Wives of Windsor; Mrs Hardcastle in She Stoops To Conquer, for the National Theatre, for which she won the Variety Club of Great Britain Award; The Applecart, in which she co-starred with Peter O'Toole and Charlie Girl, with Paul Nicholas and Cyd Charisse. Amongst the dozens of films in which she has appeared, she won a BAFTA Award for her outstanding performance in A Taste Of Honey. She frequently appears on television, has been the subject of Desert Island Discs and This Is Your Life twice and, in 1992, was awarded an MA by Manchester University.

VICTORIA WOOD

Thirty-nine year old Victoria Wood is one of the few British performers who can consistently sell out the biggest theatres in the land. She has toured regularly since 1984 and every show has been sold out. The same is true of her West End appearances at the Strand Theatre and The Palladium and she looks set to complete a hat-trick when she appears at the Albert Hall in September 1993. Her career began in 1974 on local news programmes and her BBC shows, As Seen on TV, netted top rating, with three BAFTA Awards for Best Light Entertainment Programme and two for Best Light Entertainment Performance. An Audience With Victoria Wood, for LWT, won another two BAFTAs. Between 1987 and 1991, Victoria was awarded the Variety Club award for BBC Personality of the Year, the TV Times Readers Award for the Funniest Woman, the Radio Times Funniest Woman Award and the British Comedy Award for best stand-up comedian. In 1991 she was a major contributor to the LWT special, Julie Walters and Friends, which won the 1992 Writers Guild Award for the best light entertainment script. Victoria's books, Barmy and Up To You, Porky, continue to be very popular and her latest BBC special, Victoria Wood's All Day Breakfast was played on Christmas Night. Her future plans include a countrywide tour in 1993, and a film which she is writing for herself and Julie Walters, Pat and Margaret.

BRENDA LARENTY

The "Ballerina on the tight wire", Brenda Larenty's act varies according to the venue. It may consist of the one point arabesque on a wire, jumping through paper hoops, unicycle, skipping, juggling and dancing. She has worked in Billy Smart's Circus, the Hippodrome Circus and in many other circuses in the UK as well as in Germany and Hungary, where she worked at the Hungarian State Circus in Budapest. More unusually, Brenda has worked for the English National Opera, the Royal Opera House, Covent Garden and the Cologne Opera, and has frequently appeared with the Welsh National Opera.

FAY PRESTO

Appearing on the entertainment scene, as if by magic, several years ago, Fay Presto rapidly established herself as one of the leading exponents of the magician's art. She is now to be seen regularly perfoming at Langan's Brasserie and other top restaurants, on stage at various West End theatres or in front of audiences of celebrities all over the country. Fay is one of the few performers ever to have received a standing ovation at the Magic Castle, in Hollywood. She has appeared on the QEII, yachts in Cannes harbour, at the National History Museum and has even been brothel mother in a German night club.

BECKY TRUMAN

Artistic director of the Skinning The Cat Aerial Theatre workshops, Becky Truman has trained with the Circus Senso, Ecole de Trapeze Volant and Archaos. She founded Skinning The Cat in 1988 and has toured festivals extensively in Britain and Europe for the past four years. Workshops comprise: aerial skills; trapeze; acrobatics; innovative rope work; cloud swing; choreography; character work and stage make-up. As artistic director, Becky is a leading exponent of experimental aerial techniques used in contemporary circus theatre.

VALERIE FLEET

Valerie Fleet is a social worker with a difference. In her working life she helps find foster-homes for children and, when relaxing, she finds nothing more soothing than a spot of fire-eating and fire-breathing. She learned the art some years ago and, since she became proficient, there has been no dampening of her enthusiasm. She has performed at charity functions and on yachts in the Mediterranean and, recently, she used her skills to light the barbecue at a party for her foster parents and their children, who all think she's hot stuff.

MARILYN WATERHOUSE

Marilyn Waterhouse is a housewife and mother, a partner in the family marketing business, where she specialises in beauty products and services, and a lion-tamer. She had always been fascinated with big cats, but in her youth she had to make do with small ones. However, on her 35th birthday, her husband, David, organised a trip to the circus where, to her surprise, she discovered she was to be apprentice lion-tamer for the afternoon. Since then she has got together with lions whenever possible.

JANE WATSON

Mult-talented Jane Watson was born in 1964, and educated at the Jacques Lecoq School of Movement Theatre in Paris, the Etienne Decroux and Daniel Stein Schools of mime, also in Paris and the Arts Educational School in Tring, Hertfordshire, where she studied singing, voice and modern dance. Her performances have taken her all over the Far East, notably to Japan, where she has made language educational videos as well as starring on the stage and on television. Amongst her Japanese successes were Charlie and the Chocolate Factory and One Day Maybe Tuesday in Tokyo, in 1989. Doris Jones' Diary, which she performed at the Hong Kong Fringe in 1990, later transferred to the Finborough Arms Theatre, in London. Jane has also done a great deal of voice-over and radio work, including language tapes for the Oxford University Press.

ROSY THE CLOWN (ROSY GIBB)

Held by many to be Britain's leading woman clown, Rosy Gibb was born in 1942 and brought up in the Channel Islands and in Africa, where she taught Haille Sellassie's grandchildren to ride. She was educated at Trinity College, Dublin and the London School of Economics; acquired an MA and MPhil, saved a dog from drowning in the Liffey, became Ireland's first ever twisting champion, started a society to teach literacy skills to gypsies and became a record breaking swimmer. Married with two children, as the age of 40 loomed she decided she wanted to find her true vocation. She went out busking, visualising fame and fortune, and collected 7½p in her hat, but she was not deterred. She taught herself magic, juggling, mime and acrobatics and bookings started to come in from festivals, schools and theatres, gathering momentum all the time. She has now performed all over the UK, Europe and the USA.

SARAH HB

A DJ at Kiss FM, Sarah HB started collecting records at the tender age of 14, a passion that has progressed to the point where she now has two rooms overflowing with vinyl. She began DJing in 1989 at London's Limelight club and from there became involved in the capital's burgeoning pirate scene, starting with a half hour show and progressing to two permanent weekly slots. She joined Kiss in 1990 as a programme assistant but was soon to be found behind the microphone where she can now be heard playing a selection of house, soul and garage music. Sarah remains a familiar figue on the club circuit where her DJing talents are constantly in demand.

ANNIE NIGHTINGALE

Starting out as a journalist with the Brighton Argus, Annie Nightingale "fell into" radio in the late 1960s and was soon offered the job of Radio 1's only female DJ. She presented various slots on the network during the 1970s and established the Request Show in 1982. One of Britain's most respected broadcasters, Annie paved the way for the growing band of women DJ's that followed and is a frequent guest on Pick of the Week, Start the Week and Woman's Hour. She has written rock columns for the Daily Express and Cosmopolitan and her television credits include The Old Grey Whistle Test (at the time one of the few music programms that did not slavishly follow the charts) and Late Night in Concert. She is a regular guest on Pop Quiz and was the presenter for the Philadelphia end of the historic Live Aid concert in 1985. In 1982 Annie published an anecdotal semi-autobiography, Chase The Fade. She has two children and still lives in Brighton.

LIZ KERSHAW

After gaining a degree in Business Studies and a spell at British Telecom during which she also became well-known on Leeds' Radio Aire, Liz Kershaw broke into network broadcasting as a reporter on The Whistle Test and then as a presenter of Open Space. In 1986 she set up BT's pop service, Livewire, achieving a £3 million turnover in the first 12 months. From 1987 to 1988, she hosted Radio 1's first teenage magazine programme, Backchat, which was nominated for a Sony Award for best magazine programme. She has contributed to numerous television and radio shows and written for The Guardian and The Independent among others.

ANGIE GREAVES

Angie is one of London's up an coming presenters with a strong background in independent radio. After working for Capital Radio for five years, Angie joined the newly formed ethnic station, Spectrum Radio, hosting the breakfast show on the first day of broadcast and thus launching the station. On departure from Spectrum she joined Choice FM where she has chaired live discussions and talk shows on a wide range of topics.

LYNN PARSONS

Lynn Parsons joined TV-am as a sound engineer in 1983, becoming a vision mixer within a year and gaining a thorough understanding of live television. At this time Lynn was also presenting weekend shows for County Sound Radio and auditioning for other presenting work. Her first big break came with Capital Radio where Lynn produced and presented a three hour programme five nights a week, interviewing such luminaries as Cliff Richard, Al Jarreau and Billy Joel. In March 1990 she compered the LWT Arts Festival which became a 90 minute programme with Melvyn Bragg.

JAKKI BRAMBLES

After growing up in Essex, Ayr and then the Isle of Arran, Jakki Brambles found her first job presenting a Saturday evening show for Westsound Radio in Scotland whilst also working as an assistant producer of commercials. After moving to London and working in local radio for 18 months, she became one of Radio 1's youngest presenters when she hosted the Weekend Early Show in 1989, contributing travel and weather news for Simon Mayo's breakfast crew during the week. Jakki's next slot was the early evening Drivetime Show before she moved to the popular weekday lunchtime show. Jakki lives with her husband in North London but often returns to Arran to visit her family.

BARONESS THATCHER OF KESTEVEN

Margaret Hilda Thatcher was born on 13th October, 1925, daughter of a politically active grocer in Grantham. She was educated locally at Somerville College, Oxford, where she obtained a degree in chemistry. She was also President of the University Conservative Association. On leaving Oxford she worked as a research scientist. Reading for the Bar in her spare time, she was called to the Bar by Lincoln's Inn in 1954, and practised as a barrister specialising in taxation law. After unsuccessful attempts in 1950 and 1951, she was elected to the House of Commons in 1959 as Member for Finchley. Lady Thatcher's first ministerial post came in 1961 and from 1964 until her November 1990 resignation she sat on the Front Bench. She became Leader of the Opposition in 1975 and Britain's first woman Prime Minister in 1979. With her election victory in 1987, she became the first British Prime Minister to win three consecutive General Elections. A Master of the Arts at Oxford University, in 1983 she was elected Fellow of the Royal Society. In 1990 she was awarded the Order of Merit by Her Majesty the Queen, and in 1992 was elevated to the House of Lords.

RACHEL HEYHOE-FLINT

Rachael Heyhoe-Flint is unique in that people who know nothing of cricket – certainly not women's cricket – know her as a cricketer. Captain of England from 1966-77, she has toured throughout the cricketing world and, in 1976, averaged 85.5 against Australia. She scored 22 centuries during her career and has also played hockey for England and coached it in America. She has written two hockey books, the Definitive History on Women's Cricket and "Heyhoe"!, her autobiography. In 1973, she was nominated Best After Dinner Speaker by the Guild of Professional Toastmasters and is a regular broadcaster and speaker.

RABBI JULIA NEUBERGER

Julia Neuberger has been Rabbi at the South London Liberal Synagogue since 1977. She was educated at Cambridge (MA, BA), and the Leo Baeck College, London, where she has been a lecturer and Associate Fellow since 1979. Apart from her myriad appointments within the Jewish community, she sits on the Council of St. George's Hospital Medical School and is Chairman of the Patients' Association; was Convenor of the SDP/Liberal Lawyers Working Party on Legal Services 1985-87, and holds many other secular appointments.

ANGELA RIPPON

Born in Plymouth, Angela Rippon moved into television in 1966 as a reporter and presenter following three years in newspaper journalism. Via various programmes, in 1973 Angela Rippon returned to the BBC as a news reporter and in 1976 introduced the "new look" Nine O'Clock News and did so until 1981, winning Newscaster of the Year in 1976, 77 and 78. In 1982 she left he BBC to be a founder of TV AM, leaving amid controversy and winning a court action against the Company. Other broadcasting credits are too numerous to mention, and she is currently working on a dozen regular radio and TV programmes.

ROSIE SWALE

In Rosie Swale's vivid talks, she likes to feel that her audiences are sharing her adventures "without the blisters and wet socks". Her early adventures included overland expeditions to Russia, Nepal and India. She lived at sea for many years, and her son was born on board the boat, with the help of the Emergency Childbirth section of Reed's Almanack. She sailed the Atlantic single handed – for seventy days – to raise money for the Royal Marsden Hospital Cancer Scanner Fund, and has since developed a further hunger for exploring on land, leading to journeys through South America on horseback.

JUDITH CHALMERS

Judith Chalmers was born in Manchester, and started her broadcasting career there on Children's TV at the age of 13. She is probably now most famous for "Wish you were here . . .?" the holiday programme which has been running since 1973. Outside broadcasting, Judith is chairman of the Appeals Committee of the Women's National Cancer Control Campaign, and of the Holiday Care Service. She is a member of the National Consumer Council and honorary Lady Taverner. She holds the distinction of being the only lady member of the Peacock Committee, investigating the financing of the BBC.

SUE ARNOLD

Columnist for the Observer and member of the Chelsea Arts Club, Sue Arnold originally trained as a ballet dancer. She was educated at Trinity College Dublin where she received an honours degree in English. She worked originally for the Lancaster Evening Telegraph and has written columns for the London Evening Standard and the Teheran Journal as well as the London Observer, for 15 years.

CLAIRE RAYNER

Claire Rayner started her career in nursing at the Royal Northern Hospital, London, where she became State Registered in 1954 winning the hospital Gold Medal for Outstanding Achievement. She studied midwifery at Guy's and was sister in the Paediatric Department at the Whittington. Best known as the quintessential "Agony Aunt", in the Press and on Television, she is the author of an incredible 75 books on nursing, sex education, family health, etc., many of them translated into several languages. She is also a published novelist, and much in demand as a speaker.

Photograph by Amanda Rayner

DEANNE KEENE

Deanne Keene is England's Diana Ross lookalike. She is 25 years old, and has been Diana full time for the past five years. Since being discovered, she has travelled the world doing promotions, TV, films and personal appearances, and has forged a singing career of her own, backing top singers. In 1992 she took part in the European Promotional Tour for Virgin Megastores, and this year is travelling to the US, Japan and Australia.

JEANNETTE CHARLES

Although the most famous lookalike of them all, Jeannette Charles did not enter the acting profession because of her uncanny resemblance to HM the Queen, although she would be the first to admit that it has done her career no harm at all! Born in London in 1927. Jeannette's first appearances were in tap dancing contests at seaside resorts. She then worked in her father's restaurant and appeared in Rep emigrating to Texas to work in the office of an oil company. It was in July 1971 that a portrait of her was mistaken for one of the Queen, and subsequent publicity launched her into the world of international entertainment. In addition to commercials, TV and films in ten countries over the last 20 years, Jeannette makes appearances as the "Special Guest" at all kinds of functions. Her book, The Queen and I, was published in 1987.

All photographs courtesy of Susan Scott
LOOKALIKES
26 College Crescent
London NW3 5LH
Tel: 071-387 9245
Fax: 071-722 8261

GLADYS CROSBIE

Gladys Crosbie is the Queen Mother lookalike and has appeared as Her Royal Highness on television many times.

PAULINE BAILEY

Pauline Bailey is 24, and has been a fan of Marilyn Monroe since she was five. She really does look uncannily like Marilyn, and works here and abroad doing TV appearances, commercials, photographic advertising, pop videos and personal appearances. She also sings and dances like Monroe. She has been a professional lookalike for five years, and recently acted the part of Marilyn Monroe in a play about her at the Edinburgh Festival.

BARBARA KEALY

Barbara Kealy has been a Joan Collins lookalike for six years and has worked abroad several times as well as in Great Britain. People have been telling her she looks like "Joanie" for years. She is a secretary during the day and belongs to a well-known Old Time Muisc Hall group for fun.

DEBBIE ROSLYN

Debbie Roslyn is a professional Steffi Graf lookalike which, when you think about it, is a stroke of luck and unlikely to have been determined on at a very early age. She used to own her own hairdressers and still works part-time in someone else's, but works as a lookalike whenever she can because, she says, it is interesting and good fun. She is 29 years old and lives in Lancashire.

CHRISTINA HANCE

Christina Hance is the Princess Diana lookalike. She and Peter Hugo, the Prince Charles lookalike, are always in great demand and have made many "Royal" appearances together.

SHELLEY SILAS

Shelley Silas is 33. After a variety of jobs, she decided to concentrate on a writing career, and has ten published stories to her credit. She became the Liza Minnelli lookalike four years ago, when a magazine chose her to take part in a feature. She also works part-time for a casting director, and has recently started a degree course in English Literature at Birkbeck College.

MARIE LLOYD

Thirty-one year old Marie Lloyd is the Cher lookalike. She lives in Manchester and runs Fantasia Productions, organising Theme Nights, and travelling with other lookalikes in a musical roadshow. She studied theatre and drama and has her own show, impersonating Piaf, Monroe and Carmen Miranda. She is currently making children's educational videos.

DAME FREYA STARK

One of our most esteemed travellers and travel writers with more than 30 titles to her name, Dame Freya Stark was born in Paris and spent her childhood in England and Italy. She read literature under W. P. Ker at London University until her studies were interrupted by WWI which she spent working as a nurse on the Italian Front. After a course in Arabic at the School of Oriental and African Studies she was invited to Baghdad by the prime minister where she worked on the Baghdad Times, followed the Crusader routes and mapped the Valley of the Assassins in Luristan. During WWII she worked for the ministry of information in Aden and Cairo, and was personal assistant to Lady Wavell, describing her experiences in West Is East (1945). She has travelled extensively, always financed by her writing, in Europe, the Middle East and Asia.

Photograph Royal Geographical Society, courtesy of the Expedition Advisory Centre

ALISON JANE HARGREAVES

Widely admired as one of the world's best women technical mountaineers Alison grew up in a family of keen hill walkers and learnt to rock climb at school. She has achieved a formidable list of alpine climbs including three of the classic north face climbs, The Eiger, The Matterhorn and the Grandes Jorasses. In 1988 she climbed the North Face of the Eiger, the Matterhorn and the months pregnant. In 1993, along with her family, she is setting off on a three part, two year journey before her small children get settled into school – they will go first to the Alps for a unique solo attempt, then Alison will make a solo climbing journey from the lowest to the highest point of North America to acclimatise her for an attempt on Mount Everest in the autumn of 1994.

ZOE HILL

Zoe Hill describes herself as an "unlikely specimen to be found wandering around a jungle". She really "fell" she says, into her adventure. In 1990 she was a member, with her medical officer husband, of an expedition looking for a Mayan temple in the rain forests of Belize. She became seriously ill and was advised to return to base. Their Belizian guide, William, accompanied her and she believes it was his care and knowledge of medicinal herbs that saved her life. Wanting to do something for the local people (suffering from diabetes and without a fresh water supply) who cared so well for her and to find out more about how these herbs could be used by Westerners she got in touch with Kew Gardens. They offered to investigate any plant material she could collect. She returned to the settlement and William taught her how to survive in his world using "plants and instinct" instead of a compass. Back in England she has raised around £1,000 to fund research into several promising plants, two showing anti-HIV activity, one anti-cancer and several anti-diabetic.

HELENA DRYSDALE

When Helena Drysdale discovered family papers in the attic of her crumbling house in Devon revealing that her 19th century ancestors traded in Madagascar she decided to set out for the islands of the Indian Ocean with her photographer husband Richard Pomeroy. Together they uncovered tales of piracy and slave trading, ancestor worship and the annual ceremony of dancing with the dead. The book of the journey was made into a TV documentary, shown in America and on ITV last April. Helena has travelled extensively in India, the Far East, China, East Africa and Eastern Europe. She is also the author of Alone Through China and Tibet. Since 1985 she has given over 100 talks about China and Tibet to groups throughout Britain and Ireland.

CHRISTINA DODWELL

Christina Dodwell's wanderlust is inherited from her grandmother, an unconventional lady who travelled the length and breadth of China during the era of the Warlords. Born and bred in the African bush Christina is the author of seven books describing her time exploring Africa on horseback, white-water rafting in Papua New Guinea, canoeing down the Congo and visiting remote tribes in China. Her book, Travels with Pegasus (published in 1989), covers a 7,000 mile flight, the first crossing of West Africa by Ultralight, during which she met Pygmies, duck-billed women, Nomads and Moors, discovered a dinosaur skeleton and learnt to fly! Her latest book, Beyond Siberia, is due out in May. Her work for television includes a film in the BBC TV series of River Journeys which won three international awards, and a Channel 4 film in the South Pacific in 1990.

ROSIE SWALE

Rosie Swale had an unconventional start to life. Brought up by a grandmother who didn't believe in school and managed to keep her out of one until she was 13 years old, she lived in Ireland until she was 17 when she moved to London and kept herself with a variety of modelling and typing jobs. Her travels began in earnest at the age of 20. Hitch-hiking through Europe, Turkey and Iran to Delhi and back and then to Scandinavia and Russia she covered 16,000 miles before her marriage and twice as many again before her divorce. She lived at sea for many years and her son was born on board a boat, with the help of the Emergency Childbirth section of Reed's Almanac! In 1983 Rosie made a solo trip across the Atlantic in a 17-foot yacht (raising money for the Royal Marsden Hospital Cancer Scanner Fund) and a year later began a pioneering journey on horseback through Chile from the Atacama Desert to Cape Horn. She often lectures and gives talks about her travels – she likes to feel her audiences are sharing her adventures "without the blisters and wet socks".

JULIE-ANN CLYMA

New Zealand born Julie-Ann Clyma has climbed extensively on rock and ice in Britain and Europe and has completed new routes and winter ascents in the Alps. She has also led and participated in many expeditions to high and remote mountains, including trips to the Andes, Alaska, Tien Shan, the Himalayas and the Karakoram, where she has climbed new routes and made first British ascents. In her most recent expeditions to some of the world's highest mountains in Pakistan, exploration has been combined with development work in local villages, introducing micro-hydro energy schemes with the support of Eastern Electricity plc. A graduate in physiology, she combines climbing and expeditions with work in medical research at the Christie Hospital in Manchester.

SANDRA LEVY

A counselling astrologer for over 13 years, Sandra Levy holds the Diploma of the Faculty of Astrological Studies, and was Vice-President of the Faculty's Council for three years. After gaining the Diploma in Counselling Skills from South West London College, she helped set up and tutored on the Faculty's first astrological counselling course. Middlesex-based Sandra also has a keen interest in alternative therapies. A founder member of the Association of Professional Astrologers, Sandra is a long-standing student of Eastern philosophies and often draws on spiritual themes in her work.
Photograph by George Wells Studio

BABS KIRBY

London-based Babs Kirby has a private psychotherapy practice and an astrological consultancy. She also teaches astrology at beginner and advanced levels for the Faculty of Astrological Studies, of which she is currently Vice-President. She teaches counselling to experienced astrologers and supervises counselling astrologers. With Janey Stubbs, Babs has co-written Love and Sexuality, An Exploration of Venus and Mars and Interpreting Solar and Lunar Returns, a Psychological Approach and has published numerous articles in journals including the Astrological Journal. Throughout Britain, Europe and the USA she has lectured and run workshops which combine humanistic and transpersonal psychology with astrology.

MAGGIE HYDE

Maggie Hyde graduated in literary studies and has a background in teaching and educational administration. She is a founding member and Director of the Company of Astrologers, writes regularly for magazines in the field and is the author of Jung and Astrology and Jung for Beginners, both published in 1992. She lectures widely in Britain and abroad and lives in London, where she practises as a consultant.

LIZ GREENE

Best known for her writing and teaching of astrology, and its links with mythology and psychology, Dr Liz Greene has worked as a professional astrologer for over 25 years. Among her 15 books are The Astrology of Fate, novels and children's books, and she has created and written, with Dr Alois Treindl, the text for two computerised horoscope interpretation programmes. She has also made a video, Liz Greene's Guide to Astrology. In 1982, with the late Howard Sasportas, Liz founded the Centre for Psychological Astrology in London, which she now co-directs with Charles Harvey. She has given seminars, workshops and lectures all over Europe, the USA and Australia, and in 1987 was made a lifetime patron of the Faculty of Astrological Studies. The holder of a doctorate in psychology from Los Angeles University and a diploma from the Association of Jungian Analysts in London, Oxfordshire-based Liz has a private practice as an analyst.

BEATA BISHOP

After a varied career in journalism and broadcasting, Beata Bishop embarked on the twin paths of astrology and psychotherapy, and holds diplomas in both. Her interests include holistic medicine and the psychosomatic connection in sickness and health, the understanding of which, she believes, will be the next great breakthrough in the art of healing. Beata is in private practice in West London and runs many workshops and seminars in Britain and abroad.

Photograph by Caroline Forbes

OLIVIA BARCLAY

Her early reading of classical literature led Olivia Barclay to conclude that all life is one and that the analysis of heavenly positions reveals the nature of events on Earth. She subsequently devised and now teaches a worldwide correspondence course, the Qualifying Horary Diploma Course, and her US-published book Horary Astrology Rediscovered gained for her the Professional Astrologers Inc 1991 Award for her outstanding contribution to astrology. Olivia, who lives in Kent, belongs to several astrological organisations for whom she has both written and lectured, as well as speaking in Europe and the USA.

JULIA PARKER

Julia Parker's interest in astrology dates from 1965, spurring her on to gain the Diploma of the Faculty of Astrological Studies, of which she was later President for six years. With her husband Derek she published in 1971 The Compleat Astrologer, which became a bestseller in several languages and has sold over two million copies worldwide. They have since written over 40 books on subjects including astrology, dream interpretation and popular psychology, and published Parker's Astrology in 1991. Julia is a consultant astrologer, and was for some years astrological columnist for Cosmpolitan and Good Housekeeping. With Derek she wrote a column for Woman, and now writes for the Singapore and Hong Kong editions of Tatler. Julia and Derek have lectured widely in Europe, North America and Australasia, and broadcast regularly on breakfast television and the radio in Britain.

MAVIS KLEIN

Psychotherapist and astrologer Mavis Klein graduated in Philosophy and Clinical Psychology from the University of Melbourne before becoming in 1974 a founder member of the British Institute of Transactional Analysis and, the following year, of the European Association for Transactional Analysis. She qualified as a certified psychotherapist in 1975, since when she has been in private practice. Mavis, who lives and works in north London, gained the Mayo School's Diploma of Astrology in 1983 and in 1991 was a founder member of the Association of Professional Astrologers. She has published several books including, in 1992, Pain and Joy in Intimate Relationships.

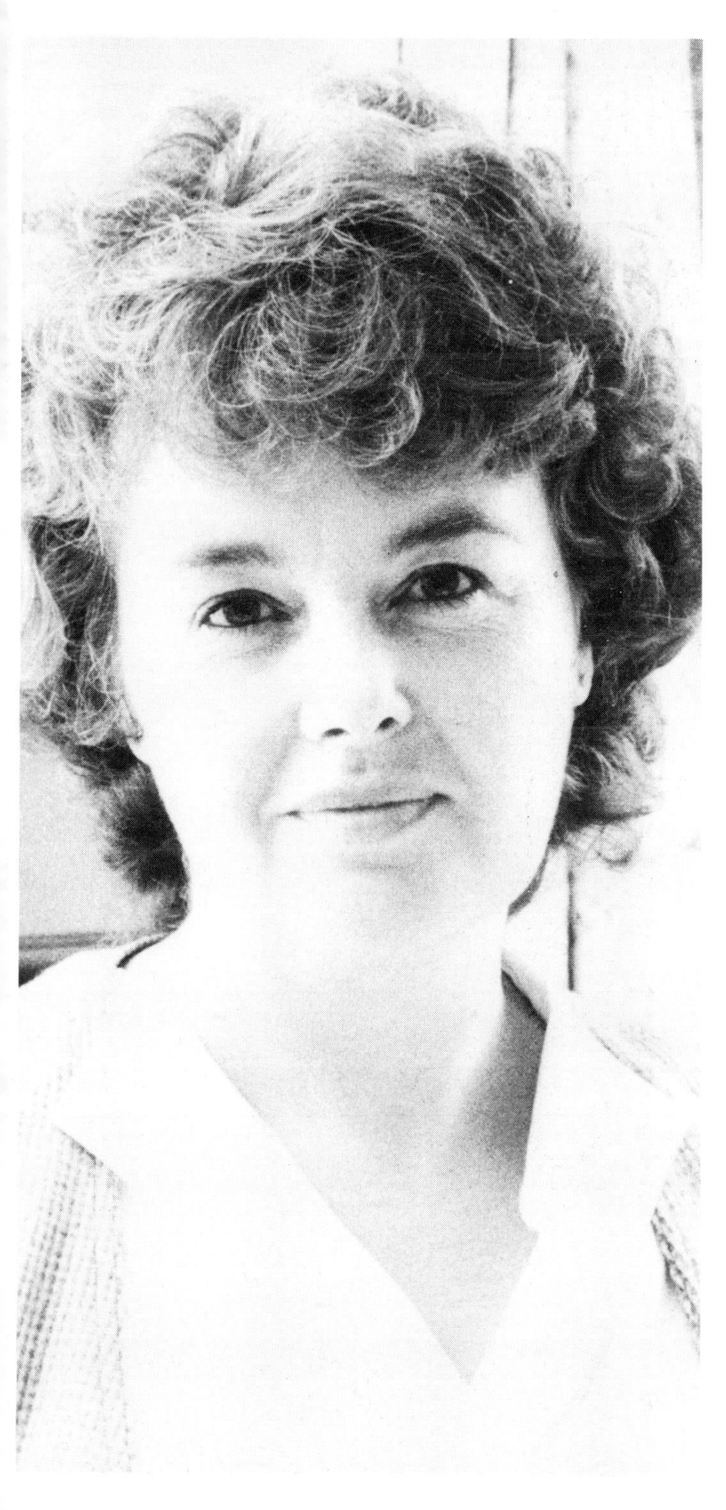

LINDSAY RADERMACHER

After studying at Somerville College, Oxford, and working as a publisher's editor, Lindsay Radermacher developed an interest in astrology. Intensive study led her to gain the Diploma of the Faculty of Astrological Studies in 1976, for which she has tutored for 15 years as well as lecturing widely and running workshops. She is currently President of the Faculty. Lindsay, who holds the Diploma in Counselling Skills from the South West London College, was a founder member of the Association of Professional Astrologers and of the Advisory Panel for Astrological Education, and taught astrology in adult education for 11 years. As well as devoting herself to her London practice, Lindsay has become increasingly involved in group and supervision work, particularly with the Faculty's recently launched counselling course for astrologers.

CHRISTINA ROSE

During the 1970s Christina Rose pioneered the growth of counselling astrology in Britain. With diplomas from the Faculty of Astrological Studies and in counselling and guidance, she is often consulted by other professional astrologers. She is the author of Astrological Counselling, a set book for students of astrology worldwide.

LADY SMITH

Co-founder of the Landmark Trust in 1965, Lady Smith is still responsible for the decoration and soft furnishing of all the historic buildings which have been rescued by this remarkable charity. The Trust not only rescues neglected buildings, but gives them a new lease of life by letting them for self-catering holidays so that anyone may experience the pleasure of living in them. All the 137 buildings adopted by the Trust are of historical or architectural interest, but widely differing character, from mediaeval castles, through Gothic temples to Victorian follies. The quality of workmanship and finish on all the buildings and, particularly, the high standard of appropriate decor all reflect the loving care of Lady Smith, who still personally carries out the silk screening of the hand designed curtain fabrics. There is a history album in each building providing an insight into the personalities and lifestyles of former residents.

SUSIE WORTHY

Susie Worthy has been in the travel business most of her working life. In the 1960s she started as a ski rep, but soon set up exclusive special interest holidays for visitors to Britain. Her early trademark was arranging for guests to stay in privately-owned country homes and castles. In 1986 she started her own business, Worthy International Travel Ltd. Susie's clients tend to have special requirements; she will arrange for the best tickets to apparently fully-booked events and upgrading on flights. Places which are closed will miraculously open their doors for her. Among the special interest trips she is currently arranging for her British Breaks are horse-drawn carriage rides, including tuition; cookery demonstrations by leading London chefs; VIP theatre evenings, including dining at the theatre before the show and, of course, the best seats in the house.

ARLETTE BANISTER

Arlette Banister and her husband, John, own and run Ackergill Tower, a 15th century castle in Caithness, Scotland, overlooking the sea. Originally in the packaging design business in London, in 1970 they started a company specialising in corporate entertainment, and were always on the lookout for the ideal venue. They bought Ackergill Tower in 1986 from the Dunbar Estate and set about years of intensive restoration work. Although almost all the furniture and fittings now in the house were part of the purchase, everything needed a great deal of loving care. Ackergill Tower opened for business in 1989. Definitely not a hotel, Ackergill Tower provides the ultimate in house parties. It is only available to private groups, and is tailored to individual needs to ensure such details as your size (for boots, kilts, Barbours and, possibly, shotguns), sporting predilections (golf, shooting, fly fishing, archery), and tastes in food are established long before your arrival. At Ackergill Tower you truly feel King of the Castle.

PRIMROSE STOBBS

Abercrombie & Kent in London was started in 1973 by Primrose Stobbs, an ex-colonial farmer from Kenya, as a purveyor of stylish safaris in Africa. Twenty years later, the company has grown into an up-market travel organisation selling exotic holidays around the world and, not least, in the UK. Exclusive to A&K is the Royal Scotsman train, with all its traditional wood-panelled luxury, which takes passengers on leisurely tours of the Highlands, stopping for excursion trips, bedding down in sidings and providing immaculate service and cuisine. The same quality is provided on the company's two luxury river cruisers on the Thames and the Caledonian Canal. Primrose Stobbs' high reputation has never been better served than by these unique British travelling opportunities.

Photograph courtesy of Thistle Photography

HEATHER CHAPMAN

Heather and Nigel Chapman have been married for 11 years and have four small children. Frustrated over being unable to find a hotel that served good food and welcomed children, they decided to open a hotel of their own. They were initially gazumped on one they wanted near Bath but decided to stay in the area. An estate agent showed them the details of a 17th century manor house at Bradford-on-Avon and, in 1989, Woolley Grange opened as a country house hotel. Nigel, a chartered accountant, still commutes twice a week to his London office and the hotel has been a great success, with a nursery and resident nanny.

MORNA FLETCHER

Twenty-seven year old Morna Fletcher went to Edinburgh from Yorkshire to take a zoology degree at Edinburgh University and has been in the city ever since. She had various jobs after graduating and travelled widely, particularly in the Far East. In May 1992 she started Spice (Scotland East). Spice is a club providing unusual events for people who want to do them, but don't have anyone to do them with, or for groups of people who want to do something different but don't know how to set about it. A few examples of the things Morna organises are: fire eating workshop, tandem skydiving, microlighting, rock climbing, magic workshop, racing and rally driving, bungee jumping and white water canoeing.

REBECCA MERRIAM

Extrovert Rebecca Merriam is well known in the city of Bath, where she lives, and her strong and spontaneous views are frequently sought by the Council and the local press among others. She is a self-made person and has received no formal business training. Her tour operator/language course business started in a small way nine years ago and continues to flourish despite the recession. She is always seeking fresh outlets for her boundless energies and many new business ideas are in the offing.

JANE VINCENT AND HILARY DATCHENS

Jane Vincent worked for Grecian Holidays as an overseas manager in Greece for eight years before returning to Cornwall. She is now a part-time gunner in the Royal Auxiliary Airforce Regiment. Hilary Datchens moved from Hertfordshire to Cornwall 17 years ago and worked as secretary/PA to the editor of The Ecologist magazine for 11 years. Jane's return from Greece coincided with Hilary losing her job due to the magazine's move to London and, two years ago, they set up Alternative Cornish Holidays. They specialise in walking tours and mini-bus tours to less accessible parts of the county, using local guides.

SALLY INCHBALD

Prior to setting up Heritage Touring in 1988, Sally Inchbald worked as company secretary for a leisure management company. This experience, which included financial controls, proved invaluable in setting up a new company during a recession. She started the company on a business expansion scheme involving London and Dorset investors. She offers an unusual "home hosting" service for overseas clients who take lunch, tea and dinner in private houses. The company, which specialises in literary tours, has also obtained the touring rights to the books of historical novelist Edward Rutherford.

GEORGINA HUNTER-JONES

Having qualified as a pilot while at university, Georgina Hunter-Jones went on to fly helicopters, including performing aerobatics, and is currently the only woman to be both a helicopter and a fixed-wing instructor. In 1988 Georgina raised £19,000 for the Women's National Cancer Control Campaign, flying her mother in the world's first all-female wing-walk. The following year she won the White Waltham Pilot of the Year Cup, started the Flying Fizzios aviation company, of which she is managing director, and became an aerobatic pilot for Mithral racing. Georgina has displayed at air shows in Britain, Ireland and Europe, and in 1991 masterminded and captained the All-Female Aerobatic Wingwalking Team.

EVE JACKSON

The first person to fly a microlight aircraft from London to Sydney, Eve Jackson made the journey between 26 April 1986 and 1 September 1987, visiting 22 countries on the way. Flying a Shadow aircraft with a Rotax 447 two-stroke engine, she covered the 12,500 miles (20,100km) at around 60 knots (75mph). On her return Eve received numerous awards, including the Segrave Trophy, a Gold Medal from the Royal Aero Club, the Founders Medal of the Air League, the Barbazon Cup at the British Women Pilots Association and the Sword of Honour of the Guild of Air Pilots and Air Navigators.

SALLY WELLS

Since her first solo glider flight in 1975, Buckinghamshire-based Sally Wells has put in over 3,000 hours of gliding and power flying. Currently a radar controller at the London Air Traffic Control Centre, in 1988 she was the British Standard Class National Champion, an honour which has only served to fuel her ambition to glide farther, faster and over ever more dramatic terrain.

SARAH FENWICK

Sarah Fenwick was taught to hang-glide by her cousin Mike McMillan, formerly of the British Hang Gliding Team, and grew to love the sport. Sarah, who works as sales and marketing manager for Airwave Gliders Ltd, went on to learn to paraglide and in 1992 finished second overall in the British Paragliding National Championship, was the women's champion and set the women's world distance record of 63km (39 miles).

ANN JACKSON

It was at the age of 47 that Ann Jackson took up the intrepid sport of wing-walking. Having joined the WRAF during the war, only to find that women were not eligible to learn to fly, she later took private lessons in order to gain her pilot's licence. In the 13 years she has been practising the sport, Ann, who lives in Devon, has raised a great deal of money for Hospice Home Care and entertained countless people. When she is not wing-walking, with the stunt pilot Brendan O'Brien at the controls, Ann loves parascending – she has a certificate of proficiency to prove it – and go-karting.

JUDY LEDEN

The current women's World, European and British hang-gliding champion, and women's record holder in each of those spheres. Judy Leden was the first woman to fly in the British National Championship and the first woman to serve in the British team, which she has also captained. The first woman to cross the Channel by hang glider and the first person to hang glide from the world's highest active volcano, Ecuador's Cotopaxi, Judy is Britain's only professional, commercially sponsored, hang-glider pilot. Judy, who lives in Surrey, has received two Sportswoman of the Year awards and the Silver Medal of the Royal Aero Club. She was awarded the MBE in 1989.

LINDSAY MUIR

Lindsay Muir first became involved in ballooning while researching for a PhD. In 1989, having flown balloons for six years, she gave up her career in biochemistry to become a full-time commercial balloon pilot. She is currently chief pilot for London-based Ballooning World. For specific classes, Lindsay set British women's distance records in 1987 and 1989 and British women's duration records in 1988 and 1989. She also set a women's world distance record for her class of balloon in 1989. Lindsay was the only female competitor in the World Championship in 1989 and 1991, and won the British National Championship in 1988 and the Ladies World Cup in 1990 and 1991.

Photograph by Chris Smith

LIZ BAUWENS

Liz Bauwens, the Design Director of Good Housekeeping magazine, has never lost her love of the sound, smell and thrill of motorbikes which she acquired during her youth at her brother's motorcycle garage. She rides a Harley Davidson 1200, which she customised last year. Like her room-sets, she wants her bike to be unique, stylish and constantly changing.

Photograph by Simon Brown

LOUISA YOUNG

Louisa Young was eight years old when her love affair with motorcycles started on the back of a Moto Guzzi ridden by an Italian farm boy. At the age of 15 she was in love with a boy with a custard-yellow Honda 750 and matching socks. She started buying her own bikes to establish some independence, and now rides a Harley Davidson 1200 Sportster. Louisa has been contributing editor to Bike magazine and has contributed to publications as various as The Times and Just Seventeen on the subject of motorcycling. Her first novel was entitled The Biker's Lovesong. Her second book, due out in 1994, is a biography of Kathleen, widow of Scott of the Antarctic.

Photograph by Jacek Jan Zaluski

ELAINE FORD

Elaine Ford has been an Equity registered stunt performer since 1983. She is proficient in all forms of driving and motorcycling, horse riding, snow and water skiing, gymnastics, swimming, sub-aqua, power boats, jet skiing, trampolining, abseiling, climbing, judo and karate. She speaks French and Spanish and is a singer and guitarist. Elaine has been riding motorcycles for ten years and is a member of the Triumph Owners Motorcycle Club. Her favourite is a 1962 Triumph Trophy 650cc TR6R, which has been completely rebuilt, and which she is currently running-in.

KATE PARKINSON

Born in 1968 Kate Parkinson grew up in rural Yorkshire, where she was a keen horserider from the age of five. She began competitive motorcycle road racing in 1990 and had her first full season in 1991, when she won the Aintree Club's Most Promising Newcomer trophy, and the Best 250 Newcomer trophy. She finished third in two championships and in the Newcomers' class in the Manx Grand Prix, becoming the first solo woman to win a silver replica. In 1992 she competed on the major short circuits in the UK and, on a Honda 400, became the first woman to lap the Manx TT course at over 100mph. Her aims for 1993 are to compete in the UK National Championships in the 250 Open class, with a view to Europe in 1994 – sponsorship welcome!

ANDREA COLEMAN

Thomas Bullus, Andrea Coleman's maternal grandfather, a man who became famous when he shot dead a runaway bull in what legend insists was a china shop, was one of the pioneers of motorcycle sport in Britain. His son, Tommy, was a factory rider for NSU before the war and his daughter, Thora, married Jack Williams, one of the engineers who would have saved the ailing British motorcycle industry if it had done as he said, which the Japanese did. Jack's daughter, Andrea, started as a racer, but stopped when she found out how much it could hurt and went on to run a highly successful grand prix team. In the early 1980s she was asked by several leading riders to change the image of the sport once and for all. She started raising money, through motorcycling, for the Save the Children Fund and quickly founded Riders for Health, which uses the unique expertise of the motorcycle community to set up and manage transport programmes for health ministries in Africa. Throughout the year money is raised under Andrea's guidance and, at the end of the season, the whole community comes together for the Day of the Champions, a massive party celebrating all that is good about two wheels and an engine.

MITCH EBELING

Mitch Ebeling is an artist, upholsterer, motorcycle stunt rider, ex-lead singer and record promoter. She has travelled the world in the course of these various careers, largely on her Triumph motorcycle. Mitch has several British bikes, one of which she races, and sufficient mechanical skill to maintain them all. Her passion for British motorcycles and experience in the pop world have led to her starting her own business providing classic motorcycles and "Rocker" imagery, and performing and co-ordinating stunts for film, TV and video. She has also employed her artistic skills to paint and customise leather jackets for various pop and film stars.
Photograph by Ken Copsey

SUE MINTER

Sue Minter is the curator of the Chelsea Physic Garden. She graduated from Cambridge in 1971, with an MA(Hons) in history, and took up a Fulbright Scholarship at the University of California. From 1973-75 she worked as editor of encyclopaedias, and children's and horticultural books for a publisher in Milan, but moved into specialised horticulture when she became house plant buyer for Syon Park Garden Centre in London in 1976. From 1978-79 she was a freelance editor of horticultural books. She joined the Royal Botanic Gardens at Kew in 1983, as propagator in the Temperate Nursery, moving to be supervisor of the Palm House until taking up her present position four years ago.

BETH CHATTO

One of the great women gardeners of our time, Beth Chatto is celebrated for her use of unusual perennials and the way she groups them, as well as for her mastery of difficult situations such as very wet or very dry conditions. She was born in Essex where she has lived ever since and, 30 years ago, set about transforming several acres of her husband's fruit farm near Colchester into a garden in which she now grows a range of plants from Mediterranean sun-lovers to waterside bog plants. Her interest in species plants led her to start her now famous nursery of unusual plants. A well respected author, her books include the classics, "The Dry Garden" and "The Damp Garden". Beth holds the Victoria Medal of Honour from the RHS, and was awarded an honorary doctorate at Essex University in 1988.

See front cover for photograph

PENELOPE HOBHOUSE

Penelope Hobhouse is a garden designer of international reputation. She has designed gardens in England, Scotland, Europe and the USA (Texas, Maine, Vermont, Michigan and New York). She is a contributor to gardening journals and magazines in the UK and the USA, where she conducts lecture tours. She has also been a guest lecturer on Italian renaissance and baroque gardens in Europe. Educated at Cambridge, Penelope Hobhouse and her husband, Professor John Malins, are the National Trust tenants of Tintinhull House Garden. Amongst her many books are The National Trust; A Book of Gardening (1986), Private Gardens of England (1986), Garden Style (1988), Painted Gardens (1988) and The Gardens of Europe (1990).
Photograph by Andrew Lawson

PHILIPPA RAKUSEN

Philippa Rakusen was the director of gardens for the Northern Horticultural Society from 1980 to 1992. She has been a council member of the National Gardens Scheme since 1987, and is an active member of the Garden History Society. In 1972 she was the founder chairman of the Leeds Decorative and Fine Art Society, of which she is now president. Her own garden is frequently featured in books, magazines and on television. A writer speaker and advisor on gardens, Philippa Rakusen is a Fellow of the RSA, and has been awarded the Veitch Memorial Medal by the Royal Horticultural Society for services to horticulture in the North.

JULIA CLEMENTS

Julia Clements' life stood in tatters at the end of WWII. She had lost her child, and her husband had failed to return from the war. A meeting of the Kent Area Women's Institutes which she was invited to address transformed her life, faced with a room full of drab, dispirited women, all suffering the effects of wartime deprivation gave her a purpose in life; flowers, she decided, were available to everyone, and floral art could brighten everyone's life. From touring the bombed cities of Britain with an almost evangelical fervour, Julia Clements has become the world's leading expert in floral art, a judge, teacher and speaker, she has written 20 books on the subject which have sold over a million copies worldwide. A judge and Fellow of the Royal Horticultural Society, she holds their highest award, the Victoria Medal of Honour, and was awarded the OBE in 1989. Julia Clements has the unique distinction of having three roses named after her.

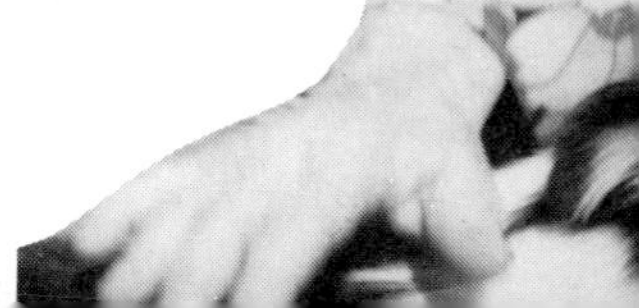

MIRIAM ROTHSCHILD

Born in 1908, Miriam Rothschild is a woman driven by a consuming interest in the mysteries of the physical world. She is almost entirely self-taught, and has always worked independently of established institutions. Perhaps best known as the world's leading expert on fleas, and for her studies on the plant derived defence poisons of insects, she has also made notable contributions in the fields of marine biology, chemistry, pharmacology, neurophysiology, horticulture and zoology. In 1985 she was elected a Fellow of the Royal Society, and she is an honorary Doctor of Science at Oxford and at five other universities. She holds the Victoria Medal of Honour from The Royal Horticultural Society. A lady of seemingly limitless energy, she is the author of many books and articles on science and horticulture, fascinating to expert and layman alike.

DAME SYLVIA CROWE

Dame Sylvia Crowe trained at Swanley Horticultural College and has spent most of her life in private practice as a landscape architect. From 1964 tyo 1976 she was the first landscape consultant to the Forestry Commission, she was secretary to the International Federation of Landscape Architects (1948-59), president of the Landscape Institute (1957-59), and chairman of the Tree Council (1974-76). Dame Sylvia has received honorary degrees from the Universities of Newcastle, Herriot-Watt and Sussex, and was awarded the Victoria Medal of Honour by the Royal Horticultural Society in 1991. Dame Sylvia was appointed CBE in 1967, and OBE in 1973. A prolific author, her books include The Landscape of Power (1958), The Landscape of Roads (1960), The Landscapes of Forests and Woodlands (1979), and Patterns of Landscape (1986).

Photograph by The Landscape Institute

ROSEMARY VEREY

Rosemary Verey graduated from University College, London, and married architectural historian David Verey in 1939. Her garden at Barnsley House, near Cirencester, is open to the public throughout the year. Special features of the garden are the vegetable garden, or Potager, the Laburnum Walk and the Knot Garden. The garden has been featured in many books and magazines including, in the USA, Garden Design, Architectural Digest and House & Garden. In 1988 she won the Christie's/Historic Houses Association Garden of the Year Award. Rosemary Verey is also an author and lecturer. Of her eight books written since 1981, the most recent is "A Gardener's Book of Days", which was published in 1992.

JACKIE ELLIOTT

When the Peak District park authorities decided to set up a wildflower nursery resident in 1982 Jackie Elliott rang to ask if she could help and was invited both to start and run the nursery. He efforts at the nursery won her the European Conservation Award in 1985. These days, in addition to growing wildflower plants for sale, she lectures to women's groups, horticultural societies and universities and runs day schools and weekend courses for Derbyshire Adult Education service and YHA. She has a weekly piece on Radio Sheffield, based around the wildlife garden she made for them (listed in BBC Gardner's World magazine), writes regularly for the Yorkshire Post and Sheffield Telegraph, and has been featured in the Sunday Times magazine and the Guardian, on Woman's Hour and BBC TV. Her landscaping includes a wood for David Mellor Cutlery, a woodland edge around 33 acres of a Sheffield crematorium, a quarry for a mineral company and planting 28 acres of meadow for an oil company.

JANET HARVEY

The Harveys, who married in 1968, sold their house six years later to buy the nursery from their former employer. They lived in a caravan while they modernised the half-acre of traditional tomato greenhouses in 2½ acres of land, which was yielding 80 tons to the acre. They went over to nutrient film technique (plants grown in troughs of water) in 1980 when the greenhouse area expanded to an acre. Since then, the Buckland Gardens Nurseries in Broadway, Worcestershire, has expanded in three further stages to its present four acres of modern aluminium structures. The nursery is computer-controlled and heated by natural gas. Plants are pollinated by bumble-bee and biological control is used when needed. The expected yield is 180-200 tons to the acre. Janet and Chris now employ a full-time staff of seven, plus seasonal workers in the summer.

PENELOPE KAIN

Penelope Kain and her husband Edward have been running Dittisham Fruit Farm and Capton Vineyard, near Dartmouth, South Devon, since 1988. Their main business is producing top quality soft fruit but the region's higher rainfall forced them to find another outlet for their "mushy" strawberries – thus Devon pure fruit liqueurs was born. Dittisham plum liqueur was added later, along with sloe gin made from sloes from their own hedgerows. A typical bottle of liqueur contains the juice from ½ kilo of fresh fruit. As Penelope puts it: "Basically, we grow anything that no-one else can be bothered to grow." Nevertheless, their produce can be found only in the very finest restaurants and shops.

FRANCES SMITH

A fascination with things horticultural gripped Frances Smith while still a schoolgirl. At the age of 14 she grew runner beans and flowers in her mother's roof garden in Kensington, London. Yet it was not until she was married, with two children and five years in the advertising business behind her, that she became truly vegetable-mad. Fellow allotment holders in Beckenham, Kent, "fired my enthusiasm", she says. Today she runs Appledore Salads and Park Hill Produce in Ashford, planted with a wide selection of unusual salad leaves, herbs and vegetables. Seeds from all over the world continue to improve the range and the firm's produce can be found in more than 30 fine restaurants in London and the South East.

MORAG RENDALL

Farmer's wife Morag Rendall helps to run the long-established family business David Rendall and Son, now in the third generation of fruit growing in Blairgowrie, Perthshire. It is a small company but widely acclaimed for the excellence of its raspberries and strawberries. Two years ago Rendalls introduced Harvest fruit salad, a unique blend of selected fruits. Careful harvesting and quality selection has kept them in the forefront of the industry, a fact recognised by the producers of the TV series Scottish Larder, which has featured their produce. Mother of two daughters and grandmother of two.

JOY LARKCOM ▲

Despite gaining a degree in horticulture, Joy Larkcom then pursued an early career she now says was "utterly irrelevant in horticulture". She was a teacher in Thailand, a librarian in Canada and a journalist on The Observer. When she married and settled in East Anglia, she began experimenting with vegetable growing, spending a year travelling around Europe to study old and modern methods. On their return, they established a small experimental organic market garden. A fascination with Oriental vegetables led to a trip to China, Japan and Taiwan in 1985. The result was a standard work on the subject, Oriental Vegetables: The Complete Guide for Garden and Kitchen, published in 1991. She recently revised the Royal Horticultural Society's wartime classic The Vegetable Garden Displayed.

Photograph by Malcolm Birkitt

ROSEMARY TITTERINGTON ▼

With a herbalist grandmother and a father who worked as a herbal vet Rosemary had a fairly wide knowledge of her subject when she set up Iden Croft Herbs in 1969 with her husband. Since then she has played a major role in raising the image of herbs here and abroad. She was a 1990 SMART winner (DTI Small Firms Merit Award for Research and Technology), won an Energy Efficiency Award in 1991, and is a Fellow of the World Master Chefs' Society and an Agricultural Training Board instructor. From Iden Croft Rosemary runs hundreds of herb courses and workshops and has developed gardens for the blind and handicapped. She has exhibited at the Chelsea Flower Show and RHS shows and was selected for the Women in Britain Marquee at the Stoneleigh Royal Show in 1991. She has also chaired a committee to set British Standards on pot herbs sold to the public and developed systems for growing now used in the UK and overseas.

DEVORA PEAKE ▲

Born in 1915 near Tel Aviv of Russian parents Devora studied Business and Economics at the American University in Beirut. After working for United Artists and Lloyds Underwriters she married her first husband, a fruit grower, in 1938, and came to Suffolk, where she still farms. She was a founder member, with her second husband Bill Peake, of the Soil Association. They grew fruit, cereal and vegetables, reared poultry, pigs and a Jersey herd and made cheese and yoghurt. The produce was delivered direct to consumers' homes and to outlets such as Harrods, Fortnum and Mason and Selfridges. In 1958, realising that they couldn't farm as successfully as they would like to with the small amount of rainfall in East Anglia, they installed one of the most extensive irrigation systems in England. In 1969, prior to England joining the EEC, they launched Copella apple juice which provided a much needed market for third grade fruit for English growers. Copella won the NFU Marketing Award in 1984. In 1983 Devora won a Joseph Nickerson Husbandry Award for adding value to farm produce and in 1991 she was made an associate of the RASE for her achievements in the farming industry. Devora, her family and businesses were featured in Sir John Harvey-Jones' BBC TV Troubleshooter series in 1990 and 1992.

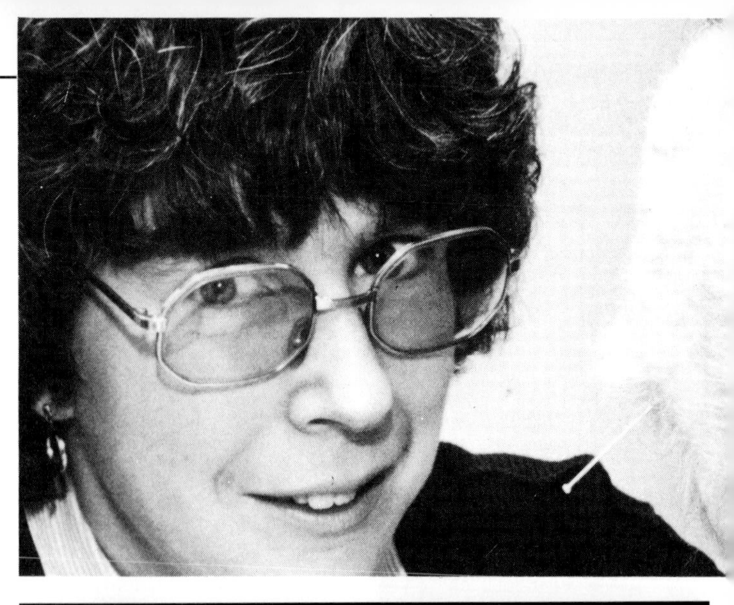

MRS B. M. WILLIAMS, BVSc, MRCVS

Trixie Williams qualified at the Liverpool Veterinary School in 1974, and set up her own practice in Wiltshire in 1979, a small animal and equine practice. In 1979 she became interested in acupuncture, and trained at the Southampton Centre of Alternative Therapies. She now runs a twice yearly basic introductory veterinary acupuncture course at her Wiltshire practice to enable other veterinary surgeons to train. She has also attended the homeopathic course run at the Royal Homeopathic Hospital, and believes in using acupuncture and homeopathy alongside orthodox medicine and surgery.

JENNIFER POLAND, OBE, BVSc, PhD, MRCVS, DTVM

Jennifer Poland qualified as a veterinary surgeon from Bristol University in 1956 and worked in practice and for MAFF for five years. In 1962 she obtained the Diploma of Tropical Veterinary Medicine from Edinburgh University before travelling to Brazil for seven months. She joined the Royal Veterinary College in 1963 as a lecturer in microbiology and submitted a PhD thesis on porcine mycoplasmas to London University in 1972. In 1980 she started the Unit for Veterinary Continuing Education at the Royal Veterinary College. This unit has produced many audio tapes, slides, videos, etc., and is now the largest audio-visual library in Europe and increasingly used by veterinarians worldwide. In 1988 she was awarded the OBE, which she sees as recognition of the work of all the unit's staff over the preceding eight years.

CHRISTINE MAY MORTON, BVMS, MRCVS

Christine Morton was born and educated in Glasgow, and graduated from Glasgow University in 1982. Her first position was as an assistant at Rutland House Veterinary Hospital in St. Helens, where in 1988 she became a partner. The Society of Practising Veterinary Surgeons invited her to join as a Council member in 1989, and she was elected treasurer and membership secretary in 1990, a position she still holds. Christine was also elected a Council member of the British Veterinary Hospital Association in 1990. Christine says that managing an extremely busy veterinary hospital as well as an interest in medicine presents a continual, but satisfying challenge.

PATRICIA JILL NUTE, BVSc, MRCVS

The immediate past president of the Society of Practising Veterinary Surgeons, Jill Nute qualified from Liverpool University in 1970, married fellow graduate Geoff and from 1970-76 worked in mixed practice in the Lake District. In 1976 they moved to Geoff's native Cornwall, where they started their own mixed practice, doing locums in the early days to help pay the bills. She later spent some time at Polwhele VI Centre, as temporary veterinary inspector, doing post mortems on badgers, which led to the Nutes co-authoring the publication "First Aid and Care of Wildlife" with Richard Meyer. Jill is still in mixed practice, but is also official veterinary surgeon for North Cornwall District Council, she has sat on the BVA Council as representatives for the SWVS on various committees. She is past chairman of the Cornwall branch of the Friends of the VBF. Jill and Geoff have also found time to have three children.

KATHERINE ANNE HOVERS, BVSc, MRCVS

Kate Hovers qualified from Liverpool University in 1983, and has been in mixed general practice ever since. Kate's principal interest has always been in sheep and cattle, and her first job was a six month locum in Wales, which included work at the greyhound track! She then spent 4½ years in Rugby, gaining all round experience, playing hockey and having back surgery. In 1988 she moved back to Wales, to concentrate on sheep and cattle, running a branch practice in Llandovery, which she bought in 1991. She currently employs a nurse and two part time staff, is a committee member for the South Wales Division of the BVA, and says that she has less time for hockey, although she still plays.

SUE J. DYSON, MA, VetMB, DEO, FRCVS

Sue Dyson graduated from Cambridge in 1980 with a first class hons degree in applied biology and a degree in veterinary medicine with distinction. She was awarded a Thouron Scholarship, which permits British graduates to study at the University of Pennsylvania. She completed an internship at the School of Veterinary Medicine at Pennsylvania, and then spent a valuable year in specialist equine practice there. In 1982 she returned to Britain to take up a post in the Equine Clinical Unit of the Animal Health Trust at Newmarket, and she has since worked there, specialising in equine orthopaedics with special interests in lameness diagnosis and treatment, radiography and ultrasonography. She was awarded a Fellowship of the Royal College of Veterinary Surgeons in 1986 for submission of a paper on equine shoulder lameness and, in 1988, acquired the RCVS Diploma in Equine Surgery (Orthopaedics). Sue has published many scientific papers pertaining to lameness, co-authored a text book on radiology and lectured widely

JANE MARGARET DOBSON, MA, BVetMed, DVetMed, MRCVS

Jane Dobson graduated from the Royal Veterinary College in 1982, and joined the Beaumont Animal Hospital at the College as a houseman, initially progressing to registrar in 1983. In 1984 she transferred to the Royal Marsden as a veterinary research assistant in the Department of Surgical Pathology, and in the same year, she transferred to the University Department and MRC Unit of Clinical Oncology and Radiotherapeutics at the Medical Research Council Centre in Cambridge, where she was appointed on a Cancer Research Campaign grant to investigate the use of hyperthermia in combination with radiation in the treatment of spontaneous tumours in domestic animals. Jane Dobson has held the post of Lecturer in Clinical Veterinary Oncology at Cambridge University since 1987 (when she was 28 years old). Apart from lecturing and post graduate supervision, she is Resident in Clincial Oncology and an MSc student, undertaking research into clinical veterinary and comparative oncology. She is an examiner, deputy hospital superintendent and a member of the curriculum committee. Outside the university, Dr. Dobson is chairman of the Small Animal Veterinary Association Scientific Committee, a Council member of the Royal Veterinary College Alumnus Association, Treasurer of the Society for Comparative Oncology and much more. She is also a wife and mother.

FRANCES JENNIFER BARR, MA, VetMB, PhD, DVR

Frances Barr graduated from Cambridge University Veterinary School in 1979. After four years general practice in Kent, she moved to take up a post in the Department of Veterinary Surgery at the University of Bristol, to concentrate on diagnostic imaging. She was awarded the Diploma in Veterinary Radiology in 1985, and a PhD in 1990 for her thesis entitled: "The Evaluation of Ultrasound As An Imaging Modality for Abdominal Soft Tissues in the Dog". Her book entitled: "Diagnostic Ultrasound in the Dog and Cat" was published in 1990. Frances continues to work at Bristol in the field of diagnostic imaging and is active in post graduate education, giving lectures and courses throughout the UK and Europe. She is married with two children.

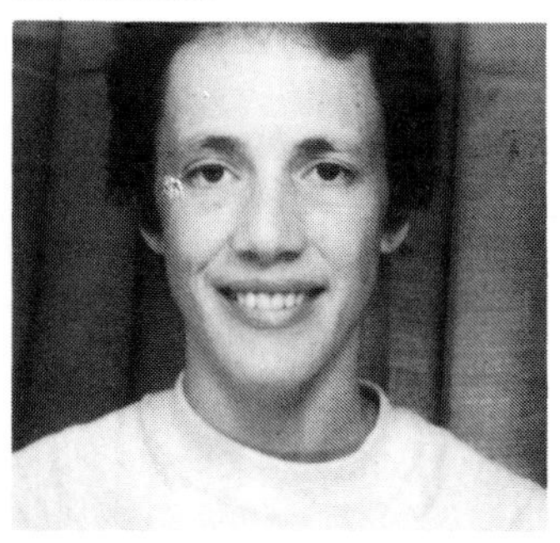

GINNI LITTLE

Ginni Little owns and runs the country's only bat hospital and sanctuary based in Penzance, Cornwall. Born in 1939, and with a life-long interest in wildlife, Ginni first established an empathy with these endangered mammals with the advent of "Batty", who had been abandoned and probably dying. She popped "Batty" into her bra where she lived and thrived. That was five years ago and "Batty", along with more than 50 other bats from all over the country, now resides with Ginni in rather larger accommodation.

JULIE DEPTFORD

Julie Deptford is the owner and trainer of Gwen, the Champion of Champions Sheepdog, and Bess and Mell the 1991 and 1992 Scottish Brace Champions. Gwen has been runner-up in BBC's One Man and His Dog, and Julie was the first lady ever to win the Scottish National in 1991.

CAROLINE BROWN

Born in 1950 in Paris and educate in Hampshire, Caroline Brown is the curator of The Wildlife Breeding Centre in Hertfordshire. She has worked at the centre for 20 years specialising in the breedin and hand-rearing of endangered species such as Ocelots, Servals, Scottish Wildcats, Fennec Foxes, Golden and Sea Eagles, Sparrowhawks and Great Grey and Barn Owls, and care and rehabilitation of injured British wildlife. She keeps a flock of rare Soay sheep and part-owns an islan in Chile where she is conducting a detailed study of its wildlife and ecology. She has hand-reared, from day-old, over 2,000 birds of prey o over 20 different species.

PATRICIA SIMPSON

Clinically dyslexic and labelled as backward at school, Patricia Simpson has been sensitive to animal cruelty since early childhood. As an adult she developed into an outspoken campaigner for animal rights and, in 1979, she took control of an anti-vivisection group in Blackpool and spearheaded a national campaign for the removal of animals caged in the infamous Tower Circus.

She founded the International Animal Welfare Alliance and is widely recognised for her major contribution in reforming public opinion on the welfare of captive animals.

PATRICIA NEVINES

In 1979 Patricia Nevines' late husband started breeding endangered species of ornamental pheasant as a retirement hobby. Patricia was then domestic bursar to Queen's University, Belfast, and after 16 years the opportunity for early retirement arose. She joined her husband and, in 1981, their collection of birds was opened to the public when, soon after, injured wild birds were being brought to them for attention.

Now the walled garden of her Co. Antrim house is home to long-eared owl, peregrine falcon, kestrel, sparrowhawks, ibis, ducks, rabbits and even a red fox roams freely.

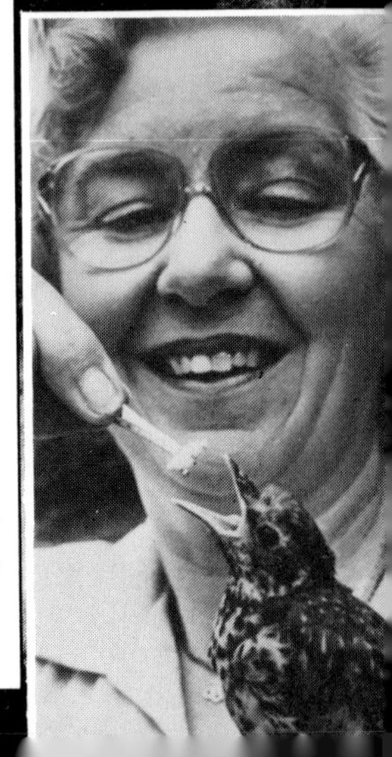

LEONIE VEJJAJIVA

Born in Aldershot in1936 and educated at Eastbourne, Leonie Vejjajiva married a Thai accountancy student and went to Thailand in 1958. In 1985 she began caring for wild animals, starting with a baby stump tailed macaque then a baby gibbon, rescued from cruel animal dealers. In 1990, at the suggestion of the President of the Orang Utan Foundation, Leonie and some friends set up The Wild Animal Rescue Foundation of Thailand, now licensed by the Thai Government as a charity. Also, for 20 years Leonie has worked with Thailand's oldest and largest independent law firm and is now a Senior Paralegal.

CELIA HAMMOND

Celia Hammond initially found fame as one of the super-models of the 1960s. Concerned about cruelty in the fur-trade, she visited Canada, saw seal-clubbing for herself and persuaded all the top models of her day to boycott fur. In 1970 she gave up modelling to devote herself full time to helping animals. She has rescued and rehoused thousands of cats, and in 1987, set up CHAT, a registered charity providing low-cost crucial neutering. She sees a drastic reduction in cat and dog birth rate as the only way to alleviate the suffering of 2½ million strays.

LYNN CORNICK

Born in 1945, Lynn Cornick was always devoted to animals. From the age of 12 she helped out at breeding kennels at weekends and, after leaving school, worked for a veterinary surgeon as an animal/veterinary nurse for nine years. Now, with husband Graham, who lectures full-time on wildlife to schools, clubs, etc., she runs the Hydestile Wildlife Hospital in Godalming, caring for the thousands of wild animals, injured or orphaned, that come to them. They have a staff of three and a phone that never stops ringing.

DR. ELIZABETH SVENDSEN

Born in Yorkshire in 1930, Elizabeth Svendsen moved with her family to Devon after a successful business career, where they purchased a country hotel. Here she started to rescue mistreated donkeys and obtained charitable status for The Donkey Sanctuary, which has so far taken into care more than 5,400 donkeys. In addition, she runs three other charities, The International Donkey Protection Trust, a worldwide organisation, The Slade Centre, an indoor riding centre for the handicapped, and The Elizabeth Svendsen Trust, aiming to provide donkey-riding for the disabled countrywide. She was appointed MBE in 1980 and received an Honorary Degree of Doctor of Veterinary Medicine and Surgery in 1992.

MARGARET FREARSON

Margaret Frearson is the daughter of an agricultural merchant and comes from a long line of farmers. However, Margaret started her company, Frearson Farm Feeds, not for reasons of heredity, but more out of desperation. In 1982 her husband was forced to retire from his building society job due to ill health, and Margaret could see that, without her becoming the breadwinner, they would not be able to manage. She started on the road as an agricultural merchant, visiting farms regularly and trying to build a regular clientele at the same time as nursing her husband through three heart attacks and two major cancer operations. Gradually, the business grew, and when it reached a £½m turnover, her son joined to do the administration, leaving her more time on the road. £1m turnover was passed, and the business continued to grow in the face of appalling domestic hardship. In 1991 Margaret won the Daily Mail Women into Business Award. In 1992 Margaret's husband died. In the ten years since the business started, through milk quotas and recession, Margaret's business has grown year by year.

ANNE PETCH

Anne Petch bought her Devon farm in 1971, with a view to breeding a variety of pig which would thrive outside battery conditions. By 1978 she had built up a sizeable herd of Gloucester Old Spots. Realising that she was not receiving the rewards she deserved for producing superior park, Anne set up a modern, tiled butchery on the premises, and started to market her own meat. She oversees everything "from cradle to table", including curing and smoking bacon and ham and making sausages and pies. Everything is done by hand, and the pork, she says, is as good as it would have been 50 years ago.

RACHEL ROWLANDS

Rachel Rowland's family represents the third generation at Brynllys in Dyfed. Rachel and Gareth farm their 250 acre sheep and dairy farm organically. The farm gained Soil Association status in 1948, and its pedigree Guernsey herd has been established since 1946. Rachel's Dairy came into being by accident in 1982, when snow prevented the tankers getting to the farm. Rachel delivered milk and cream free to the locals, and revived her grandmother's buttermaking equipment. By the time the snows had cleared, a market had been created. Rachel's Dairy now employs 30 people, and distributes organic dairy products throughout the country.

BARBARA SMITH

Barbara Smith describes herself as "dairy farmer and general slave". Born in Lancashire, Barbara farms in Middlewich, Cheshire. Amongst the appointments which she holds are: deputy chairman of the Cheshire NFU; chairman of the National Council of Women's Animal Welfare Working Party; secretary for the Northwest Agricultural and Countryside Forum; member of the Regional CBI Council; past national chairman, Women's Farming Union Dairy Committee; member of the European Union of Women and chairman of Byley Parish Council. She was the first woman to stand for election to the Milk Marketing Board.

TRICIA WAKEM

Tricia Wakem obtained a BSc in biometrical genetics at Birmingham University, and taught science for many years before buying a guest house in Keswick. This was followed by a residential hotel near Wastwater, and now the Routen Llama Farm in Ennerdale. With husband Michael, a nuclear scientist, Tricia farms the 72 acre hill property with sheep, Dexter cattle and llamas. They breed Polwarth sheep imported from Tasmania as embryos and live from New Zealand, together with Ryelands and Shetlands and market finished quality products in natural undyed colours, produced from what they believe to be the only coloured flock in Europe. Tricia has one of the largest llama herds in the UK, producing fibre which is warm and incredibly soft. Llamas thrive in these difficult conditions and, she says, the spare males make ideal pets.

GINNY MAYALL

Ginny Mayall farms in partnership with her father in Shropshire. Their's is one of the country's largest organic farming operations and was converted in 1949. Before going farming Ginny trained in stage management, while helping to establish Organic Farm Foods, a fruit and vegetable wholesaling business based originally in London. Returning to the farm in 1987, she started by taking on the marketing of home produced flour and oat products but is now fully involved in running the dairy herd and in all aspects of the farming business. She is on the council of Oxford Farming Conference and the Ministry of Agriculture's regional panel.

CAROLYN FAIRBAIRN

Carolyn Fairbairn is the daughter of a West Suffolk farmer. On leaving school she studied photography in London, and worked there for six years. In 1969 she married and settled in Cumbria. She lives in a converted barn with six acres of land, on which she originally kept four goats. After the birth of her children, she decided to expand the herd to 30, and converted the basement of the house for cheesemaking and storage and, in 1979, made her first cheese. Her output has now increased to 30 tons a year.

ELIZABETH HENSON

Born in 1958, Elizabeth Henson has an MA in zoology from the University of Oxford, and an MSc in domestic animal breeding from the University of Edinburgh. Since 1981 she has been involved within the management of the Cotswold Farm Park, which is the premier rare breeds survival centre in the country, with over 30 endangered breeds. Elizabeth was secretary of the Castlemilk Moorit Sheep Society from 1982 to 1988 and of the Cotswold Sheep Society from 1983 to 1990, and where she is currently chairman. She has been secretary of the Gloucester Cattle Society since 1981, and the Longhorn Cattle Society since 1984. A Founder Life and Governing Council Member of the Rare Breeds Survival Trust, she has been a member of its Technical/Project Development Committee since 1984, and its Breed Liaison Committee from 1988 to 1991. In 1985 Elizabeth became the first executive director of the American Minor Breeds Conservancy, and carried out the first national census of breeds in the USA. She has been on various US committees in conjunction with this work and, in 1992, published her manual on the "in situ Conservation of Livestock and Poultry" for the Food and Agricultural Organisation of the United Nations.

Photograph by Cheltenham Newspaper Co Ltd

KATHERINE MONBIOT

British women's armwrestling champion Katherine Monbiot gained her title soon after taking up the sport in 1990, having previously armwrestled simply as a party piece and with friends. At one time she suffered from anorexia nervosa and weighed only five and a half stone, but now she travels abroad several times a year to attend international competitions and has won a silver medal at European level. She is currently rated fourth in the world in the under 70kg (154lb) class. In 1990 she was selected to compete in Japan in the Search for the World's Strongest Woman, which involved not only armwrestling but truck-pulling, man-throwing and Roman soldier battles. London-based Katherine, in addition to running an armwrestling and fitness-training course, is a practitioner of alternative medicine, specialising in nutritional therapy and colonic irrigation.

SUSAN ARKELL

As a teenager Susan Arkell regularly won National Girls' chess titles and represented England in the under-18 girls team events. But her career really blossomed when she became an International Woman Master during the year she took off between A levels and university. Abandoning her plans to take a degree, Susan married Keith, who was at the time an International Master and chess professional. She quickly rose from being the third best British woman player to the top-rated British woman player ever. Every year since 1986 Susan has won both the Commonwealth Ladies Championship and the British Ladies Prixette. She has won the British Ladies Championship several times in the same period, losing it once, and is currently the British Ladies Champion. Susan, who lives in Derbyshire, achieved Woman Grandmaster status in 1988.

MONICA BECKERSON

Monica Beckerson was the top lady player in the contest for the 1992 British Open Backgammon Trophy. She was knocked out of the competition in the quarter-finals, having beaten a former two-times British Champion in the second round. London-based Monica was introduced to backgammon by her husband Alan, and the couple are joined at all BIBA tournaments by their 12-year-old son Tony.

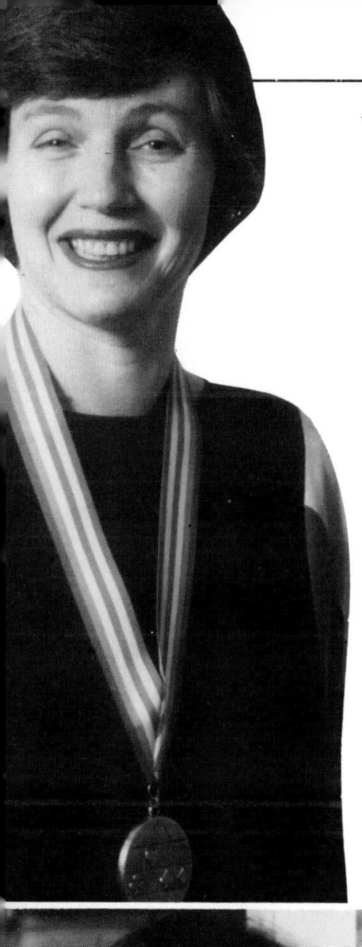

NICOLA SMITH

The daughter of international bridge champions, Nicola Smith was taught to play at the age of 11 by her father, at the school which he founded, and won her first bridge pot at 16. She has won every major event in England with various partners, but her regular partner since 1981 has been Pat Davies. Nicola, three times European Champion – in 1975, 1979 and 1981 – and twice World Champion – in 1981 and 1985 – won a bronze medal in the 1980 Olympics and a silver in 1976, 1984, 1988 and 1992. Presenter of the Channel 4 series Master Bridge, Nicola has also appeared in three other television series and broadcast on radio, and was formerly the bridge correspondent for Now! magazine. Based in London, Nicola currently teaches the game to 150 students a week, including beginners.

SANDRA LANDY

Currently rated No. 1 bridge player in the world ladies ratings, Sandra Landy has regularly played internationally for the British ladies team since 1967. East Sussex-based Sandra was a member of the team which won the Venice Trophy (World Championship) in 1981 and 1985 and has played in five Olympiads, winning four silver medals and one bronze.

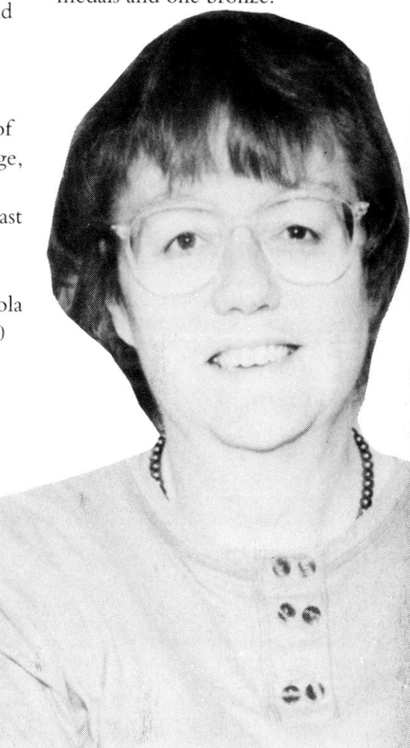

SHEILA SPATE

Sheila Spate helped form the Nottingham Scrabble Club in 1978 and enjoyed success in tournaments, including three wins in the Nottingham Open. She went on to win the Wilmslow Matchplay contest in 1990 and the Women's Matchplay in 1992, having the previous year been runner-up in the second. With her husband Clive, rated among Britain's top players, Sheila belongs to the six-strong Nottingham Nomads. The Nomads are also members of the APSP which, with a total membership of over 330, organises tournaments all over the country.

JOAN CAWS

Joan Caws played her first draught tournament in 1968, in the company of 50 men, and there met her future husband, Ian. The following year she entered the English Open Championship and has competed in every one since then. Her first major success came in 1979, when she won the British Ladies Championship. In 1986 Joan, who lives on the Isle of Wight, took the World Ladies Championship title, which she has successfully defended three times and intends to retain when it is contested in 1993. She became the first lady in over a century to play for England's national team – in 1992, at Morecambe, against Scotland, Wales and the Republic of Ireland.

PROFESSOR JOCELYN BELL BURNELL

It was while studying for a PhD at Cambridge in 1967 that Jocelyn Bell Burnell discovered pulsars, later identified as a completely new phenomena – the neutron star. The discovery opened a major field of astrophysics and earned her a number of prestigious prizes, including the Royal Astronomical Society's Herschel Medal. Currently a Professor of Physics at the Open University, her concern is to make astronomy and physics more accessible, and to this end is a frequent lecturer and broadcaster. Active in the management of science in the UK, with considerable experience of Science and Engineering Research Council committees, Professor Bell Burnell's 30 year career has involved significant contributions in the fields of X and gamma-ray astronomy, as well as the publication of numerous papers including a number on the UK's Ariel 5 satellite.

PROFESSOR GILLIAN GEHRING

Professor of Solid State Physics at Sheffield University, Gillian Gehring specialises in theoretical condensed matter physics, particularly magnetism and superconductivity. Born in 1941, Professor Gehring moved to Sheffield from Oxford in 1989 after 21 years as a lecturer in the Department of Theoretical Physics and a fellow and tutor in Physics at St Hugh's College. She is a member of the Council of the Institute of Physics; an advisory editor of both the Europhysics Letters and the Journal of Physics, and is a member of the National Committee for Superconductivity, currently one of the most challenging and active areas of research. Professor Gehring is also involved in the drive to encourage more women to study science and to increase the number of women scientists employed at all levels.

DR YVONNE ELSWORTH

Born in 1959, into a family with a strong tradition of medicine, Yvonne Elsworth was nonetheless drawn to physics by the research discoveries being made while she was an undergraduate at Manchester. When it was pointed out that she could observe a total eclipse of the sun from the Sahara Desert, she decided to take a PhD in Upper Atmosphere Physics and Optical Instrumentation. After a three year stint at Perkin Elmer, Dr Elsworth moved to the School of Physics and Space Research at Birmingham University where she lectures in Solar Physics and studies solar oscillations.

DR MARGARET J PENSTON

Born in Aberystwyth in 1941, Dr Margaret Penston took a BSc in Physics at Edinburgh before moving to Sussex University for her MSc and eventually, DPhil. A Fellow of Lucy Cavendish College, Cambridge, her present position, which she has held on and off since 1963, is senior scientific officer at the Royal Greenwich Observatory, Cambridge, and she was founding editor of their newsletter, Gemini, from 1982-88. Dr Penston's research has included the study of the optical variability of RR Lyrae stars (in the Lyra constellation) and of Seyfert galaxies (a class of small galaxies with very bright nuclei).

She is currently part of an international team working on the European Space Agency's Hipparcos project which seeks to provide accurate positions, motions and parallaxes for 120,000 stars, providing information which will improve our understanding of the scale of the universe.

DR MARION STORM

Marion storm was born and brought up in Scotland, graduating from St Andrews University in 1979 with a first-class honours degree in Applied Mathematics. She took a PhD in theoretical Nuclear Structure Physics at Glasgow University in which she used quark theory to explain the behaviour of sub-atomic particles known as nucleons. Moving to London, Dr Storm pursued a varied career that included scientific publishing, industrial research and computer systems development. She now works for National Power as a consultant specialising in the management implications of new computer systems. She is a member of the Institute of Physics and has served on the Women in Physics Committee for the last five years.

DR DOLORES BYRNE

Originally from Northern Ireland, Dr Dolores Byrne read Physics at Queens University, Belfast, gaining a first-class degree, and was awarded a scholarship to undertake research into electro-optics, work which earned her a Doctorate in Physics in 1978. After a two year lectureship appointment at Queens, Dr Byrne joined the Defence Research Agency in Portsmouth. Here, she has undertaken research in radar, computing and artificial intelligence, as well as laterally managing a research group. In 1992 she studied Business Administration at Southampton University, returning with a diploma in Business Administration, to the Defence Research Agency where she is now Business Manager in Operational Studies. Dr Byrne is a member of the Institute of Phsyics and is the current chair of the Women in Physics Committee.

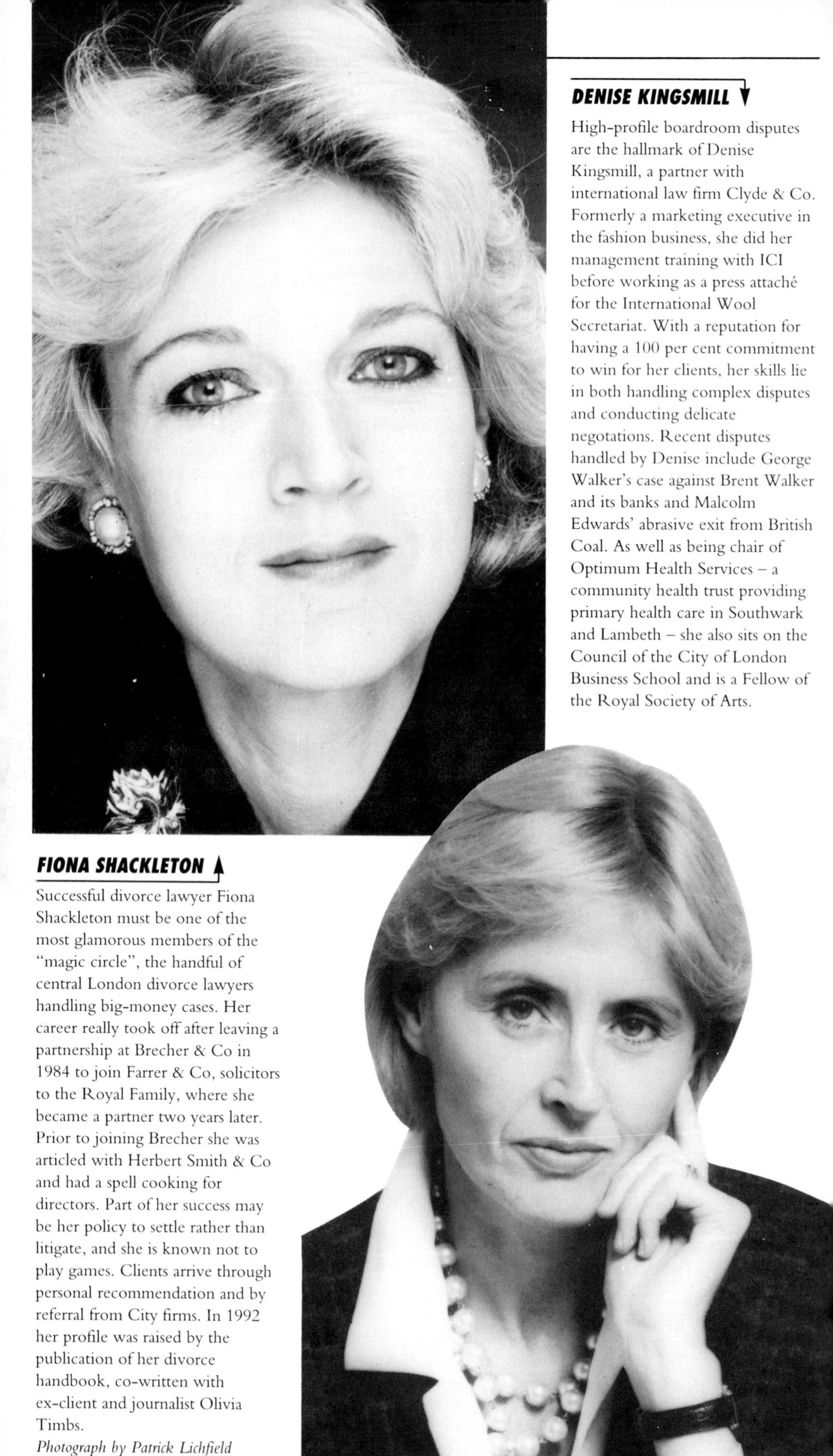

DENISE KINGSMILL

High-profile boardroom disputes are the hallmark of Denise Kingsmill, a partner with international law firm Clyde & Co. Formerly a marketing executive in the fashion business, she did her management training with ICI before working as a press attaché for the International Wool Secretariat. With a reputation for having a 100 per cent commitment to win for her clients, her skills lie in both handling complex disputes and conducting delicate negotations. Recent disputes handled by Denise include George Walker's case against Brent Walker and its banks and Malcolm Edwards' abrasive exit from British Coal. As well as being chair of Optimum Health Services – a community health trust providing primary health care in Southwark and Lambeth – she also sits on the Council of the City of London Business School and is a Fellow of the Royal Society of Arts.

FIONA SHACKLETON

Successful divorce lawyer Fiona Shackleton must be one of the most glamorous members of the "magic circle", the handful of central London divorce lawyers handling big-money cases. Her career really took off after leaving a partnership at Brecher & Co in 1984 to join Farrer & Co, solicitors to the Royal Family, where she became a partner two years later. Prior to joining Brecher she was articled with Herbert Smith & Co and had a spell cooking for directors. Part of her success may be her policy to settle rather than litigate, and she is known not to play games. Clients arrive through personal recommendation and by referral from City firms. In 1992 her profile was raised by the publication of her divorce handbook, co-written with ex-client and journalist Olivia Timbs.

Photograph by Patrick Lichfield

KAMLESH BAHL

As Company Secretary and Manager Legal Services with Data Logic Limited, Kamlesh Bahl is directly responsible for managing all legal work for the company's two divisions. She joined Data Logic in 1987 and for two years held the post of Legal and Commercial Manager before being promoted to her present position. Her first foray into industry was in 1981 when she joined the British Steel Corporation as Legal Advisor. Subsequently, she joined Texaco Ltd as a solicitor. Highly articulate and efficient, she currently has a number of other professional commitments which include serving as a Council Member of the Law Society, non-executive director of Parkside Health Authority, member of the Ethnic Minorities Advisory Committee and Tribunals Committee of the Judicial Studies Board and member of the Justice Sub-Committee on Judiciary. She is also advisor to the BBC radio soap The Archers, and has edited a book called Managing Legal Practice in Business.

HELENA KENNEDY

Elected to the Bar Council in 1990, in which year she established a set of Chambers in London (her third establishment), Helena Kennedy is also known for her frequent broadcasting on issues connected with law, civil liberties and women. In 1990 she presented The Trial of Lady Chatterley's Lover on Radio 4, Raw Deal on BBC 2 and co-produced Women Behind Bars for Channel 4. She was also the creator of the award-winning drama series Blind Justice for the BBC and is a regular host of After Dark. The most recent of several publications to her credit is Eye Was Framed, a book about women, crime and law published by Chatto Windus in 1992. In addition, she is on the Board of the Women's Legal Defence Fund and creator of an equal opportunities committee to counter the handicaps facing women at the Bar.

HILARY BROWNE-WILKINSON

Now a specialist in Family Law, Lady Browne-Wilkinson has pursued three different careers during her working life. Her first venture was to establish a group of small retail and manufacturing clothing businesses, but she then decided to realise her ambition to become a pianist and trained as a professional musician in Australia. After coming to live in England in 1970 she travelled extensively, meanwhile studying externally for a law degree. A year after qualifying as a solicitor in 1984 she became a partner in the Family Law Department of the law firm Charles Russell. In her present capacity her work includes divorce, separation, finance, children and cohabitation, with a considerable international element where there is a conflict of jurisdiction. As a trained family mediator her approach is concilitory.

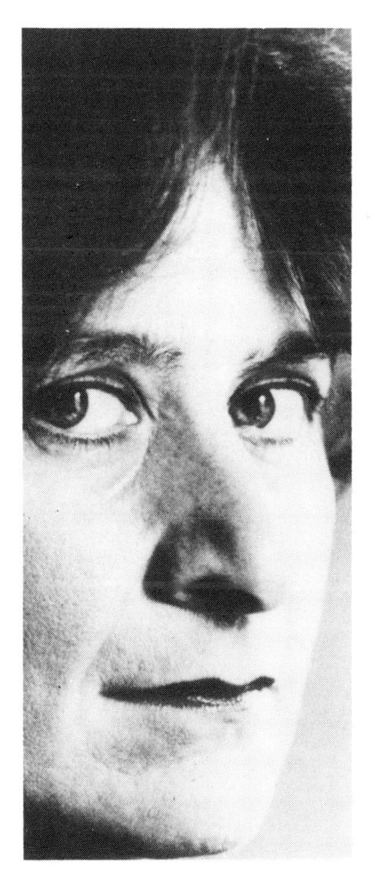

BARBARA MILLS

Since being called to the Bar in 1963, Barbara Mills has followed a distinguished career in criminal law and in 1992 was appointed Director of Public Prosecutions and head of the Crown Prosecution Service. She came from the Serious Fraud office where she served as Director for 18 months, and prior to that she was a barrister in private practice, specialising in criminal trials with a particular emphasis on commercial criminal law. In 1982 she became a Recorder of the Crown Court, took silk (became a Queen's Counsel) in 1986, became a Bencher of the Middle Temple in 1990 and, in 1991, became a QC (Northern Ireland). During 1990 she was also a member of the Parole Board and from 1991 to 1992 was a member of the General Advisory Council of the BBC.

THE RT HON THE BARONESS BLATCH

Educated in Birkenhead, Emily Blatch served in the WRAF from 1955 until 1959, when she transferred to the Ministry of Aviation until 1963. She was elected to Cambridge County Council in 1977 and was its leader from 1981 until 1985. During this time, she was a member of the Schools' Council of the Association of County Councils, a board member of the Peterborough Development Corporation, chairman of the Huntingdon Citizen's Advice Bureau and a member of the regional policy committee of the CAB. In 1986 she was appointed to the European Economic and Social Committee where she served until being created a life peer in 1987. Her first government appointment was as Baroness-in-Waiting to the Queen in 1990 and government whip for the Departments of Health, Social Security and Education. Later in the same year, she became Under Secretary of State in the Department of the Environment and, in 1991, she was appointed Minister of State for Heritage. After the 1992 general election, Emily Blatch was appointed Minister of State for Education and she was made a Privy Councillor in the 1993 New Year's Honours List.

JULIET LODGE

European Woman of Europe, 1992-93, and UK Woman of Europe 1991-92, Juliet Lodge was born in London. She attended Reading University, where she attained BA, MA, MPhil and DLitt degrees and read for her PhD at the University of Hull. She is currently Professor of European Politics, Jean Monnet Professor of European Integration and co-director of the European Community Research Unit at the University of Hull. She was formerly visiting Fellow in IR at the London School of Economics and lecturer in politics at the University of Auckland, New Zealand. Current areas of research for Professor Lodge are: the EC and Yugoslavia (NATO Fellow; plus modest EC funding); EC foreign and security policy (co-director of the Free University of Brussels based team on Europe 2000); EC judicial co-operation (with special reference to the Four Freedoms, EC counter-terrorism, asylum and refugees) and European Union. Professor Lodge has published several books and papers on: common foreign and security policy/EC defence; terrorism and internal security and European union/architectures.

CAROLYN PLUNKETT

Winner of the 1992 Times Educational Supplement Maths Teacher of the Year Award, Carolyn Plunkett's only formal maths qualification until recently was a C grade pass at O level. Carolyn has been teaching for more than 20 years; she trained at St Ostyth's College, Clacton, from 1966 to 1969 and then taught infants in Greenwich. In 1973 she took a job in Singapore, where she met her husband and they went to live in Australia, where she continued to teach in Commonwealth and Catholic schools, developing her ideas of teaching infants through stories. The family returned to England in the 1980s and Carolyn took a job, first in Croydon and then in Biggin Hill where she remains today. Tragically, her husband died in 1987. What finally singled out Carolyn as the winner of the TES Award was her refusal to underestimate the abilities of her pupils and her capacity to translate advanced mathematical ideas into terms easily understood by young children.\

LOUISE KIDD

Born in Glasgow, Louise Kidd was the only woman in her year to take a BSc in chemistry at Strathclyde University. She taught at St Pius High School in Glasgow in 1968-69 and then moved to North Manchester High School, where she taught all three sciences and where her commitment to balanced science teaching had its origins. In 1973 she moved to St Alban's High School as head of science and took her masters degree in education, with her thesis topic, The Testing of Skills and Abilities in A-Level Chemistry Papers 1968 to 1978, which was the origin of her concern in a curriculum which reflects the whole range of student needs. In 1979 she moved to Penworhtam Girls' High School as deputy head and joined the Senior Heads Association. 1985 saw her as vice-principal of Newman Sixth-Form College, Preston, and, in 1989, she became principal of Rutland Sixth-Form College. Louise Kidd was elected president of the Senior Heads Association in 1992.

MARGARET MADEN

County Education Officer for Warwickshire County Council since 1989, Margaret Maden was born in 1940, and educated at Leeds University (BA Hons) and the University of London (PGCE). From 1962 until 1966, she was a geography teacher at a London comprehensive and, from 1966 until 1971, a lecturer at the Sidney Webb College of Education. She went from there to become deputy head of Bicester Comprehensive (1971-75); headmistress of Islington Green Comprehensive (1975-82) and director of the Islington Sixth Form Centre (1983-86). She entered local government service as principal adviser on tertiary development at ILEA, until 1987, when she joined Warwickshire County council. Amongst Margaret Maden's publications are contributions to: Dear Lord James (1971); Teachers for Tomorrow (1971); Education 2000 (1979) and The School and The University.

DENA COLEMAN

Born in London in 1952, Dena Coleman gained a BSc in Zoology and Botany and a PGCE from Manchester University, an MA, with distinction, from Chelsea College, London, in 1985 and her PhD from King's College, London, in 1991, where the subject of her thesis was Science Education in Victorian Times. Her first teaching post was at a co-educational comprehensive in Middlesex, where she taught science. She then spent six years as a home teacher for the Child Guidance Services of the Barnet and Harrow Local Education Services, while her children were young. She returned to teaching science at a boys' independent school and thence a girls' public school as head of science. In 1990 she took up her present post as deputy head teacher at Hasmonean High School, in Barnet, where she is responsible for the 400 girl pupils. The all Jewish school has a reputation for close links with parents and the local community and the pupils are very active in community service. The academic standards achieved are extremely high and, in 1992, the school was top of the Sunday Times league table of A level results in state schools.

MO USHER

Mo Usher has trained as a complementary therapist in reflexology, aromatherapy and Bach flowers. In 1987 she became chair of the Association of Reflexologists, responsible for coordinating a huge team of people on an international scale. She is also the coordinator for the International Council of Reflexologists, is on the Executive Board of the British Complementary Medicine Association and is a member of the International Society for Pre-natal and Perinatal Psychology. She is dedicated to helping complementary medicine play a larger part within the community, so that everyone, rich or poor, young or old, black or white, sick or healthy, can have access to its philosophies.

CAROL HORRIGAN

After training as a beauty therapist, Carol Horrigan took her SRN in 1977, specialising in plastic surgery and oncology. She has studied and practised hypnosis, relfex zone therapy, aromatherapy, healing and yoga. A nurse tutor at Bloomsbury and Islington College of Nursing and Midwifery, she also designs and presents specialised workshops and courses on complementary therapies for health care workers at many other universities, colleges and medical charities. She is part of a team planning the complementary therapy components of nursing degree courses at the Royal College of Nursing and is a tutor for both the British School of Reflex Zone Therapy and the Tisserand Institute of Aromatherapy. Her role as a nurse tutor includes providing complementary therapy treatments as part of the students' support system. She has a private practice in London and is at present completing an MSc in Oncology at the University of Surrey. She is a regular contributor to international nursing journals and has written for several nursing text books.

MARY MARTIN

Prior to becoming a reflexologist, Mary Martin ran a wholefood business and worked with cancer patients as a Gerson therapist. Inspired by the tremendous healing potential she found in reflexology she formed the Association of Reflexologists which soon provided a network of well trained practitioners throughout the UK. Formerly chair of the Association she is now an honorary life member. In 1987 she was invited to work in an NHS hospital as a practitioner with pregnant women. Here she began teaching midwives and health visitors and later students from all backgrounds through the Mary Martin School of Reflexology. Her future plans include instigating further research into the effects of reflexology on infertility, Multiple Sclerosis and Parkinson's Disease.

JACQUELINE YOUNG

Jacqeline Young trained and worked as a clinical psychologist in the NHS before moving to Japan for five years. During this time she completed a three year diploma in Oriental Medicine and took a second advanced course in acupuncture at the Academy of Traditional Chinese Medicine in Beijing. She returned to the UK in 1985 and co-founded the Whole Woman Clinic, an integrated multi-disciplinary clinic for women in central London and took up the post of faculty coodinator and lecturer at the International College of Oriental Medicine, East Grinstead. She also worked as a consultant to the New Momentum Health Care Centre in Hilversum, Holland. She currently runs a private practice in London, is a visiting lecturer at the Department of Complementary Health Studies at the University of Exeter and lectures widely at acupuncture and massage colleges in the UK and other European countries. She also runs many practical workshops for lay groups on acupressure, Qi gong, Oriental exercises, self-care and natural health techniques. She is a past member of the Executive Council of the British Acupuncture Association and currently a member of the Research Committee for the Council for Acupuncture. She has had three books published: Vital Energy, Self Massage and The Acupuncture Workout, and is currently completing a text book on Oriental Medicine and a Natural Pregnancy book.

RITA BENOR

Ritá Benor has 25 years of nursing experience in both hospital and community settings, specialising in bereavement counselling. She was one of the first nurses to be exclusively employed within the NHS to provide bereavement support for parents experiencing losses during pregnancy and birth. Over the past ten years she has focused her clinical and teaching within the field of palliative care, between the Hospice movement and the NHS. She teaches nationally and internationally on holistic practice. psychoneuro-immunology and the use of complementary therapies for people (and their families) who are facing life threatening illness, who are in the palliative phase of an illness or those who are dying. She offers autogenic training and psychotherapy, particularly emphasising the use of relaxation and imagery to enhance control of pain. She runs workshops on stress management through the use of complementary therapies, specialising in teaching meditation, visualisation and Therapeutic Touch. She is chair of the new British Holistic Nurses Association, an organisation seeking to encourage, support and promote the practice of holistic nursing and to lobby for the integration of holistic practice and research in nurse curricula. She co-facilitates the Doctor-Healer Network of conventional and complementary health care professionals, clergy and healers. DHN members meet regularly at seminars on clinical and theoretical issues concerning the integration of holistic healing in patient care.

SHEENA HILDEBRAND

Born in Pakistan, Sheena Hildebrand's family dealt with minor health problems and stress with massage and oils. She trained as a registered general nurse at Charing Cross Hospital and qualified in 1986. It was while working at St Christopher's Hospice, nursing patients with cancer, that her desire to improve the quality of life for terminally ill patients emerged. Her interest in aromatherapy, massage and the use of touch to enhance patient care, motivated her to complete a diploma in aromatherapy while training for her Oncology Nurse Certificate. She now works part time as a clinical nurse specialising in therapeutic massage at the Royal Marsden Hospital, Sutton, using massage with essential oils as a means of aiding relaxation in the rehabilitation of cancer. She also runs a private practice and lectures on aromatherapy. She is a member of the Royal College of Nursing Steering Group for Complementary Therapies.
Photograph by Henry Gee

SHIRLEY PRICE

Shirley Price has always had a keen interest in natural therapies, sparked initially by her father who was a strong believer in natural healing. She trained as a beauty therapist and then ran a salon while teaching beauty therapy. Keen to learn about health as well as beauty she enrolled on various courses including aromatherapy, reflexology, orthobionomy, shiatsu and touch for health. With her husband, Len, she began to construct a specialist massage technique using lymphatic drainage methods which were not widely taught at the time. Shirley is now focusing attention on educating the general public about aromatherapy and is writing her third book on the subject. Her first, Practical Aromatherapy, written in 1983, has never been off the Thorson best seller list; her second, Aromatherapy for Common Ailments has also been extremely successful. This year she presented the first aromatherapy video for general release.

MICHELINE ARCIER

Born in the south of France and brought up in Africa and France Micheline Arcier has lived in England since 1948, when she married a British dental surgeon. She has practised aromatherapy for 30 years, having learned her craft from Marguerite Maury (the pioneer of modern aromatherapy techniques) and Dr Jean Valnet (the leading aromatherapist in Frnace) and is considered a leading authority in the field. She is a devoted believer in the three Ps – the powers, potentials and perfumes – of essential oils. She now divides her time between her clients and training, lecturing, researching and creating new products. She shares the running of her clinic in London with her daughter, Marie-Christine.

SALLY GILBERT WILSON

Sally Wilson has been in practice for 30 years. She opened her first health and beauty clinic in 1962 in North London and her Harley Street clinic 19 years ago to treat weight, figure and facial problems, providing advice and treatments for today's stress related illnesses. She uses a combination of treatments to treat skin conditions including enzyme rejuvenation, AHA peel, RNA and Embryo Therapy, chemi-peel and collagen implants. Also at the clinic are practitioners treating patients using iridology, kinesiology, diet and nutritional therapy, medical herbalism, hypnosis, acupuncture, laser therapy, Qi-gong and homoeopathy. Sally is a member of the Health Practitioners Association and the National Register of Advanced Hypnotherapists.

SU HAGAN

Su is an accredited aromatherapist, Swiss reflexologist and remedial masseuse. She teaches aromatherapy to International Diploma Standard and frequently assists new therapists with their practices. Her experience has included both the practice and financial management of international community therapy. Prior to initiating the therapeutic divison of the SEED Institute she was a marketing assistant with SD-Scicon. She is deeply concerned with immunological therapy and is retained by The Crescent within their HIV/Aids support programme. Su trained in Ayurvedic medicine in Nepal, is an advanced student of Hemi-Sync audio-technology for achieving hemispheric synchronisation in brain-functioning and is a specialist in its use in the ambient support of therapy and education.

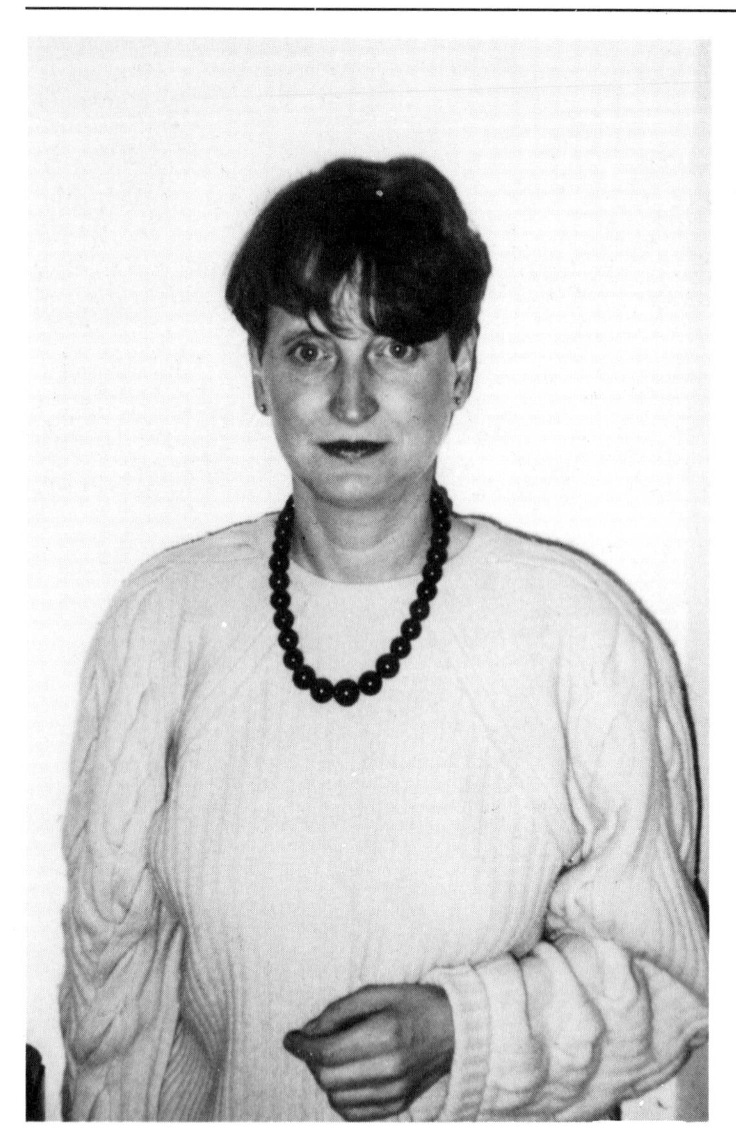

JILL PURCE

Jill Purce is well-known throughout the world for her pioneering Inner Sound and Voice Workshops, and as the author of The Mystic Spiral: Journey of the Soul, a book about the evolution of consciousness in spiritual traditions and in psychology. She has written many articles, and lectures all over the world. She is the general editor of Art and Imagination, an extensive series of books on sacred traditions, art and cosmology. After receiving an honours degree in Fine Art she was awarded a research fellowship in King's College Biophysics Department at the University of London. She then spent a year in Germany working with Karlheinz Stockhausen investigating the spiritual dimension of music. Interested in the magical properties of the voice, she learned Mongolian and Tibetan overtone chanting (producing chords or simultaneous notes octaves apart). She studied this in the Himalayas with the chantmaster of the Gyuto Tibetan Monastery and Tantric College. She has been following the philosophy and practice of Dzogchen since 1978 when she first met the Tibetan Lama. She has also worked with American Indians and Shamans from different traditions.

JANE RIDDER-PATRICK

A pharmacist, herbalist, naturopath, reflexologist, person-centred counsellor and astrologer, Jane Ridder-Patrick has a practice in natural therapeutics near Glasgow, from where she runs a series of innovative experiential workshops in astrology, self-awareness and wholeness/health. Her main work and research is interdisciplinary, aimed at investigating and integrating the essentials of naturopathy, the orthodox medical sciences, depth psychology and astrology for practical application. She was the founding editor of the newsletter Astrology and Medicine and is the author of A Handbook of Medical Astrology, published by Penguin/Arkana in 1990.

PAULINE GIESBERTS

Pauline graduated from The International College of Oriental Medicine (ICOM) 17 years ago and has been in full-time practice ever since. She has taught and practised at the Colleges in England and Holland and has travelled all over the world to increase her knowldege of acupuncture, to the US, Europe, China, Autstralia, Taiwan, Thailand, Mexico and South America. In 1990 she became principal of ICOM (UK). She is actively involved with the British Accreditation Board (BAAB) to try to gain wider acceptance for ICOM and acupuncture in general. She is still practising at the College and has her own small practice, which she runs from home.

ROSALIND BLACKWELL

After an early career as a beauty therapist and aromatherapist, Rosalind trained as a medical herbalist with the School of Herbal Medicine (phytotherapy). On finishing the four-year course and qualifying in 1986 she was admitted as a member of the National Institute of Medical herbalists and went straight into private practice. She now divides her time between her practice and an NHS medical centre. She trained further in advanced soft tissue manipulation and scientific aromatherapy with Pierre Franchomme and Dr Daniel Penoel from France which led to her setting up a training course in Aromatic Medicine for medical herbalists and doctors, the first of its kind in the UK, to teach the medical use of essential oils as practised by French doctors.

JANE CORY-WRIGHT

A professional painter and art teacher, Jane Cory-Wright has been running workshops and teaching art therapy for some 20 years. She has found, having worked with hundreds of people, that 'when someone has painted out a past trauma and healing images start coming in there is always a corresponding healing in the outer life'. Jane leads groups in Europe, the Middle East and the US, runs courses in London and Devon and has just begun a workshop with The Cancer Help Centre in Bristol. She was recently the subject of an ITV documentary.

CAROLINE WISE

Various psychic and paranormal experiences as a child sparked Caroline Wise's interest in the wider aspects of the subject. Now aged 35 she was a founder member of the Assocation for the Scientific Study of Anomalous Phenomena, and was involved for several years in the Dragon Project, which investigates the properties of ancient sacred sites. She now organises conferences on folklore, psychic questing, goddess spirituality and anomaly research, as well as publishing and editing for Neptune Press at the Atlantis Bookshop in London. Her main interests are in Earth Mysteries, Ancient Religion and Shamanism.

JENNY RANDLES

Jenny Randles is Britain's leading expert on the phenomenon of UFOs. Born in 1951 she trained initially as a science teacher but later became a professional researcher and writer on the paranormal. She has written 21 books on UFOs, ESP, life after death, unsolved disappearances and related subjects, as well as articles for the Guardian, New Scientist and other publications. She is a director of the British UFO Research Association, heading the investigation team since 1981, and is a consultant for other UFO-based organisations worldwide. Since 1989 she has been a paranormal agony aunt for the ITV Teletext service's problem panel. Jenny is unmarried and lives in Cheadle Heath, Cheshire.

JANET BORD

Leicester-born Janet Bord worked as a legal secretary before joining a book publisher and learning editorial work. After moving to London in 1970 she married photographer Colin Bord and their mutual interest in all aspects of the paranormal resulted in 14 co-authored books over a 20-year period. These include Ancient Mysteries of Britain, Atlas of Magical Britain and Life Beyond Planet Earth? Janet has also written several on her own, notably Astral Projection, Mazes and Labyrinths of the World and the children's book Ghosts. In 1978 the couple moved to Wales and they now run the Fortean Picture Library, a "pictorial archive of mysteries and strange phenomena".

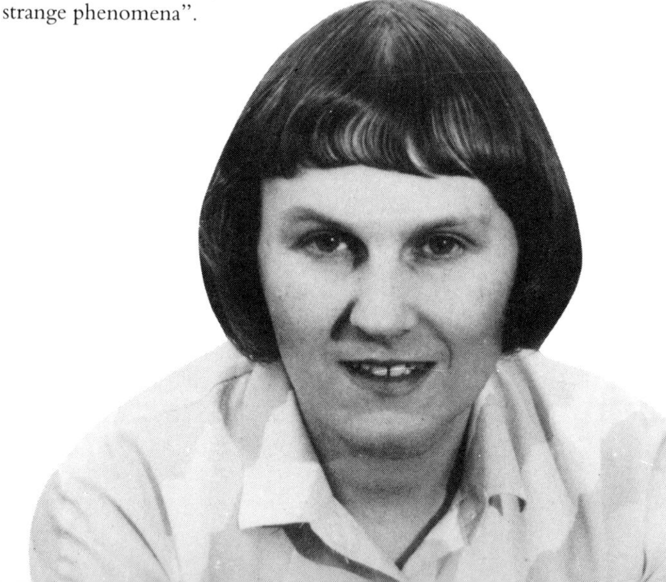

MARY CAINE ↓

Retired art lecturer Mary Caine became well-known for articles in Prediction and other publications on the Glastonbury Giants, which she later wrote about and illustrated in The Glastonbury Zodiac. She discovered another Earth-Zodiac at Kingston-upon-Thames, Surrey, and has made films and videos about these phenomena. Now aged 76, she is currently working on a video about Britain's ancient myths and legends. Although actively involved in lecturing and demonstrating at events like the Festival of Mind, Body and Spirit, she has also raised five children and has painted ecological murals which have been displayed at the Glastonbury Festival and other "green" events.

SUSAN BLACKMORE ↑

Dr Susan Blackmore is senior lecturer in psychology at the University of the West of England in Bristol, where her research interests include all aspects of parapsychology, the origins of belief in the paranormal, out-of-body and near-death experiences and related subjects. She is a member of the Council of the Society for Psychical Research and the Committee for the Scientific Investigation of Claims of the Paranormal. She is the author of Beyond The Body and The Adventures of a Parapsychologist. Another book, Dying to Live: Science and the Near-Death Experience, is imminent. Born in 1951 and a mother of two, Dr Blackmore has won several awards including the Distinguished Sceptic's Award (California, 1991) and the Alexander Imich Essay Prize (London, 1991).

SERENA RONEY-DOUGAL ↓

The hippie culture of the 1960s provided the teenage Serena Roney-Dougal's first taste of an alternative world in which she eventually made her career. At university she studied psychology, specialising in comparing telepathy with subliminal perception for her final year project. Her early life had been peripatetic because her father was in the Army (she was born in Tripoli) and she later spent a year in India before marriage and the birth of the first of her two daughters. She did nine years of postgraduate work in parapsychology at London's City University and Surrey University. She now teaches parapsychology, yoga and mental development and has her own research organisation in Glastonbury, Somerset. She has lectured in the USA and Europe and is the author of When Science and Magic Meet.

RENNA NEZOS

Renna Nezos, who came to Britain from France in 1969, is founder of the British Academy of Graphology and the London College of Graphology, which has some 100 students taking its Academy Diploma course. The main objectives of the Academy, she says, are to promote the development and research of the science of graphology and act as an academic body for it. It publishes its own quarterly journal, Graphology, and organises research into such disorders as dyslexia and psychosomatic pains as defence mechanisms. Renna's book, Graphology: The Interpretation of Handwriting, has been translated into Italian, Greek, Hebrew and Spanish. She has practised for 20 years and has taught in the UK since 1975.

ROSEMARY WILSON

As a personnel executive with several leading companies over a period of 30 years (J. Lyons and Co, Hallmark Cards and tobacco giant Gallaher), Rosemary Wilson knows the importance of graphology in assessing the character of short-listed candidates for managerial positions. In 1984 she established her own consultancy, assisting management selection for a cross-section of British industry and commerce. In addition to her "headhunting" work, she has helped to identify forged-cheque writers and anonymous letter writers. A founder member of the British Institute of Graphologists and a member of the Graphology Society, she has also represented the CBI on industrial tribunal panels over the past 17 years. Rosemary, who is unmarried and lives in Kings Langley, Hertfordshire, retains her membership of the Institute of Personnel Management.

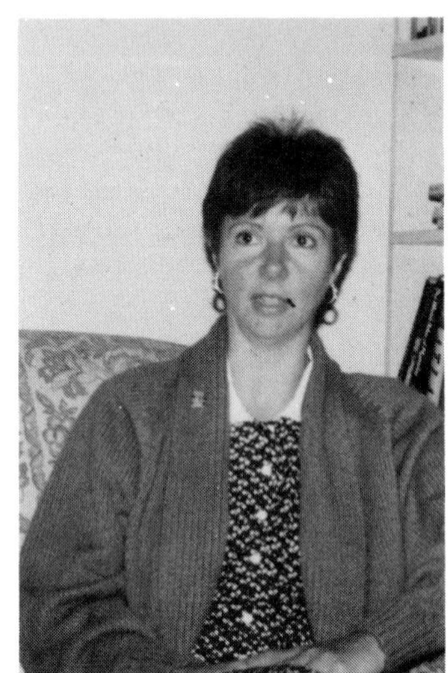

SUE BIDDLE

As someone who always had an interest in people and their motivations, Sue Biddle studied psychology and discovered graphology by way of an adult education course. At first it was a hobby – just "another means of learning about people and relationships". But she found it fascinating and went on to formal training. She has continued to develop her knowledge and understanding of graphology through private studies and lectures. Now handwriting analysis is her career – she travels around lecturing, doing analyses and giving introductory courses at adult education centres. Her real interest, she says, is in using graphology to help people in their self-development. Sue, who is 40 years old, is married and lives in Woking, Surrey.

LINDA LAWRENCE

Linda Lawrence became interested in all esoteric subjects because of psychic experiences which, she says, she had from her late teens onwards. As a Catholic she was wary of these but still fascinated enough to read widely on the subject. In 1984 she joined a psychic development class at the Spiritualist Association of Great Britain and later went on to the College of Psychic Studies. She says she is "clairvoyant, clairaudient and mediumistic" and has been reading Tarot since 1985. She also teaches and lectures on Tarot, which she views as a means of self-development as well as a method of divination. Linda has been tested by the British Astrological and Psychic Society and is now one of their consultants. Divorced, she lives in Pimlico, London, and has one son.

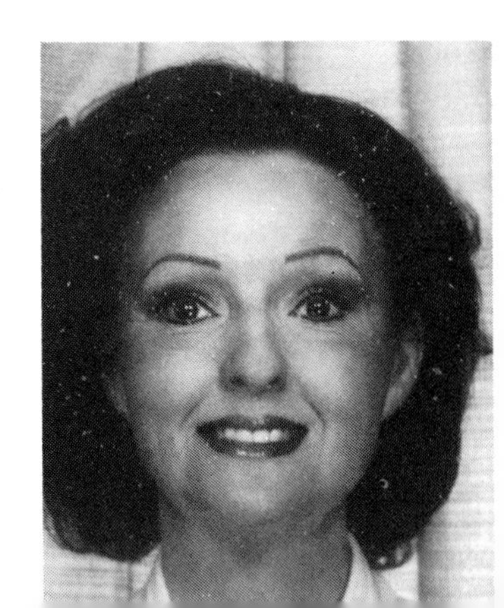

MARY ANDERSON

Always interested in "the Occult in all its expressions", Mary Anderson started working as a psychotherapist in 1963. To widen her understanding she studied astrology and took the Faculty examination in 1970. She was librarian for the Society for the Study of Psychological Patterns and studied hand analysis under its chief tutor, William Atkinson. She has since used both astrology and hand reading in her work.

JULIE HINTON

Julie Hinton discovered graphology by having her own writing analysed when she was a teenager. This reading proved so accurate that she was inspired to learn more about it. She read avidly on the subject, attended lectures and took private tuition. In 1982 she turned professional. She was also working in the personnel field at the time and found graphology extremely useful when employed in conjunction with interviewing techniques. True personality, strengths and weaknesses were determined in order to identify the best job applicants. Julie has gradually built up her own clientele, specialising in compatability (relationships, business partnerships, etc), recruitment and general character assessment. Married with three children, she lives in East Grinstead, Sussex.

SASHA FENTON

Sasha Fenton has worked as a professional palmist, astrologer and Tarot card reader since 1973 and is the author of several books. She is astrologer for Woman's Own magazine and has worked for the Sunday People and Sunday Times. She is a regular broadcaster and had her own spot on the Pete Murray show on London's LBC for four years. She has "read" for the casts of the TV shows EastEnders, The Bill and Howards' Way. A former president of the British Astrological and Psychic Society and former chairman of the Advisory Panel on Astrological Education, Sasha teaches and lectures all over the world.

LORRAINE DAVIES

Seeing thousands of different signatures while working in the banking world sparked Lorraine Davies' interest in handwriting and 11 years with St John Ambulance as teacher and nurse expanded her knowledge of people, their personality make-up and structure of their bodies. In the 1980s she took a three-year course on graphology and gained a diploma while studying with the late Frank Hilliger, founder of the British Institute of Graphology. Lorraine, mother of three sons and a daughter, lives in Bristol and practises there as a graphologist, teaching, lecturing and running seminars.

LILLA BEK

Lilla Bek has a rich medical tradition in her family and, from a early age, showed a natural interest in medicine, healing and therapy. Her life has been dedicated to communicating and practising natural therapeutic medicines such as yoga, therapeutic art, dance and movement. Born in 1933, from 1951 Lilla worked as a research analyst for the scientific and medical department of the NCB, until her marriage in 1958. She then worked as an auxiliary nurse in a psychiatric hospital near London. She studied therapeutic yoga at the London School of Yoga and, for the past 20 years, ha established her own European circuit of conference and worksho venues. Currently her most popula workshops are on therapeutic art and dance and participants at all he workshops are introduced to a rich blend of yoga, natural healing movement, art and creative self-care.

PHILIPPA PULLAR

Philippa Pullar was born in 1935 and is the author of Consuming Passions (1970), Frank Harris (1975), Gilded Butterflies (1978) and The Shortest Journey (1981) and co-author, with Lilla Bek, of To The Light (1985) and the Seven Levels of Healing (1988). The turning point in her life came when she travelled to India in the late 1970s, in the course of researching The Shortest Journey, and her healing work is a natural outcome of the spiritual experiences which she underwent at that time. She has been a member of the National Federation of Spiritual Healers since 1982. A further powerful influence on her life in recent years has been a near-death experience in the Philippines where she had gone to address a life-threatening tumour. Current interests in Philippa's life include a fascination with the wisdom of ancient Egypt and its resonances in our time. Two facets of this are the study of hieroglyphics and of Middle Eastern dance. Other interests include gardening, tapestry, riding, cats and Jungian psychology.

JUDY FRASER

Born in 1943 Judy Fraser runs her training company, Second Aid Ltd, from her base in West Sussex. Her workshops are designed to help participants to learn to live life more effectively through better communication, understanding behavioural patterns and developing intuition, as well as examining and coming to terms with relationship problems at home and at work. Judy also encourages the use of natural healing methods to relieve stress and tension. She regularly runs courses for the largest employer in Canada and, in Switzerland and Holland, her Second Aid techniques have been introduced into industry, commerce, schools and self-help groups. Second Aid produces a whole range of accessories, available by mail-order, including oils, books, tapes and teas. Judy has published a book entitled Second Aid – A Short Guide to Self-Awareness, which is also available.

ELIZABETH ST JOHN

Elizabeth St John has been in private practice in etheric healing and biofeedback meditation training since around 1980. She studied with C. Maxwell Cade, author of The Awakening Mind, Andrew Watson, author of Healing Music, and Suprapto Suryadamro, the founder of Daily Life Practice in Java. She has run healing classes in a number of adult education centres and also teaches Movement Healing, a form of energy balancing through movement. Her current focus is on helping dancers, actors and musicians develop their healing gifts in the context of performance. Although deeply involved in her work with the chronically sick and dying, 54 year old Elizabeth's special interest is in spiritual healing as a preventative therapy and a pathway to self-development. She is training co-ordinator for the Association for Therapeutic Healers, which she co-founded in 1984, and supervisor for the ATH Drop-in Healing Clinic at Neal's Yard Therapy Rooms in Central London.

JESSICA MACBETH

Born in 1937 Jessica Macbeth has been healing for over 50 years and teaching for over 20. She learned healing as a child from her grandmother and, in an effort to understand more about it and to improve her healing skills, has studied shiatzu, massage, psychology (BA degree), philosophy, anthropology, meditation and other related subjects, with a wide variety of teachers. Jessica teaches healing, meditation and psychic and spiritual development in Scotland, England and California, and practises healing by laying on of hands in Scotland. She is the author of Moon Over Water: The Path of Meditation (1990) and Sun Over Mountain: A Guide to Creative Imagery (1991) and co-editor and a regular contributor to Crann Beathadh, a quarterly journal for healers. Jessica is a member of the Association for Therapeutic Healers and senior instructor of the Order of the Ascending Spirit in the UK and the USA. Jessica lives in Scotland, where her hobbies are hill watching *sic*, breeding Abyssinian cats and sculpting.

JEAN SAYRE-ADAMS

Born in the USA, Jean Sayre-Adams trained as a nurse in San Francisco. She first came to Britain in 1982, when she started teaching the healing arts to health care professionals. In 1989 she founded the Didsbury Trust, a charitable organisation which encourages self-development in nurses and health care professionals and educates them in holistic concepts. As well as being director of the Didsbury Trust, she serves on many committees that further the integration of complementary therapies with existing health care systems. She is the principle teacher in the UK of Therapeutic Touch, a technique similar to laying on of hands, the basic concepts of which come from the Rogerian model of nursing.

DR HELEN FORD

Helen Ford trained in traditional Western medicine, with a scholarship and double first degree in Natural Sciences at Cambridge University. After practising within the British and Canadian NHS, she moved gradually into her own personal approach to illness, seeing it as a manifestation of spiritual imbalance. Helen now works with her own naturally intuitive healing abilities as well as vibrational remedies (homeopathic, flowers, trees), crystals, herbs and traditional chemical treatments in order to heal the whole rather than just the physico-chemical part of the individual. Happily unmarried, with five children, 49 year old Helen believes in "a polyamorous approach to life and relationships, with the ultimate goal of creating and being part of the flow of pure love between beings, thereby ending disease and unhappiness and recreating Paradise". Helen runs the annual Uniting in Healing conference, which embraces all therapies. She spends her spare time planting trees on her Welsh mountain farm.

SOOZI HOLBECHE

Born in Ceylon in 1937, Soozi Holbeche became fascinated by the ability of local people to walk through red-hot coals without burning themselves. This led her to study the power of mind and spirit to effect change in the physical body. She spent six years as assistant to Paul Solomon, the founder of Inner Light Consciousness in the USA, taught at the Edgar Cayce Association, ran a clinic with a doctor and three Jungian psychologists and worked for three years with Lynn Buess, psychologist and metaphysical teacher. Soozi is an internationally respected intuitive diagnostician and healer. She uses dreams, psychotherapy, crystals, colour and sound as well as meditation, movement and drawing to effect her therapeutic work. She has been associated with the Dalai Lama, E Kubler Ross, Sir George Trevelyn, Sun Bear, Peter and Eileen Caddy, Swami Satchidananda and Gerald Jampolski. Soozi works in Europe, Australia, New Zealand, South Africa and the USA. She is the author of The Power of Gems and Crystals and The Power of Your Dreams, and is working on Surviving in a Changing World, on reincarnation. Along with Prince Philip, the Dalai Lama and Jonathon Porritt, Soozi was one of 50 contributors to the book, The Way Ahead.

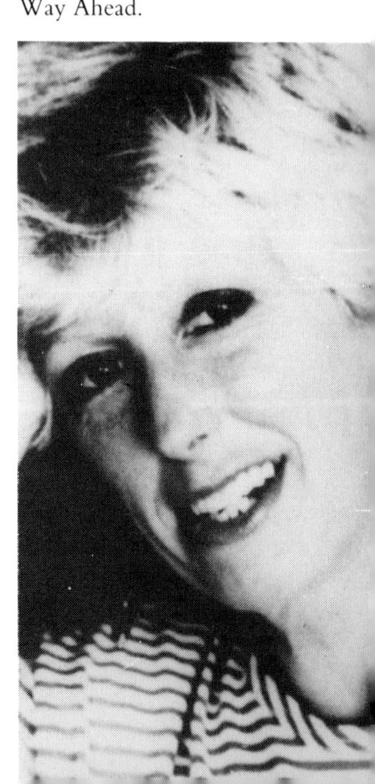

BETTY SHINE

Betty Shine was born in Kennington in 1929 and had a grandmother who was a spiritualist. For 25 years, she practised vitamin and mineral therapy, hand analysis and yoga, while pursuing a career as a professional singer. Fourteen years ago she discovered a remarkable gift; a clairvoyant ability for medical diagnosis. In 1976 she began her taining as a healer. Working from her clinic on the South Coast, she has helped thousands of people with her healing powers. Her patients have included Michael Aspel, Michael Bentine and Michael Crawford. In his autobiography, Tomorrow Is Too Late, Ray Moore tells of the help and comfort that Betty was able to give him when he had cancer. Since the publication of Mind To Mind, she has received thousands of appreciative letters from readers. The hardback edition of Mind Magic hit the No 1 slot in the Sunday Times Best Sellers list and the new paperback ensures that even more people will enjoy the benefits of mind energy.

NERYS DEE

Jungian psychology started to interest Nerys Dee when she discovered that some dreams come true. In 1974 she began writing about them and analysing 60 or more dreams a month, through the magazine Prediction. This experience enabled her to write three books, Your Dreams and What They Mean, Disocver Dreams and Understanding Dreams, and gives hundreds of talks and seminars on the subject. A seasoned journalist and radio and television broadcaster, she has had regular slots on the Pete Murray and Derek Jameson shows and has written for foreign and British papers, including the Sunday Times Colour Supplement. Nerys teaches self-help and healing for adult education centres and she started the SE Cancer Centre, where patients can talk about their dreams. As a qualified radiographer, she has collected many dreams from those who have cancer and has found that working with them and understanding the messages which they send from "self to self", can bring peace of mind and, often, forms of self-healing.

IVY NORTHAGE

Eighty-three year old Ivy Northage started as a medium as a result of her husband's experiment with table turning, when she received information from her father, whom she had never known, which her mother was able to confirm.
She developed her gift through her spirit guide, Chan, who undertook all her training. After a request to conduct a development class, which necessitated a further two years training from Chan, teaching became her priority. Her main contribution to mediumship has been to promote in students the ability to use their gift in the best possible way. In 1970 she was invited to join the College of Psychic Studies, as both teacher and medium. She has participated in teleivision and radio programmes and is still conducting workshops, demonstrations, lectures and private sittings.

DORIS COLLINS

World famous clairvoyant and healer, Doris Collins, is now 74 years old. She has toured Europe, Australasia, South Africa and the USA, addressing large theatre audiences and small, intimate groups. She helps and inspires the people she treats with her strong and sensitive attitude. She welcomes people of all faiths, saying that it is love and unity that she strives for and proves, to her audience's satisfaction, that there is life after death, and that those in the spirit world çan return to give reassurances to their loved ones.
Doris Collins has had a daily column in the Sun newspaper and the newspaper sponsored her worldwide farewell tour. However, since then she has been inundated with letters and, as Doris says, "How can I retire when there are so many needy people in the world?"

RENEE HINDLE

A founder member of the British Astrological and Psychic Society, which was founded in 1975, Renee Hindle was a natural psychic from an early age and came into spiritualism after her marriage. She was president of a Spiritualist Church for seven years and has demonstrated clairvoyance and mediumship in exhibitions throughout this country and America and taken part in television programmes in both. Renee gives spiritual healing and guidance on spiritual, emotional and material problems to those in need, particularly in the case of bereavement, and runs an advanced psychic and spiritual development group. During the past 12 years, she has founded and run a charity for people in need. Since her retirement from the NHS, Renee has worked as a full-time psychic and undertaken voluntary work at her local hospice.

BERENICE WATT

Aware of the spirit dimension since early childhood, Berenice Watt, 47, has been a professional in spiritual fields for over 20 years, working in the UK, Spain and the Canary Islands. After many years working in Spiritualist Churches, Berenice moved on to exhibitions, and has worked at the Festival of Mind Body Spirit for ten years, and travels the country teaching. As a medium, using trance, mental inspiration and clairsentience, Berenice's speciality is channelling higher wisdoms. She is the principal of Berkana Institute of Universal Light, teaching all aspects of spiritual awareness either in person or via personalised tapes. Spiritual regression is Berenice's speciality within therapy, taught by her spirit guides. She is a qualified hypnotherapist, psychotherapist and neuro-linguistic programming practitioner. She is a consultant member and executive secretary of the British Astrological & Psychic Society.

MAVIS PITTILLA

Mavis Pittilla started to see and hear the spirit world when she was suffering illness at the age of 13. With the help and guidance from the spirit world and earthly teachers, she has enhanced her gifts of mediumship. She has travelled extensively and made television and radio appearances and is soon to be seen in the film, Reunion, about spiritualism. Mavis may often be found at Stanstel Hall, the home of the Arthur Findlay College, where students can study and participate in psychic, mediumistic and spiritual awareness.

MARY DUFFY

Born in 1924, Mary Duffy started her career as a medium, but did not join the spiritualist movement until the 1950s. She worked exclusively in Scotland until 1960, when she went to Australia, continuing to work as a medium in a limited way. Her work as a medium began in earnest in 1965, and she became known throughout the UK. She has worked in many other countries, particularly South Africa, and for various organisations in her home town of Edinburgh, including the College of Parapsychology, as well as in individual churches. She has taken classes over 30 years. Mary became a minister of the SNU in 1980 and has been awarded her certificates for public speaking and demonstrating clairvoyance.

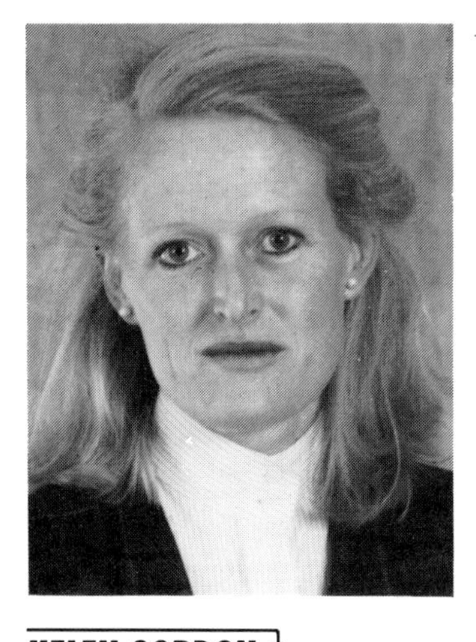

HELEN GORDON

A qualified chartered surveyor and a director of John Laing Developments, Helen Gordon was born in Cheshire in 1959 and educated at Sale Girls Grammar School and Oxford Polytechnic, where she gained a degree in Estate Management. She worked in private practice in Manchester before joining the development team of Milton Keynes Development Corporation in 1981, eventually becoming Head of Office Development for the the new city. She joined Laings in 1987 and worked on a variety of office and retail development and financing projects. She was appointed to the Board in 1990 and given responsibility for managing the London office the following year. A founder member of the working party to encourage women into the construction business (established by Laings), she is also a member of Opportunity 2000.

VICTORIA MITCHELL

Victoria Mitchell has done very well for someone who says she had hardly any education (her father was a Colonel in the Army and they moved a lot) and left school with a handful of O levels. Having joined the international property consultants Savills as a secretary in 1967, she has risen through the ranks to her current position as executive director, sitting on the executive committe and the main Board. She is Head of London Region, Residential Agency and responsible for international residential associations. The residential department which she started in 1972 now has five offices. She is Savills' Business in the Community representative and a member of the Royal Society of Arts. Married to David Mitchell, Partner in Dreweatt Neate, she lives in London while David lives and works in Newbury, Berkshire. "We meet at weekends," she says. They have a 20-year-old daughter at university.

JENEFER GREENWOOD

Jenefer Greenwood joined Hillier Parker in 1978 as an assistant in the Local Authority Consultancy department, concentrating on shopping developments. In 1981 she transferred to the retail department to be responsible for day-to-day letting co-ordination on a number of town centre shcemes. She is now a partner heading a team to act for development clients seeking overall co-ordination of marketing advice on shopping centres. She is a Fellow of the Royal Institution of Chartered Surveyors, a member of the Board of Management of the British Council of Shopping Centres and Chairman of the Retail Liaison Committee.

AVRIL BUTT

Avril Butt's most notable achievement in 1992 was the sale of one of the most expensive houses ever to change hands in London – Ancaster House in Mayfiar, which fetched around £20 million. Born in Warwickshire and educated at Sibford Gower Quaker School and at Banbury Grammar School, she did a three-year management course before taking six years off to see the world. She joined Knight Frank & Rutley in 1972 and six months later moved to De Groot Collis to help build up the residential side of the agency. She took over the opeation in 1981 and became an associate partner. In 1986 she became the only woman equity partner. At the beginning of 1992, De Groot Collis merged with Chesterton International, the UK's largest property consultants, and this offers enormous expansion potential for the Residential Agency division, especially in the Far East. Married with two children, she lives in London.

LINDA BEANEY

Linda Beaney, a partner in Beaney Pearce, began her career in 1969 with Edward Erdman and Company, working in the residential department. In 1976 she joined Hamptons and became managing director of their London operation. During this time she became the most experienced residential development expert in London and widened her broad knowledge of estate agency. Later she formed Beaney Pearce as a new independent partnership, handling sales and lettings, providing survey, valuation and development consultancy services. Linda has acted for major estates, including the Howard de Walden Estate and the Crown Estate Commissioners. The agency's success is reflected in a move at the end of 1982 to new offices in fashionable Sloane Square.

JOANNA EMBLING

With responsibilities for City and Docklands propeties for Healey & Baker, Joanna Embling has seen these areas boom spectacularly and tumble into a depressing slump since the mid-1980s. Like everyone else, she will welcome the recovery when it comes. Born in 1949 and educated at Benenden School in Kent, on a scholarship in the USA and at the Polytechnic of Central London (where she gained a BSc in Estate Management), Joanna has worked for Chesterfield Ronson in Paris, Chesterfield Properties in London and HRO International in New York. She joined Healey & Baker's City office in 1984 and was invited to become an equity partner in 1992. She is on the Steering Committee of Women in Property, of which she has been chairman for the year 1992-93. Married with two children, she lives in London.

PATRICIA FARLEY

The world of advertising could have claimed Patricia Farley, for that was where she found her first two jobs after leaving school. After moving into the residential property business, she worked for two years with other agencies before joining the family firm in 1972. She is now a partner and runs the residential property sales department of Farley and Company, as well as overseeing the running of both the rentals and management departments with a staff of 25. She has lived and worked in South Kensington, London, since 1968 and says she has always enjoyed the area's village atmosphere. She is married and much of her spare time is taken up by her two dogs.

EDWINA CURRIE

Born in 1946, Edwina Currie was educated at St Anne's College, Oxford and the London School of Economics. Mrs Currie worked in the Department of Trade and Industry as an economic assistant (1970-71) and afterwards held various teaching posts, including Head of Business Studies at Bromsgrove School (1978-81). She was a member of Birmingham City Council from 1975 until 1986 and chairman of the Central Birmingham Health Authority from 1981 to 1983. Mrs Currie was elected as Conservative MP for South Derbyshire in June 1983 and was the first maiden speaker of the 1983 intake. She became PPS to Sir Keith Joseph, Secretary of State for Education, in 1985. From 1986 to 1988 she was Minister of State at the Department of Health and Social Security, later the Department of Health. She was appointed a trustee of the Marie Curie Cancer Care Organisation and continues her health interest by raising funds for asthma research. In 1989 her first book, Life Lines, was published and, in 1990, came her second, What Women Want. In 1989 Edwina Currie became the first president of Women in Business and was voted Speaker of the Year by The Association of Speakers Club.

ANGELA RUMBOLD

Angela Rumbold's political career started when she was elected to Kingston Council in 1974. She became deputy leader of the Council and chairman of the Education Committee and the Policy and Resources Committee. She has been MP for Mitcham and Morden since 1982 and was appointed PPS to Nicholas Ridley, then Secretary of State for Transport, in 1983, and was Parliamentary Under Secretary of State for the Environment from September 1985. In September 1986, Mrs Rumbold was appointed Minister of State at the Department of Education. In July 1990 she was appointed Minister of State at the Home Office, with responsibility for prisons and chairman of the Ministerial Group for Women's Issues. Dame Angela Rumbold was appointed deputy chairman of the Conservative Party in April 1992 and was also awarded the DBE. She became a member of the Privy Council in 1991.

Photograph by Carole Latimer

VIRGINIA BOTTOMLEY

In April 1992, at the age of 44, Virgina Bottomley was appointed Secretary of State for Health. She has been MP for Surrey South West since 1984. She was PPS to Sir Geoffrey Howe, the Foreign and Commonwealth Secretary, from 1987 to 1988 and had been PPS to the Minister of State for Education and Science during 1985-86 and to the Minister of Overseas Development from 1986 to 1987. She was appointed Minister at the Department of the Environment in 1988 and Minister of Health in 1989. She was co-chairman of the Women's National Commission from January 1991 and until April 1992. Prior to entering Parliament, she was a researcher for the Child Poverty Action Group between 1971 and 1973, and a psychiatric social worker at Brixton and Camberwell Child Guidance Units. She was also a magistrate in inner London from 1975 and chairman of Lambeth Juvenile Court from 1981 to 1984. She was a member of the Medical Research Council in 1987-88 and is a governor of the Ditchley Foundation and of the London School of Economics. She is a graduate of Essex University and the London School of Economics and Political Science.

LADY OLGA MAITLAND

Lady Olga Maitland began her career as a journalist with the Blackheath and District Reporter in 1965, at the age of 21, and went on to write her own column for the Sunday Express for 14 years, until 1991. Elected as MP for Sutton and Cheam in 1992, Lady Olga's political experience includes: Islington South & Finsbury executive and ward chairman (1970-87); founder and chairman of pro-NATO Families for Defence (from 1983); ILEA candidate in Holborn & St Pancras (1986) and the contesting of the Bethnal Green & Stepney for the Conservative Party in 1987. Born in 1944, Lady Olga is the author of Margaret Thatcher: The First Ten Years and a contributor to Peace Studies in Our Schools, by Dr John Marks.

GILLIAN SHEPHARD

Born in 1940, Gillian Shephard won a scholarship to St Hilda's College, Oxford, where she read Modern Languages. On leaving Oxford, Mrs Shephard taught in both the public and private sectors, and then worked in administration in a variety of posts, including that of senior inspector for schools and senior education officer. She left full-time employment when she married in 1975, because her husband, Tom, was a widower with two young sons and she wished to devote time to bringing them up. In 1977 she was elected to Norfolk County Council and was immediately elected vice-chairman of the Social Services Committee and subsequently became its chairman and chairman of the Education, Personnel and Museum Committees. She left the council in 1989, having been elected to Parliament in 1987. Mrs Shephard's progress through the ranks has been rapid: in 1988 she became PPS to Peter Lilley, the Economic Secretary to the Treasury; in 1989 she was appointed Parliamentary Under-Secretary of State at the Department of Social Security; in 1990 Minister of State at the Treasury; in 1991 she was appointed deputy chairman of the Conservative Party and in 1992 she became Secretary of State for Employment.

EMMA NICHOLSON

Emma Nicholson was a computer programmer, software engineer and management consultant in the UK and Africa before joining the Save the Children Fund, where she was director of fund raising from 1977 until 1985. She became vice-chairman of the Conservative Party with special responsibility for women in 1983. She was elected MP for Devon West and Torridge in 1987 and was a member of the Select Committee on Employment from 1990 until 1991 and was an alternate member of the British delegation of the Council of Europe and the Western European Union before becoming PPS to Michael Jack, the Minister of State for Home Affairs. Outside Parliament, Miss Nicholson holds more than 50 non-governmental organisational honorary posts. She was patron and trustee of the Suzy Lamplugh Trust, a member of the Council of the Howard League and patron of the Plymouth and District Relate. She is also a Fellow of the Royal Society of Arts and of the Industry and Parliament Trust.

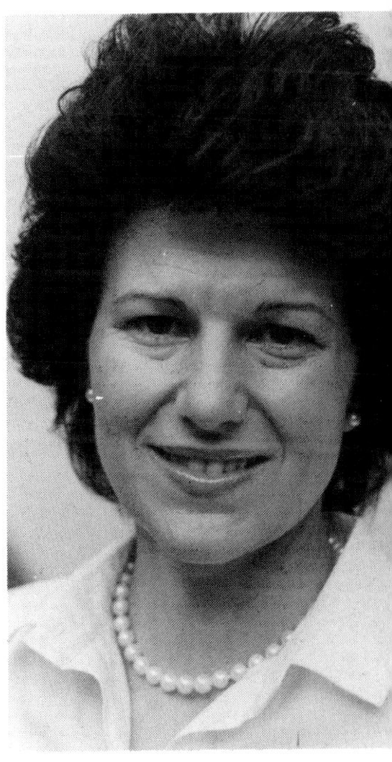

GLENDA JACKSON

Born in Birkenhead in 1936, Glenda Jackson won a place at RADA after two years of working as a shop assistant. As an actress, she has won international acclaim and two Oscars for her performances in Women in Love and A Touch of Class. She was a member of the Royal Shakespeare Company from 1963 to 1967 and 1979 to 1980. Awarded a CBE in 1978 Glenda Jackson joined the Labour Party in that year and was elected MP for Hampstead and Highgate in 1992, sponsored by ASLEF.

MARJORIE MOWLAM

MP for Redcar since 1987, Marjorie Mowlam was born in 1949 and educated in Coventry and at Durham University. She joined the Labour Party in 1969 and was Opposition front bench spokesperson for Northern Ireland from 1988 to 1989. She has been front bench spokesperson for Trad and Industry since 1989. Marjorie Mowlam is a member of the Transport and General Workers Union, the Tribune Group and th Socialist Education Association. She is sponsored by COHSE.

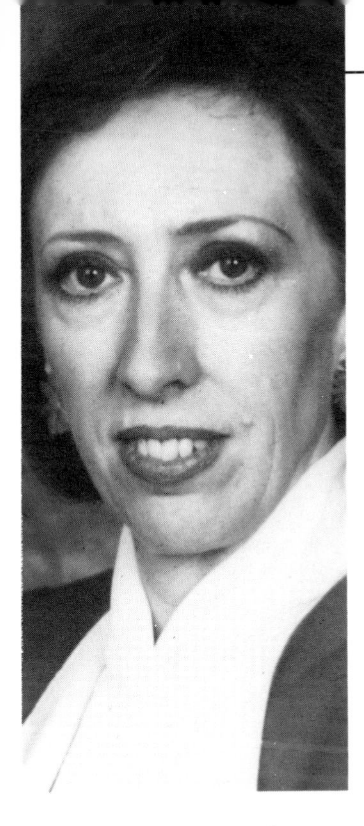

MARGARET BECKETT

Margaret Beckett was born in 1943 in Ashton-under-Lyne and was educated at Notre Dame High School and the Manchester College of Science and Technology. She has been the MP for Derby South since 1983 and has been Shadow Chief Secretary to the Treasury since 1989. A former metallurgist and industrial policy researcher at Labour headquarters, she was MP for Lincoln from 1974 until 1979. She joined the Labour Party in 1961, was PPS to the Ministry of Overseas Development in 1974-75, assistant Government Whip, 1975-76, Under Secretary for Education Committee, 1976-79 and Shadow Minister for Social Security, 1984-89. She is a member of Labour's National Executive Committee, and has been so intermittently since 1980. Margaret Beckett is a member, and sponsored by, the TGWU and is a member of the NUJ, BECTU, the Fabian Society, the Anti-Apartheid Movement, the Tribune Group, the Socialist Education Association, Labour Women's Action Committee, the Derby Co-operative Party, SERA, Amnesty International and the Common Market Safeguards Campaign. She is deputy leader of the Labour Party.

HARRIET HARMAN

Harriet Harman, MP for Peckham since 1982, was born in 1950 and has been Opposition front bench spokesperson on Health since 1987. She was educated at St Paul's Girls School and York University and is a qualified solicitor. She worked for Brent Community Law Centre from 1975 until 1978 and was legal officer at the National Council for Civil Liberties from 1978 until 1982. She is a member of, and sponsored by, the Transport and General Workers Union and is a member of the NCCL. Health, women's and trades unions' rights and civil liberties are her particular political interests.

CLARE SHORT

Labour MP for Birmingham Ladywood since 1983, Clare short was born in1946 and educated at Keele and Leeds universities. She holds a BA honours degree in Political Science. She worked at the Home Office from 1970 until 1975 and joined All Faiths for One Race, in Birmingham, as director in 1976 and, from 1979 until her election to Parliament, was director of Youth Aid and the Unemployment Unit. She was the chair of the All Party Parliamentary Group on Race Relations from 1985 to 1988 and a member of the Home Affairs Select Committee from 1983 until 1985. She has been Opposition spokesperson on Employment (1985-88) and on Social Security (1989-91). She is currently Opposition frontbench spokesperson on the environment. She has published Talking Blues: a study of young West Indians' views on policing (1978); A Handbook on Immigration Law (1978) and Dear Clare . . . This is what women think about page 3 (1991).

EMILY ANDERSON

Emily Anderson is a graduate of the Royal College of Art. She held her first exhibition, New Contemporaries, at the Institute of Contemporary Arts in 1982; since then her work has been seen at a number of galleries in London and around the UK. Her latest exhibition, Ecstatic Antibodies, commissioned by the Impressions Gallery in York, toured the UK for two years between 1990 and 1992. Emily has had numerous editorial commissions, including a cover for Art Monthly, and work for Blueprint, Elle, ES magazine, the Guardian, the Observer, the Sunday Times and Vogue. She is regularly commissioned by record companies for art work and has several books to her credit. She has been a visiting lecturer at the Institute of Contemporary Arts and the Special Photographers' Gallery in London and at New Jersey College in New York. In 1983 she won the Chestertons Prize, the 3M Colour Prize and the J Walter Thompson Award.

ANNABEL WILLIAMS

Annabel Williams is noted for introducing the Cover Girl makeover and photo session. Working with her sister, Lucinda Layton, a professional make-up artist, Annabel's photographs are intended to give people what they want from photography. Formerly a teacher of emotionally disturbed children who took wedding photographs at weekends, she became a professional portrait photographer in the early 1980s. As well as taking portraits of children, she also practices carte blanche photography – taking photographs of clients wherever they choose. Her studio, the Picture House, was featured on The Clothes Show in 1988. Annabel is an Associate of the British Institute of Professional Photography and has won its Peter Grugeon Award.

CHRISTINE HANSCOMB

Christine Hanscomb joined Conde Nast Publications in the late 1960s; she was the art director of Vogue magazine and of the Vogue Beauty Book. She has been a photographer since 1980. Her commercial commissions include advertising work for all the major agencies and editorial work for Vogue magazine and the Sunday Times. Christine, who is well-known for her still-life and work with children, specialised in taking photographs of food and is noted for her exquisite sense of composition. Her work often appears in cook books and she has more than 20 book credits. With a substantial commercial portfolio as a photographer, she is now also directing TV commercials.

Photograph by David Burnham

ANITA CORBIN

A precocious photographer, Anita Corbin took her first pictures in 1965, when she was only seven years old. She decided to become a professional at the age of 18 after spending time in India. A first-class honours graduate of the Polytechnic of Central London and a postgraduate student at the Royal College of Art, Anita has been a freelance photographer since 1981, when she won the Nikon/Sunday Times Under 25 Photo-Journalist Competition. In 1983 she spent three months in Sumatra and won the Observer Award. Her unique working relationship with partner John O'Grady began in 1985. They specialise in work for designers, corporate portraiture and annual report photography.

LINDA BURGESS

Born in Portsmouth, photographer Linda Burgess grew up in Australia. She studied graphic design at the Maidstone College of Art, where she left before completing the course. Linda has been a professional photographer for 12 years and has published several books. Her subjects are flowers and fruit, which she photographs, meticulously arranged, against hand-painted canvasses or stylised backdrops. She makes even the most mundane flowers look beautiful, with her grainy, highly textured finishes, echoing the still-lifes of the Renaissance painters she so admires.

Photograph by kind permission of At Home magazine

CLARE PARK

Forced to retire through injury from the Ballet Rambert, Clare Park became a model in 1977 (after winning the Vogue Model Competition) and worked with photographer Barry Lategan. Inspired by his vision and the dance imagery created by choreographer Pina Bausch, Clare began taking her own photographs. After working for several years as a dance photographer and winning Vogue's Sotheby/Beaton Award in 1984, she studied at the Royal College of Art. Her first solo exhibition was held at the Special Photographer's Company in 1991. Memories, Dreams, Reflections. She used her experience as a dancer and model to examine the distorted ideals of the female form. The work took silver in the 1992 AFAEP Awards and an image from the exhibition was used on the cover of Naomi Wolf's book The Beauty Myth. Her new colour work has already been selected for the 1993 AFAEP Awards.
Photograph by Robert Barber with kind permission of the Special Photographers Company

JAN BALDWIN

Jan Baldwin worked as a photographer's assistant before studying photography at the Royal College of Art, where she graduated with a Master's degree in 1981. She was first commissioned by Good Housekeeping and then by a major leisure group to shoot hotel interiors. Perhaps best known for still-life and photographs of food, Jan has travelled extensively for corporate clients while working on her commercial portfolio. Her editorial work includes commissions from the Sunday Times and Elle Decoration, book publishers penguin and Time-Life, graphic design groups and advertising agencies. Her book (with Felicity and Roald Dahl), Memories with Food at Gypsy House, was shortlisted for the 1992 Glenfiddich Awards.
Photograph courtesy of Peter Bailey Company

SANDRA LOUSADA

Sandra Lousada, photographer of the people, was born in London in 1938. A black and white portrait photographer in the 1960s, she also worked on films, including Tom Jones and A Taste Of Honey, and with the English Stage Company at the Royal Court. She went on to join Whitecross Studios, adding work with children to her fashion and beauty portfolio. A freelance since she was 21 years old, Sandra set up her own studio in 1980. Her work has appeared in Country Living, Harpers & Queen and Tatler, and her corporate clients include the Body Shop and Next.
Photograph by Susan Griggs

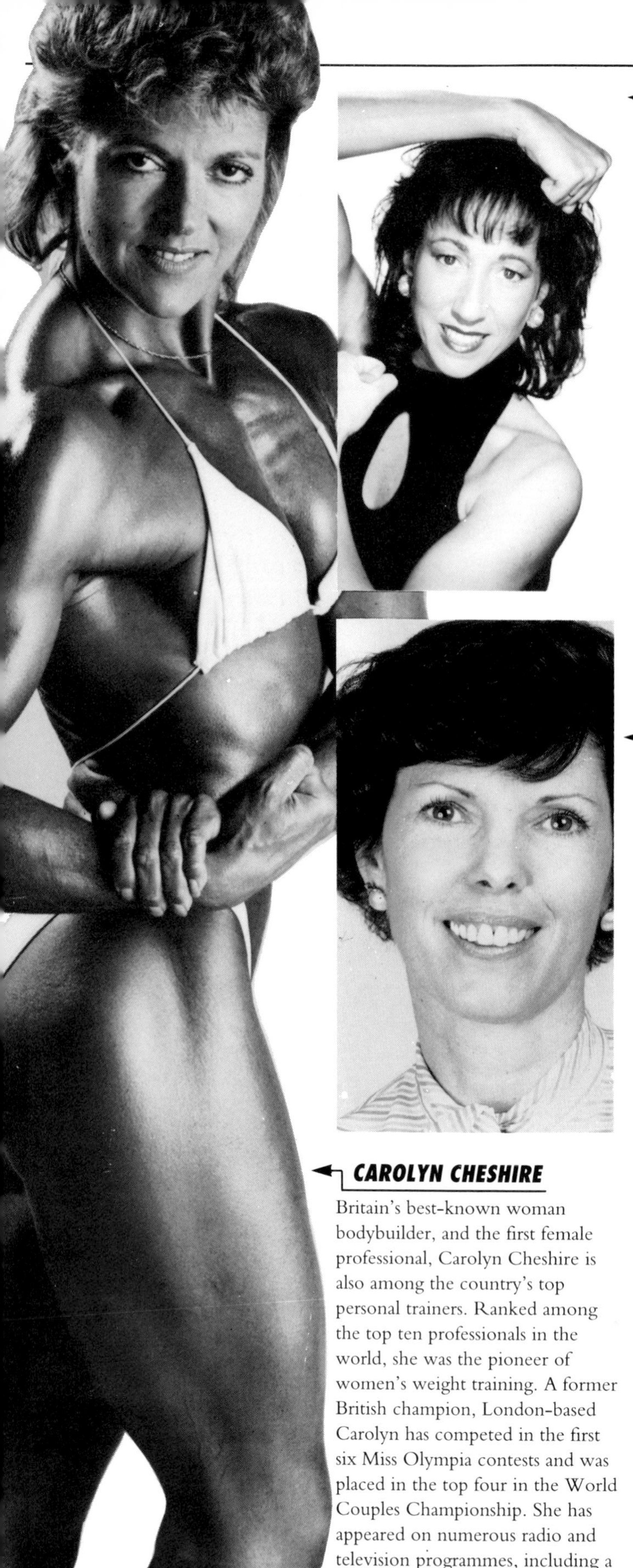

CAROLAN BROWN

The Way Ahead Ltd, the company that Carolan Brown founded in 1987 and now directs, is helping Britain rank alongside the USA in the international fitness industry. In addition to her workshops, held all over Britain and Europe, Carolan's projects include events such as the first European Fitness and Business Weekend, which took place in 1992 and attracted the top 180 British and European exercise teachers. Carolan has choreographed and presented five exercise videos – the most recent, Total Body Programme, in 1993. The winner of the National Association of Exercise Teachers' 1990 Business Award, she is also an international presenter for the fitness industry and since 1990 has been personally training the Princess of Wales.

JENNIFER HALL

After a career in ballet embracing seven years with the Royal Ballet Company, work as a choreographer in film, television and theatre, and principal roles with the Royal Opera Ballet, Jennifer Hall turned to Tai-Chi as a method of maintaining her strength and suppleness. For a number of years Jennifer, who lives in Somerset, has been studying Tai-Chi under a Chinese Master and is an instructor herself.

CAROLYN CHESHIRE

Britain's best-known woman bodybuilder, and the first female professional, Carolyn Cheshire is also among the country's top personal trainers. Ranked among the top ten professionals in the world, she was the pioneer of women's weight training. A former British champion, London-based Carolyn has competed in the first six Miss Olympia contests and was placed in the top four in the World Couples Championship. She has appeared on numerous radio and television programmes, including a documentary on her preparation for the 1981 World Championship, and in 1985 published her book Body Chic.

HARRIET ALEXANDER

From an early age Harriet Alexander studied classical ballet, eventually gaining her teaching qualifications at the Royal Ballet. Having developed an interest in sport and fitness, and competing in athletics at county level, she became an aerobics instructor – a discipline linked to dancing experience. Since 1990 Harriet has represented various areas in physique competitions, but at present concentrates on running her London gym.

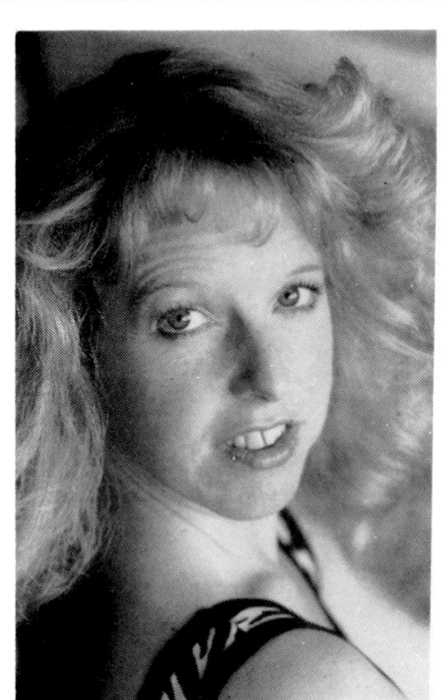

CAROL HAMPTON

One of London's foremost personal trainers, Carol Hampton is frequently featured in the press as an authority on fitness and health. She is an international presenter at fitness conventions, lectures on training courses all over Britain and is co-director, with Floyd Brown, of the National Register of Personal Trainers, a unique London-based organisation that lists the qualified fitness teachers in Britain who offer personal training. Convinced that fitness should be fun, Carol formulates an individual plan of action that will keep the client happy while achieving results.

JENNI RIVETT

Jenni Rivett is a personal trainer and nutritionist who views the body from the inside out. With over 13 years' experience in the fitness industry, including running two top London health clubs, she now has her own company, Jenergy. Operating solely by word of mouth and on a one-to-one basis, this enjoys a 95 per cent success rate. With certification from the Institute of Optimum Nutrition, the Vail Centre for Human Performance, the American Council on Exercise and the Aerobics and Fitness Association of America, Jenni presents workshops all over Britain on fitness and related subjects. She is currently researching the development of a new fitness product and in the second year of her clinical nutrition studies.

LINDA RAYNER

A presenter, instructor, teacher trainer and personal trainer, Linda Rayner was a lead dancer for 12 years and then a choreographer before founding the Body Workshop, which she still runs. Every year Linda launches a new exercise concept – Pumped on Classics was the theme in 1992 – and is currently the fitness consultant to several fitness centres and organisations, as well as a tutor and examiner. Resident in Hampshire, Linda is a member of the USA's International Dance Exercise Association and Aerobics and Fitness Association of America, and of the UK's National Association of Exercise Teachers, whose Instructor of the Year award she won in 1992.

JANETTE KIDD

As a result of training as a yoga teacher while studying German at university, Janette Kidd later developed an interest in exercise in general which led to her gaining qualifications in exercise training for ante-natal and post-natal women and the over 50s. RSA Course Director for Lifeworks Unlimited, and since 1990 has been a personal trainer.

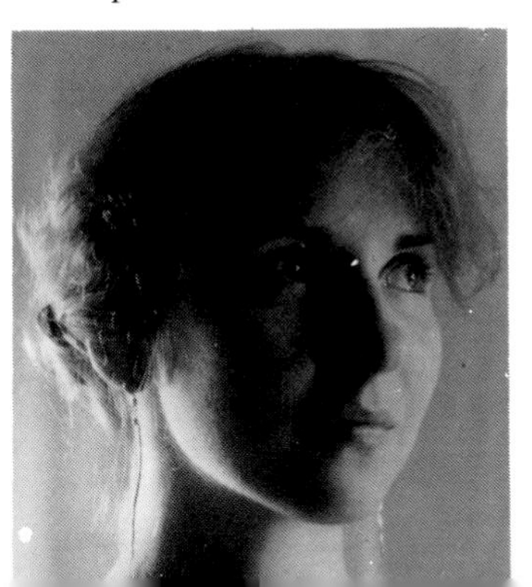

JANET THOMSON

As fitness consultant to Rosemary Conley, Janet Thomson worked on the Whole Body Programme 2 and 3, as well as the 1992 BBC series. She also choreographed Cosmopolitan's aerobics workout video, The Great Body Shape Tape, in addition to choreographing, designing and presenting the videos for the Kettler Step'n'Tone, for which she is currently designing a training programme. Originally trained at Farnborough College of Technology, Janet is now a part-time lecturer and course director for its Diploma in Fitness and Exercise Studies. She also designed and runs Pinks Teacher Training, RSA and Sports Council-approved exercise-to-music courses. A national representative for Fitness Professionals, Janet is also a freelance lecturer for many fitness companies and runs her own classes in Basingstoke.

NICHOLA FLETCHER

Glasgow-born Nichola Fletcher was trained as a jewellery designer, winning several major awards. She married John Fletcher, a vet researching wild deer, and together they started Britain's first deer farm. Reacting against the way other meats were intensively farmed at the time, they decided to produce quality meat with sympathy for animal welfare and the environment. Nichola became more involved in production and cooking of venison and now runs that side of the farm. She has written two books – Venison, The Monarch of the Table and Game for All, as well as editing another. She believes meat animals should be raised and fed on a diet of unprocessed food. After stress-free slaughter, the Fletchers' designer venison is carefully matured to bring out the characteristic flavour. She also offers a hotline advisory service.

GILLY METHERELL

Gilly Metherell is co-founder and managing director of the Real Meat Company. Born in Hampshire in1954, she spent her childhood in the New Forest and a year working on farms in Canada. After gaining a diploma in Agricultural Merchanting from Berkshire College of Agriculture, she started to rear pigs in 1978. She held various commodity trading positions in Sandy, Bedfordshire, and in the City of London before becoming non-contract grain manager for the Southern Counties Agricultural Trading Society. She married tenant farmer Richard Guy in 1985 and moved with her pigs to his Wiltshire farm. They co-founded the Real Meat Company and run it from there. The couple have two young daughters.

Photograph by David Wiltshire

HELEN BROWNING

Still only in her early 30s, Helen Browning had had the tenancy of her Wiltshire farm since 1989. With experience gained during earlier research work on a large organic farm and a degree in Agricultural Technology, she began large-scale conversion to organic methods, adding pigs and poultry to an already complex system. She bought her first shop in 1989 and began retailing organic meats, eggs, etc. Next came home curing and speciality sausage making. All her meats and eggs are now sold through her own outlets and she has a mail-order service. In 1990 Helen was named the Farmers' Weekly/BOCM Farming Woman of the Year. She is currently chairman of British Organic Farmers and a council member of the Home Grown Cereals Authority. She is married with a young daughter.

ANN REES

Ann Rees was brought up on a farm near Carmarthen. After education at the local grammar school, she married and began to help her husband's family with their Welsh produce business – cured bacon and hams, cooked meats, cheese, etc – which has markets all over West Wales. In 1989 her parents-in-law retired and Ann (with husband Chris) took over half the business, including a shop in Carmarthen. A mother of two, Ann has been a church organist for over 20 years and is an enthusiastic fundraiser for charity.

JUDY GOODMAN

The wife of a dairy farmer in Worcester, Judy Goodman started out in 1982 with 26 geese, as a hobby, and built Goodman Geese into a successful business with more than 2,000 free-range geese and 750 bronze turkeys. Because the goose is a seasonal bird, she encourages people to eat it at the "correct" times of the year – Christmas and Michaelmas (September 29). She is vice-chairman of the British Goose Producers Association and a member of the Advisory Board of the National Rural Enterprise Centre. The mother of three grown-up children, Judy takes a lively interest in husband Geoff's dairy farm and says she feels very strongly that consumers should buy British-produced food "so we can narrow the trade gap". The Financial Times recently described her as the most practical, down-to-earth, businesslike farmer you could hope to meet . . . fizzing with energy, good humour and marketing ideas.

LESLEY WARD

Lesley Ward saw 1992 as being an eventful year. She moved her shop into her own freehold premises. With the help of her husband, the Horsham Cheese Shop in Horsham, West Sussex, is a dream come true for Lesley – at one point she had two shops, so she feels she has exceeded her goal. Her success, she believes, is built on reputation, articulate staff and giving free samples. Lesley started with a small unit in an arcade and quickly moved into a proper shop. She holds an HND in Hotel & Catering Management and has experience of industrial catering management. Lesley's shop has won many awards. The most recent are 1990 South of England Winner, Best Delicatessen and 1991 National Winner of Retail Cheese Display Award. Married with one daughter, she lives in Cranleigh, Surrey.

MICHELLE BERRIEDALE-JOHNSON

It was after her son developed dairy product allergies that company director and writer Michelle Berriedale-Johnson launched her company, Berrydales, in 1987. For some years Michelle had run an up-market catering company specialising in authentic historic dinners set in period houses. She sold the company in the late 1980s to concentrate on writing and broadcasting. She has written over ten books – The Victorian Cookbook, Pepys at Table, special diet cookbooks, cookbooks for the disabled and How to Rescue Culinary Disasters. Michelle has a degree in history. She is an active member of the Guild of Food Writers and contributes regularly to magazines and newspapers as well as broadcasting on television and radio. She shares her busy life with her son and lives in London.

ZOE SAYER

Cheesemaker Zoe Sayer insists her success has come with the assistance of husband Peter and daughter Gemma. Zoe claims that Gemma, aged 17, must be one of the youngest cheesemakers in the country. The Welsh Farmhouse Cheese was already an established company when Zoe took over in 1990. She is still learning the craft and since taking over has added three more cheeses to the list. Zoe takes pride in claiming that all the milk is unpasteurised and that everything is done by hand. Some of her cheese is now exported to Germany. Husband Peter drives all over Wales and to parts of England to other outlets. Zoe considers herself very fortunate to live and work in the beautiful Teifi Valley in Dyfed with Peter and their daughter Gemma and son Jeremy.

NICOLETTE READ

Born in 1950, Nicolette Read married into the food business in 1975. She is currently chief administrator and girl Friday of Tastemasters Best of British Mail-Order Foods, established in 1988 by her husband. Nicolette was educated in Switzerland and later worked as a professional cook there. She then became a personal assistant/secretary to the chairman of a large cash & carry and hypermarket chain. Married with three daughters, Nicolette lives in Lockerley, Hants.

KAREN HINDLE

Enthusiasm and a shared love of food with her husband, Mark, were the ingredients Karen Hindle had when she opened her first Mousetrap Cheeseshop in Leominster, Herefordshire. Karen studied at Loughborough University in sporting sciences and took up teaching appointments in Leicester, Cambridge and Coggershall in Essex. Eight months after the opening of the Mousetrap Cheeseshop, its success and her disillusionment with the teaching profession encouraged her to resign as a supply teacher in Herefordshire and open the second Mousetrap Cheeseshop.

JUNE FOLDER

June Folder specialised in art at teacher training college. She taught the youngest boys in a prep school for several years. She met her husband, Joe Scottish country dancing, and they married in 1962. They started married life on a Cairmarthenshire smallholding, where June looked after the animals, grew vegetables and reared two children, while Joe ran a construction team, erecting grain silos. June also started a successful holiday business. They moved to Tything Barn, at West Williamson on the Milford Haven Estuary, in 1980, and, while continuing to run an enlarged and successful holiday business, started farming pacific oysters. They now produce a million oysters a year, of which half go for export, a quarter to distributors and by mail order and a quarter to other producers. In addition to providing all the round-the-clock back up to the business, June runs two holiday cottages and two caravans, with facilities for campers and independent caravanners, for visitors from Britain and five European countries.

MEG DORMAN

As a single mother with three children to support, Meg Dorman has set up and made a success of her own business under extremely difficult circumstances. She always baked delicious fruit cakes and was prompted by friends and family to turn her hobby into a business. In 1988, she opened her tiny shop and bakery in the village of Tysoe, in south Warwickshire, and Meg Rivers Cakes was born. It soon became clear that the greatest potential for the business lay in mail order and she now provides a unique, very personal and efficient service to customers all over the world. Meg publishes two illustrated catalogues each year and offers special occasion cakes: a Simnel cake at Easter; cakes for Mother's Day; Father's Day; Valentine's Day and a range of interesting variations for summer picnics, sporting events and special celebrations. Accompanied in the package by an appropriate bottle of wine, or a carefully chosen cup and saucer or cake plate, a Meg Rivers cake makes a memorable and unusual gift. For the more extravagant, she will provide hampers filled with cakes, shortbread, home-made jams, chutneys and mincemeat, spices, teas and wines. Meg Dorman's achievements were recognised in 1991, when she won the Women Mean Business – Best Newcomer Award and was overall winner of the Small Business Bureau's Women Into Business Award.

ROSEMARY KEEN

With her farmer husband, Roger, Rosemary Keen set up Sandridge Farmhouse Bacon six years ago, in response to complaints that English bacon and ham was lacking in flavour. Grain is grown on the 300 acre farm and mixed with whey for pig feed. Rosemary has named her selection of hams after the local towns and villages as they are spelt on a 17th century map of Wiltshire: The Brumham – the longest maturing ham, steeped in molasses and juniper berries, with a ruby red centre and strong flavour; The Trubridge – a dry cure similar to York ham; The Devyses – cured in beer and molasses, with the sweet flavour of hops and The Chipnam – the traditional Wiltshire cure, deep pink and firm when cut. In response to articles in the national press, Rosemary has now set up a mail order service from her farm shop, where visitors are very welcome to admire the pig herd.

JANE STAFFORD ALLEN

Jane Stafford Allen was born in Cheltenham in 1946, and brought up in India, where her father was in the jute trade. It was in India that she developed her interets in herbs and herbal remedies. Jane is a State Registered Nurse, a trained cook and has been awarded the Certificate of Herbal Studies by the National Institute of Medical Herbalists School of Herbal Medicine. With husband John, she started Candlesby Herbs from a kitchen garden, but now grows them on a five acre smallholding. In her workshop, wher the public is made welcome, she dries the herbs and prepares them for their various uses – medicinal, both internally and externally, decorative and culinary. The herbs are grown in the traditional way, and consist of old fashioned wild flowers, such as marsh mallow, as well as the more commonly associated plants. Jane lectures frequently on the benefits and practical uses of herbs, and has a regular spot on Radio Lincoln.

JANE FORESTIER-WALKER

Minola Smoked Products is a husband and wife partnership, founded and run by Jane Forestier-Walker and her husband Hugh. They started the business in 1984, having previously been in trout farming. Jane received tuition in smoking from the late Richard Pinney at the renowned Orford Smokery and Oysterage in Suffolk. The Minola Smokery is one of the few remaining traditional smokehouses, using whole English oak logs in traditional smoke pots. Jane's smoking technique produces a smoked salmon which is smoky without being salty, with a teriffic colour and texture. One customer comments: "Minola smoked salmon pleases many and offend a few, wheras the majority of smoked salmon pleases nobody and offends nobody." The Forestier-Walkers send many of their 40 smoked foods worldwide by air courier or first class mail. In the UK, individual caterers and private customers are supplied by overnight carrier. Jane and Hugh have recently opened a farm shop at the smokery, which is in the Cotswolds, near Burford, and where a tour of the smokehouses is welcomed.

Photograph by James Hawkins

INTRODUCTION

Welcome to the BEST OF BRITISH WOMEN HALL OF FAME. Most of the people who appear on the following pages do so, not necessarily because of any outstanding achievements in 1992, but because of long-term achievement, and the lasting impact which they have had on the lives of the British people. Some of their names will be very familiar and some, perhaps, virtually unknown. There are also women here who have achieved a degree of popularity or notoriety which makes them impossible to ignore in 1993. So here we have it, an amalgam of the great and the good, the famous and the infamous.

DIANE ABBOTT

Britain's first black woman MP, Diane Abbott, born to a Jamaican welder in Paddington, London, on 27 September 1953, was elected as Labour MP for Hackney North and Stoke Newington in 1987, part of the first intake of MPs from the Afro-Caribbean communities. Her 1989 attempt to set up a parliamentary black caucus, along the lines of the congressional group in America, was criticised by senior Labour Party members as a "party within a party" and petered out within a few months. After reading history at Newnham College, Cambridge, she worked for the National Council for Civil Liberties and was a TV researcher with Thames Television and reporter for TV-am. She is married to architect David Thompson and has a young son, James.

SHIRLEY WILLIAMS

One of the original Gang of Four who left the Labour Party in 1981 to found the Council for Social Democracy, which eventually became the SDP, Shirley Williams was born in 1930, daughter of political scientist George Caitlin and author Vera Brittain, studied at Oxford University and Columbia University, New York. After standing unsuccessfully in Harwich and Southampton Test, she was elected Labour MP for Hitchin in 1964. She had various junior posts in the Labour government of 1964-70 and was subsequently Secretary of State for Prices and Consumer Protection (1974-76) and Education Secretary (1976-79). She lost her seat, renamed Hertford and Stevenage in 1979 and, two years later, left to form the SDP. She was its president from 1981-88. She stood for the SDP as an MP in 1987. She was elevated to the House of Lords with a life peerage in 1993.

DAME SHIRLEY PORTER

Controversial former leader of Tory Westminster Council, Dame Shirley Porter, born on 29 November 1930 to the founder of the Tesco chain,She resigned in 1991, but was Lord Mayor for the next two years. During her leadership she had particular success in campaigns to clean up London's streets but was criticised for actions such as selling three cemetries for 15p. She was late entering politics, becoming a Tory councillor in 1974 after two years as a magistrate. Made a dame in 1991, she is married to Sir Leslie Porter and has two children, John and Linda.

BARONESS WARNOCK

Former mistress of Girtop College, Cambridge, Baroness Warnock was born Mary Wilson on 14 April 1924. She has become a leading authority on education. She read philosophy at Oxford and subsequently taught the subject, before becoming headmistress of Oxford High School. She chaired committees of inquiry into special education and human fertilisation, and a standing advisory committee on animal experimentation. Made a dame in 1984 and given a life peerage a year later, she is married to Sir Geoffrey Warnock, former vice-chancellor of Oxford University, and has two children.

DAME ANNETTE PENHALIGON

Widow of former Liberal MP David Penhaligon, who died in a car crash in 1986, Dame Annette Penhaligon has since been a tireless worker for the party. In 1992 she helped to start Cornwall's first commercial radio station, Pirte FM, which raises money for local charities. Husband David had been Liberal MP for Truro since 1974 and, during that time, was the Party's spokesman on employment, energy, industry and the treasury. She was made a dame in the 1993 New Year's Honours List.

BETTY BOOTHROYD

The House of Commons made history when, in 1992, it elected Betty Boothroyd as its first female Speaker. Born in Dewsbury, West Yorkshire on 8 October 1929, she was a member of the Tiller Girls dance troupe in the 1940s and had four attempts at getting into Parliament before finally becoming Labour MP for West Bromwich West in 1973. She was also a British member of the European Parliament for two years from 1975.

PRINCESS MARGARET

Younger daughter of George VI and the present Queen Mother, Princess Margaret was born at Glamis Castle, Tayside, on 21 August 1930, became a Sea Ranger during WWII and was subsequently the organisation's commodore. In October 1955, after two years of press stories that she wished to marry Group Captain Peter Townsend, an equerry to the Queen, she announced that she would not be doing so. He was a divorcee and she would have had to give up her right of succession to the throne. Such a marriage would also have been unacceptable to the public less than 20 years after the abdication of her uncle, Edward VIII, so that he could marry Mrs Wallis Simpson. In 1960 she wed Antony Armstrong-Jones, later to become Lord Snowdon, and subsequently had two children, Viscount Linley and Lady Sarah Armstrong-Jones, but the couple divorced in 1978. She lives at Kensington Palace and has a house on the Caribbean island of Mustique.

PRINCESS ALEXANDRA

Born in London on Christmas Day, 1936, daughter of Prince George and Princess Marina, Duke and Duchess of Kent, Princess Alexandra was only five when her father died in a plane crash during active service in the war. She became the first British princess to be taught in an ordinary school when she went to Heathfield and was one of the eight bridesmaids at the then Princess Elizabeth's wedding to the Duke of Edinburgh in 1947. She herself married Sir Angus Ogilvy at Westminster Abbey on 24 April 1963 and subsequently gave birth to two children, James and Marina.

THE QUEEN

After more than 40 years of rule, Queen Elizabeth II has been on the throne longer than all but five of her 39 predecessors since the Norman Conquest. Born at her grandmother's home, 17 Bruton Street, London, on 21 April 1926, daughter of the future George VI and Queen Elizabeth, Princess Elizabeth married Lt Philip Mountbatten – formerly Prince Philip of Greece – in 1947 and acceded to the throne five years later. The high point of her monarchy was the Silver Jubilee year, 1977, when she toured 36 counties in the United Kingdom in three months.

PRINCESS OF WALES

Lady Diana Spencer, born in Sandringham on 1 July 1961, third daughter of the then Viscount and Viscountess Althorp, is descended from both Charles II and James II. Her late father was a former equerry to George VI and the Queen. After her parents divorced, Viscount Althorp married Raine, Countess of Dartmouth, daughter of novelist Barbara Cartland. In 1981, after attending a Swiss finishing school and working as a nanny and kindergarten teacher, Lady Diana married Prince Charles. The couple announced their separation 11 years later.

THE QUEEN MOTHER

Daughter of Lord and Lady Glamis, Elizabeth Bowes-Lyon was born in London on 4 August 1900 and during WWI helped to run the family's home, Glamis Castle, as a hospital for the wounded. She married Prince Albert, Duke of York, second son of George V, at Westminster Abbey on 26 April 1923 and had a daughter, Princess Elizabeth, three years later. Following the death of George V and abdication of Edward VIII, the Duke and Duchess of York took over the throne as George VI and Queen Elizabeth and remained on it until the King's death in 1952, when they were succeeded by their daughter.

COUNTESS SPENCER

Born on 9 September 1929, daughter of Alexander McCorquodale and novelist Barbara Cartland, Raine, Countess Spencer, was only 19 years old when she married Gerald Legge – later Lord Dartmouth – and five years later began her own political career by winning a seat on Westminster City Council and adding to it another on the old London County Council in 1958. She was subsequently a member of the Greater London Council and in 1976, after her divorce, she married Earl Spencer, father of the Princess of Wales. She remained in the family home at Althorp until his death in 1992.

CAMILLA PARKER BOWLES

Shortly before the announcement of the Prince and Princess of Wales's separation in 1992, Camilla Parker Bowles was thrust into the limelight when the Australian magazine, New Idea, published the transcript of an intimate, bugged telephone call alleged to have taken place between her and Prince Charles in December 1989. She had been an early girlfriend of his before her wedding to Brigadier Andrew Parker Bowles and his to Diana. Charles is godfather to their son, Thomas, and the couple also have a daughter, Laura.

MARCHIONESS OF BLANDFORD

Estranged wife of the Marquess of Blandford, Jamie Spencer-Churchill – son of the Duke of Marlborough – Becky Few Brown married her husband in 1990 and subsequently had a baby son, George. The couple split up and she subsequently took legal action to enforce maintenance payments from the Marquess, a former junkie who had been addicted to heroine and cocaine.

LADY HELEN WINDSOR

Second child of the Duke and Duchess of Kent, Lady Helen Windsor, born in Buckinghamshire on 28 April 1964, followed an A level art course at Gordonstoun, where she was a contemporary of Prince Edward, with a job as a receptionist at the Mayor Gallery in Mayfiar, London. She subsequently worked in Christie's contemporary design department in London and moved to its New York office, before returning to London to work at the Karsten Schubert Gallery.

HON CAMILLA ASTOR

As the daughter of Lord Astor of Hever, whose father owned The Times, the Hon Camilla Astor stepped out as a 17-year-old débutante in 1992 while studying at St Geroge's, Ascot, for her A levels. At the end of the year, she was one of five débutantes flying off to New York for the International Debs' Ball, before leaving Britain to study history of art at the British Institute in Florence, Italy. Following her appearances on the catwalk at the Berkeley Dress Show during her Season, she was planning a career in modelling.

DUCHESS OF YORK

Daughter of Major Ronald and Susan Ferguson, Sarah Ferguson, born in London on 15 October 1959, took a secretarial course on leaving college and worked in a public relations firm, then a Covent Garden picture gallery, before joining a fine-art company and subsequently running its London office. Her parents divorced and both later married again, her mother wedding Argentine polo player Hector Barrantes. Her own marriage, to Prince Andrew, followed at Westminster Abbey on 23 July 1986 and the couple had two daughters, Beatrice and Eugenie. The announcement of the Duke and Duchess of York's separation, in 1992, came as a surprise to press and public alike.

JILL MORRELL

Girlfriend of Beirut hostage John McCarthy, Doncaster-born Jill Morrell campaigned relentlessly for his release after being captured in 1986. The couple both worked for the agency World Televison News. In January 1988, she formed the Friends of John McCarthy to fight for his freedom, but had to wait five years to be reunited with him, after his 1,943-day ordeal. She had originally worked as a secretary at WTN, before being promoted to the newsroom. By the time of John McCarthy's release, she had become a fully fledged television producer and was working on the Channel 4 current affairs programme The World This Week.

SALLY BURTON

Widow of actor Richard Burton, Sally Hay was educated at a convent in Birmingham and was a production assistant when she met the star in a studio canteen while he was filming Wagner, in 1982. She became his third wife the following year, but the couple had been married for only 13 months when he died of a cerebral haemorrhage. She subsequently made a BBC documentary, The Real Life of Hollywood Wives, and wrote a novel, The Barren Patch.

NORMA MAJOR

The wife of Prime Minster John Major, Norma Wagstaff was the daughter of a sergeant in the Royal Artillery who died in Holland in 1945, just three days after VE Day. Her mother subsequently reverted to her maiden name of Johnson. After going to boarding school, she attended Oakfield School, in Dulwich, South London, where actor Michael Crawford was a contemporary. In 1970 she married John Major and, since her husband became Prime Minister 20 years later, she has been writing a book about Chequers and has plans to turn Audrey Erskine Lindop's novel the Way To the Lantern into a film script.

JULIA MORLEY

Nicknamed Mrs World, Julia Morley saw the Miss World contest that she had organised for 40 years disappear from British TV screens in 1991. It had once been a spectacle that attracted some of television's biggest audiences, but ITV dropped it at the end of the 1980s, following protests that it was outdated and sexist. The BBC had previously axed it when, in 1984, Michael Grade declared the contest "an anachronism". The managing director of the Miss World Group, married to co-organiser Eric Morley, has four sons. Their daughter, Katy, died of an incurable disease of the central nervous system at the age of 17.

LADY ARCHER

Wife of best-selling novelist Jeffrey Archer, Dr Mary Archer, born Mary Weeden in Surrey on 22 December 1944, has had an equally distinguished career as a chemist. After graduating from Oxford, she lectured both there and at Cambridge University. She gave up lecturing to sit on various committees and boards of directors, including that of Anglia Television. She was the first woman to be elected to the Council of Lloyd's. In 1992 she demonstrated another of her talents, releasing a record of Christmas carols, with royalties split between two choirs and the Iris Fund for prevention of blindness.

FAY WELDON

Born in Alvechurch, Worcestershire, on 22 February 1931, Fay Birkinshaw grew up in New Zealand and was later educated in Britain. She was a writer for the Foreign Office and the Daily Mirror, before working in advertising. Her first novel, The Fat Woman's Joke, was published in 1967 and her feminist writing has mainly concentrated on women as mothers and men exploiting women in domestic circumstances. Her other novels include Down Among the Women, The Life and Loves of a She-Devil, The Heart of the Country and The Cloning of Joanna May, the last three all adapted for television. In 1961 she married antiques dealer Ron Weldon, who has since become a painter and jazz trumpeter.

DAME CATHERINE COOKSON

Growing up amid poverty in the North East, Catherine Cookson, born illegitimately in Tyne Dock on 20 June 1906, moved to Sussex at the age of 18 to get a job in a workhouse, becoming its laundry manager. She married Tom Cookson in 1940 and suffered the tragedy of losing four babies and subsequently had a nervous breakdown. She started writing in her mid-40s and uses the working classes of the North East as her subject. He 90-plus books include the Mallen series, The Fifteen Streets, The Black Velvet Crown and The Black Candle. She was made a dame in 1993.

LADY ANTONIA FRASER

Distinguishing herself by writing both fiction and historical works, Lady Antonia Fraser, born Antonia Pakenham, daughter of Lord Longford, in London on 27 August 1932, read history at Oxford University, before going into publishing. She started writing children's history books and books for collectors of dolls and toys, before writing her first biography, Mary Queen of Scots, and following it with books on Oliver Cromwell and Charles II. She has also written fiction, including A Splash of Red and other books on which the Jemima Shore Investigates TV series was based. She married playwright Harold Pinter after her divorce from Sir Hugh Fraser.

BERYL BAINBRIDGE

After 11 years as an actress in repertory theatre, Beryl Bainbridge, born in Formby, Lancashire, on 21 November 1934, worked as a cellarwoman in a bottle factory and as a clerk. By then she had already had some success with her fiction, with two of her books runners-up for the Booker prize. Her writing usually centres on a death or act of violence, and her books have included The Dressmaker, Sweet William, Young Adolf and Forever England. Divorced from Austin Davies, she has one son and two daughters, one of whom, Rudi Davies, is the actress who played the author as a teenager in a stage version of her autobiographical novel An Awfully Big Adventure. She has also written various plays, including Tiptoe Through the Tulips, The Warriors Return and Journal of Bridget Hitler.

DAME IRIS MURDOCH

On leaving Oxford University, Iris Murdoch, born in Dublin on 15 July 1919, became a civil servant in the Treasury, before spending two years working in a Displaced Persons Camp in the French zone of Austria after the war, where she met Jean-Paul Sartre. In 1953 she wrote her first book, Sartre – Romantic Rationalist, and her subsequent novels, filled with philosophy, have included Under the Net, A Severed Head, The Black Prince and The Sea, The Sea. She was made a dame in 1987.

JILLY COOPER

Born in Hornchurch, Essex, on 21 February 1937, Jilly Cooper was a junior reporter on the Middlesex Independent, in Brentford, and worked as a copywriter and publisher's reader, before becoming a columnist for the The Sunday Times, Mail On Sunday and Daily Mail. After writing books about class and country life, she turned to racy novels full of steamy affairs and torrid romances. They were an instant hit, with titles such as Riders, Rivals and Polo.

DORIS LESSING

A writer whose work has focused on the politics and culture of the post-modern world, Doris Lessing, born in Persia on 22 October 1919 and raised in Southern Rhodesia, wrote her first novel, The Grass Is Singing, in 1950. She followed it with books such as The Golden Notebook, five Children of Violence novels and The Memoirs of a Survivor. Less successful were her attempts at science fiction, including Landlocked and Briefing for a Descent Into Hell. Divorced twice, she has three children.

MURIEL SPARK

After working in the Political Intelligence Department of the British Foreign Office during WWII, Edinburgh-born Muriel Spark became general secretary of the Poetry Society and editor of Poetry Review. She wrote many poems and biographies of Mary Shelley and the Brontës, before turning to novels. Her books include The Prime of Miss Jean Brodie, The Mandelbaum Gate and The Abess of Crewe.

RUTH RENDELL

The queen of crime writers, Ruth Rendell, born in London on 17 February 1930, started her career as a newspaper journalist but, at the age of 33, wrote her first novel, From Doon with Death, which introduced Inspector Wexford to the world. Her Wexford books have been adapted for TV, as was Gallowglass. She has written some novels under the pseudonym Barbara Vine.

JEANETTE WINTERSON

One of Britain's most promising up-and-coming novelists, Jeanette Winterson, born in Lancashire on 27 August 1959, left Oxford University to do make-up in a funeral parlour, drive an ice-cream van and work in a mental hospital. After a spell working at the Roundhouse theatre in London, she became an editor for Brilliance Books, the gay publishers, and while there wrote her first novel, Oranges Are Not the Only Fruit, an autobiographical work recounting her break with Pentecostal Church as the result of a lesbian affair. The book was a best-seller and subsequently adapted for television, winning a BAFTA award. She followed it with The Passion, Sexing the Cherry and Written On the Body. She also wrote the screen play for the film Great Moments In Aviation.

TWIGGY LAWSON

In a career that has spanned modelling, singing and acting, Twiggy, born Lesley Hornby in London on 19 September 1949, came to prominence in the late 1960s. She made her film debut in The Boy Friend, in 1971. Her greatest acting success came on stage, appearing on Broadway in My One and Only. On record, she has a Top 20 single with Here I Go Again. After the death of her first husband, she married actor Leigh Lawson.

FIONA FULLERTON

Since making her professional debut in the film Run Wild, Run Free at the age of 11, Fiona Fullerton, born in Daduna, Nigeria, on 10 October 1956, has appeared in films such as the James Bond drama A View To a Kill, on TV in Angels and mini-series such as To Be the Best, and on stage in Gypsy and The Boy Friend. Divorced from actor Simon MacCorkindale, she was also the girl in the Max Factor advertisements.

ANITA DOBSON

Since making her name as landlady Angie Watts in EastEnders, Anita Dobson, born in the East End of London herself, on 29 April 1949, has had mixed fortunes, starring on TV in the hairdressing comedy Split Ends and as a stripper in The World of Eddie Weary, as well as in a flop stage version of Budgie and My Lovely... Shayna Maidel, as a concentration camp survivor.

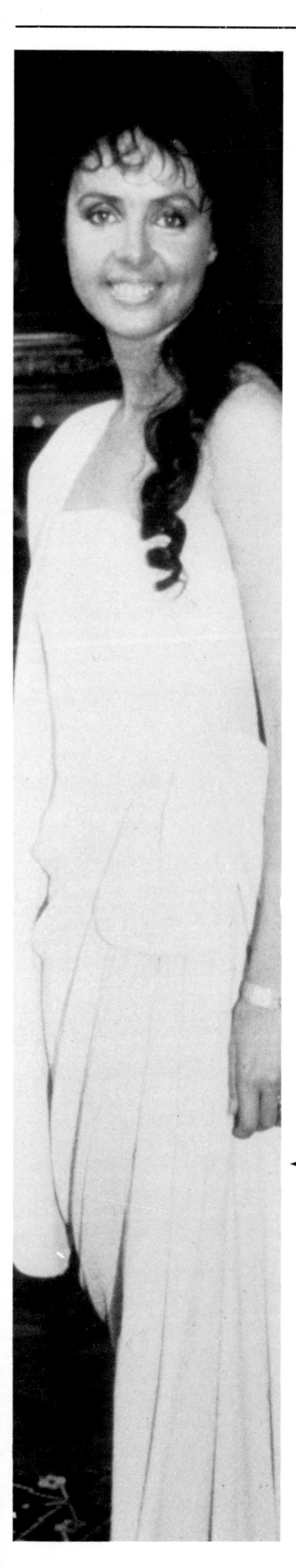

CILLA BLACK

Beginning her career at The Iron Door Club in her native Liverpool, Cilla Black, born Priscilla White on 27 May 1943, went on to become a pop star of the 1960s with hits such as Anyone Who Had a Heart, You're My World and Alfie. After her own light-entertainment show on television, she branched out with a situation-comedy, Cilla's World of Comedy, before becoming one of Britain's top TV presenters, hosting Surprise, Surprise and Blind Date. Married to her manager, Bobby Willis, she has three sons, Robert, Banjamin and Jack.

SARAH BRIGHTMAN

After leading the raunchy dance group Hot Gossip to Top 10 success with the single I Gave My Heart To a Starship Trooper, Sarah Brightman, born on 14 August 1961, rose the dizzy heights of musical theatre from dancing in Andrew Lloyd Webber's Cats to starring in the première of his Requiem and, ultimately, The Phantom of the Opera. She and the composer were divorced in 1990, after seven years of marriage, but she still starred in his musical Aspects of Love.

JOAN COLLINS

Daughter of the late theatrical agent Joe Collins and sister of novelist Jackie, Joan Collins, born in London on 23 May 1933, boosted her flagging film career in the 1970s with the soft-porn cinema hits The Stud and The Bitch, before starring as Alexis in Dynasty. Four times married and divorced, she has also written half-a-dozen books, including the novel Prime Time.

RULA LENSKA

Born Rozamaria Lubienska in St Neots, Huntingdonshire, on 30 September 1947, Rula Lenska trained as a secretary but switched to acting and eventually made her name in the TV series Rock Follies, about an all-girl group. She subsequently starred in the comedy series Take a Letter Mr Jones, as the boss dictating letters to secretary John Inman. After her marriage to actor Brian Deacon ended in divorce, she wed another actor, Dennis Waterman, but the couple have since split up. She has a daughter, Lara, from her first marriage, and is fluent in Polish, French, Italian and German.

MARTI CAINE

A winner on the TV talent show New Faces in 1975, comedienne Marti Caine, born in Sheffield on 26 January 1945, went on to star in her own series and a situation-comedy, Hilary, before hosting a revival of New Faces. She started her career as a photographic model, before becoming a singer in working men's clubs. Divorced from her manager, Malcolm Stringer, with whom she had two sons, Lee and Max, she is now married to TV producer Kenneth Ives.

LYNSEY DE PAUL

As a singer and songwriter, Lynsey de Paul had hits with singles such as Sugar Me and No Honestly – theme from the TV comedy series – as well as a Eurovision song contest duet, Rock Bottom, with Mick Moran in 1977. She gave up singing and left Britain for America, living with actor James Coburn for four years, before returning home to set up a music publishing business, as well as writing and producing. She also starred in the London West End musical Pump Boys and Dinettes. In 1992 she made a TV documentary on self-defence, Eva Strikes Back, after being attacked herself by another woman.

CATHERINE ZETA JONES

As Mariette in ITV's adaptation of H E Bates' The Darling Buds of May stories, Swansea-born Catherine Zeta Jones was cast as the perfect English rose, although the role came only a year after she had stripped off to play a slave girl in the French film Scheherazade. She also appeared topless in Out of the Blue, a BBC play, and acted on stage in a tour of The Pyjama Game and the London West End hit 42nd Street, progressing from the chorus line to be its star. Her professional career began at the age of 11, in the musical Annie.

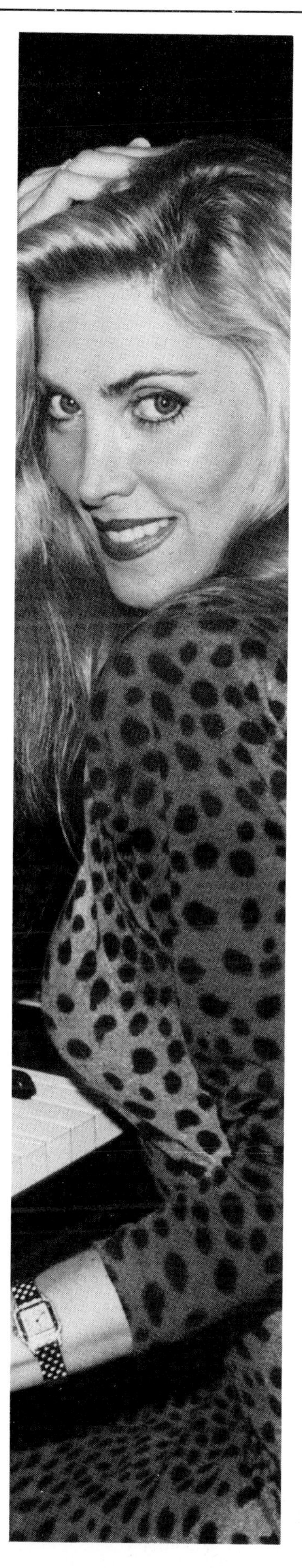

JANE SEYMOUR

Born Joyce Frankenberg in Hillingdon, Middlesex, on 15 February 1951, Jane Seymour began her career as a dancer with the London Festival Ballet at the age of 13, before turning to acting. She made her name as the heroine in the 1973 James Bond film Live and Let Die and subsequently became the star of many TV movies, most notably East of Eden, Jamaica Inn and The Woman He Loved, as well as the television series War and Rembrance.

SUSAN HAMPSHIRE

Before finding success in TV period dramas such as The Forsythe Saga and The Pallisers, Susan Hampshire, born in London on 12 May 1938, appeared in the film The Woman In the Hall at the age of nine, then trained as a ballet dancer and spent a year with the Festival Ballet when she was 15 years old. When she grew too tall for ballet, she switched to acting and gained her experience in repertory theatre. She has recently had success with her gardening books

EMMA THOMPSON

Born in London on 15 April 1959, the daughter of actor Eric Thompson – who narrated the original Magic Roundabout series – Emma Thompson made her mark in the TV series Tutti Frutti and Fortunes of War, where she met actor-director Kenneth Branagh, whom she married in 1989. She has also appeared with him in the films Henry V and Dead Again and a television version of Look Back In Anger, as well as starring in her own TV show.

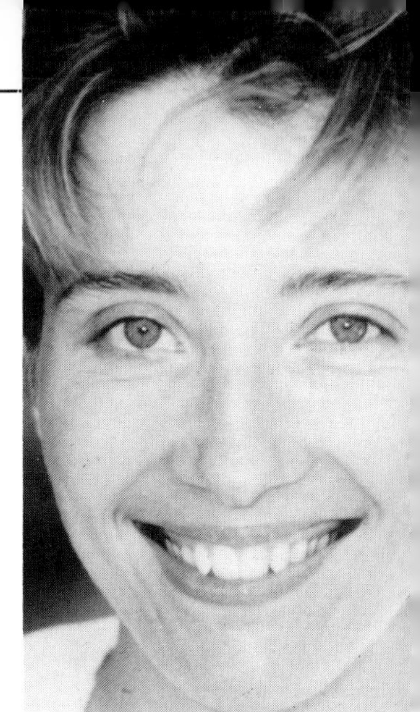

PATRICIA HODGE

Born in Cleethorpes, Lincolnshire, on 29 September 1946, Patricia Hodge was brought up in Grimsby, where her parents ran a hotel. She trained as a teacher and taught for a year before switching careers and becoming one of Britain's most in-demand actresses. On TV she has played Phyllida Erskine-Brown in Rumpole of the Bailey and the title roles in Jemima Shore Investigates and The Cloning of Joanna May. Married to musician Peter Owen, she gave birth in her 40s to two sons.

ELAINE PAIGE

Better known now as a singer, it was as an actress that Elaine Paige, born in London on 5 March began her career, even popping up as Caroline Winthrop in an episode of Crossroads. She appeared in the film Oliver! and on TV in Love Story and The Ladykillers, before making her name as Eva Peron in the Andrew Lloyd Webber musical Evita, following it as Grizabella in Cats and Florence in Chess. She and Barbara Dickson had a No 1 single with the duet I Know Him So Well, from Chess.

CHARLOTTE RAMPLING

From a career in modelling, Charlotte Rampling, born in Sturmer, Cambridgeshire, in 1946, landed a small role as a water-skiier in the film The Knack . . . And How To Get It, before getting the lead in the Boulting Brothers' Rotten To the Core. One of her most memorable roles was as a neurotic actress in Woody Allen's Stardust Memories. As a fluent linguist, she has also appeared in French and Italian films, and is married to musician Jean-Michel Jarre.

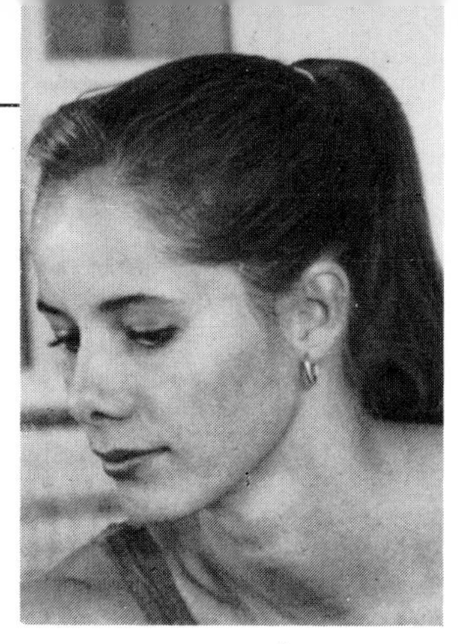

DARCEY BUSSELL

Britain's brightest young ballerina, Darcey Bussell, born on 27 April 1969, became principal dancer with the Royal Ballet at the age of 20 and is being tipped as heir to Dame Margot Fonteyn's crown. She became an overnight star in the world premiere of Prince of Pagodas, in a role created specially for her by choreographer Sir Kenneth MacMillan and performed at the Queen Mother's 90th Birthday Tribute. She recovered from a hip injury in 1992 to star as Princess Aurora in The Sleeping Beauty, at the Royal Opera House. Opera House.

PRUNELLA SCALES

Destined to be forever known as Sybil Fawlty in the classic comedy series Fawlty Towers, Prunella Scales, born Prunella Illingworth in Sutton Abinger, Surrey, on 22 June 1932, also starred on TV in Mapp and Lucia and as Sarah in the long-running comedy After Henry. Married to actor Timothy West, she has performed her favourite role in Queen Victoria: Evening At Osborne at many theatres and played Elizabeth II in the TV movie A Question of Attribution.

JULIET STEVENSON

One of the greatest talents to emerge on the British stage and screen in recent years, Juliet Stevenson has played many of Shakespeare's heroines for the RSC, appeared in the TV series Maybury and The Mallens, and made a great impression in the films Drowning By Numbers and Truly Madly Deeply, which won her the 1991 London Evening Standard Best Actress award.

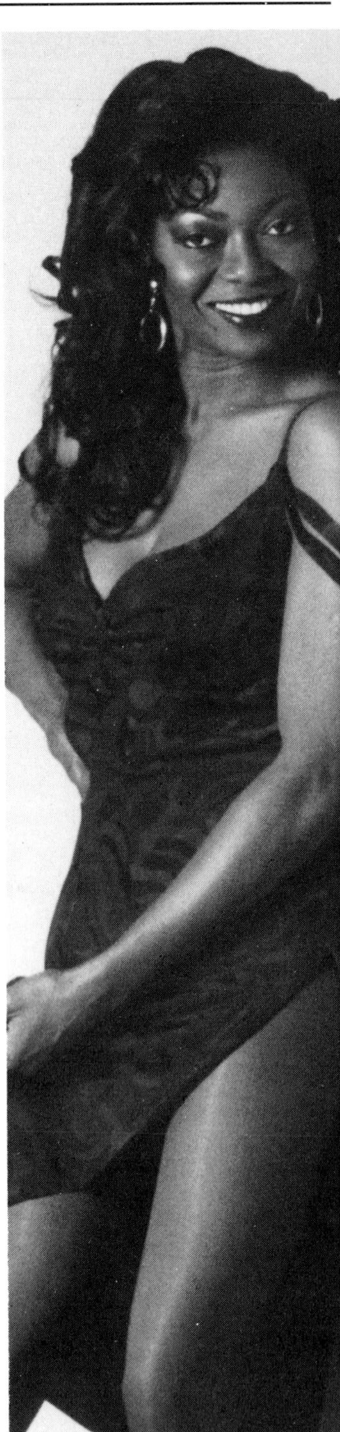

SAMANTHA FOX

Britain's most famous Page Three Girl, Samantha Fox switched from nude modelling to singing when her pop career took off with hits such as Touch Me (I Want Your Body), Naughty Girls and I Wanna Have Some Fun. She gave up her Page Three crown in 1987, at the age of 21, and has since found fame as a singer throughout Europe, Russia, India, the Far East and America. She has had No 1 records in 15 different countries. She moved to America and concentrated on touring abroad as her popularity in Britain diminished. As presenter of pop music's Brit Awards in 1989 she was less than successful.

PATSY KENSIT

As a child Patsy Kensit, born in London on 4 March 1968, appeared in TV commercials, alongside Robert Redford in the film The Great Gatsby and Elizabeth Taylor in The Blue Bird, and in TV series such as The Foundation. As she grew up she looked for fame as a pop star in the group Eighth Wonder, who had a handful of hit singles. After an appearance in the disastrous Absolute Beginners, her film career was revived with a role in Lethal Weapon 2. Following the break-up of her marriage to Big Audio Dynamite keyboards player Dan Donovan, she married Simple Minds singer Jim Kerr and has a son called James.

PATTI BOULAYE

Nigerian-born singer and actress made a name for herself in 1970s musicals such as Jesus Christ Superstar and Hair, after training at the London Academy of Music and Dramatic Art. Married to Stephen Komlosy, she has two children, Emma and Sebastian.

EMILY LLOYD

Daughter of actor Roger Lloyd Pack (Trigger in Only Fools and Horses), Emily Lloyd was born in North London in 1971. She found instant stardom as the rebellious 1950s teenager Lynda in her debut film Wish You Were Here, aged just 16. Courted by Hollywood, she appeared on Johnny Carson's American television show and subsequently starred in the films Cooke, with Peter Falk and Jerry Lewis, In Country and Chicago Joe and The Showgirl.

LESLEY JOSEPH

Finding stardom as man-eating Dorien in the BBC comedy series Birds of a Feather, after a career of bit-parts, led to actress Lesley Joseph, 44, getting the lead role of Angela Temple in the radio role of Angela Temple in the radio comedy Queen of Romance. She also appeared on television in the quiz programme Ps and Qs and presented a Lesley Joseph At Large spot on the BBC weekday programme Good Morning . . . With Anne and Nick. She played four different characters in the stage show Singular Women. A single parent, she has two children, Andrew and Elizabeth.

SANDIE SHAW

Britain's leading lady of 1960s pop, Sandie Shaw, born Sandra Goodrich in Dagenham, Essex, on 26 February 1947, worked as an IBM machine operator before being spotted and signed to a record contract. Her first single (There's) Always Something There To Remind Me, in 1964, was a No 1, as was her Eurovision Song Contest winner, Puppet On A String, three years later. She failed to make the charts in the 1970s but returned with a couple of hits in the 1980s. Divorced from Clothes Show presenter Jeff Banks, she is now married to film executive Nik Powell.

SUE LAWLEY

Since leaving the BBC in 1991, Sue Lawley, born in Dudley, Worcestershire, on 14 July 1946, has been seen only occasionally on television in her Granada interview programmes for ITV. She has continued as presenter of Desert Island Discs on radio. Starting her career in newspapers, with the Western Mail and South Wales Echo in Cardiff, she entered television with BBC Plymouth in 1970, before becoming a presenter of the early evening magazine programme Nationwide two years later. She was also a presenter of the revived Tonight, then a BBC news reader, first on the Nine O'Clock News, then the Six O'Clock News. While at the BBC she was a stand-in host of Wogan and Question Time. She is married to Roger Williams and has two children from her first marriage, to David Ashby.

ANNEKA RICE

Since making her name as the skyrunner in Treasure Hunt, regularly Channel 4's most popular programme, Anneka Rice, 34, has appeared on all BBC and commercial channels, with shows such as Challenge Anneka and Play It Safe!, although she was less successful as presenter of the Holiday programme. Married to theatre producer Nick Allott, she has two sons, Thomas and Joshua.

ANNABEL CROFT

Britain's former No 1 female tennis player, Annabel Croft, born in Kent on 12 July 1966, changed career at the age of 21 to become a television personality. She took over from Anneka Rice as skyrunner in Treasure Hunt and followed it with the less successful Interceptor series. In 1992 she returned to the tennis world by taking part in the Volkswagen National Championships. She recently became engaged to yachtsman Mel Coleman, who had been adviser on the sailing programme Cudmore's Call, her first TV series. As well as her television work she has appeared in pantomimes such as Dick Whittington and Cinderella.

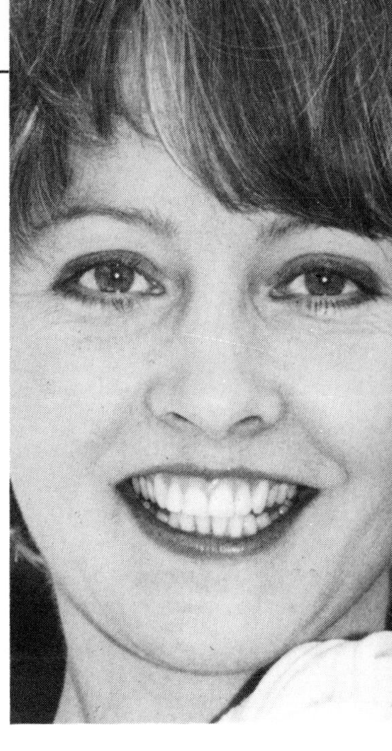

ANNE DIAMOND ▲

From a local newspaper career in Bridgwater and Bournemouth, Anne Diamond, born in Birmingham on 8 September 1954, went into television as a reporter with ATV, which later became Central Television. After a short stint on the BBC's Nationwide, she joined TV-am and boosted its flagging ratings. Since then she has presented TV Weekly and Gooding Morning . . . With Anne and Nick.

PAULA YATES ▼

Daughter of TV presenter and producer Jess Yates, Paula Yates was born in Colwyn Bay on 24 April 1960. She first made her name as co-host of the pop show The Tube in 1982. Ten years later she became a presenter of The Big Breakfast on Channel 4. In between she wrote a string of books, including the best-selling Blondes, Rocks Stars In Their Underpants and Sex With Paula, and presented programmes such as Baby, Baby. She is married to Bob Geldof and has three daughters.

DELIA SMITH ▲

After working in a hair salon and a travel agency, Delia Smith, born in Woking, Surrey, on 18 June 1941, learned the art of cookery in a London restaurant and went on to appear in TV commercials and write a cookery column in a Sunday newspaper, before landing her own instructional television programmes. Married to writer Michael Wynn Jones, she has also written many cookery books.

SELINA SCOTT ▼

Born in Scarborough on 13 May 1951, on graduating from the University of East Anglia, Selina Scott, joined publishers DC Thomson in Dundee, and was then a reporter for Grampian Television. She subsequently made her name as an ITN newscaster and has since been a presenter of Breakfast Time, The Clothes Show, West 57th (for CBS of America), Entertainment Express and Sky News.

MARINA MOWATT

Britain's most outrageous Royal, Marina Ogilvy, born on 31 July 1966, daughter of Princess Alexandra and Sir Angus Ogilvy, made headlines in 1989 when she announced that she was to have a child by her photographer boyfriend Paul Mowatt. She eventually married him before daughter Zenouska was born, but had already caused more damage to the Royal Family with hurtful allegations against her parents, which were discovered to be unfounded. A talented pianist, she graduated from the Royal School of Music and, determined to rail against the Establishment, has since posed on a dummy throne with a litter of corgis and accepted the Rear of the Year award. Turning to modelling after the birth of her daughter, she paraded Vivienne Westwood designs on the Paris catwalk.

NIGELLA LAWSON

Daughter of former Chancellor of the Exchequer Nigel Lawson, Nigella Lawson caused a stir with the National Union of Journalists when she was taken on by The Sunday Times without any previous experience. Observer editor Donald Trelford had previously vetoed an appointment there. Following her degree in modern languages from Oxford she worked for the book publishers Quartet. She has since written as a freelance for publications such as The Spectator, once edited by her father and now by her brother, Dominic. She is married to journalist John Diamond.

LYNDA LEE-POTTER

One of Britain's top columnists, Lynda Lee-Potter puts across her views on the Royal Family, celebrities and any topical issues of the day in the Daily Mail. Born Lynda Higginson in Lancashire, she trained as an actress at drama school before entering journalism. She is married to Dr Jeremy Lee-Potter, now consultant haematologist at Poole General Hospital, and the couple lived in Aden, where he was an RAF squadron leader and she wrote a column for the Aden Chronicle, Back in Britain, she became a feature writer on the Daily Mail and, when Jean Rook moved to the Daily Express, took over her weekly column.

TINA BROWN

Former editor of the glossy, high society British magazine Tatler, Tina Brown, born on 21 November 1953, daughter of film producer George Brown, moved to America in 1984 to become editor-in-chief of Vanity Fair. Eight years later, she was controversially appointed to the same job on the high-brow magazine The New Yorker. Married to former Sunday Times editor Harold Evans, she has also written two books and two plays.

MARJE PROOPS

Britain's leading agony aunt, Marjorie Proops has been with the Daily Mirror since 1939, leaving for a ten year spell after the war to work for the Daily Herald, before returning to the Mirror. She has written two books, Pride, Prejudice and Proops and Dear Marje, and was awarded the OBE in 1969.

JULIE BURCHILL

Reputed to be Britain's highest-paid female journalist, Julie Burchill, born in Bristol first came to prominence in her teens as a writer on New Musical Express during the punk era of the 1970s. She has since written columns for The Face, Arena, The Sunday times and the Mail On Sunday, and two novels. Divorced from her former New Musical Express colleague, Tony Parsons, she has since wed American writer Cosmo Landesman. She has sons from both marriages.

STELLA RIMINGTON

The first head of MI5 to be named, and first woman to hold the post, Stella Rimington, born in south Norwood, London in 1935, was educated at Edinburgh University and worked as a principal in the tariff division of the Board of Trade before being recruited by the Security Service in 1969. In the F2 branch, she monitored domestic "subversives", including trade unions, then was promoted to direct counter-terrorist activities. Separated from her husband – Health and Safety Executive director-general John Rimington – she became director-general of MI5 in February 1992.

HELEN SHARMAN

Britain's first astronaut, Helen Sharman, born in Sheffield on 30 May 1963, gained a chemistry degree from Sheffield University, before becoming a research technologist with Mars Confectionery. She joined the Anglo-Soviet Juno mission in 1991, carrying out medical and biological tests 250 miles above Earth, and was awarded the OBE two years later.

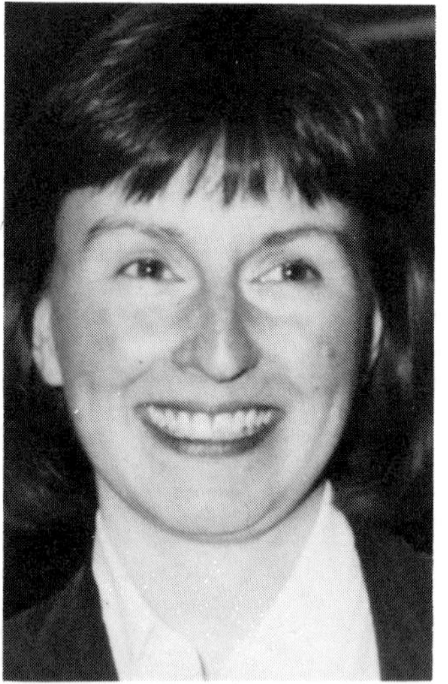

ANNE SNELLING

Moving from her position as deputy head at an Essex comprehensive to become head of Stratford School, in Newham, East London, in 1991, resulted in a head-on confrontation with the school's governors for Anne Snelling. The opt-out school was fighting for its survival when she arrived, with governors having won a battle against Newham Council for grant-maintained status, but at the expense of losing many pupils. The governors ousted the chairman and then tried to do the same to their new head, accusing her of racism in a school with a large number of Asians. She was suspended for five days for gross professional misconduct but won the battle to keep control of the school when Education Secretary Kenneth Clarke ruled the suspension groundless. She was awarded an OBE in the 1993 New Year's Honours List.

SISTER WENDY BECKETT

As a nun with a special love of art, Sister Wendy Beckett, born in Edinburgh and brought up in South Africa, became a media star in 1992 as presenter of Sister Wendy's Odyssey, a television series in which she visited galleries and museums to see her favourite paintings. After becoming a nun at the age of 16, she gained an English degree at Oxford and taught with the Nôtre Dame order in South Africa until forced to give up through ill health. She wrote a book about contemporary women artists and talked about Rembrandt in a 1991 TV programme about the National Gallery, The Much Loved Friend. She lives in a caravan in the grounds of the Carmelite Convent at Quidenham, in Norfolk.

MARY GLEN HAIG

Since her days as a sportswoman, Mary Glen Haig, born on 12 July 1918, has become one of Britain's leading sports campaigners and administrators. She was British ladies' foil champion between 1948 and 1950, captained the ladies' foil team for seven years, took part in four Olympic Games and won two Commonwealth gold medals. In 1966 she became a member of the Sports Council and has been vice-president of the Central Council of Physical Recreation since 1982, after a term as president, during which she campaigned vigorously for more sponsorship in sport and less taxation. A member of the International Olympic Committee, she was made a Dame Commander in 1993.

SCORPIO

One of the stars of Gladiators, which came to British TV screens in 1992 and was based on a successful American programme, Scorpio – real name Nikki Diamond – was one of the resident Gladiators trying to stop super-fit contestants completing gruelling tests. She and husband Mike have a young daughter, Emily.

LORRAINE CHASE

After success as a model led her to become the girl in the Campari drink commercials with the catchprase "Luton Airport", Lorraine Chase, born in South London on 16 July 1951, landed her own TV situation-comedy, The Other 'Arf, and followed it with another series, Lame Ducks, as well as guest appearances in Worzel Gummidge and quiz shows such as Blankety Blank and Celebrity Squares. She was in the Charles Bronson film Love and Bullets and on stage in the Young Vic's Pygmalion, a national tour of Little Shop of Horrors and the West End hits Me and My Girl and Run for Your Wife.

CLEO ROCOS

After finding fame as Miss Whiplash, dressed in suspenders and brandishing a whip in The Kenny Everett Show on TV, voluptuous Greek actress Cleo Rocos went on to appear in the film Number One Gun. She made a bigger splash by falling into then Liberal leader David Steel's arms at a celebrity party, with her breasts popping out from the top of her dress.

MANDY SMITH

Former teenaged wife of Rolling Stone Bill Wyman, Mandy Smith and the rock star divorced in 1992 after three years of marriage, with her receiving a £580,000 settlement, including their three-bedroom house in Muswell Hill, North London. The couple had met at the British Rock and Pop Awards in 1984, when she was only 13 years old.

ANTONIO DE SANCHA

An affair with Conservative MP David Mellor gave half-Spanish, half-Swedish actress Antonio de Sancha the publicity she so desperately needed. Since training at RADA, acting work had been scarce, with roles as a one-legged prostitute in a blue film called The Pieman and as Clytemnestra, who murdered her husband, in a fringe production of the Greek tragedy Agamemnon.

INDEX

NOMINATION FORM

I would like to nominate the following person for inclusion in the Best of British Guides 1994.

Name ____________________

Address ____________________

____________________ Postcode ____________________

Tel No. (Home) ____________________ Tel No. (Work) ____________________

Occupation ____________________

Category of Nomination

Reason for Nomination

Proposer's Name ____________________

Address ____________________

____________________ Postcode ____________________

Tel No. (Home) ____________________ Tel No. (Work) ____________________

Occupation ____________________

Signature ____________________

NOMINATION CATEGORIES

These categories change from time to time and if you feel a new category is required please let us know.

- Hoteliers
- Restaurateurs
- Chefs
- Housekeepers
- Publicans/B&Bs
- Wine and Food
- Wine Producers/Brewers
- Cooks and Courses
- Party Organisers
- TV Personalities
- Theatre
- Actresses
- Dance
- Film
- Music – Classical
- Music – Jazz
- Pop Music
- Folk
- Music Industry
- Art Intro
- Artists/Sculptors
- Applied Arts
- Craftswomen
- Country Craftswomen
- Gallery Owners
- Antiques
- Fashion Intro
- Hats, Bags and Shoes
- Ready To Wear
- Bridalwear
- Dress Hire/Secondhand Clothing
- Fashion Specialists
- Jewellery
- Hairdressers
- Beauty
- Models
- Model Agents
- Sports Intro/Rugby Union
- Skiing/Skating/Ice Hockey/Bobsleigh
- Hockey/Netball/Lacrosse
- Tennis
- Athletics
- Cricket/Golf
- Horse Racing
- Equestrian
- Yachting
- Archery/Croquet/Fencing/Bowls
- Watersports
- Martial Arts
- Shooting/Fishing
- Paralympics
- Paralympic Athletes
- Environmentalists
- Osteopaths/Physios/Chiropractors
- Nutritionists
- Alternative Therapy
- Health Clubs/Gym2
- Children's World
- Children's Fashion
- Community Services
- Charity
- Public Relations
- Advertising
- PAs and Secretaries
- Magazine Editors
- Book Publishers/Editors
- Literary, Film and Theatrical Agents
- Literature
- Entrepreneurs
- Business
- Finance
- Pawn Brokers
- Vintage Cars
- Head Hunters
- Introduction Agencies
- Recruitment
- Interior Designers/Decorators
- Florists
- Interior Designers
- Inventors/Innovators
- Media
- TV Industry
- Radio – Women
- Entertainers – Comedy
- Disc Jockeys
- After Dinner Speakers
- Lookalikes
- Adventurers
- Astrologers
- British Travel
- Pilots
- Motorcyclists
- Horticulture
- Vets
- Animal People
- Farming
- Indoor Games
- Astronomers/Physicists
- Lawyers
- Education
- Complementary Medicine
- Paranormal
- Graphologists/Numerologists/Tarot
- Healers
- Mediums/Psychics
- Property
- Politics
- Photographers
- Personal Trainers
- Food
- Hall Of Fame
- Medical Specialists

Please return form to Nominations Editor, Best of British Eldon Lodge, 52 Victoria Road, Kensington, London W8 5RQ